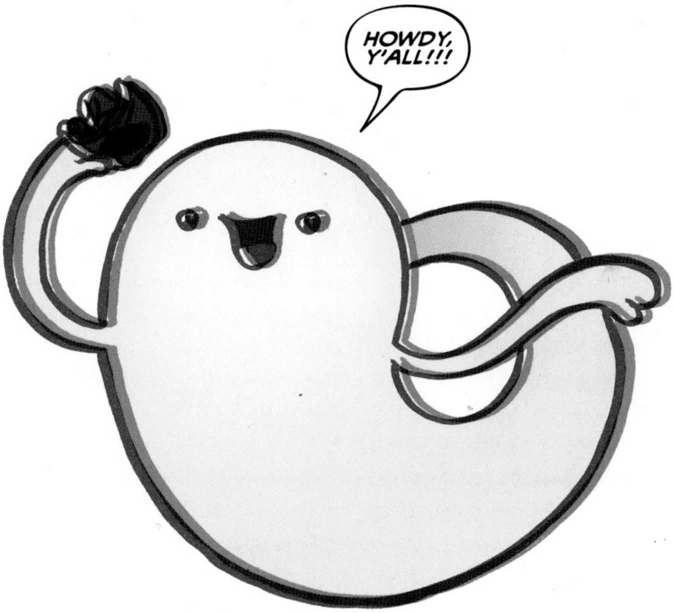
HOWDY,
Y'ALL!!!

Artisanally written and drawn for the page by the ever virtuous
RYAN "HEAD FULL OF RUSTY ARCADE TOKENS" BROWNE

Made to be in glorious color by
JORDAN "DON'T CALL ME JORDAN" BOYD

Slammed with letters in the proper order by
CHRIS "CRANK" CRANK AND RYAN "HUNTED BY WASPS" BROWNE

Edited beyond belief by
JORDAN "COP AND A HALF" BROWNE

Fanciful design elements by the ever designful
THOMAS "THE NICKNAME" QUINN

Imposiclypse Now backup art by
ALEJANDRO "SMOOTH CRIMNOWL" BRUZZESE

Goofin' With Gnarled art by
BRAD "ON THE RUN FROM NO ONE" MCGINTY AND JORDAN "XXX" BOYD

Check out everything God Hates Astronauty on the web at
GOD HATES ASTRONAUTS.COM

Follow Ryan's ass on Instagram and Twitter
@RYANBROWNEART

Download the GHA theme song by Murder By Death at
GODHATESASTRONAUTS.COM/MBD

Know that you are a great person for buying this comic
and an even greater person for telling
your friends. Ryan needs every
money in the world.

IMAGE COMICS, INC.
Robert Kirkman – Chief Operating Officer
Erik Larsen – Chief Financial Officer
Todd McFarlane – President
Marc Silvestri – Chief Executive Officer
Jim Valentino – Vice-President

Eric Stephenson – Publisher
Ron Richards – Director of Business Development
Jennifer de Guzman – Director of Trade Book Sales
Kat Salazar – Director of PR & Marketing
Corey Murphy – Director of Retail Sales
Jeremy Sullivan – Director of Digital Sales
Emilio Bautista – Sales Assistant
Branwyn Bigglestone – Senior Accounts Manager
Emily Miller – Accounts Manager
Jessica Ambriz – Administrative Assistant
Tyler Shainline – Events Coordinator
David Brothers – Content Manager
Jonathan Chan – Production Manager
Drew Gill – Art Director
Meredith Wallace – Print Manager
Addison Duke – Production Artist
Vincent Kukua – Production Artist
Tricia Ramos – Production Assistant
IMAGECOMICS.COM

GOD HATES ASTRONAUTS, VOL. 2: A STAR IS BORN. First printing. February 2015. Copyright © 2015 Ryan Browne. All rights reserved. Published by Image Comics, Inc. Office of publication: 2001 Center Street, Sixth Floor, Berkeley, CA 94704. Originally published in single magazine form as GOD HATES ASTRONAUTS #1-5, by Image Comics. "God Hates Astronauts," its logos, and the likenesses of all characters herein are trademarks of Ryan Browne, unless otherwise noted. "Image" and the Image Comics logos are registered trademarks of Image Comics, Inc. No part of this publication may be reproduced or transmitted, in any form or by any means (except for short excerpts for journalistic or review purposes), without the express written permission of Ryan Browne or Image Comics, Inc. All names, characters, events, and locales in this publication are entirely fictional. Any resemblance to actual persons (living or dead), events, or places, without satiric intent, is coincidental. Printed in the USA. For information regarding the CPSIA on this printed material call: 203-595-3636 and provide reference #RICH-602101. For international rights, contact: foreignlicensing@imagecomics.com. ISBN: 978-1-63215-196-4

GOD HATES ASTRONAUTS

VOLUME TWO
A STAR IS BORN!

SUGGESTED VOICE TALENT
IN ORDER OF APPEARANCE

ISSUE ONE

Mr. Crabtree:
Dwayne "The Rock" Johnson

Admiral Tiger Eating A Cheeseburger:
Robert De Niro

Gorilla Mustache Farmer:
Bill Bellamy

Lord Astro-Farmer:
Christopher Walken

Big Chin Farmer:
Larry "The Cable Guy"

Hennifer:
A Chicken

Chicken Vendor:
Captain Lou Albano

Cop Who Is About To Puke:
The Kid From "Cop And A Half"

Worst Woman In The World:
A Wild Raccoon

Star Grass:
John C. Reilly Doing a Cow Impression

Gnarled Winslow:
Wendell Pierce

The Impossible:
Fast Food Speaker

3-D Cowboy:
Emmanuel Lewis

Starrior:
Maggie Gyllenhaal

The Anti-Mugger:
Burt Reynolds

Dr. Professor:
Dean Stockwell

Craymok:
Rip Torn

Texas Tom:
Walton Goggins

Baseball Hat Farmer:
Rick Moranis

Horse:
A Bunch Of Cats Taped Together

Farmer On Goat:
Anthony Michael Hall

Pig:
Martin Lawrence

Cow:
A Horse

Sir Hippothesis:
John Cleese

King Tiger Eating A Cheeseburger:
James Earl Jones

Pandor:
Harry Dean Stanton

Crab Soldiers:
Daryl Hall and John Oates

ISSUE TWO

Dr. Axligator:
Ernest Borgnine

Buzz Owldrin:
Neil Armstrong

NASA Employee:
Garrison Keillor

Seal Armstrong:
Buzz Aldrin

Muggee:
Woodrow Wilson

Mugger:
Breadcrumb Man

Sittor:
Richard Karn

Starlina:
Sigourney Weaver

Time Giraffe:
Regular Giraffe

Small-Faced NASA Guard:
Gary Oldman

Harryet:
CCH Pounder

The Ghost of Crazy Train:
Dame Judi Dench

Birdgess Meredith:
Stephen Merchant

The Mugger:
Wild Grizzly Bear

ISSUE THREE

Queen Tiger Holding A Baby:
A Tigress

Tiny Robot:
A Tiny Robot

Earl:
Rick Moranis

Sheila:
Maryweather T. Snopple

Croad The Unfortunate:
Julia Roberts

The Pugilator:
Penn & Teller

Karate Rabbit:
Toshiro Mifune

Dragon Bartender:
Michael Ironside With One Arm

Multi-Boobed Shitty's Customer:
Megan Fox

Count Stockula:
Frankenberry

ISSUE FOUR

Prince Tiger Eating A Cheeseburger:
Young Robert De Niro

Crabigail:
Mae Whitman

Toad:
Hayden Christensen

Dr. Cancer The Crab:
Alan Thicke

Dr. Cyclops Rabbit:
Susan Sarandon

Detective Charles LeBronson:
Charles Bronson

Madam O'Beast:
Roseanne Barr

Dr. Appointment:
Ned Beatty

Humpback Whale:
Paul Rudd

Mr. Frog
Brad Pitt

Angry Fish:
George C. Scott

ISSUE FIVE

The Whizzard:
Jon Polito

Laughing Crab:
Some Bratty Little Kid

Pufferfish:
Sad Pufferfish

Manatee:
A Walrus

Starfish:
Jim Kelly

Simon, The Cat Lawyer:
Michael Cera

Mummy Bailiff:
Larry Miller

Judge Buffalo William:
Jeffrey Jones

Myster Marbulz:
Al Capone

Whorecules:
Hercules

Little Lady:
Michael J. Anderson

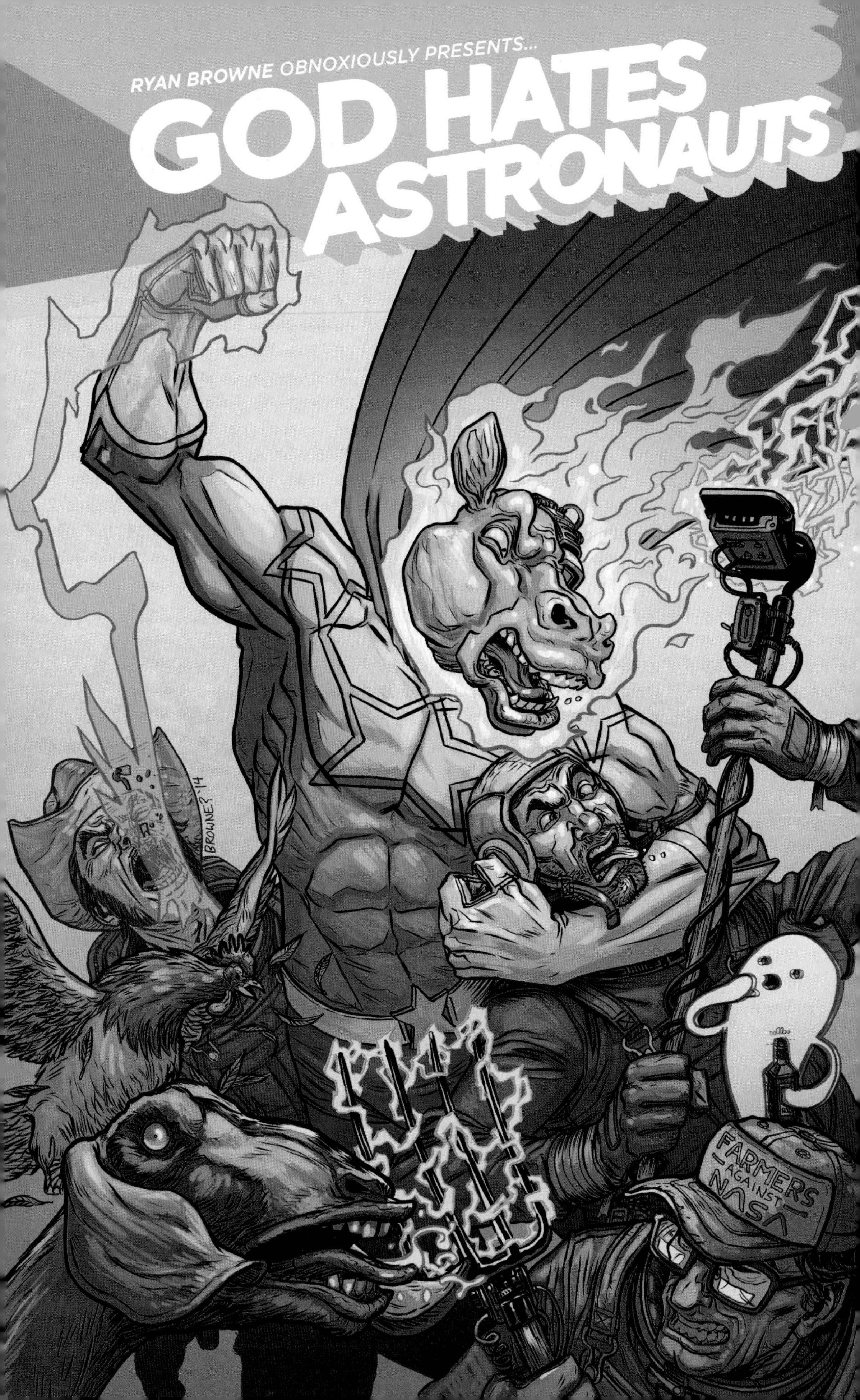
RYAN BROWNE OBNOXIOUSLY PRESENTS...
GOD HATES ASTRONAUTS
BROWNE?'14
FARMERS AGAINST NASA

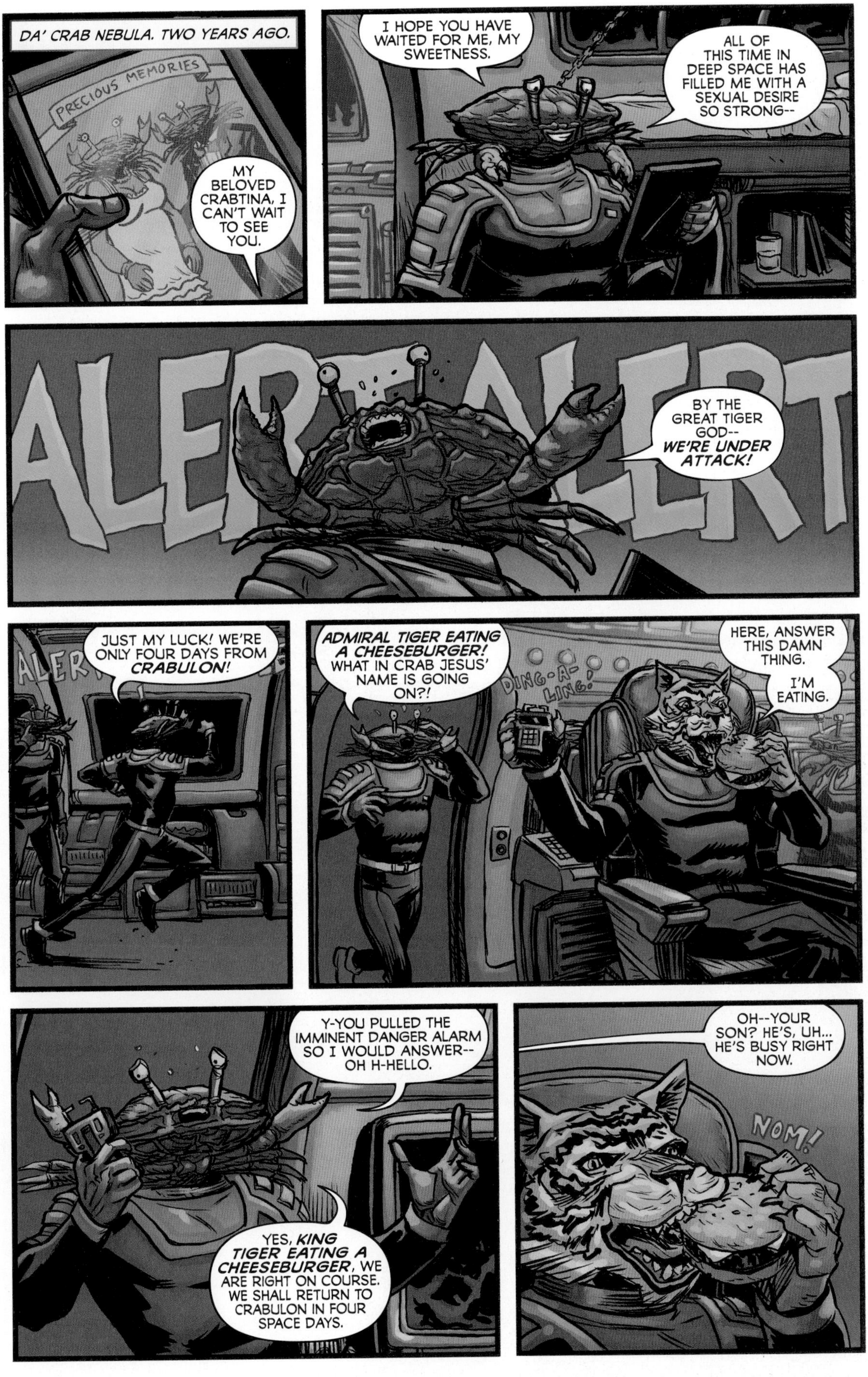
DA' CRAB NEBULA. TWO YEARS AGO.
PRECIOUS MEMORIES
MY BELOVED CRABTINA, I CAN'T WAIT TO SEE YOU.
I HOPE YOU HAVE WAITED FOR ME, MY SWEETNESS.
ALL OF THIS TIME IN DEEP SPACE HAS FILLED ME WITH A SEXUAL DESIRE SO STRONG--
ALERT ALERT
BY THE GREAT TIGER GOD-- WE'RE UNDER ATTACK!
JUST MY LUCK! WE'RE ONLY FOUR DAYS FROM CRABULON!
ADMIRAL TIGER EATING A CHEESEBURGER! WHAT IN CRAB JESUS' NAME IS GOING ON?!
DING-A-LING!
HERE, ANSWER THIS DAMN THING.
I'M EATING.
Y-YOU PULLED THE IMMINENT DANGER ALARM SO I WOULD ANSWER-- OH H-HELLO.
YES, KING TIGER EATING A CHEESEBURGER, WE ARE RIGHT ON COURSE. WE SHALL RETURN TO CRABULON IN FOUR SPACE DAYS.
OH--YOUR SON? HE'S, UH... HE'S BUSY RIGHT NOW.
NOM!

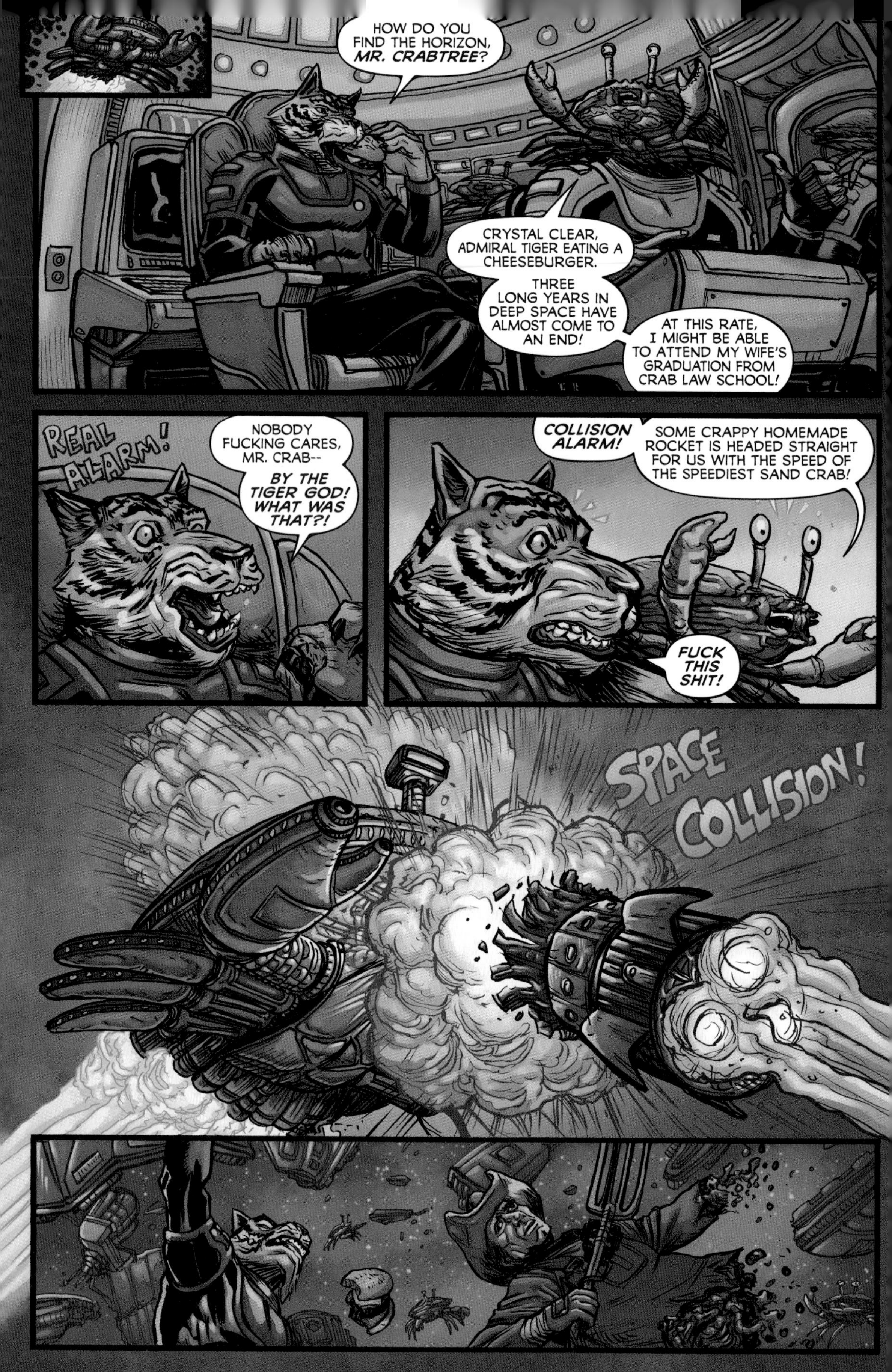
HOW DO YOU FIND THE HORIZON, MR. CRABTREE?
CRYSTAL CLEAR, ADMIRAL TIGER EATING A CHEESEBURGER.
THREE LONG YEARS IN DEEP SPACE HAVE ALMOST COME TO AN END!
AT THIS RATE, I MIGHT BE ABLE TO ATTEND MY WIFE'S GRADUATION FROM CRAB LAW SCHOOL!
REAL ALARM!
NOBODY FUCKING CARES, MR. CRAB--
BY THE TIGER GOD! WHAT WAS THAT?!
COLLISION ALARM!
SOME CRAPPY HOMEMADE ROCKET IS HEADED STRAIGHT FOR US WITH THE SPEED OF THE SPEEDIEST SAND CRAB!
FUCK THIS SHIT!
SPACE COLLISION!

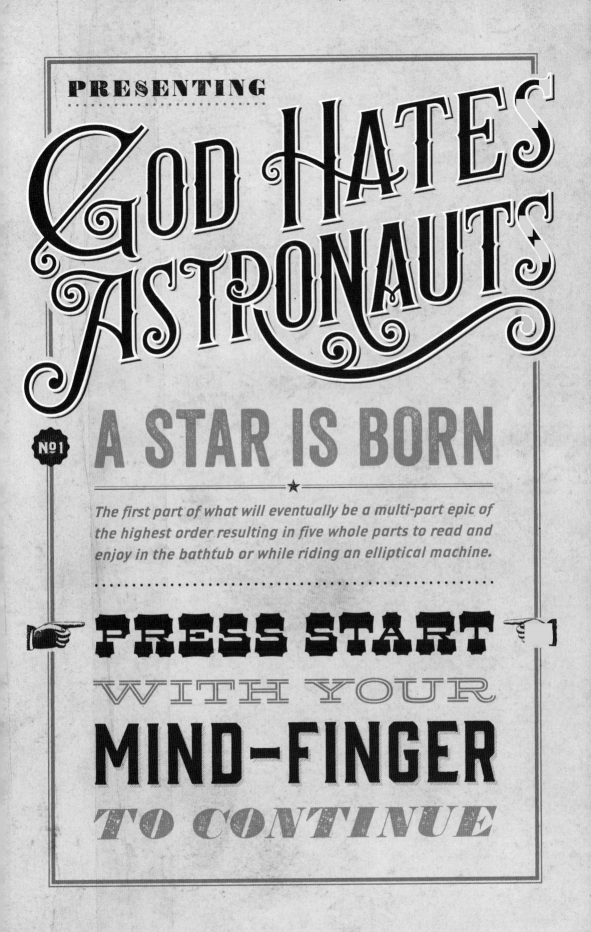

PRESENTING

GOD HATES ASTRONAUTS

Nº1 **A STAR IS BORN**

⁕

The first part of what will eventually be a multi-part epic of the highest order resulting in five whole parts to read and enjoy in the bathtub or while riding an elliptical machine.

☞ **PRESS START** ☜

WITH YOUR

MIND-FINGER

TO CONTINUE

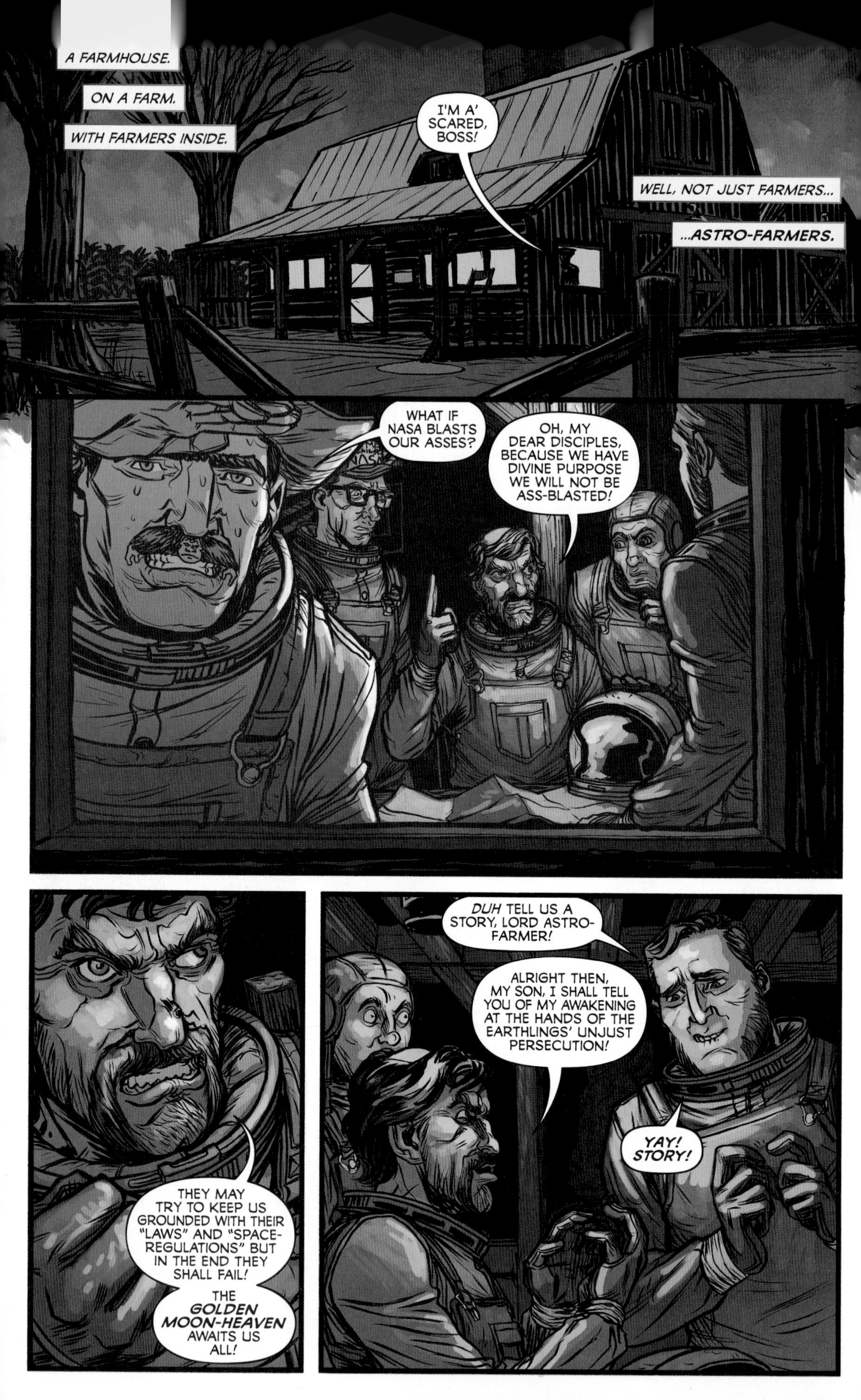
A FARMHOUSE.
ON A FARM.
WITH FARMERS INSIDE.
I'M A' SCARED, BOSS!
WELL, NOT JUST FARMERS...
...ASTRO-FARMERS.
WHAT IF NASA BLASTS OUR ASSES?
OH, MY DEAR DISCIPLES, BECAUSE WE HAVE DIVINE PURPOSE WE WILL NOT BE ASS-BLASTED!
THEY MAY TRY TO KEEP US GROUNDED WITH THEIR "LAWS" AND "SPACE-REGULATIONS" BUT IN THE END THEY SHALL FAIL!
THE GOLDEN MOON-HEAVEN AWAITS US ALL!
DUH TELL US A STORY, LORD ASTRO-FARMER!
ALRIGHT THEN, MY SON, I SHALL TELL YOU OF MY AWAKENING AT THE HANDS OF THE EARTHLINGS' UNJUST PERSECUTION!
YAY! STORY!

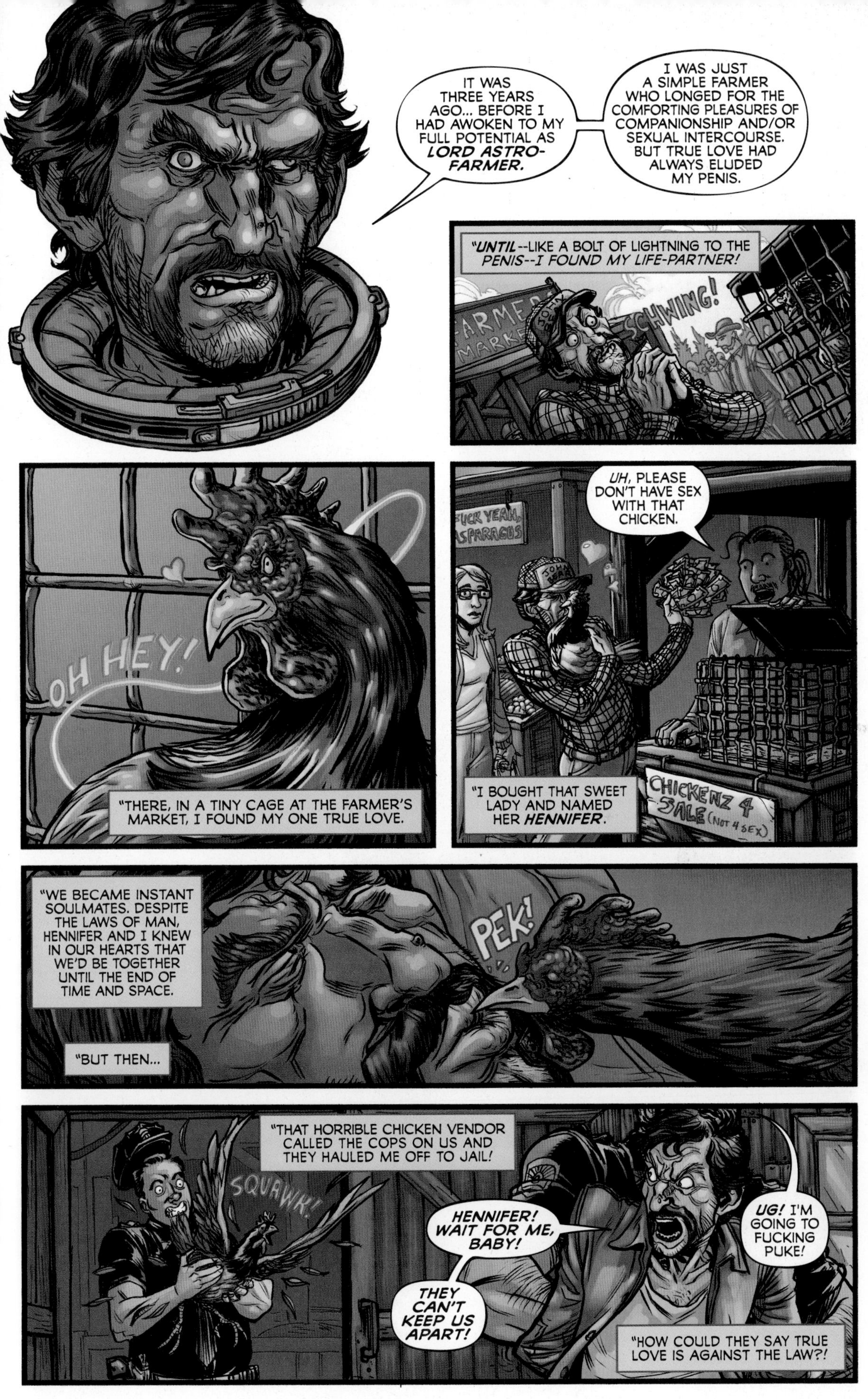
IT WAS THREE YEARS AGO... BEFORE I HAD AWOKEN TO MY FULL POTENTIAL AS ***LORD ASTRO-FARMER.***
I WAS JUST A SIMPLE FARMER WHO LONGED FOR THE COMFORTING PLEASURES OF COMPANIONSHIP AND/OR SEXUAL INTERCOURSE. BUT TRUE LOVE HAD ALWAYS ELUDED MY PENIS.
"*UNTIL*--LIKE A BOLT OF LIGHTNING TO THE *PENIS--I FOUND MY LIFE-PARTNER!*
SCHWING!
"THERE, IN A TINY CAGE AT THE FARMER'S MARKET, I FOUND MY ONE TRUE LOVE.
OH HEY!
UH, PLEASE DON'T HAVE SEX WITH THAT CHICKEN.
FUCK YEAH, ASPARAGUS
"I BOUGHT THAT SWEET LADY AND NAMED HER ***HENNIFER***.
CHICKENZ 4 SALE (NOT 4 SEX)
"WE BECAME INSTANT SOULMATES. DESPITE THE LAWS OF MAN, HENNIFER AND I KNEW IN OUR HEARTS THAT WE'D BE TOGETHER UNTIL THE END OF TIME AND SPACE.
PEK!
"BUT THEN...
"THAT HORRIBLE CHICKEN VENDOR CALLED THE COPS ON US AND THEY HAULED ME OFF TO JAIL!
SQUAWK!
HENNIFER! WAIT FOR ME, BABY!
THEY CAN'T KEEP US APART!
UG! I'M GOING TO FUCKING PUKE!
"HOW COULD THEY SAY TRUE LOVE IS AGAINST THE LAW?!

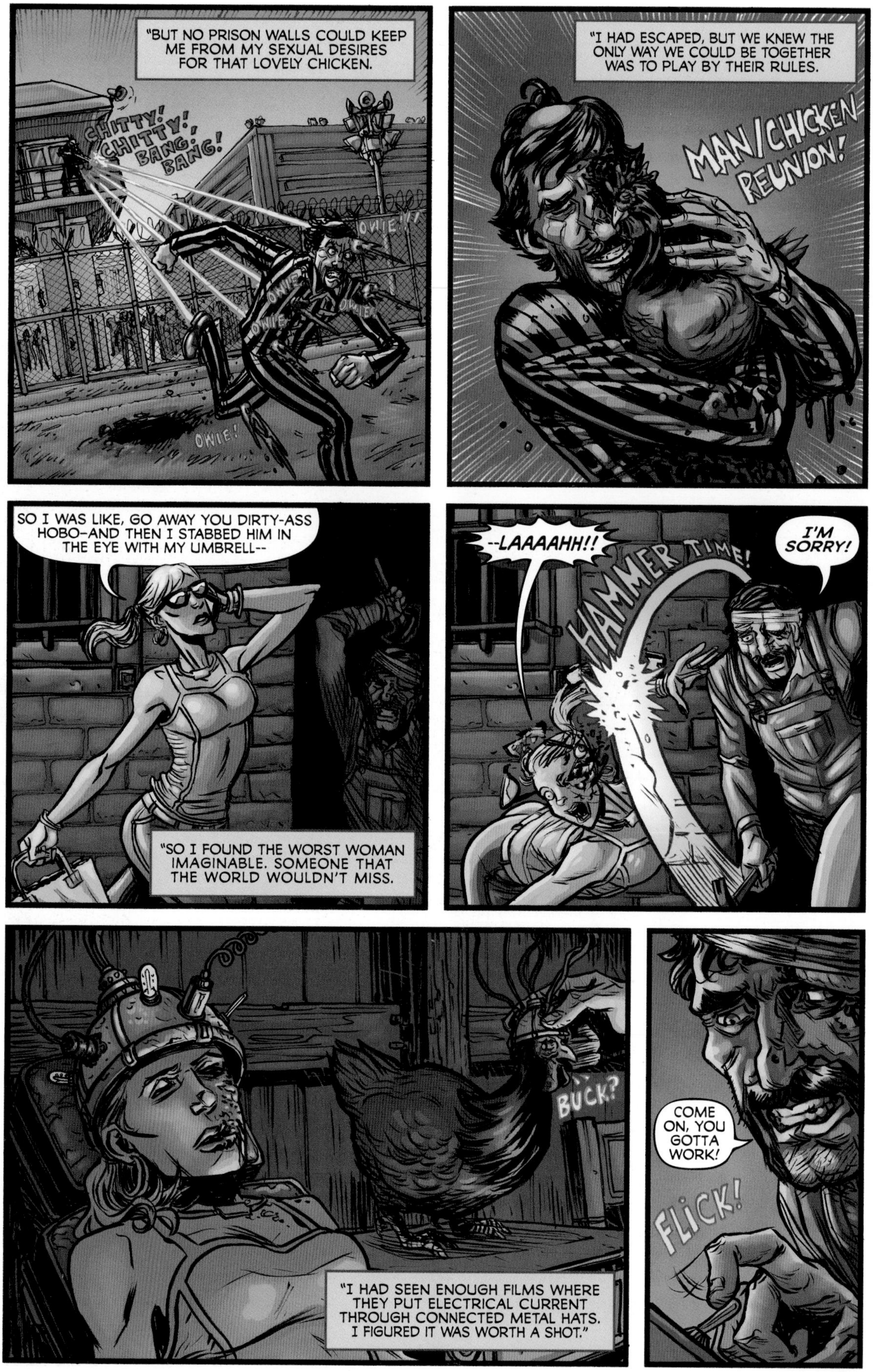
"BUT NO PRISON WALLS COULD KEEP ME FROM MY SEXUAL DESIRES FOR THAT LOVELY CHICKEN.
CHITTY! CHITTY! BANG! BANG!
OWIE!!!
OWIE
OWIE
OWIE
OWIE!
"I HAD ESCAPED, BUT WE KNEW THE ONLY WAY WE COULD BE TOGETHER WAS TO PLAY BY THEIR RULES.
MAN/CHICKEN REUNION!
SO I WAS LIKE, GO AWAY YOU DIRTY-ASS HOBO--AND THEN I STABBED HIM IN THE EYE WITH MY UMBRELL--
"SO I FOUND THE WORST WOMAN IMAGINABLE. SOMEONE THAT THE WORLD WOULDN'T MISS.
--LAAAAHH!!
HAMMER TIME!
I'M SORRY!
BUCK?
"I HAD SEEN ENOUGH FILMS WHERE THEY PUT ELECTRICAL CURRENT THROUGH CONNECTED METAL HATS. I FIGURED IT WAS WORTH A SHOT."
COME ON, YOU GOTTA WORK!
FLICK!

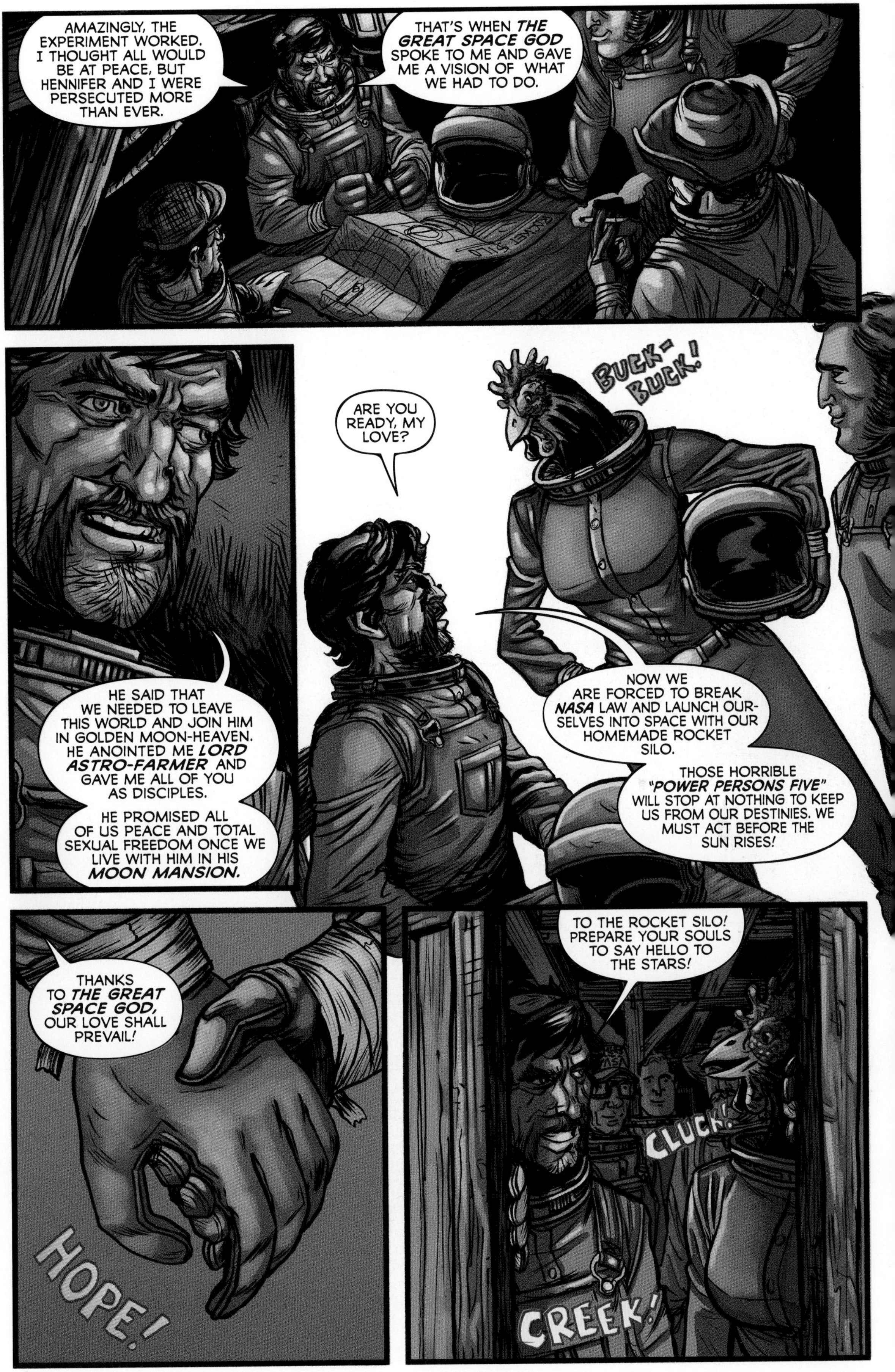
AMAZINGLY, THE EXPERIMENT WORKED. I THOUGHT ALL WOULD BE AT PEACE, BUT HENNIFER AND I WERE PERSECUTED MORE THAN EVER.
THAT'S WHEN *THE GREAT SPACE GOD* SPOKE TO ME AND GAVE ME A VISION OF WHAT WE HAD TO DO.
HE SAID THAT WE NEEDED TO LEAVE THIS WORLD AND JOIN HIM IN GOLDEN MOON-HEAVEN. HE ANOINTED ME *LORD ASTRO-FARMER* AND GAVE ME ALL OF YOU AS DISCIPLES.
HE PROMISED ALL OF US PEACE AND TOTAL SEXUAL FREEDOM ONCE WE LIVE WITH HIM IN HIS *MOON MANSION.*
ARE YOU READY, MY LOVE?
BUCK-BUCK!
NOW WE ARE FORCED TO BREAK *NASA* LAW AND LAUNCH OURSELVES INTO SPACE WITH OUR HOMEMADE ROCKET SILO.
THOSE HORRIBLE *"POWER PERSONS FIVE"* WILL STOP AT NOTHING TO KEEP US FROM OUR DESTINIES. WE MUST ACT BEFORE THE SUN RISES!
THANKS TO *THE GREAT SPACE GOD,* OUR LOVE SHALL PREVAIL!
HOPE!
TO THE ROCKET SILO! PREPARE YOUR SOULS TO SAY HELLO TO THE STARS!
CLUCK!
CREEK!

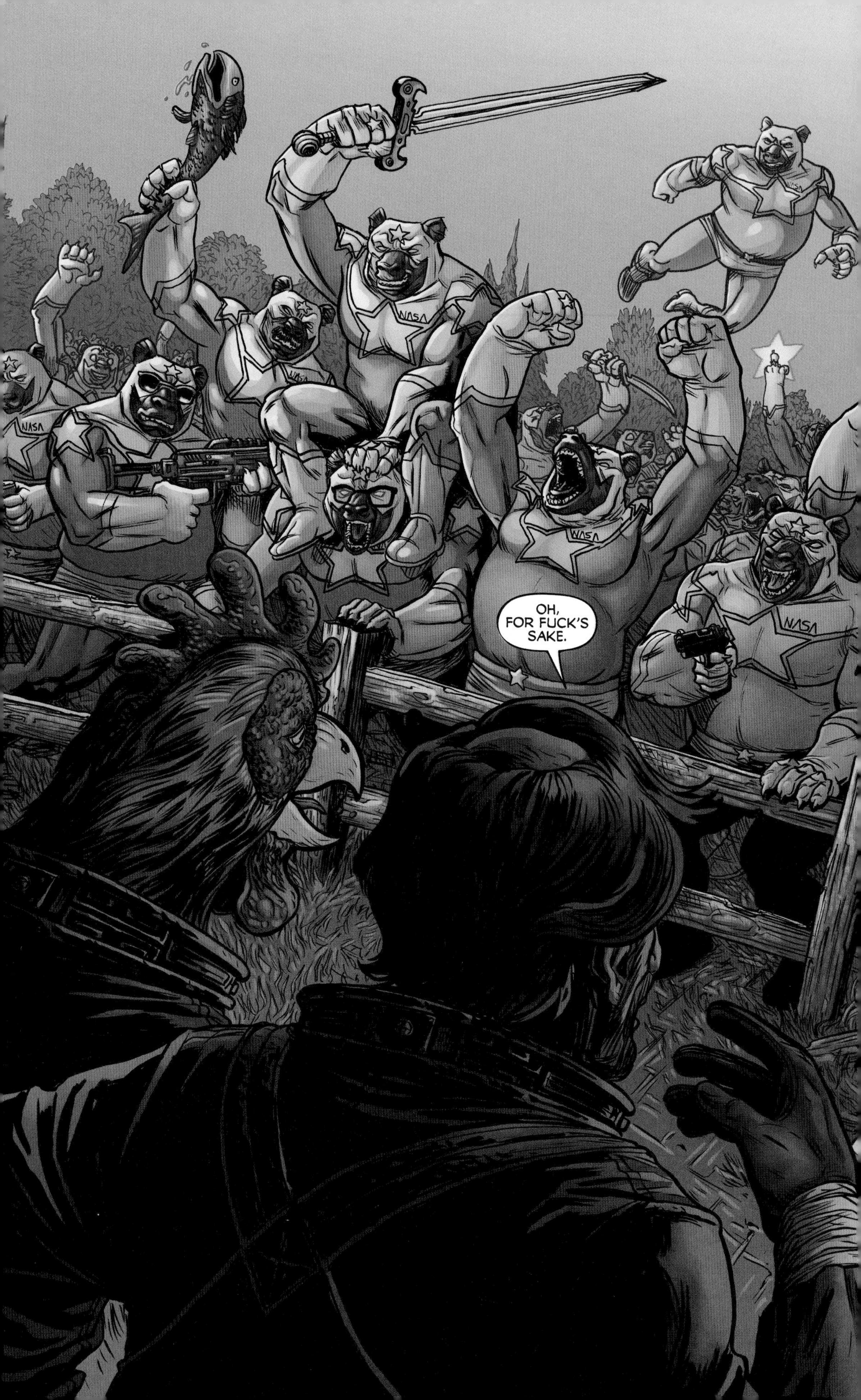
NASA
OH, FOR FUCK'S SAKE.

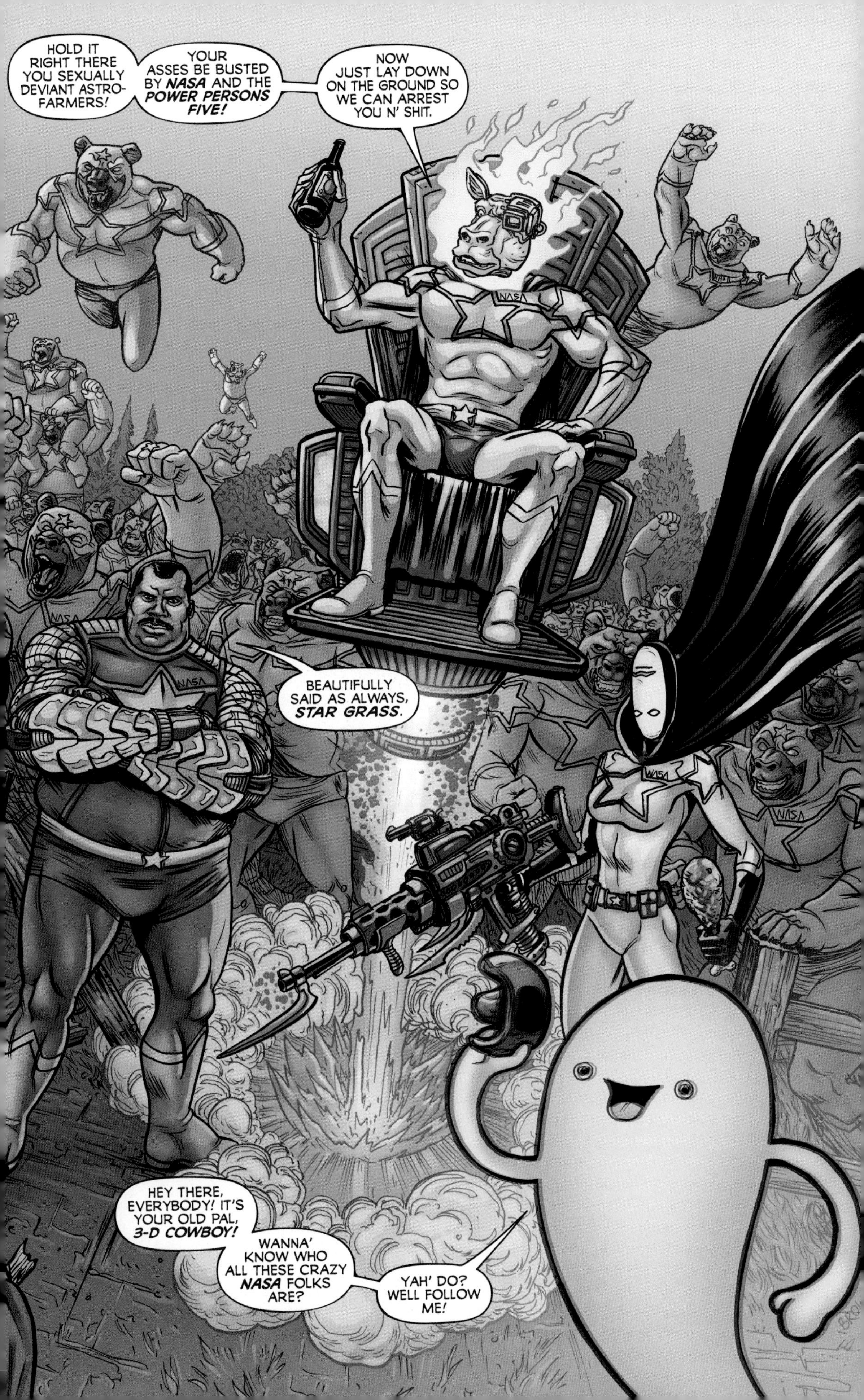

HOLD IT RIGHT THERE YOU SEXUALLY DEVIANT ASTRO-FARMERS!
YOUR ASSES BE BUSTED BY NASA AND THE POWER PERSONS FIVE!
NOW JUST LAY DOWN ON THE GROUND SO WE CAN ARREST YOU N' SHIT.
BEAUTIFULLY SAID AS ALWAYS, STAR GRASS.
HEY THERE, EVERYBODY! IT'S YOUR OLD PAL, 3-D COWBOY!
WANNA' KNOW WHO ALL THESE CRAZY NASA FOLKS ARE?
YAH' DO? WELL FOLLOW ME!

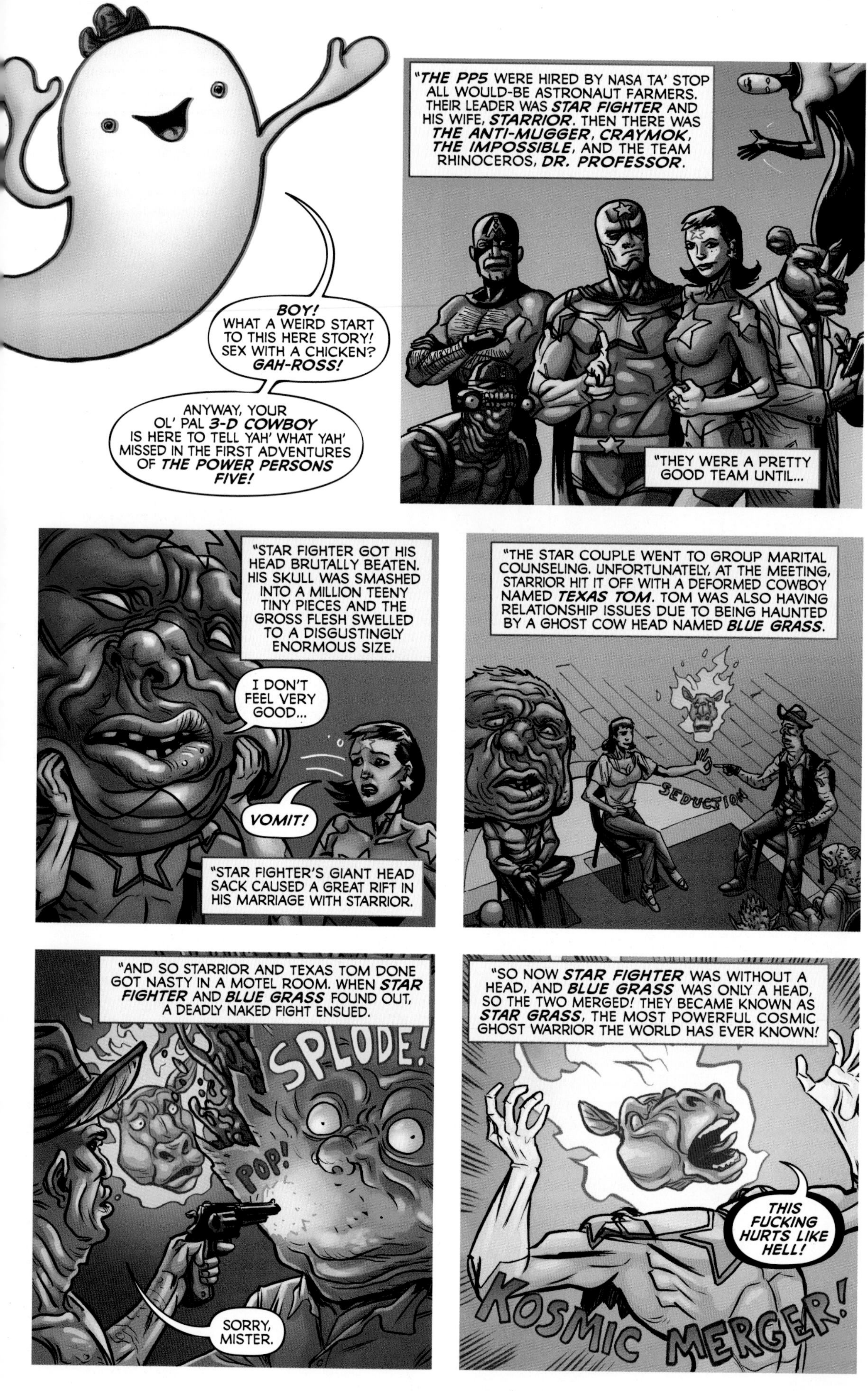
BOY! WHAT A WEIRD START TO THIS HERE STORY! SEX WITH A CHICKEN? GAH-ROSS!
ANYWAY, YOUR OL' PAL 3-D COWBOY IS HERE TO TELL YAH' WHAT YAH' MISSED IN THE FIRST ADVENTURES OF THE POWER PERSONS FIVE!
"THE PP5 WERE HIRED BY NASA TA' STOP ALL WOULD-BE ASTRONAUT FARMERS. THEIR LEADER WAS STAR FIGHTER AND HIS WIFE, STARRIOR. THEN THERE WAS THE ANTI-MUGGER, CRAYMOK, THE IMPOSSIBLE, AND THE TEAM RHINOCEROS, DR. PROFESSOR.
"THEY WERE A PRETTY GOOD TEAM UNTIL...
"STAR FIGHTER GOT HIS HEAD BRUTALLY BEATEN. HIS SKULL WAS SMASHED INTO A MILLION TEENY TINY PIECES AND THE GROSS FLESH SWELLED TO A DISGUSTINGLY ENORMOUS SIZE.
I DON'T FEEL VERY GOOD...
VOMIT!
"STAR FIGHTER'S GIANT HEAD SACK CAUSED A GREAT RIFT IN HIS MARRIAGE WITH STARRIOR.
"THE STAR COUPLE WENT TO GROUP MARITAL COUNSELING. UNFORTUNATELY, AT THE MEETING, STARRIOR HIT IT OFF WITH A DEFORMED COWBOY NAMED TEXAS TOM. TOM WAS ALSO HAVING RELATIONSHIP ISSUES DUE TO BEING HAUNTED BY A GHOST COW HEAD NAMED BLUE GRASS.
SEDUCTION
"AND SO STARRIOR AND TEXAS TOM DONE GOT NASTY IN A MOTEL ROOM. WHEN STAR FIGHTER AND BLUE GRASS FOUND OUT, A DEADLY NAKED FIGHT ENSUED.
SPLODE!
POP!
SORRY, MISTER.
"SO NOW STAR FIGHTER WAS WITHOUT A HEAD, AND BLUE GRASS WAS ONLY A HEAD, SO THE TWO MERGED! THEY BECAME KNOWN AS STAR GRASS, THE MOST POWERFUL COSMIC GHOST WARRIOR THE WORLD HAS EVER KNOWN!
THIS FUCKING HURTS LIKE HELL!
KOSMIC MERGER!

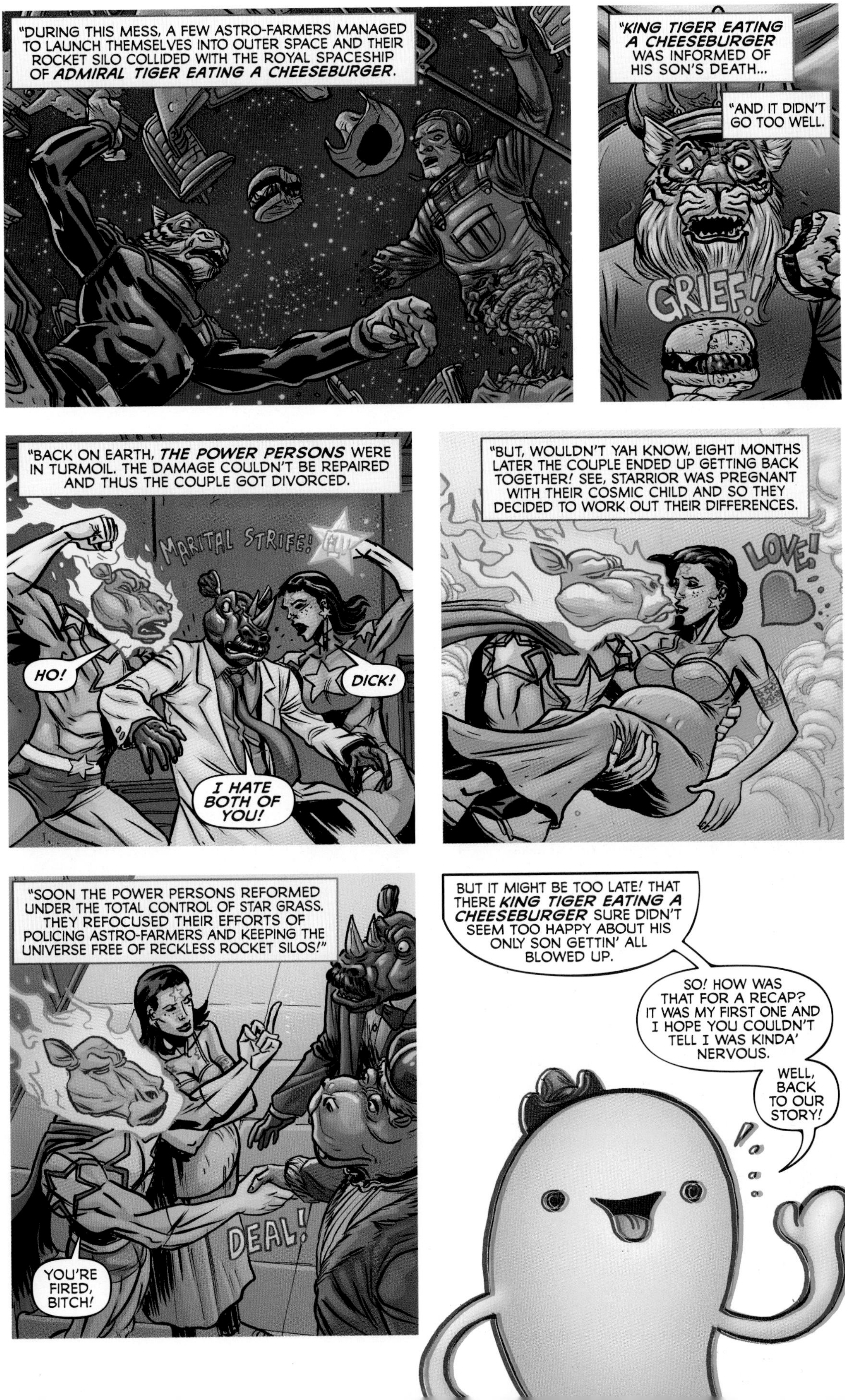
"DURING THIS MESS, A FEW ASTRO-FARMERS MANAGED TO LAUNCH THEMSELVES INTO OUTER SPACE AND THEIR ROCKET SILO COLLIDED WITH THE ROYAL SPACESHIP OF *ADMIRAL TIGER EATING A CHEESEBURGER*.
"*KING TIGER EATING A CHEESEBURGER* WAS INFORMED OF HIS SON'S DEATH...
"AND IT DIDN'T GO TOO WELL.
GRIEF!
"BACK ON EARTH, *THE POWER PERSONS* WERE IN TURMOIL. THE DAMAGE COULDN'T BE REPAIRED AND THUS THE COUPLE GOT DIVORCED.
MARITAL STRIFE!
HO!
DICK!
I HATE BOTH OF YOU!
"BUT, WOULDN'T YAH KNOW, EIGHT MONTHS LATER THE COUPLE ENDED UP GETTING BACK TOGETHER! SEE, STARRIOR WAS PREGNANT WITH THEIR COSMIC CHILD AND SO THEY DECIDED TO WORK OUT THEIR DIFFERENCES.
LOVE!
"SOON THE POWER PERSONS REFORMED UNDER THE TOTAL CONTROL OF STAR GRASS. THEY REFOCUSED THEIR EFFORTS OF POLICING ASTRO-FARMERS AND KEEPING THE UNIVERSE FREE OF RECKLESS ROCKET SILOS!"
DEAL!
YOU'RE FIRED, BITCH!
BUT IT MIGHT BE TOO LATE! THAT THERE *KING TIGER EATING A CHEESEBURGER* SURE DIDN'T SEEM TOO HAPPY ABOUT HIS ONLY SON GETTIN' ALL BLOWED UP.
SO! HOW WAS THAT FOR A RECAP? IT WAS MY FIRST ONE AND I HOPE YOU COULDN'T TELL I WAS KINDA' NERVOUS.
WELL, BACK TO OUR STORY!

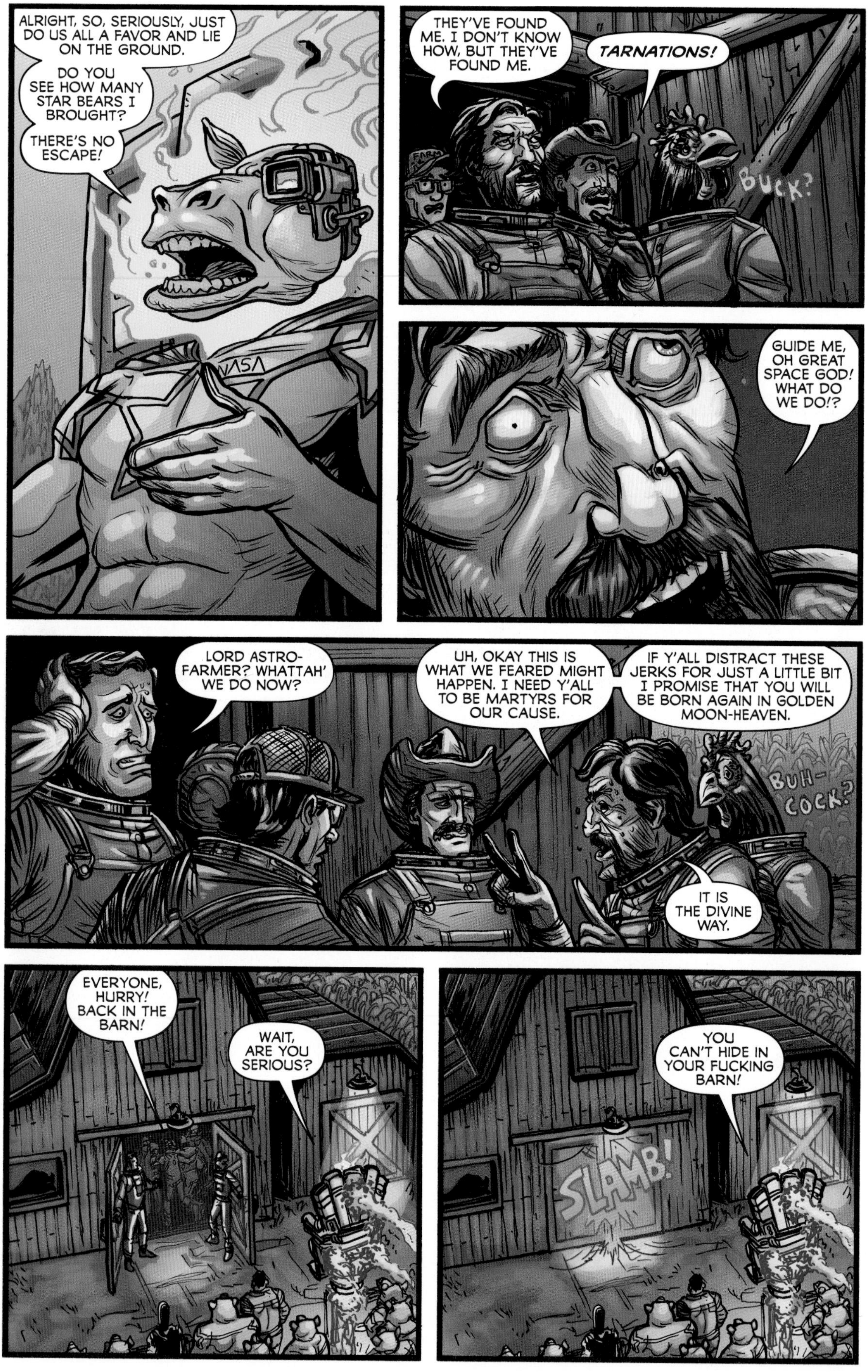
ALRIGHT, SO, SERIOUSLY, JUST DO US ALL A FAVOR AND LIE ON THE GROUND.
DO YOU SEE HOW MANY STAR BEARS I BROUGHT?
THERE'S NO ESCAPE!
NASA
THEY'VE FOUND ME. I DON'T KNOW HOW, BUT THEY'VE FOUND ME.
TARNATIONS!
BUCK?
GUIDE ME, OH GREAT SPACE GOD! WHAT DO WE DO!?
LORD ASTRO-FARMER? WHATTAH' WE DO NOW?
UH, OKAY THIS IS WHAT WE FEARED MIGHT HAPPEN. I NEED Y'ALL TO BE MARTYRS FOR OUR CAUSE.
IF Y'ALL DISTRACT THESE JERKS FOR JUST A LITTLE BIT I PROMISE THAT YOU WILL BE BORN AGAIN IN GOLDEN MOON-HEAVEN.
BUH-COCK?
IT IS THE DIVINE WAY.
EVERYONE, HURRY! BACK IN THE BARN!
WAIT, ARE YOU SERIOUS?
SLAMB!
YOU CAN'T HIDE IN YOUR FUCKING BARN!

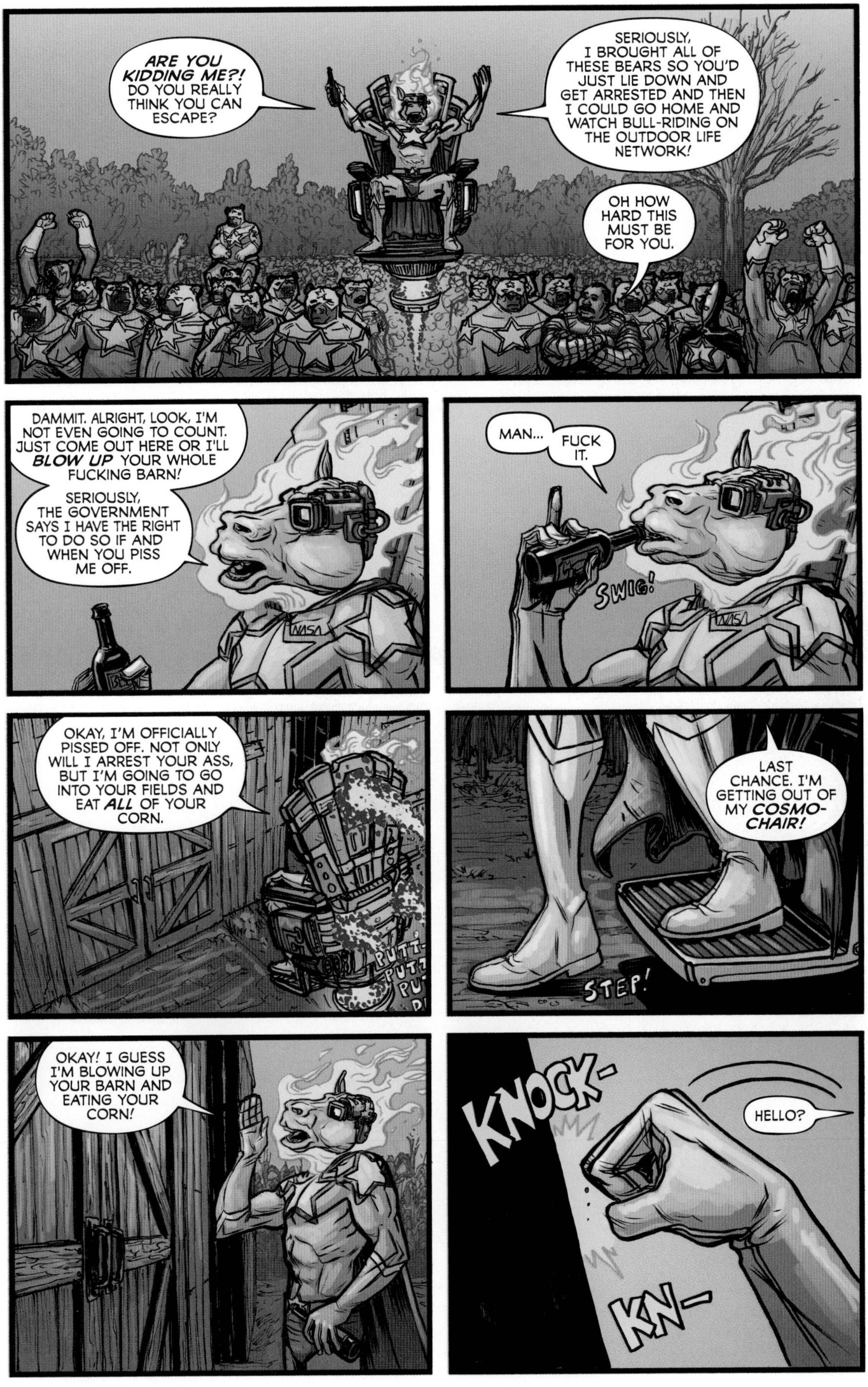
ARE YOU KIDDING ME?! DO YOU REALLY THINK YOU CAN ESCAPE?
SERIOUSLY, I BROUGHT ALL OF THESE BEARS SO YOU'D JUST LIE DOWN AND GET ARRESTED AND THEN I COULD GO HOME AND WATCH BULL-RIDING ON THE OUTDOOR LIFE NETWORK!
OH HOW HARD THIS MUST BE FOR YOU.
DAMMIT. ALRIGHT, LOOK, I'M NOT EVEN GOING TO COUNT. JUST COME OUT HERE OR I'LL BLOW UP YOUR WHOLE FUCKING BARN!
SERIOUSLY, THE GOVERNMENT SAYS I HAVE THE RIGHT TO DO SO IF AND WHEN YOU PISS ME OFF.
MAN...
FUCK IT.
SWIG!
OKAY, I'M OFFICIALLY PISSED OFF. NOT ONLY WILL I ARREST YOUR ASS, BUT I'M GOING TO GO INTO YOUR FIELDS AND EAT ALL OF YOUR CORN.
LAST CHANCE. I'M GETTING OUT OF MY COSMO-CHAIR!
STEP!
OKAY! I GUESS I'M BLOWING UP YOUR BARN AND EATING YOUR CORN!
KNOCK-
HELLO?
KN-

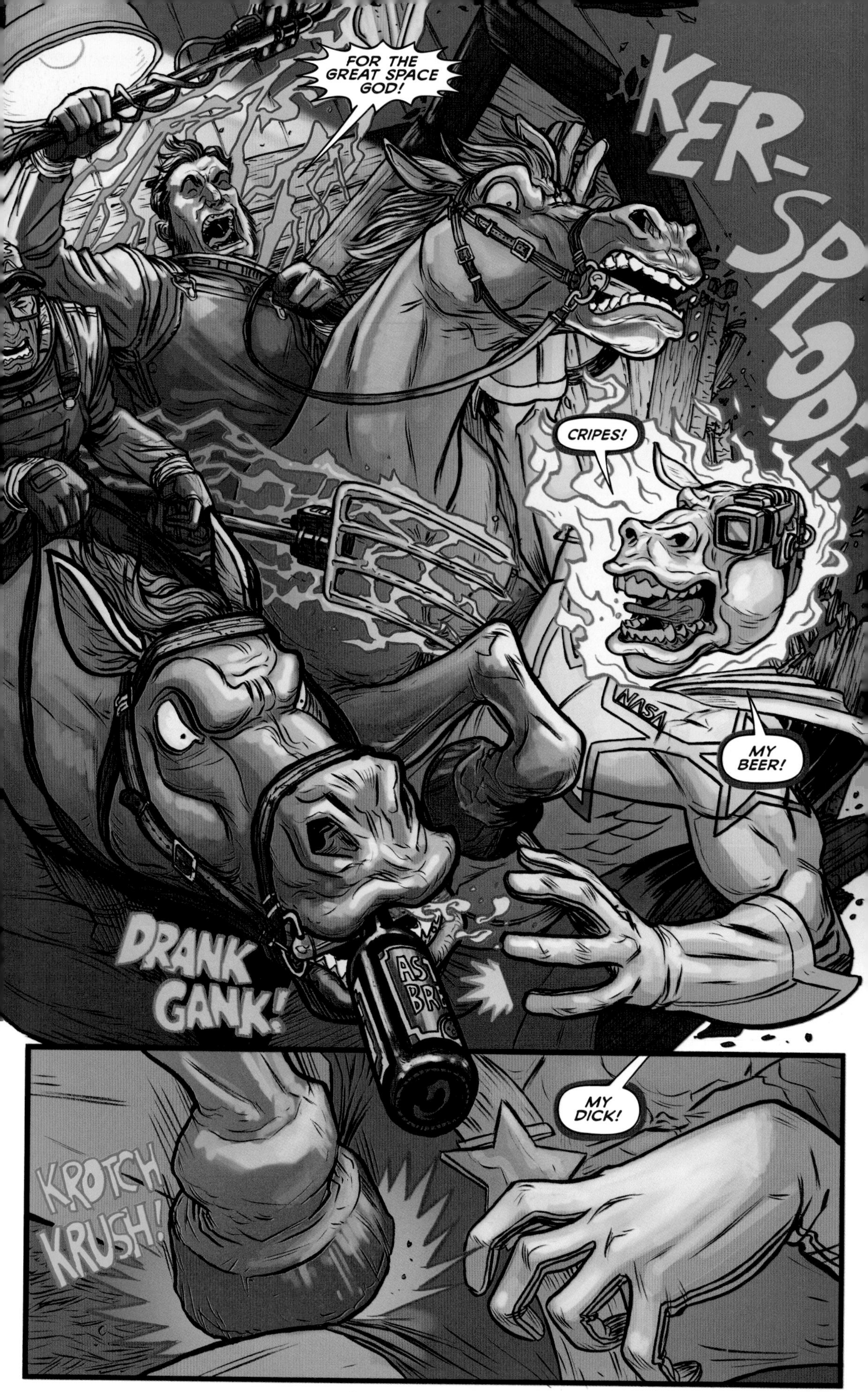
FOR THE GREAT SPACE GOD!
KER-SPLODE!
CRIPES!
MY BEER!
DRANK GANK!
MY DICK!
KROTCH KRUSH!

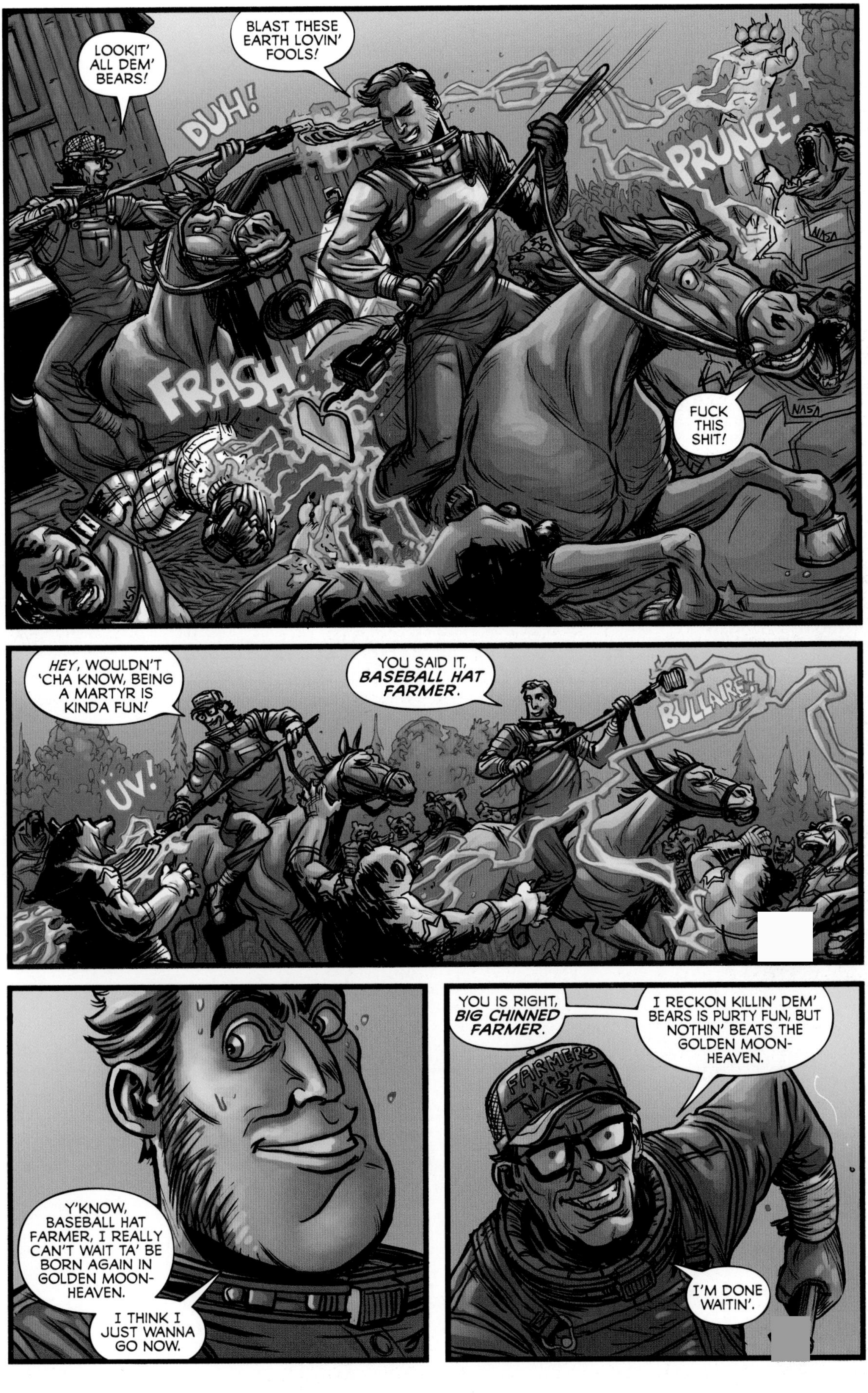
LOOKIT' ALL DEM' BEARS!
BLAST THESE EARTH LOVIN' FOOLS!
DUH!
PRUNCE!
FRASH!
FUCK THIS SHIT!
HEY, WOULDN'T 'CHA KNOW, BEING A MARTYR IS KINDA FUN!
YOU SAID IT, ***BASEBALL HAT FARMER***.
BULLAIRE!
ÜV!
Y'KNOW, BASEBALL HAT FARMER, I REALLY CAN'T WAIT TA' BE BORN AGAIN IN GOLDEN MOON-HEAVEN.
I THINK I JUST WANNA GO NOW.
YOU IS RIGHT, ***BIG CHINNED FARMER***.
I RECKON KILLIN' DEM' BEARS IS PURTY FUN, BUT NOTHIN' BEATS THE GOLDEN MOON-HEAVEN.
FARMERS AGAINST NASA
I'M DONE WAITIN'.

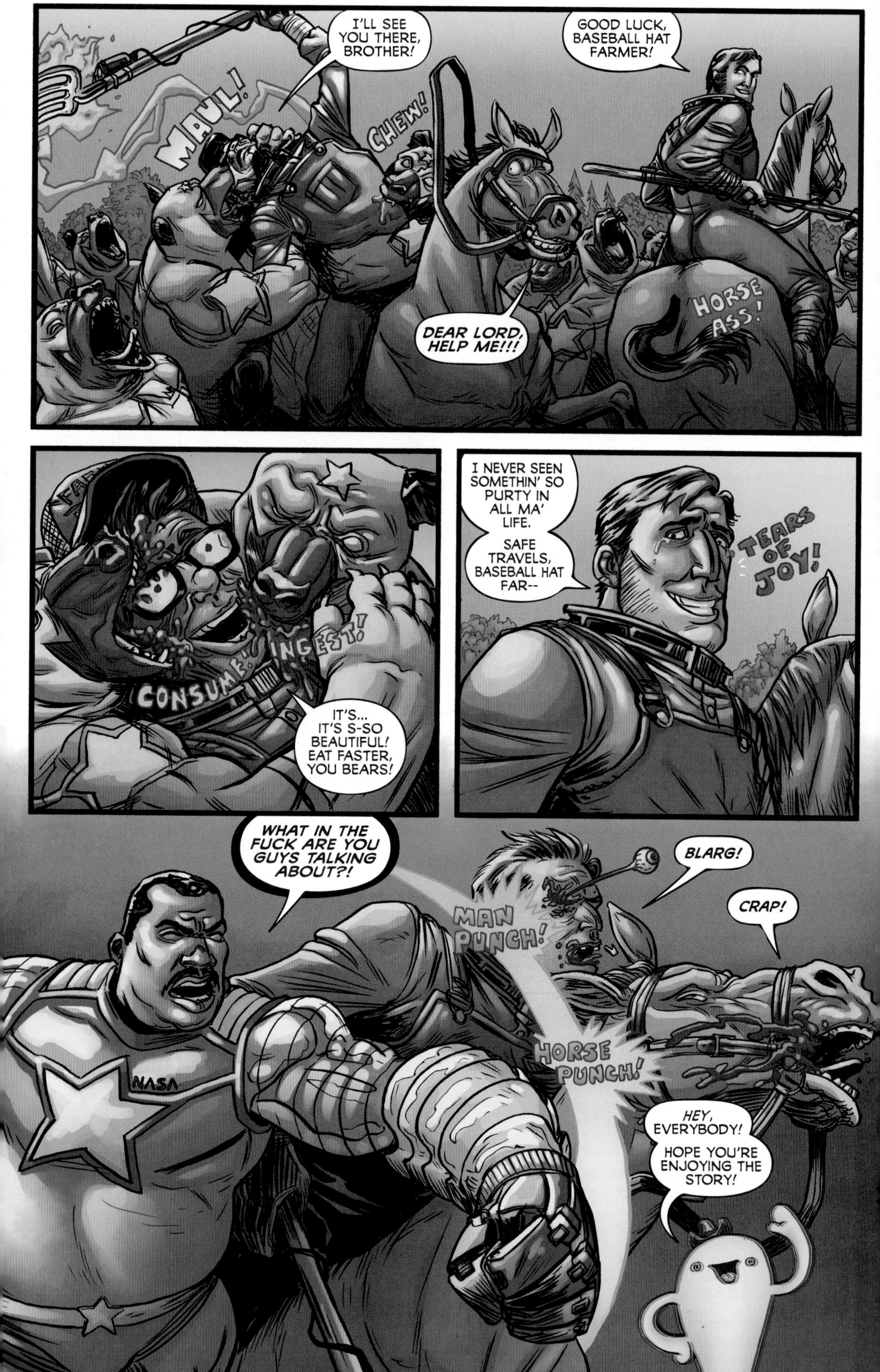
I'LL SEE YOU THERE, BROTHER!
GOOD LUCK, BASEBALL HAT FARMER!
MAUL!
CHEW!
DEAR LORD, HELP ME!!!
HORSE ASS!
CONSUME!
INGEST!
IT'S... IT'S S-SO BEAUTIFUL! EAT FASTER, YOU BEARS!
I NEVER SEEN SOMETHIN' SO PURTY IN ALL MA' LIFE.
SAFE TRAVELS, BASEBALL HAT FAR--
TEARS OF JOY!
WHAT IN THE FUCK ARE YOU GUYS TALKING ABOUT?!
BLARG!
CRAP!
MAN PUNCH!
HORSE PUNCH!
NASA
HEY, EVERYBODY!
HOPE YOU'RE ENJOYING THE STORY!

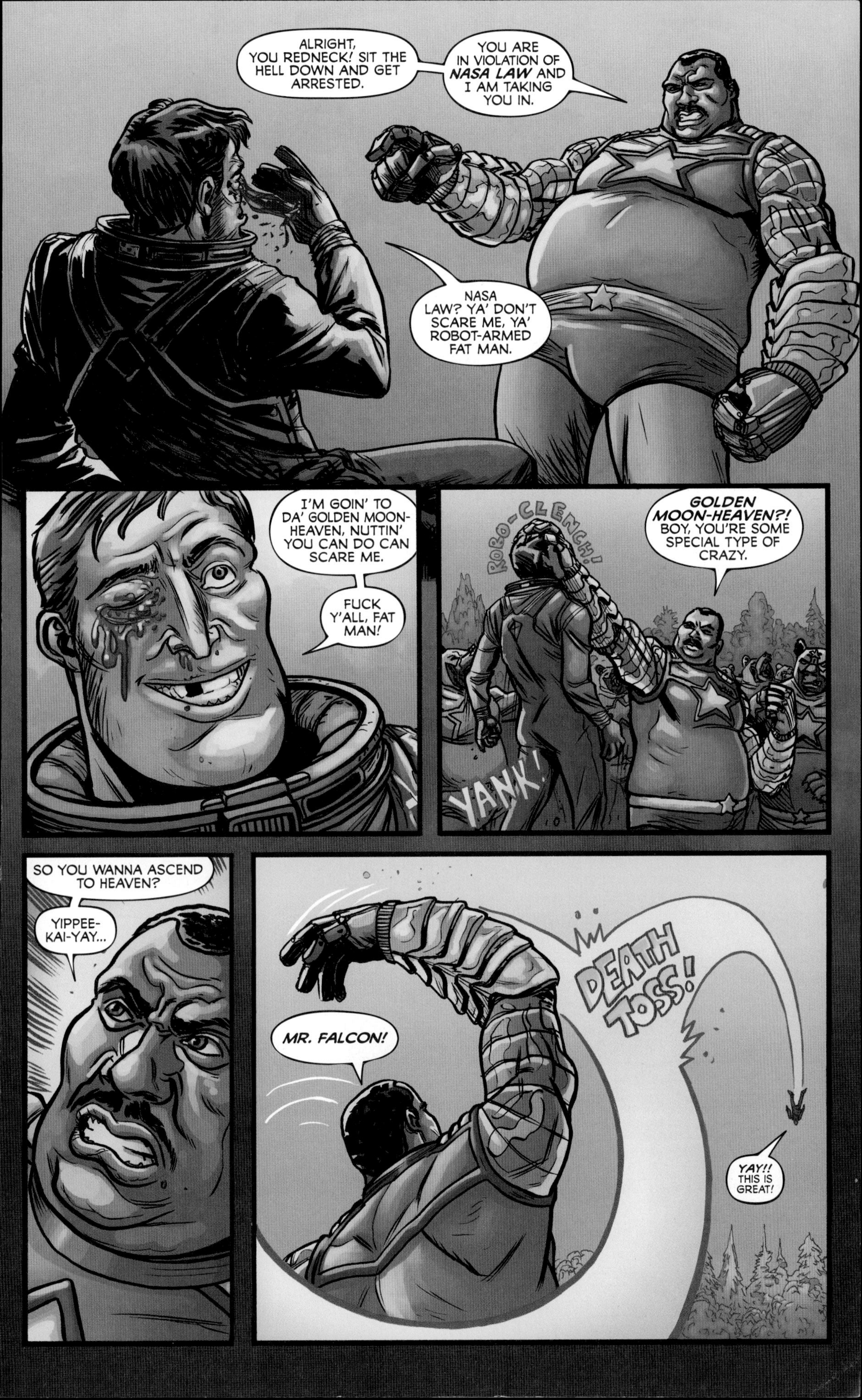
ALRIGHT, YOU REDNECK! SIT THE HELL DOWN AND GET ARRESTED.
YOU ARE IN VIOLATION OF *NASA LAW* AND I AM TAKING YOU IN.
NASA LAW? YA' DON'T SCARE ME, YA' ROBOT-ARMED FAT MAN.
I'M GOIN' TO DA' GOLDEN MOON-HEAVEN, NUTTIN' YOU CAN DO CAN SCARE ME.
FUCK Y'ALL, FAT MAN!
ROBO-CLENCH!
GOLDEN MOON-HEAVEN?! BOY, YOU'RE SOME SPECIAL TYPE OF CRAZY.
YANK!
SO YOU WANNA ASCEND TO HEAVEN?
YIPPEE-KAI-YAY...
MR. FALCON!
DEATH TOSS!
YAY!! THIS IS GREAT!

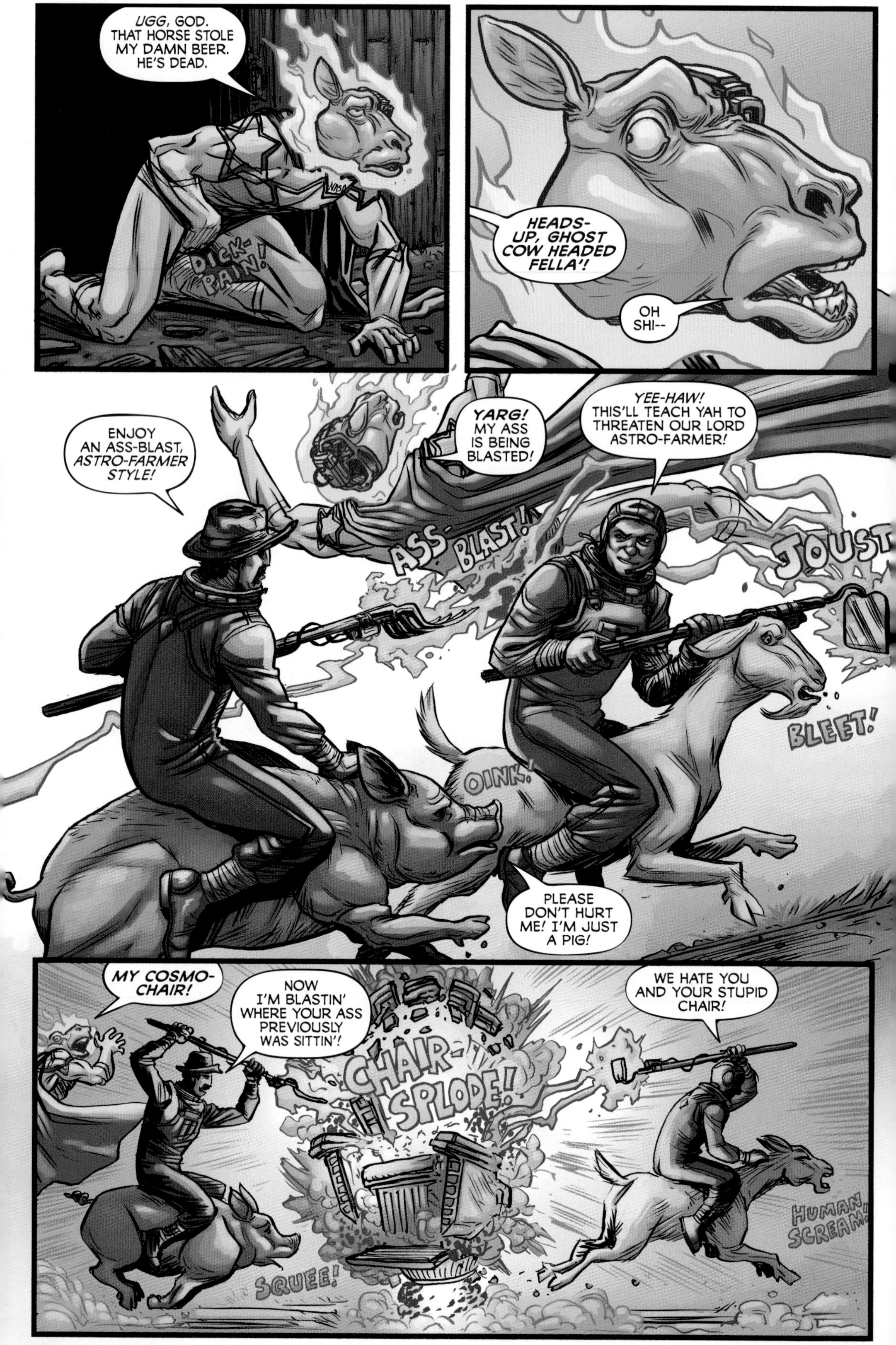
UGG, GOD. THAT HORSE STOLE MY DAMN BEER. HE'S DEAD.
DICK-PAIN!
HEADS-UP, GHOST COW HEADED FELLA'!
OH SHI--
ENJOY AN ASS-BLAST, ASTRO-FARMER STYLE!
YARG! MY ASS IS BEING BLASTED!
YEE-HAW! THIS'LL TEACH YAH TO THREATEN OUR LORD ASTRO-FARMER!
ASS-BLAST!
JOUST
BLEET!
OINK!
PLEASE DON'T HURT ME! I'M JUST A PIG!
MY COSMO-CHAIR!
NOW I'M BLASTIN' WHERE YOUR ASS PREVIOUSLY WAS SITTIN'!
WE HATE YOU AND YOUR STUPID CHAIR!
CHAIR-SPLODE!
HUMAN SCREAM!
SQUEE!

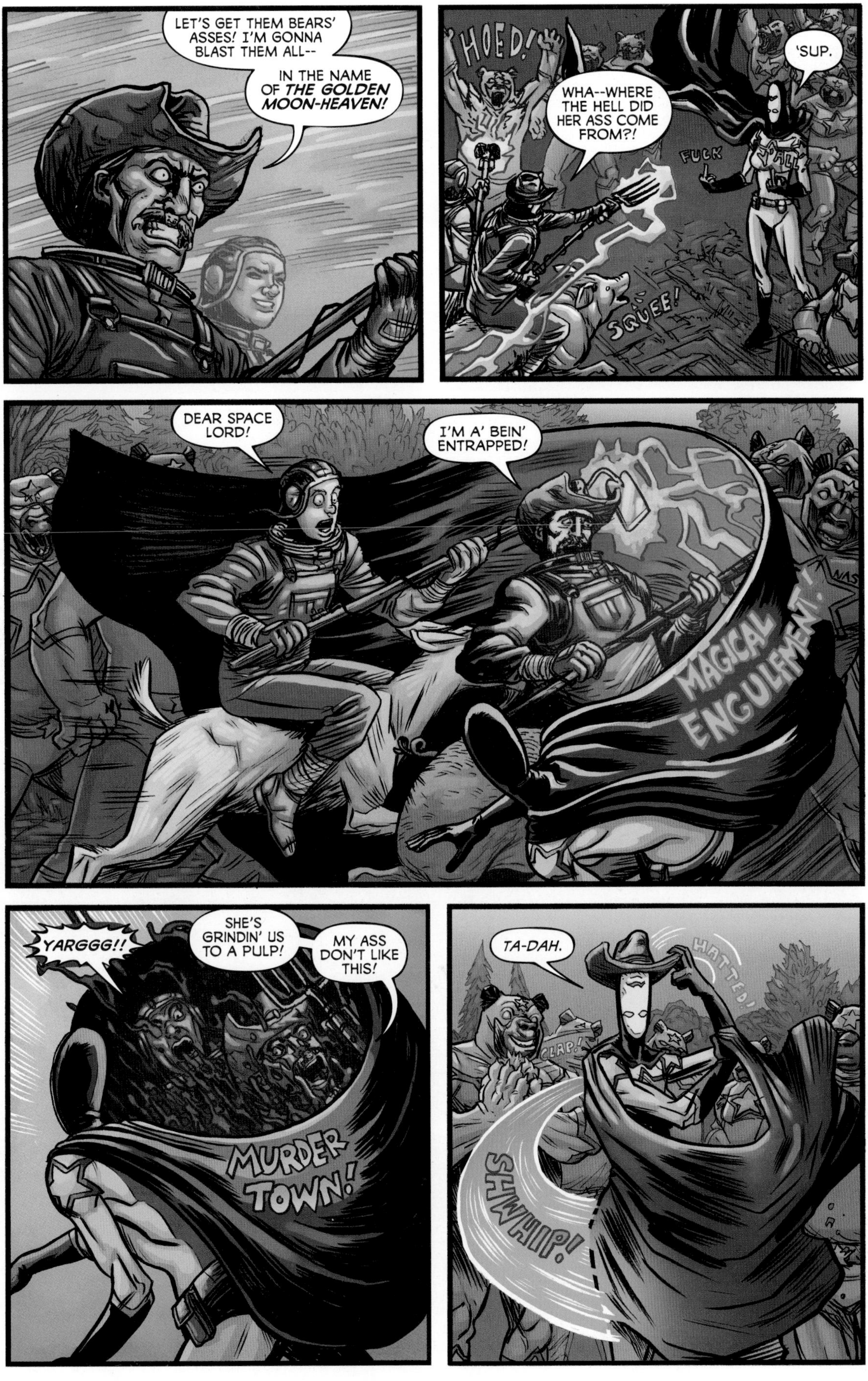
LET'S GET THEM BEARS' ASSES! I'M GONNA BLAST THEM ALL--
IN THE NAME OF *THE GOLDEN MOON-HEAVEN!*
HOED!
WHA--WHERE THE HELL DID HER ASS COME FROM?!
'SUP.
FUCK
SQUEE!
DEAR SPACE LORD!
I'M A' BEIN' ENTRAPPED!
MAGICAL ENGULFMENT!
YARGGG!!
SHE'S GRINDIN' US TO A PULP!
MY ASS DON'T LIKE THIS!
MURDER TOWN!
TA-DAH.
HATTED!
CLAP!
SHWHIP!

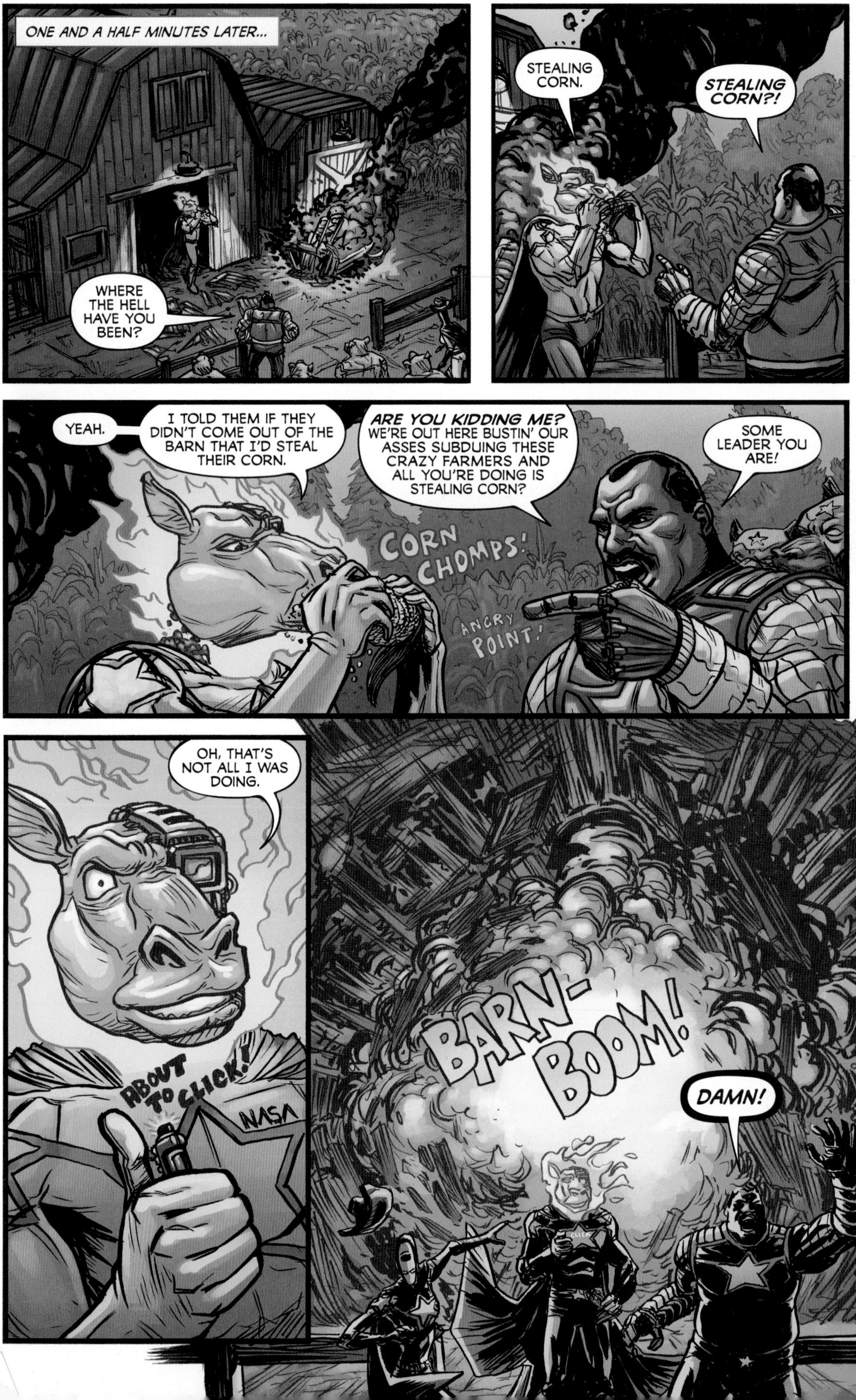

ONE AND A HALF MINUTES LATER...
WHERE THE HELL HAVE YOU BEEN?
STEALING CORN.
STEALING CORN?!
YEAH.
I TOLD THEM IF THEY DIDN'T COME OUT OF THE BARN THAT I'D STEAL THEIR CORN.
ARE YOU KIDDING ME? WE'RE OUT HERE BUSTIN' OUR ASSES SUBDUING THESE CRAZY FARMERS AND ALL YOU'RE DOING IS STEALING CORN?
SOME LEADER YOU ARE!
CORN CHOMPS!
ANGRY POINT!
OH, THAT'S NOT ALL I WAS DOING.
ABOUT TO CLICK!
BARN-BOOM!
DAMN!

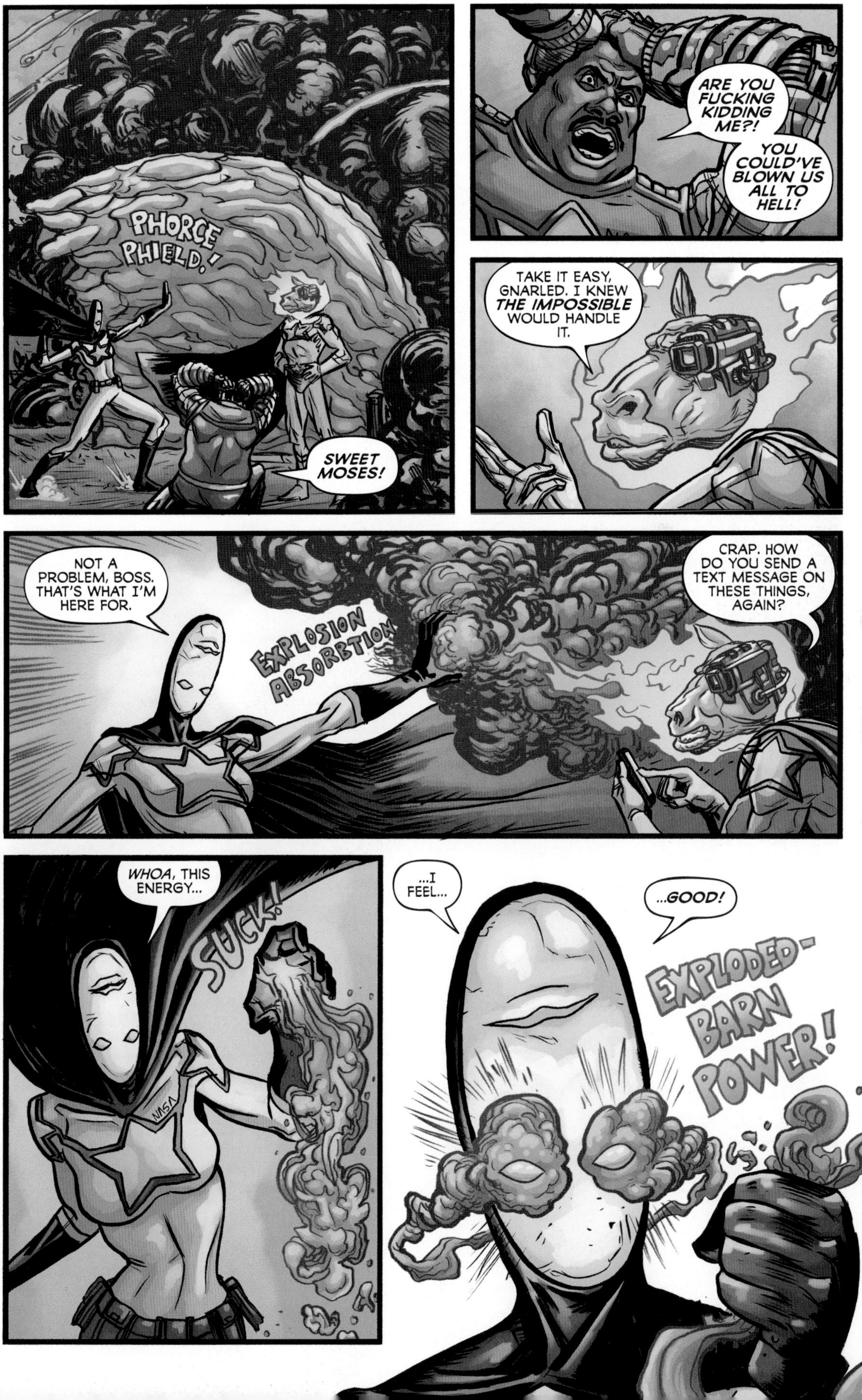
PHORCE PHIELD!
SWEET MOSES!
ARE YOU FUCKING KIDDING ME?!
YOU COULD'VE BLOWN US ALL TO HELL!
TAKE IT EASY, GNARLED. I KNEW THE IMPOSSIBLE WOULD HANDLE IT.
NOT A PROBLEM, BOSS. THAT'S WHAT I'M HERE FOR.
EXPLOSION ABSORBTION
CRAP. HOW DO YOU SEND A TEXT MESSAGE ON THESE THINGS, AGAIN?
WHOA, THIS ENERGY...
SUCK!
NASA
...I FEEL...
...GOOD!
EXPLODED-BARN POWER!

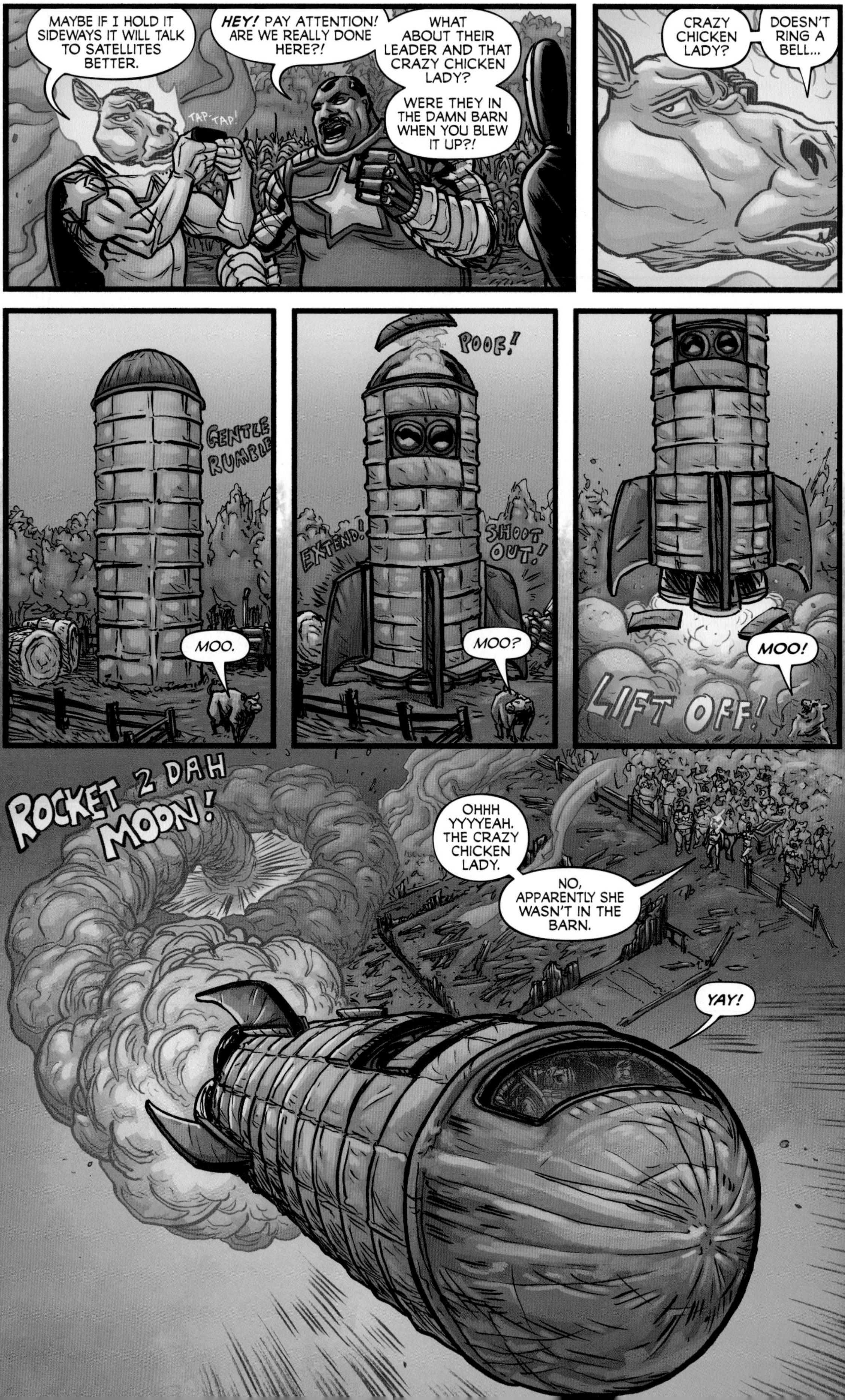
MAYBE IF I HOLD IT SIDEWAYS IT WILL TALK TO SATELLITES BETTER.
TAP-TAP!
HEY! PAY ATTENTION! ARE WE REALLY DONE HERE?!
WHAT ABOUT THEIR LEADER AND THAT CRAZY CHICKEN LADY?
WERE THEY IN THE DAMN BARN WHEN YOU BLEW IT UP?!
CRAZY CHICKEN LADY?
DOESN'T RING A BELL...
GENTLE RUMBLE
MOO.
POOF!
EXTEND!
SHOOT OUT!
MOO?
MOO!
LIFT OFF!
ROCKET 2 DAH MOON!
OHHH YYYYEAH. THE CRAZY CHICKEN LADY.
NO, APPARENTLY SHE WASN'T IN THE BARN.
YAY!

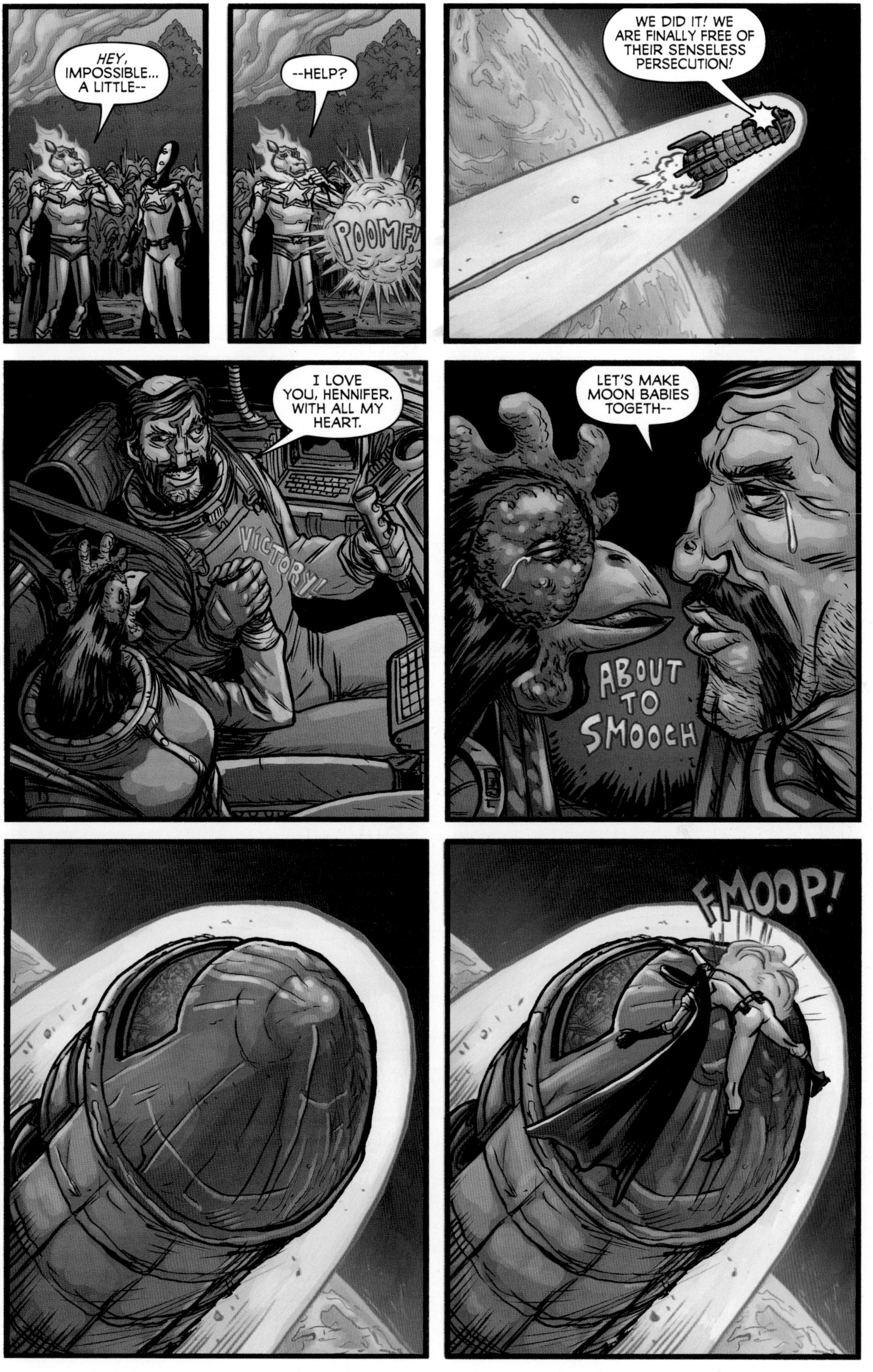
HEY, IMPOSSIBLE... A LITTLE--
--HELP?
POOMF!
WE DID IT! WE ARE FINALLY FREE OF THEIR SENSELESS PERSECUTION!
I LOVE YOU, HENNIFER. WITH ALL MY HEART.
VICTORY!
LET'S MAKE MOON BABIES TOGETH--
ABOUT TO SMOOCH
FMOOP!

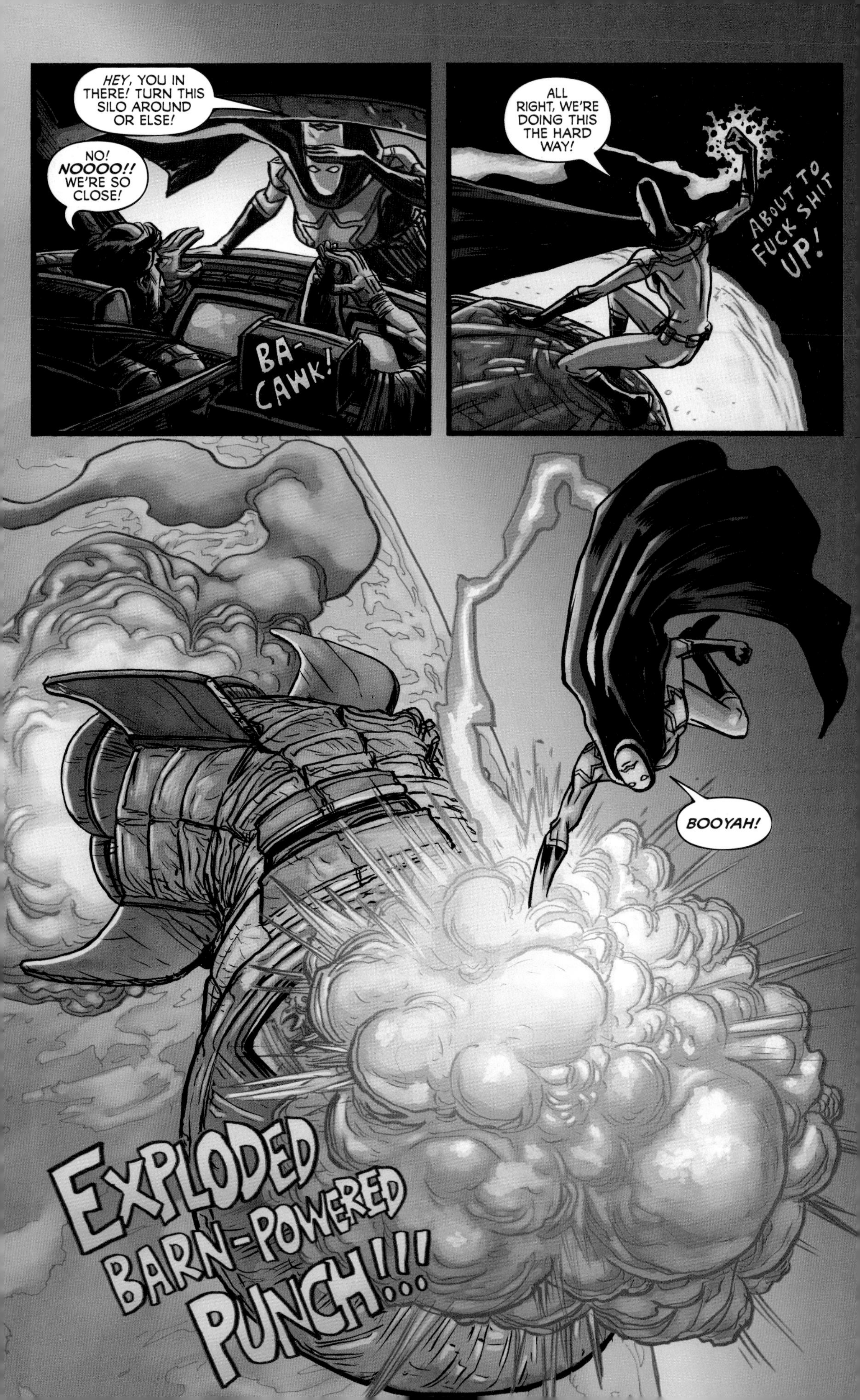

HEY, YOU IN THERE! TURN THIS SILO AROUND OR ELSE!
NO! ***NOOOO!!*** WE'RE SO CLOSE!
BA-CAWK!
ALL RIGHT, WE'RE DOING THIS THE HARD WAY!
ABOUT TO FUCK SHIT UP!
BOOYAH!
EXPLODED BARN-POWERED PUNCH!!!

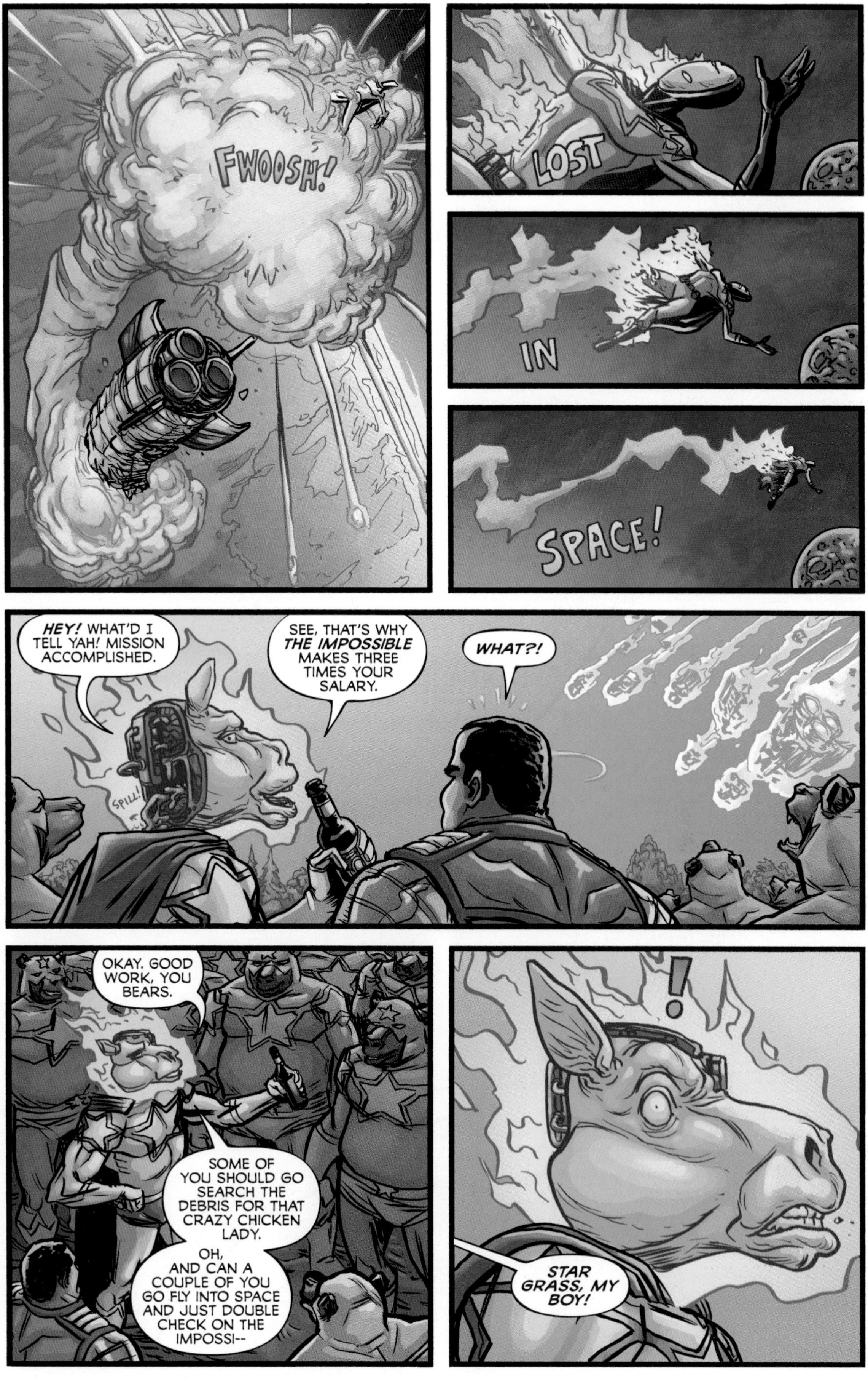
FWOOSH!
LOST
IN
SPACE!
HEY! WHAT'D I TELL YAH! MISSION ACCOMPLISHED.
SEE, THAT'S WHY THE IMPOSSIBLE MAKES THREE TIMES YOUR SALARY.
WHAT?!
SPILL!
OKAY. GOOD WORK, YOU BEARS.
SOME OF YOU SHOULD GO SEARCH THE DEBRIS FOR THAT CRAZY CHICKEN LADY.
OH, AND CAN A COUPLE OF YOU GO FLY INTO SPACE AND JUST DOUBLE CHECK ON THE IMPOSSI--
!
STAR GRASS, MY BOY!

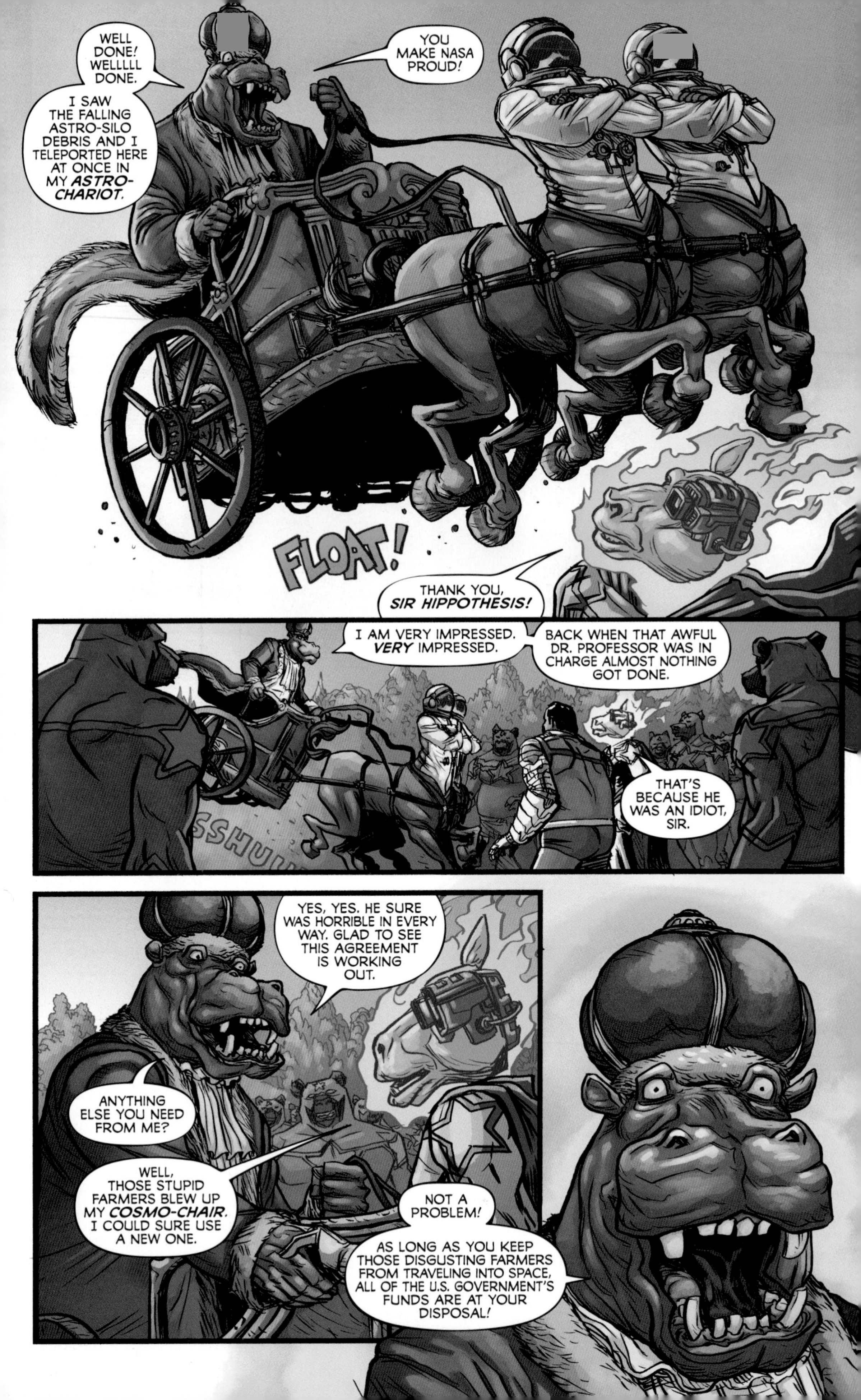
WELL DONE! WELLLLL DONE.
I SAW THE FALLING ASTRO-SILO DEBRIS AND I TELEPORTED HERE AT ONCE IN MY ASTRO-CHARIOT.
YOU MAKE NASA PROUD!
FLOAT!
THANK YOU, SIR HIPPOTHESIS!
I AM VERY IMPRESSED. VERY IMPRESSED.
BACK WHEN THAT AWFUL DR. PROFESSOR WAS IN CHARGE ALMOST NOTHING GOT DONE.
THAT'S BECAUSE HE WAS AN IDIOT, SIR.
YES, YES. HE SURE WAS HORRIBLE IN EVERY WAY. GLAD TO SEE THIS AGREEMENT IS WORKING OUT.
ANYTHING ELSE YOU NEED FROM ME?
WELL, THOSE STUPID FARMERS BLEW UP MY COSMO-CHAIR. I COULD SURE USE A NEW ONE.
NOT A PROBLEM!
AS LONG AS YOU KEEP THOSE DISGUSTING FARMERS FROM TRAVELING INTO SPACE, ALL OF THE U.S. GOVERNMENT'S FUNDS ARE AT YOUR DISPOSAL!

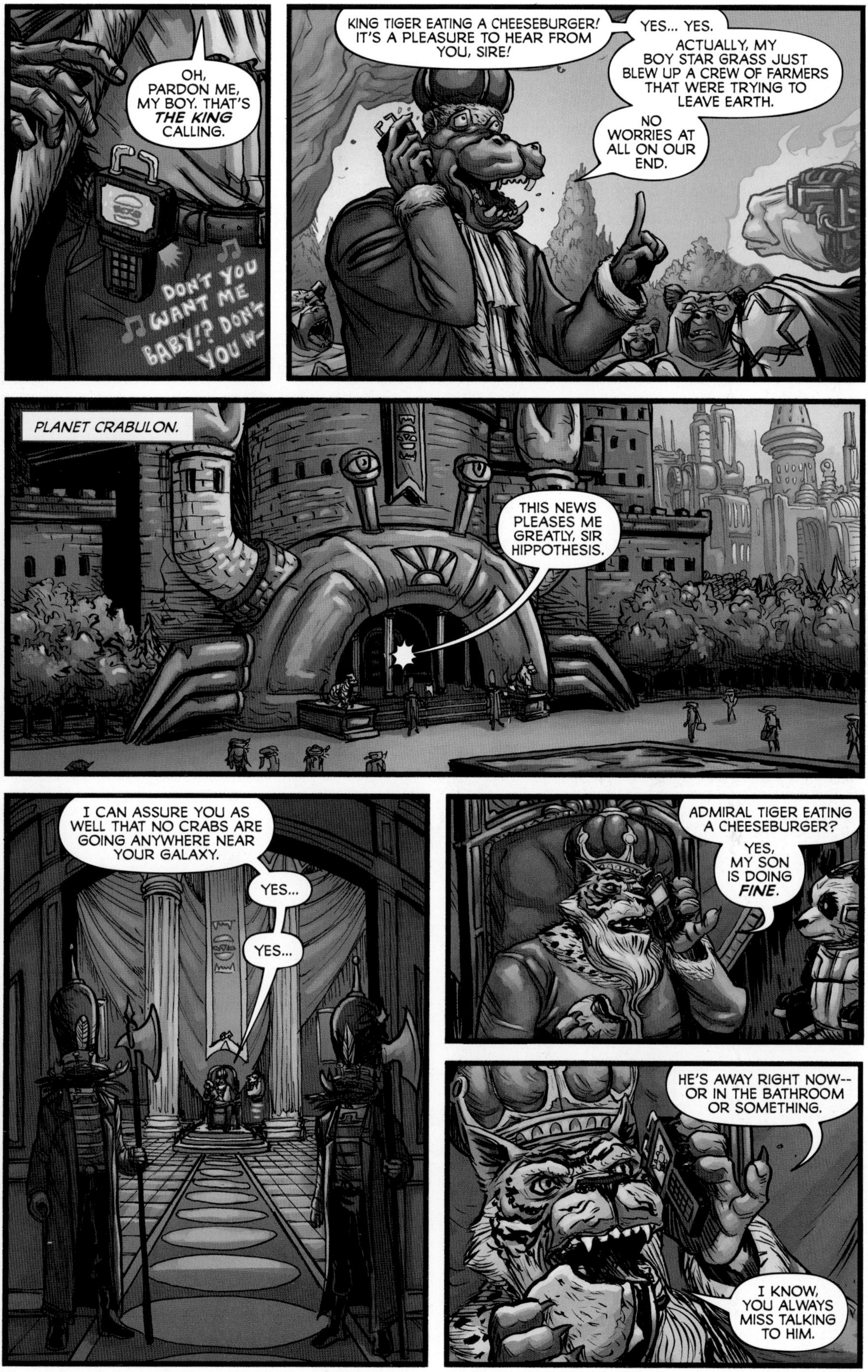
OH, PARDON ME, MY BOY. THAT'S *THE KING* CALLING.
DON'T YOU WANT ME BABY!? DON'T YOU W-
KING TIGER EATING A CHEESEBURGER! IT'S A PLEASURE TO HEAR FROM YOU, SIRE!
YES... YES.
ACTUALLY, MY BOY STAR GRASS JUST BLEW UP A CREW OF FARMERS THAT WERE TRYING TO LEAVE EARTH.
NO WORRIES AT ALL ON OUR END.
PLANET CRABULON.
THIS NEWS PLEASES ME GREATLY, SIR HIPPOTHESIS.
I CAN ASSURE YOU AS WELL THAT NO CRABS ARE GOING ANYWHERE NEAR YOUR GALAXY.
YES...
YES...
ADMIRAL TIGER EATING A CHEESEBURGER?
YES, MY SON IS DOING *FINE*.
HE'S AWAY RIGHT NOW-- OR IN THE BATHROOM OR SOMETHING.
I KNOW, YOU ALWAYS MISS TALKING TO HIM.

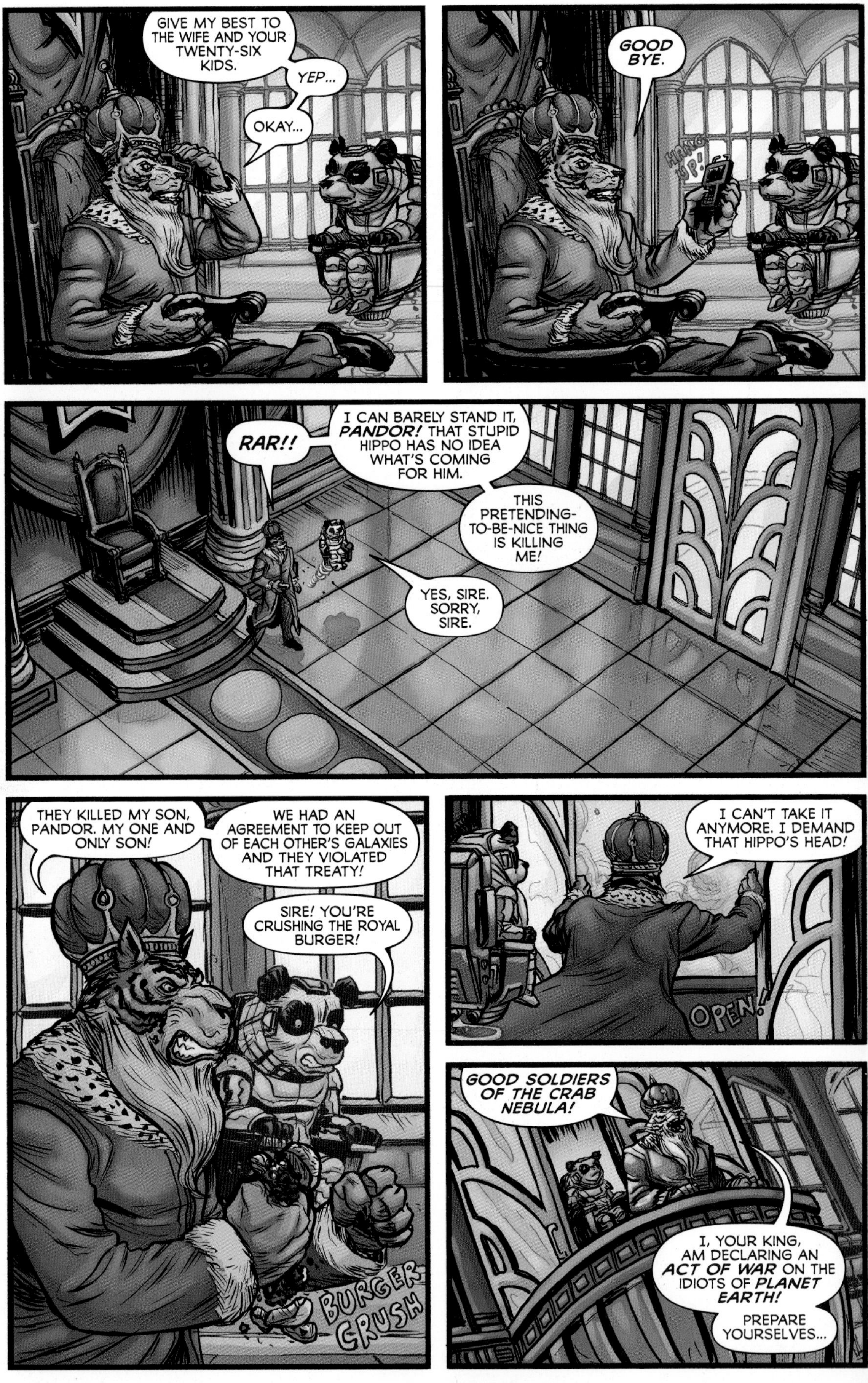
GIVE MY BEST TO THE WIFE AND YOUR TWENTY-SIX KIDS.
YEP...
OKAY...
GOOD BYE.
HANG UP!
RAR!!
I CAN BARELY STAND IT, PANDOR! THAT STUPID HIPPO HAS NO IDEA WHAT'S COMING FOR HIM.
THIS PRETENDING-TO-BE-NICE THING IS KILLING ME!
YES, SIRE. SORRY, SIRE.
THEY KILLED MY SON, PANDOR. MY ONE AND ONLY SON!
WE HAD AN AGREEMENT TO KEEP OUT OF EACH OTHER'S GALAXIES AND THEY VIOLATED THAT TREATY!
SIRE! YOU'RE CRUSHING THE ROYAL BURGER!
BURGER CRUSH
I CAN'T TAKE IT ANYMORE. I DEMAND THAT HIPPO'S HEAD!
OPEN!
GOOD SOLDIERS OF THE CRAB NEBULA!
I, YOUR KING, AM DECLARING AN ACT OF WAR ON THE IDIOTS OF PLANET EARTH!
PREPARE YOURSELVES...

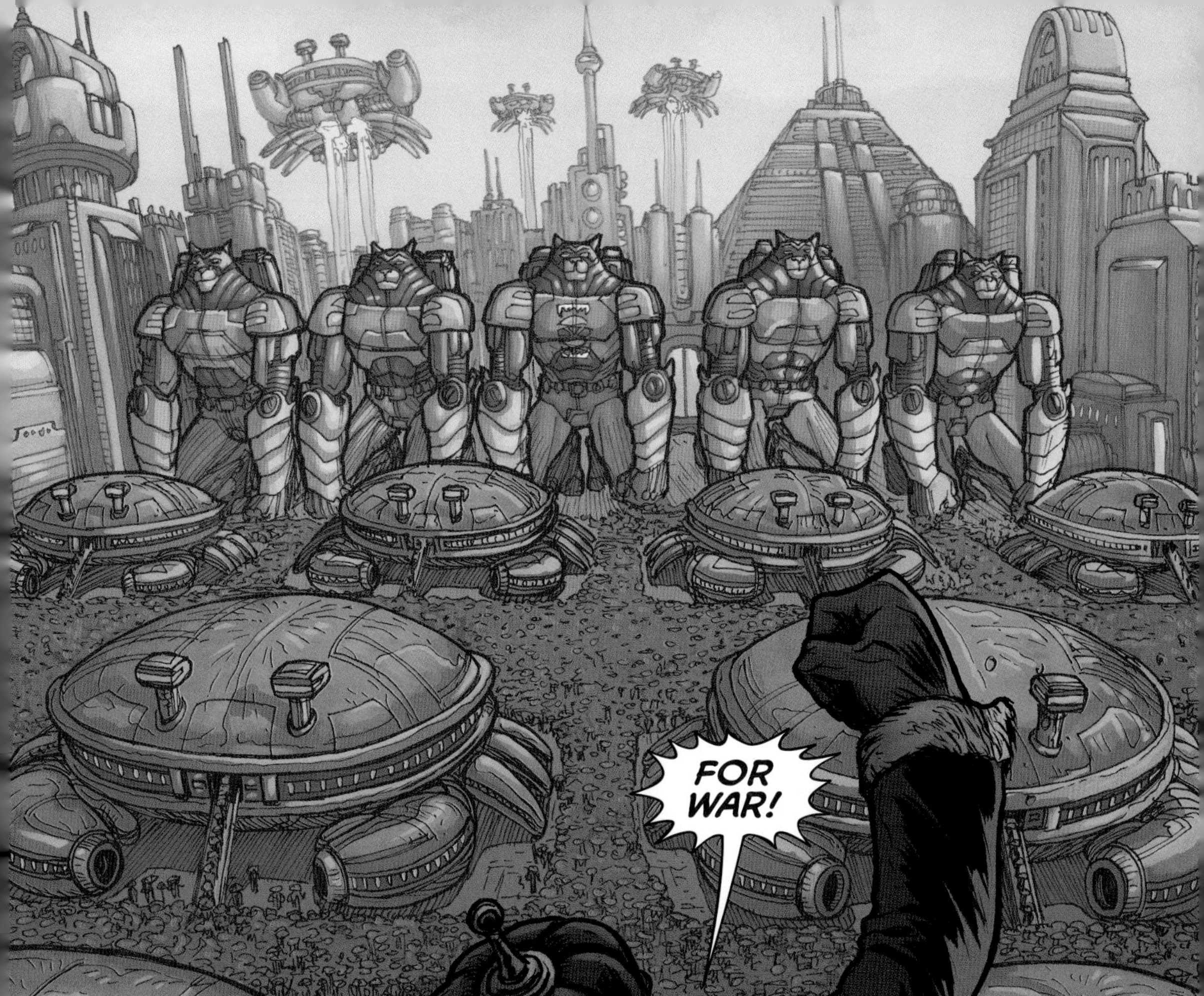
FOR WAR!

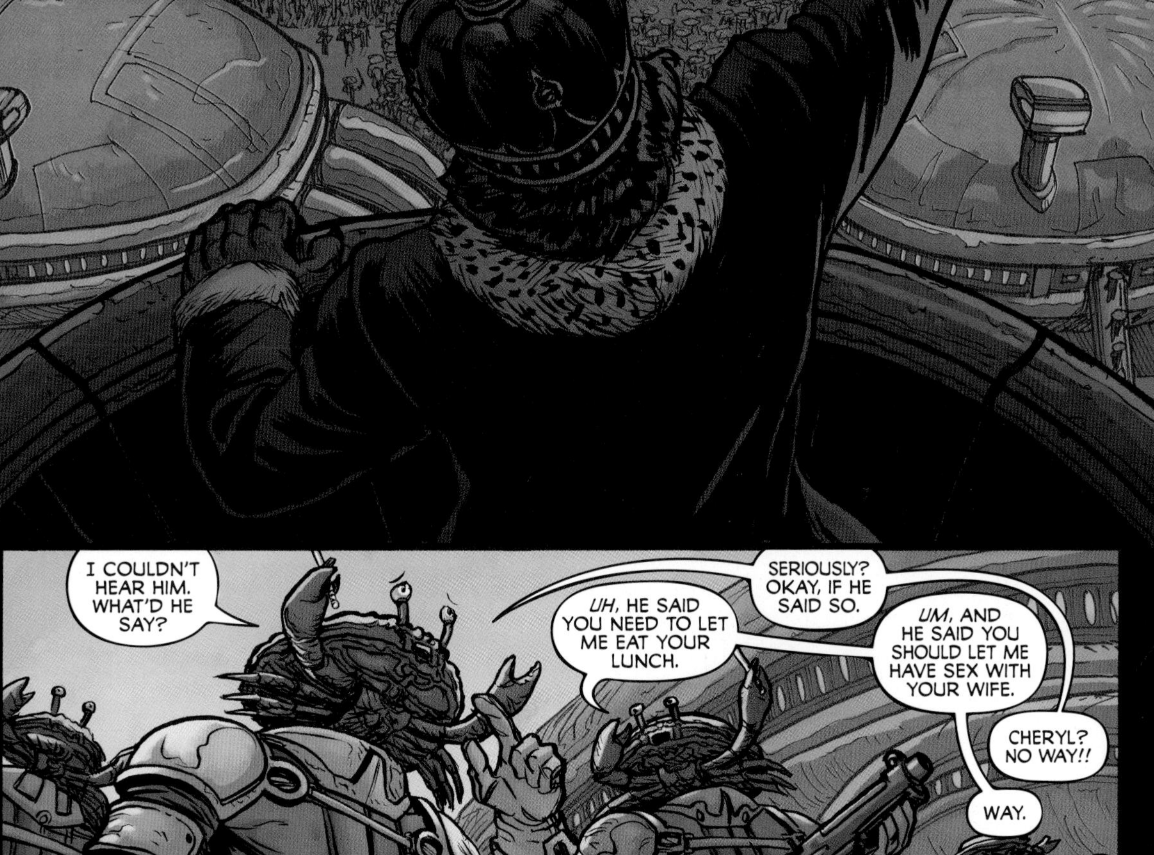
I COULDN'T HEAR HIM. WHAT'D HE SAY?
UH, HE SAID YOU NEED TO LET ME EAT YOUR LUNCH.
SERIOUSLY? OKAY, IF HE SAID SO.
UM, AND HE SAID YOU SHOULD LET ME HAVE SEX WITH YOUR WIFE.
CHERYL? NO WAY*!!*
WAY.

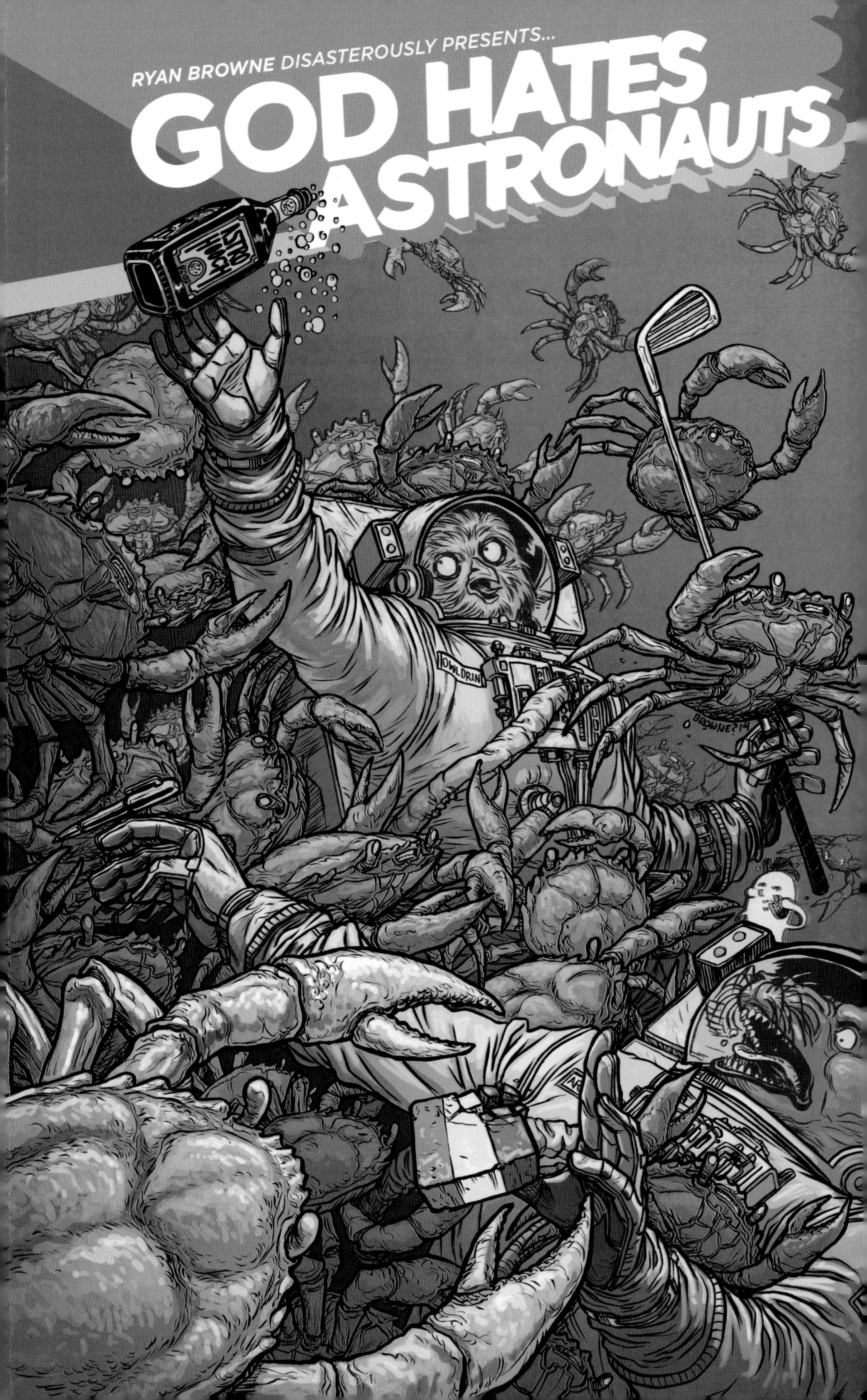
RYAN BROWNE DISASTEROUSLY PRESENTS...
GOD HATES ASTRONAUTS
OWLDRIN
BROWNE?'14

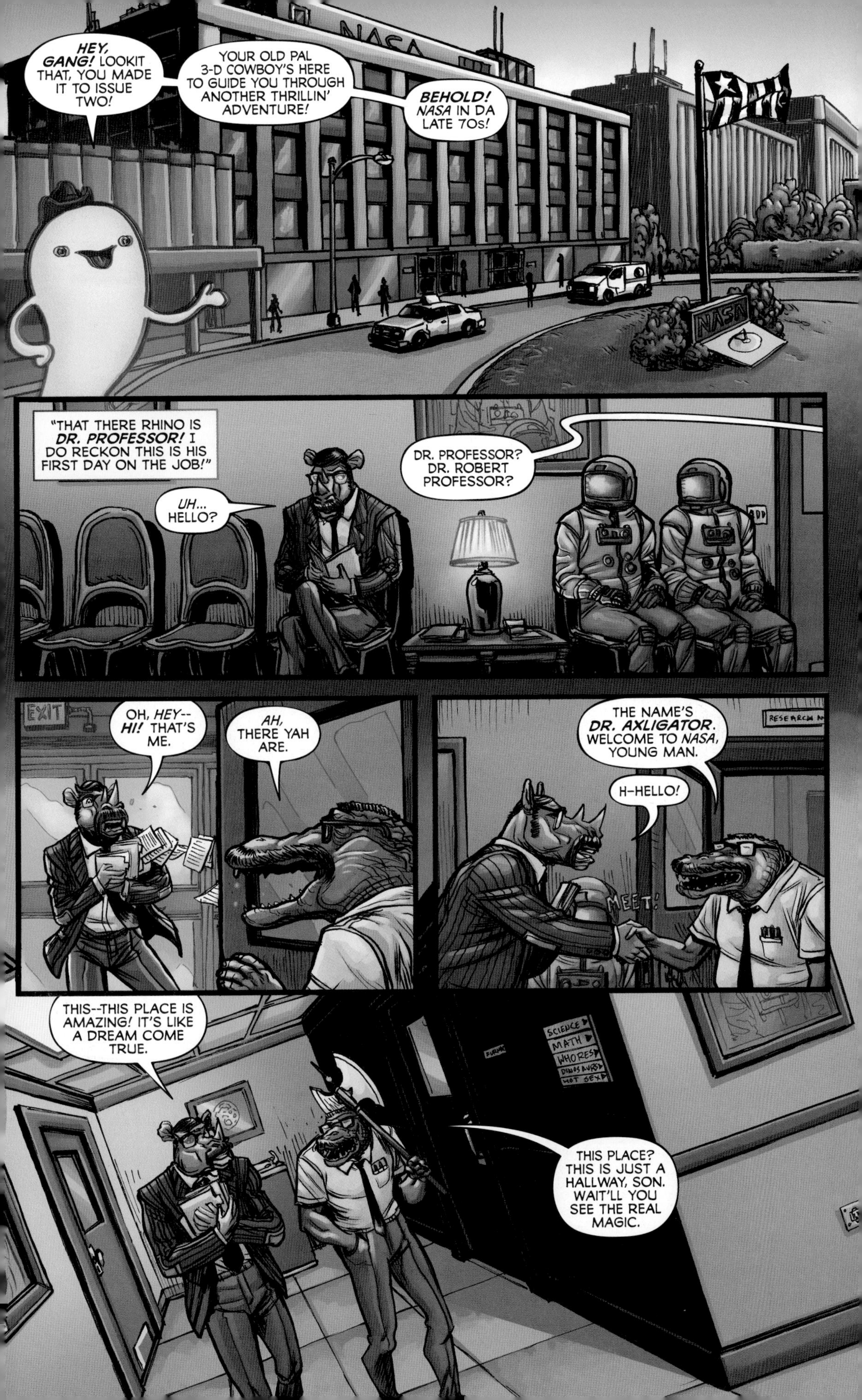

NASA
HEY, GANG! LOOKIT THAT, YOU MADE IT TO ISSUE TWO!
YOUR OLD PAL 3-D COWBOY'S HERE TO GUIDE YOU THROUGH ANOTHER THRILLIN' ADVENTURE!
BEHOLD! NASA IN DA LATE 70s!
NASA
"THAT THERE RHINO IS *DR. PROFESSOR!* I DO RECKON THIS IS HIS FIRST DAY ON THE JOB!"
DR. PROFESSOR? DR. ROBERT PROFESSOR?
UH... HELLO?
EXIT
OH, *HEY*-- *HI!* THAT'S ME.
AH, THERE YAH ARE.
THE NAME'S *DR. AXLIGATOR.* WELCOME TO *NASA,* YOUNG MAN.
H-HELLO!
MEET!
THIS--THIS PLACE IS AMAZING! IT'S LIKE A DREAM COME TRUE.
SCIENCE
MATH
WHORES
DINOSAURS
HOT SEX
THIS PLACE? THIS IS JUST A HALLWAY, SON. WAIT'LL YOU SEE THE REAL MAGIC.

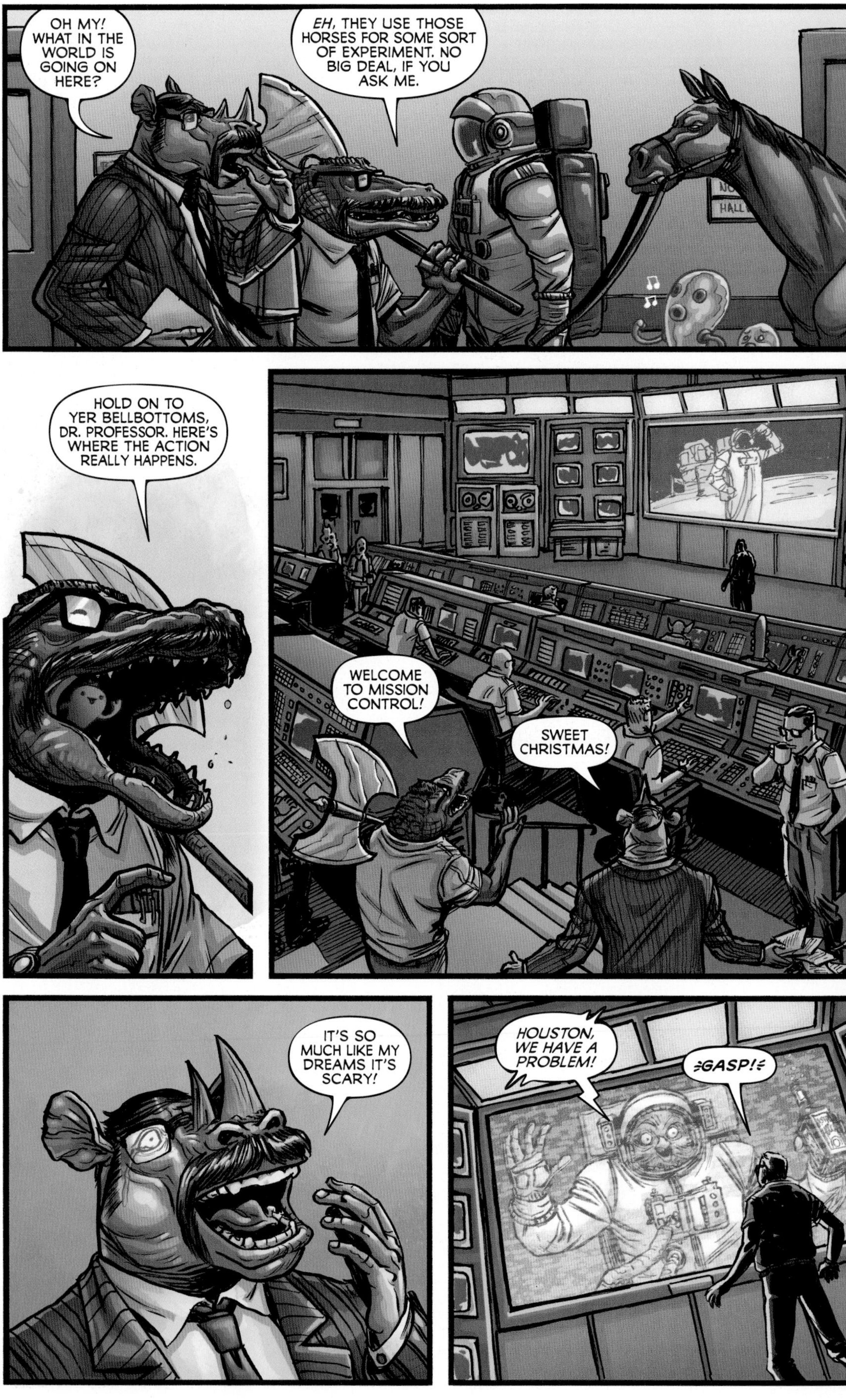

OH MY! WHAT IN THE WORLD IS GOING ON HERE?
EH, THEY USE THOSE HORSES FOR SOME SORT OF EXPERIMENT. NO BIG DEAL, IF YOU ASK ME.
HOLD ON TO YER BELLBOTTOMS, DR. PROFESSOR. HERE'S WHERE THE ACTION REALLY HAPPENS.
WELCOME TO MISSION CONTROL!
SWEET CHRISTMAS!
IT'S SO MUCH LIKE MY DREAMS IT'S SCARY!
HOUSTON, WE HAVE A PROBLEM!
GASP!

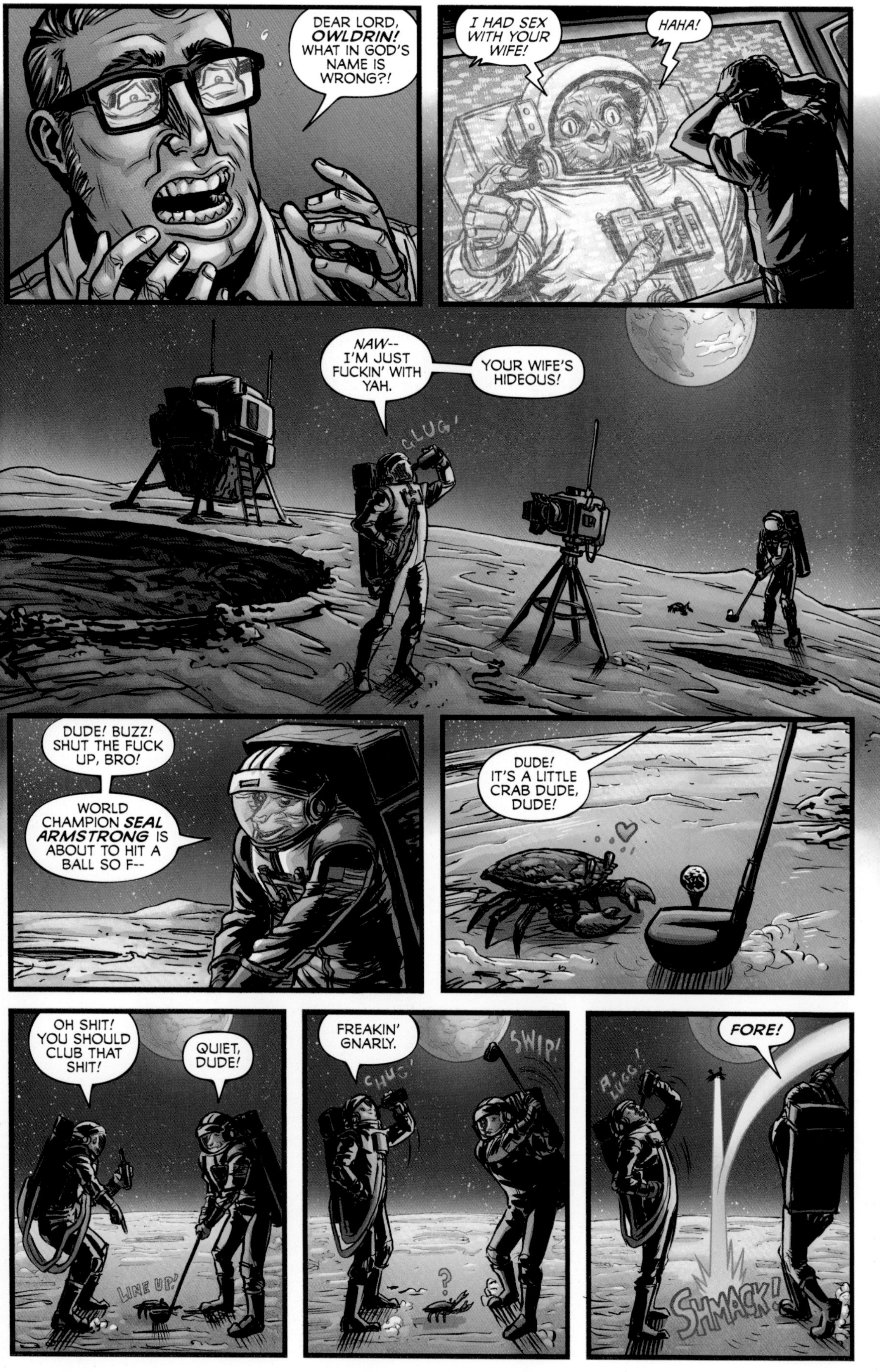
DEAR LORD, OWLDRIN! WHAT IN GOD'S NAME IS WRONG?!
I HAD SEX WITH YOUR WIFE!
HAHA!
NAW-- I'M JUST FUCKIN' WITH YAH.
YOUR WIFE'S HIDEOUS!
GLUG!
DUDE! BUZZ! SHUT THE FUCK UP, BRO!
WORLD CHAMPION SEAL ARMSTRONG IS ABOUT TO HIT A BALL SO F--
DUDE! IT'S A LITTLE CRAB DUDE, DUDE!
OH SHIT! YOU SHOULD CLUB THAT SHIT!
QUIET, DUDE!
LINE UP!
FREAKIN' GNARLY.
CHUG!
SWIP!
?
FORE!
SHMACK!

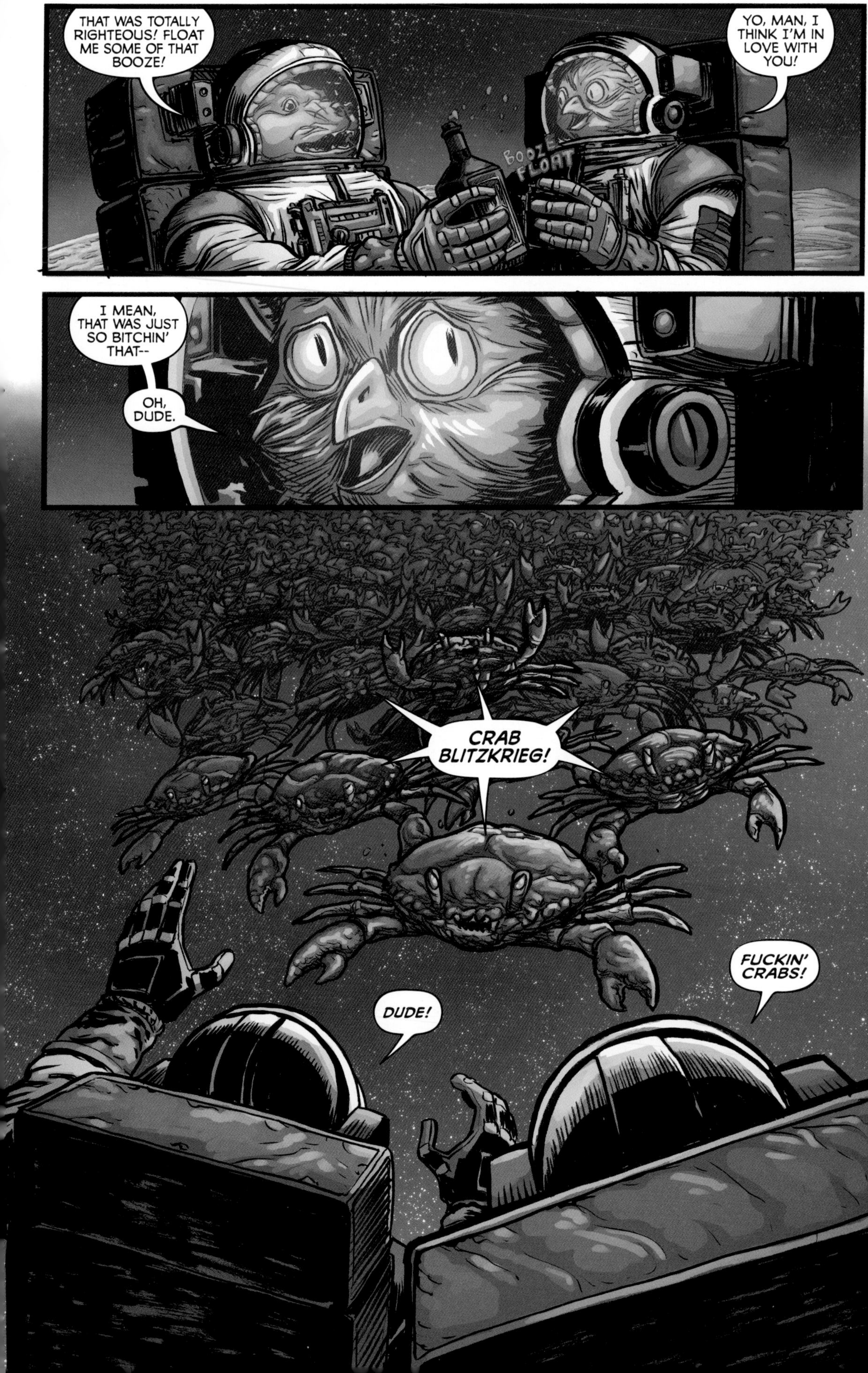
THAT WAS TOTALLY RIGHTEOUS! FLOAT ME SOME OF THAT BOOZE!
YO, MAN, I THINK I'M IN LOVE WITH YOU!
BOOZE FLOAT
I MEAN, THAT WAS JUST SO BITCHIN' THAT--
OH, DUDE.
CRAB BLITZKRIEG!
FUCKIN' CRABS!
DUDE!

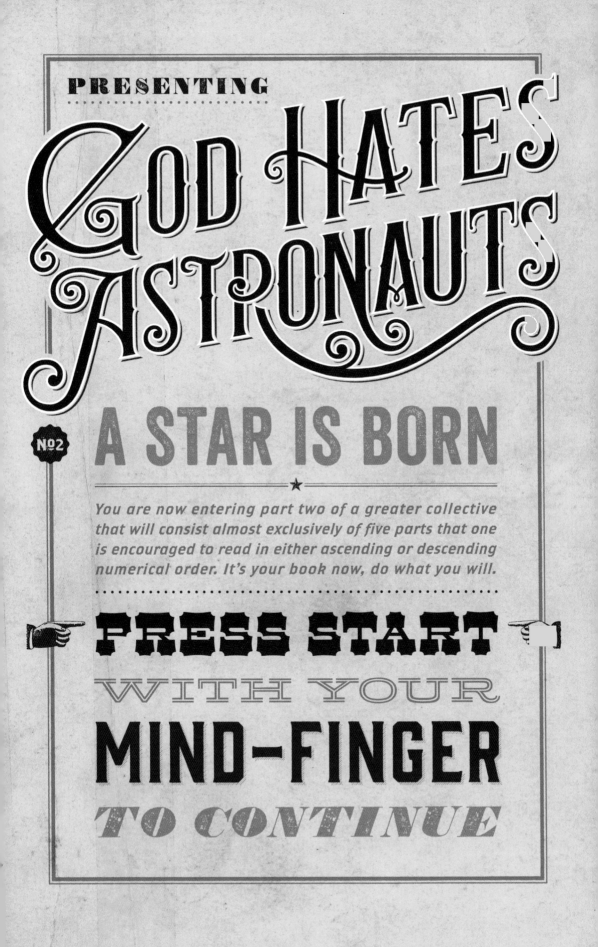

PRESENTING

GOD HATES ASTRONAUTS

Nº2

A STAR IS BORN

You are now entering part two of a greater collective that will consist almost exclusively of five parts that one is encouraged to read in either ascending or descending numerical order. It's your book now, do what you will.

☞ PRESS START ☜

WITH YOUR

MIND-FINGER

TO CONTINUE

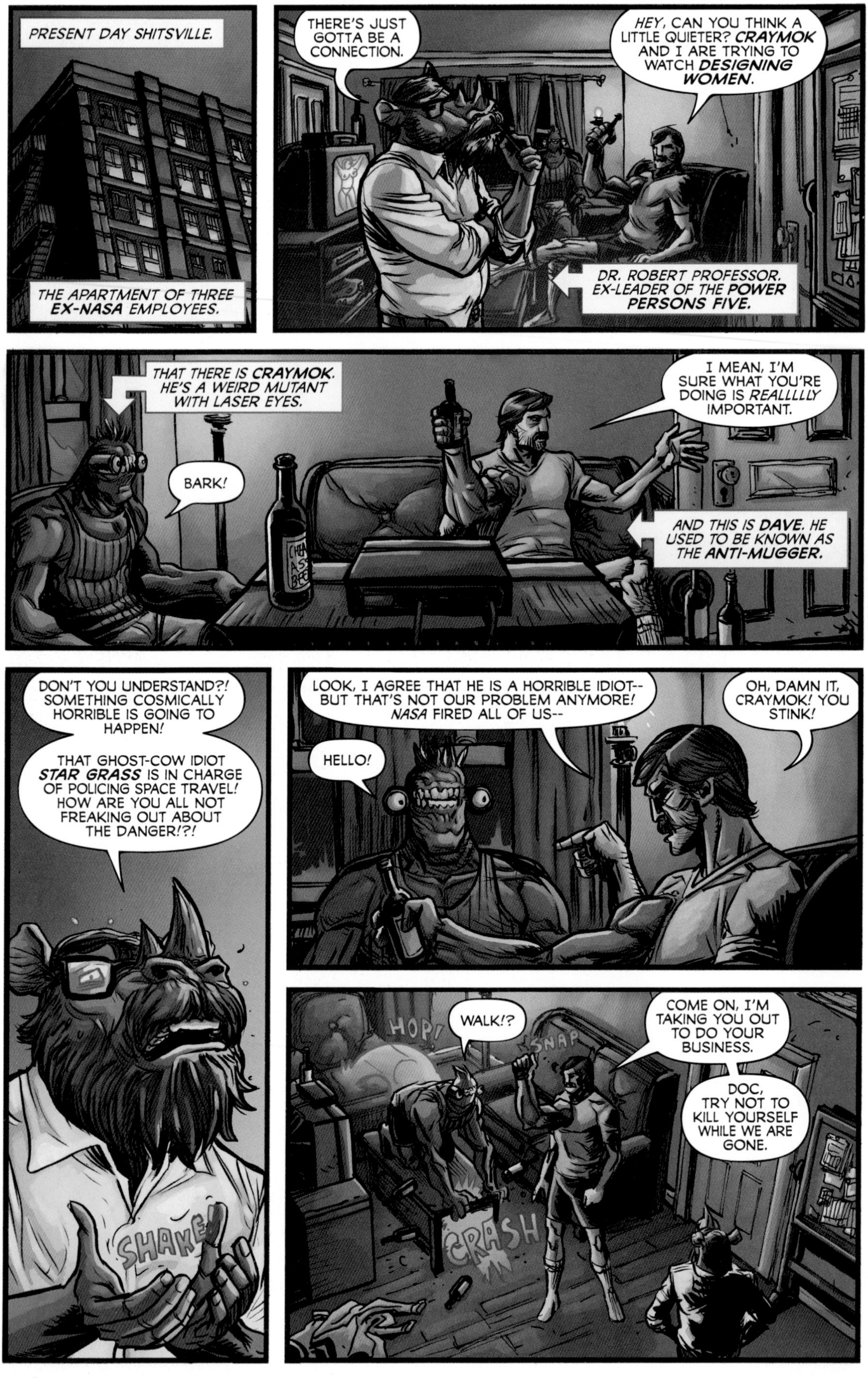

PRESENT DAY SHITSVILLE.
THE APARTMENT OF THREE EX-NASA EMPLOYEES.
THERE'S JUST GOTTA BE A CONNECTION.
HEY, CAN YOU THINK A LITTLE QUIETER? CRAYMOK AND I ARE TRYING TO WATCH DESIGNING WOMEN.
DR. ROBERT PROFESSOR. EX-LEADER OF THE POWER PERSONS FIVE.
THAT THERE IS CRAYMOK. HE'S A WEIRD MUTANT WITH LASER EYES.
BARK!
I MEAN, I'M SURE WHAT YOU'RE DOING IS REALLLLLY IMPORTANT.
AND THIS IS DAVE. HE USED TO BE KNOWN AS THE ANTI-MUGGER.
DON'T YOU UNDERSTAND?! SOMETHING COSMICALLY HORRIBLE IS GOING TO HAPPEN!
THAT GHOST-COW IDIOT STAR GRASS IS IN CHARGE OF POLICING SPACE TRAVEL! HOW ARE YOU ALL NOT FREAKING OUT ABOUT THE DANGER!?!
SHAKE
LOOK, I AGREE THAT HE IS A HORRIBLE IDIOT-- BUT THAT'S NOT OUR PROBLEM ANYMORE! NASA FIRED ALL OF US--
HELLO!
OH, DAMN IT, CRAYMOK! YOU STINK!
HOP!
WALK!?
SNAP
COME ON, I'M TAKING YOU OUT TO DO YOUR BUSINESS.
DOC, TRY NOT TO KILL YOURSELF WHILE WE ARE GONE.
CRASH

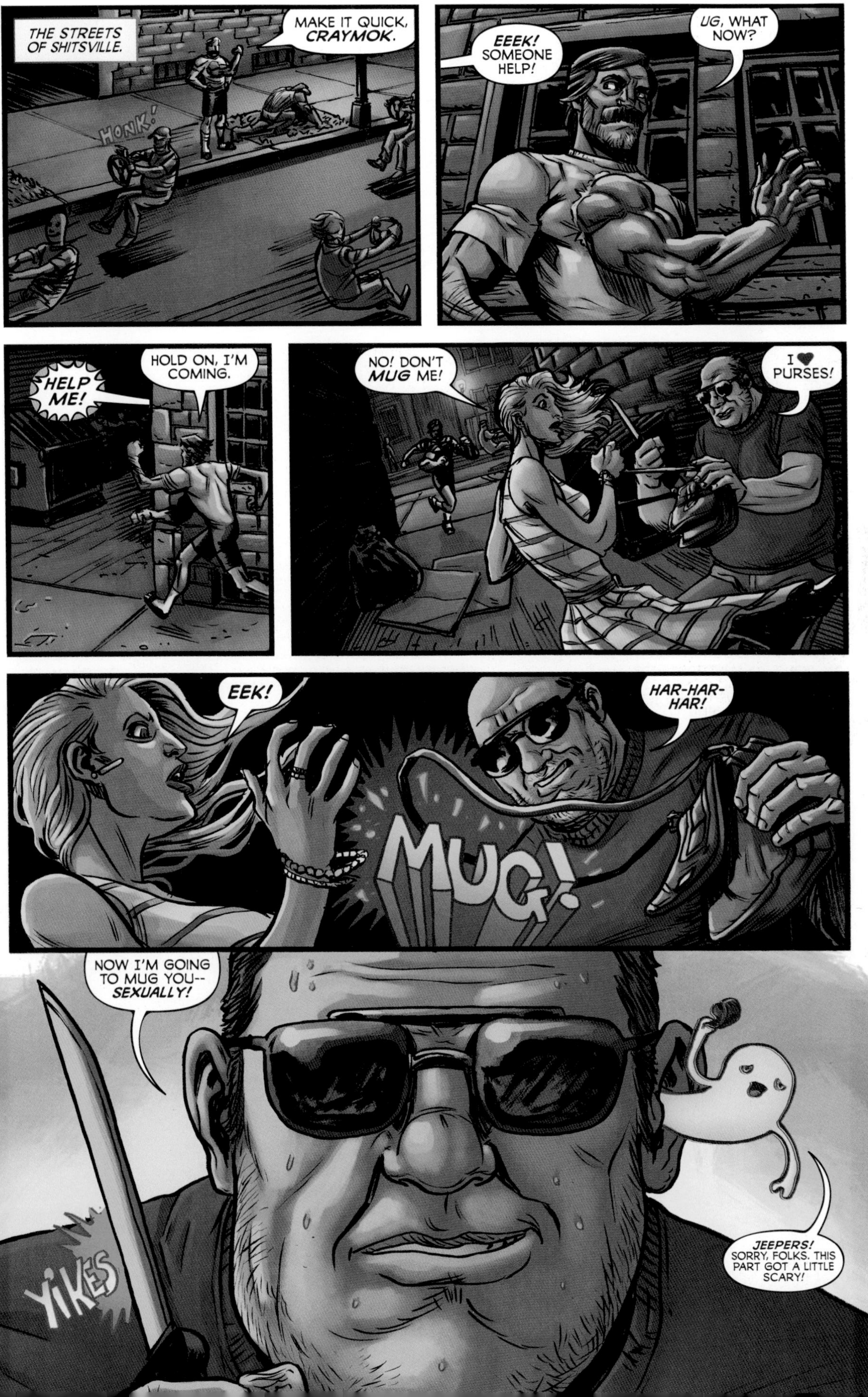
THE STREETS OF SHITSVILLE.
MAKE IT QUICK, CRAYMOK.
HONK!
EEEK! SOMEONE HELP!
UG, WHAT NOW?
HELP ME!
HOLD ON, I'M COMING.
NO! DON'T MUG ME!
I ♥ PURSES!
EEK!
HAR-HAR-HAR!
MUG!
NOW I'M GOING TO MUG YOU-- SEXUALLY!
YIKES
JEEPERS! SORRY, FOLKS. THIS PART GOT A LITTLE SCARY!

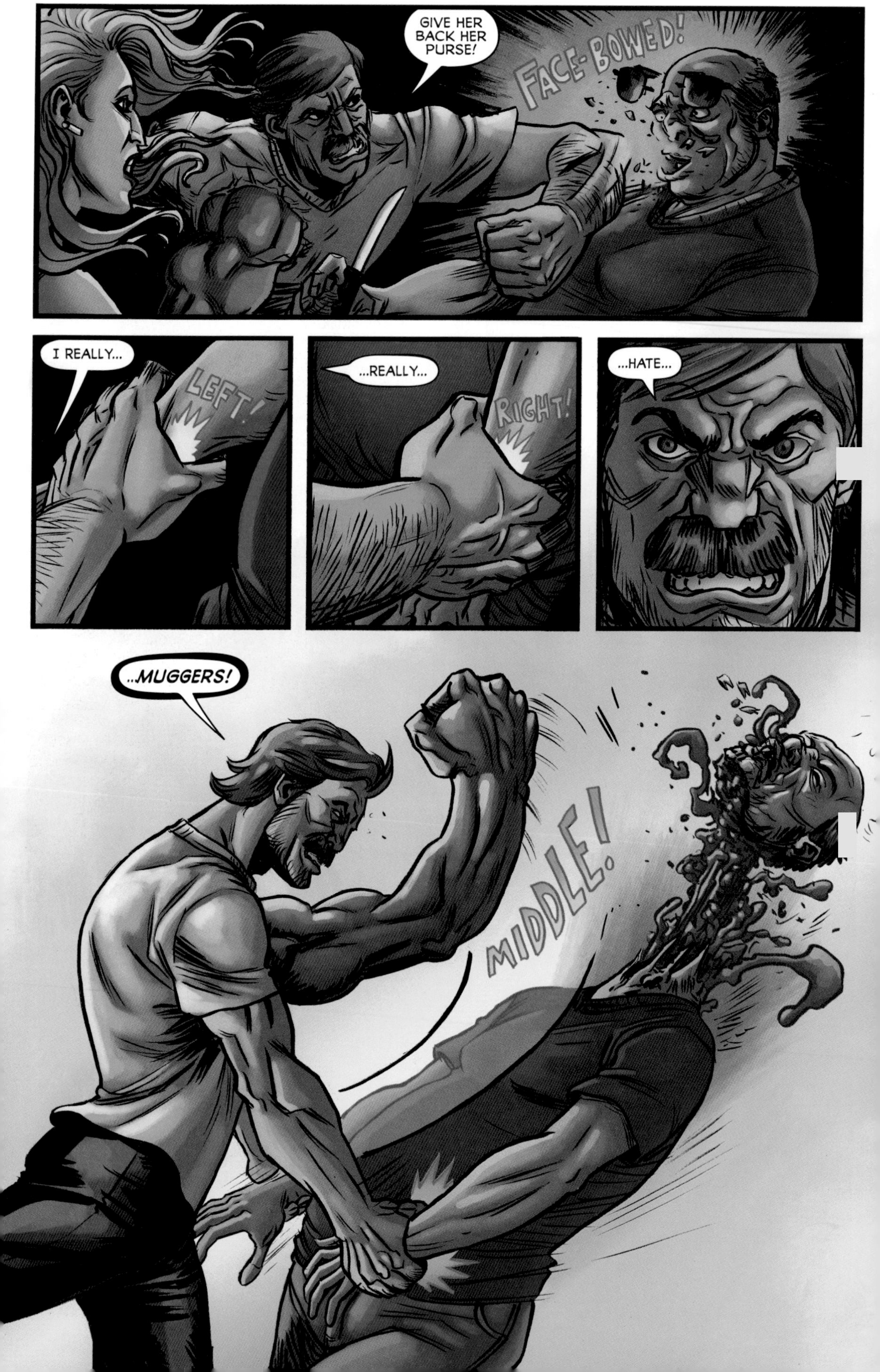
GIVE HER BACK HER PURSE!
FACE-BOWED!
I REALLY...
LEFT!
...REALLY...
RIGHT!
...HATE...
...MUGGERS!
MIDDLE!

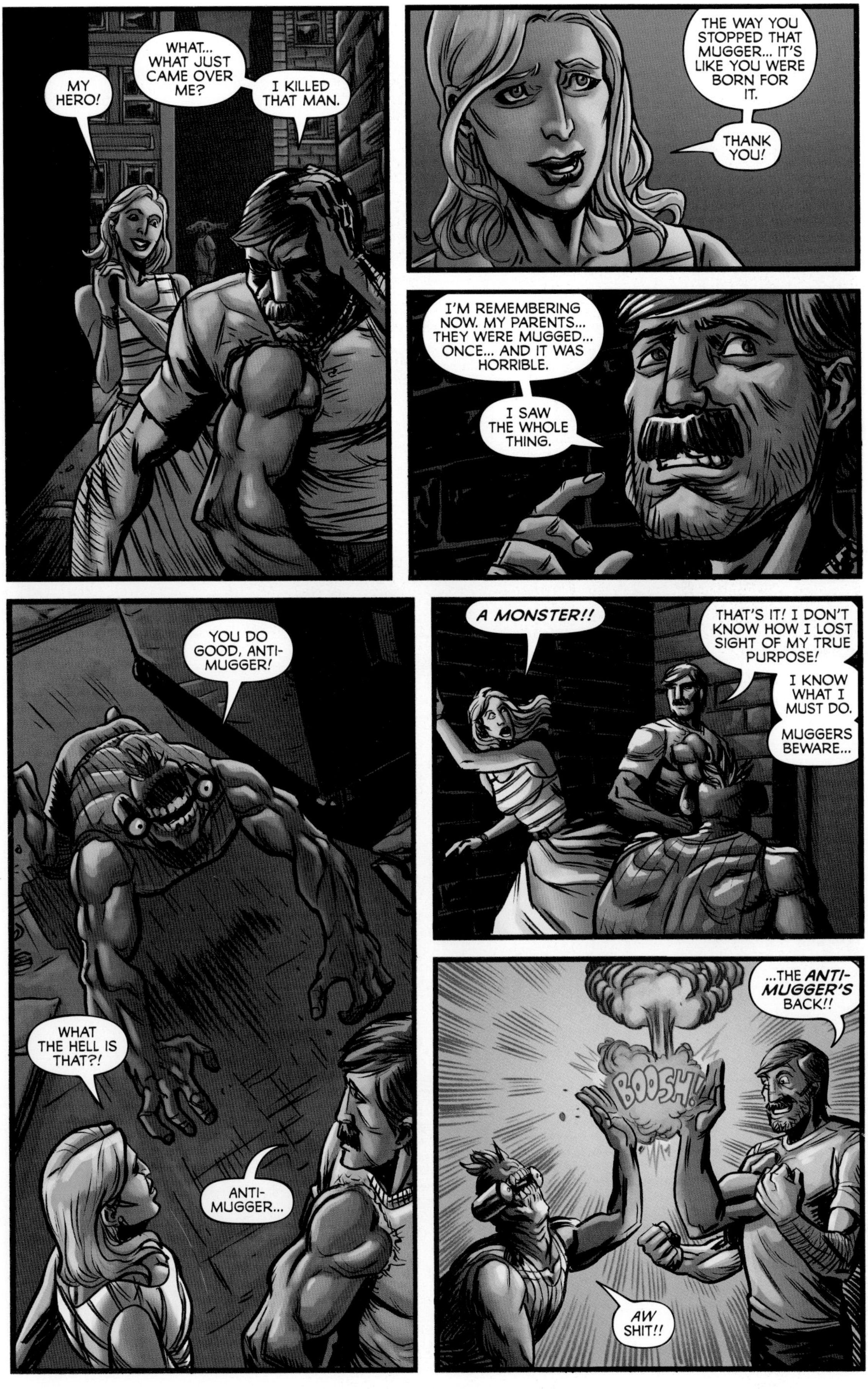
MY HERO!
WHAT... WHAT JUST CAME OVER ME?
I KILLED THAT MAN.
THE WAY YOU STOPPED THAT MUGGER... IT'S LIKE YOU WERE BORN FOR IT.
THANK YOU!
I'M REMEMBERING NOW. MY PARENTS... THEY WERE MUGGED... ONCE... AND IT WAS HORRIBLE.
I SAW THE WHOLE THING.
YOU DO GOOD, ANTI-MUGGER!
WHAT THE HELL IS THAT?!
ANTI-MUGGER...
A MONSTER!!
THAT'S IT! I DON'T KNOW HOW I LOST SIGHT OF MY TRUE PURPOSE!
I KNOW WHAT I MUST DO.
MUGGERS BEWARE...
...THE ANTI-MUGGER'S BACK!!
BOOSH!
AW SHIT!!

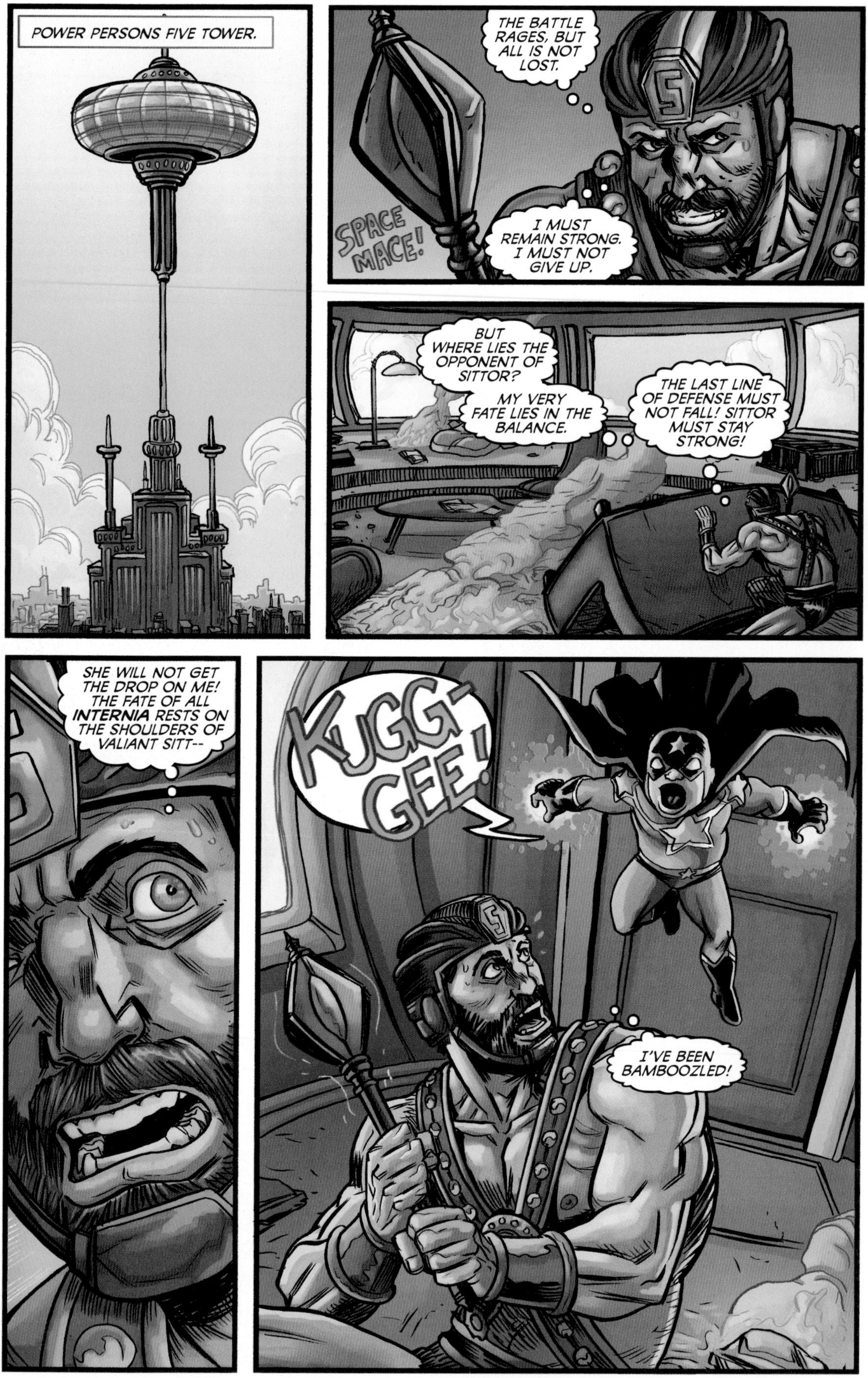
POWER PERSONS FIVE TOWER.
THE BATTLE RAGES, BUT ALL IS NOT LOST.
SPACE MACE!
I MUST REMAIN STRONG. I MUST NOT GIVE UP.
BUT WHERE LIES THE OPPONENT OF SITTOR?
MY VERY FATE LIES IN THE BALANCE.
THE LAST LINE OF DEFENSE MUST NOT FALL! SITTOR MUST STAY STRONG!
SHE WILL NOT GET THE DROP ON ME! THE FATE OF ALL INTERNIA RESTS ON THE SHOULDERS OF VALIANT SITT--
KUGG-GEE!
I'VE BEEN BAMBOOZLED!

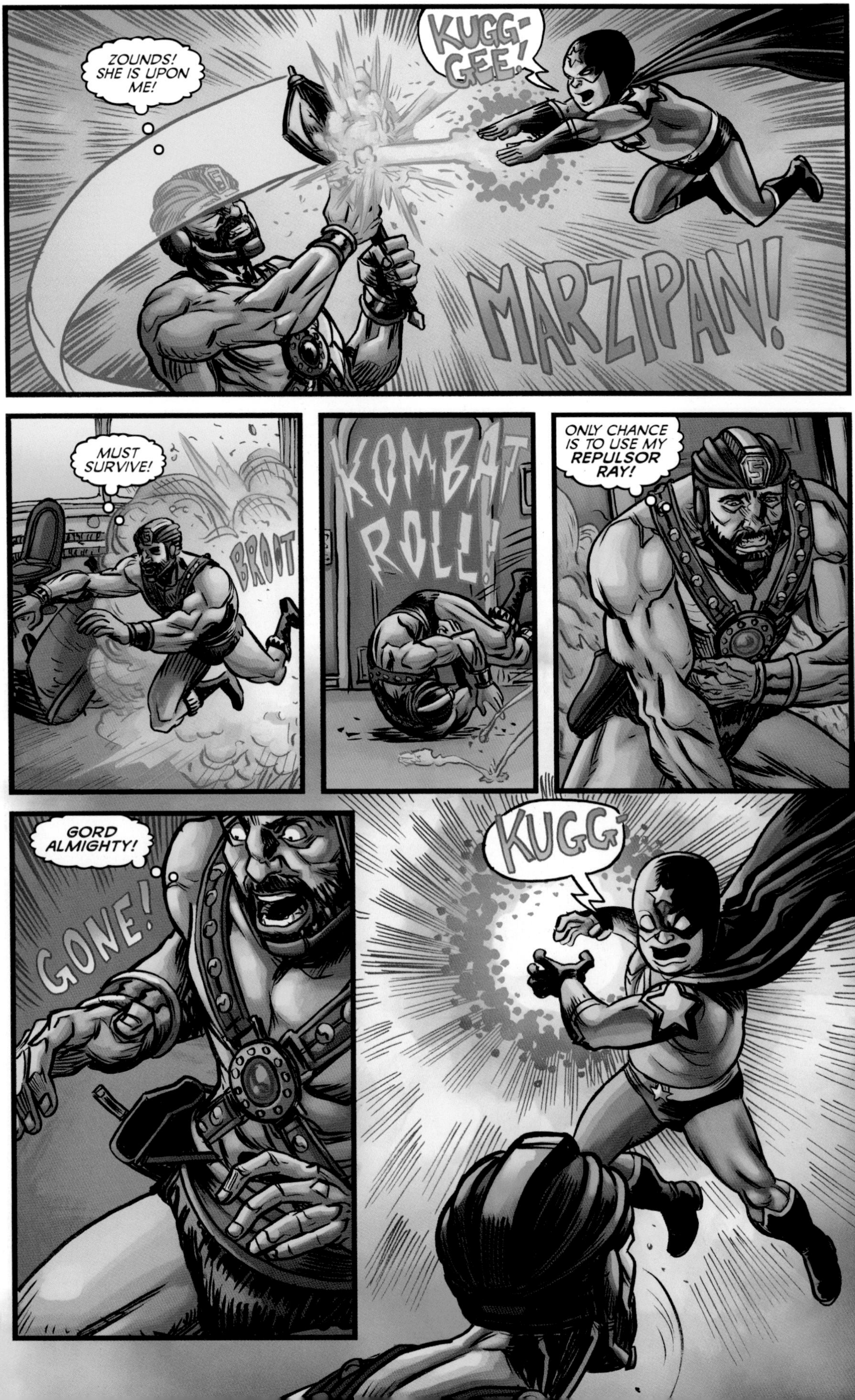
ZOUNDS! SHE IS UPON ME!
KUGG-GEE!
MARZIPAN!
MUST SURVIVE!
BROOT
KOMBAT ROLL!
ONLY CHANCE IS TO USE MY REPULSOR RAY!
GORD ALMIGHTY!
GONE!
KUGG-

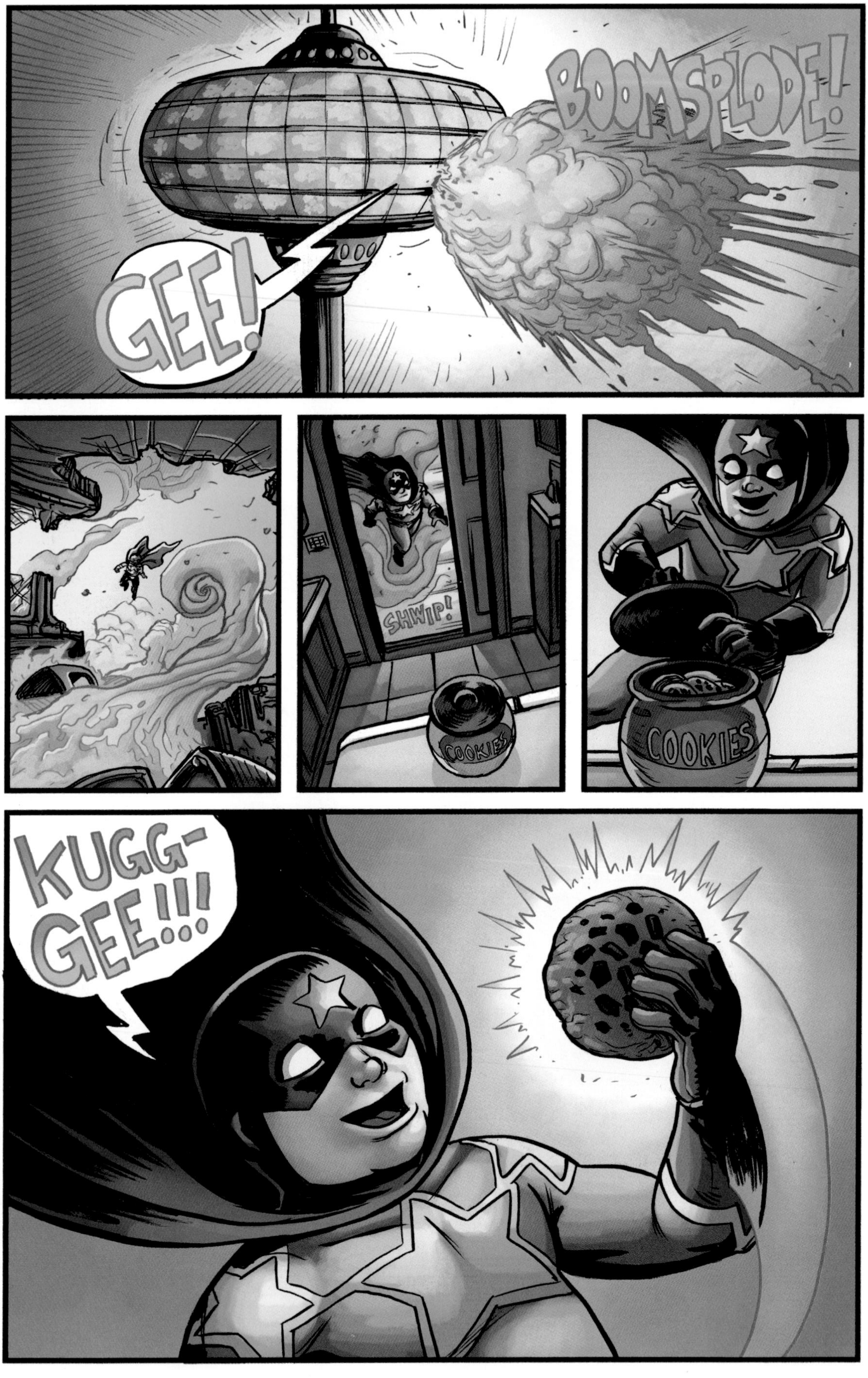
BOOMSPLODE!
GEE!
SHWIP!
COOKIES
COOKIES
KUGG-
GEE!!!

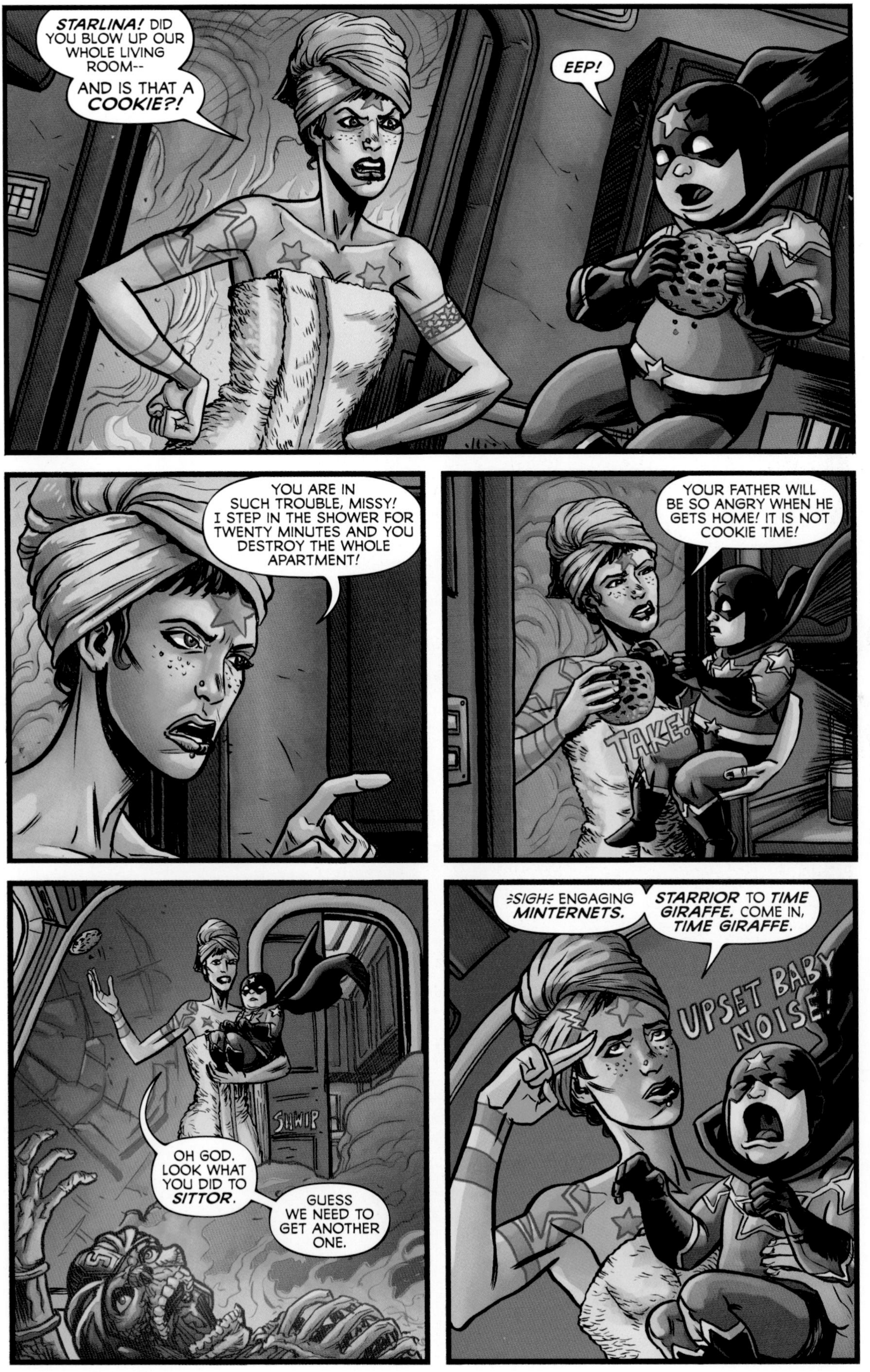
STARLINA! DID YOU BLOW UP OUR WHOLE LIVING ROOM--
AND IS THAT A COOKIE?!
EEP!
YOU ARE IN SUCH TROUBLE, MISSY! I STEP IN THE SHOWER FOR TWENTY MINUTES AND YOU DESTROY THE WHOLE APARTMENT!
YOUR FATHER WILL BE SO ANGRY WHEN HE GETS HOME! IT IS NOT COOKIE TIME!
TAKE!
SHWIP
OH GOD. LOOK WHAT YOU DID TO SITTOR.
GUESS WE NEED TO GET ANOTHER ONE.
SIGH ENGAGING MINTERNETS.
STARRIOR TO TIME GIRAFFE. COME IN, TIME GIRAFFE.
UPSET BABY NOISE!

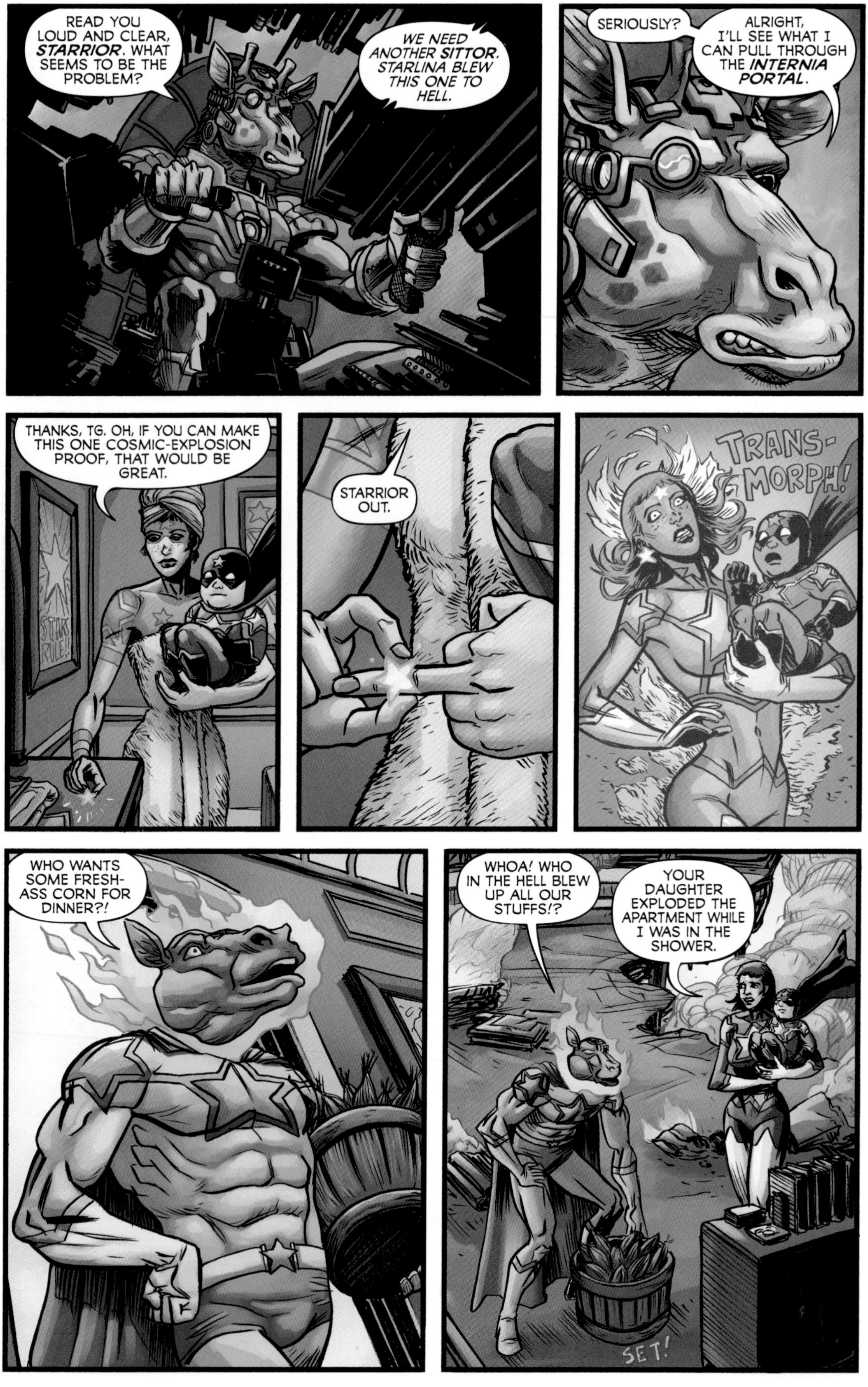
READ YOU LOUD AND CLEAR, **STARRIOR**. WHAT SEEMS TO BE THE PROBLEM?
*WE NEED ANOTHER **SITTOR**. STARLINA BLEW THIS ONE TO HELL.*
SERIOUSLY?
ALRIGHT, I'LL SEE WHAT I CAN PULL THROUGH THE ***INTERNIA PORTAL***.
THANKS, TG. OH, IF YOU CAN MAKE THIS ONE COSMIC-EXPLOSION PROOF, THAT WOULD BE GREAT.
STARS RULE!!
STARRIOR OUT.
TRANS-MORPH!
WHO WANTS SOME FRESH-ASS CORN FOR DINNER?!
WHOA! WHO IN THE HELL BLEW UP ALL OUR STUFFS!?
YOUR DAUGHTER EXPLODED THE APARTMENT WHILE I WAS IN THE SHOWER.
SET!

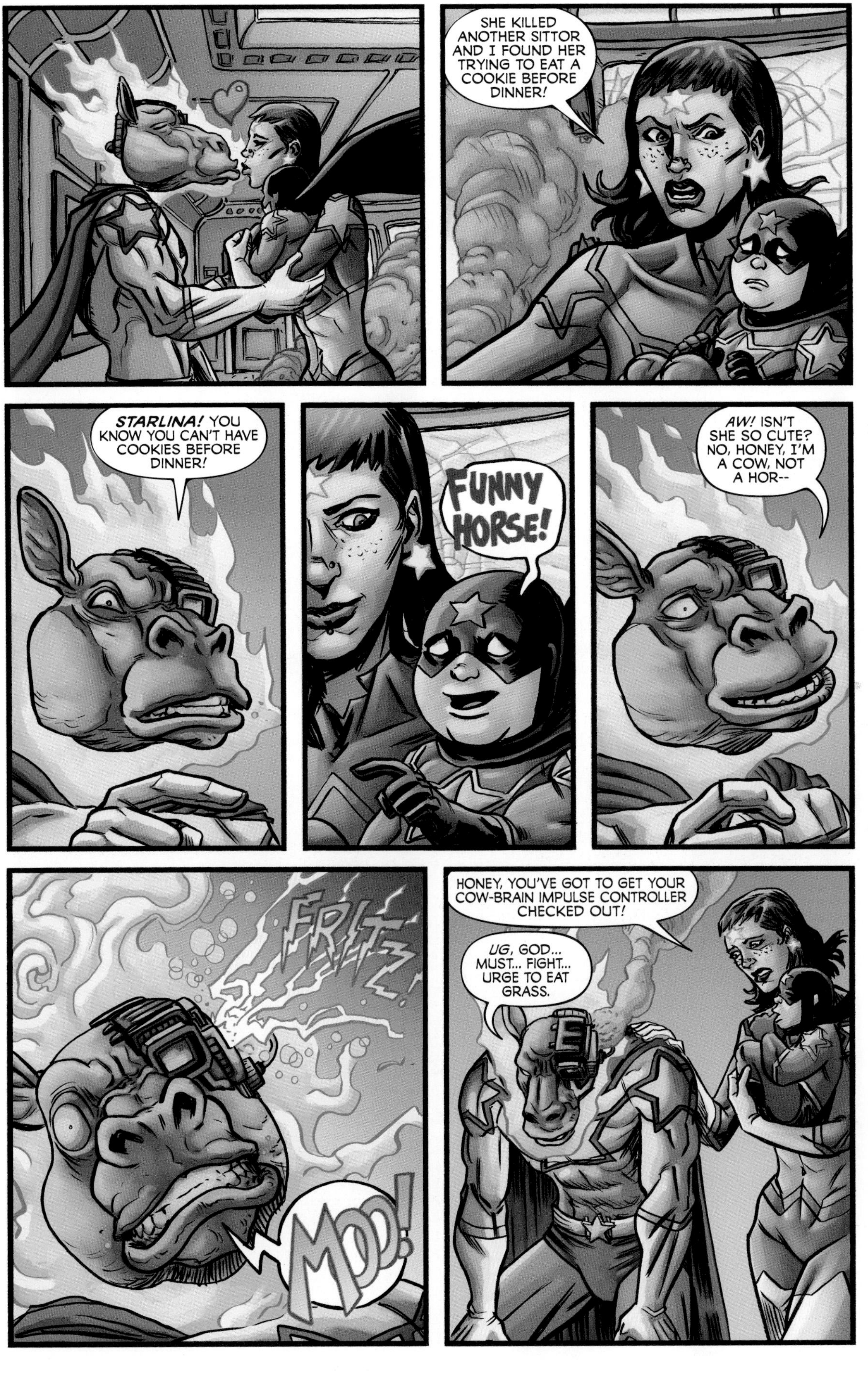
SHE KILLED ANOTHER SITTOR AND I FOUND HER TRYING TO EAT A COOKIE BEFORE DINNER!
STARLINA! YOU KNOW YOU CAN'T HAVE COOKIES BEFORE DINNER!
FUNNY HORSE!
AW! ISN'T SHE SO CUTE? NO, HONEY, I'M A COW, NOT A HOR--
FRITZ!
MOO!
HONEY, YOU'VE GOT TO GET YOUR COW-BRAIN IMPULSE CONTROLLER CHECKED OUT!
UG, GOD... MUST... FIGHT... URGE TO EAT GRASS.

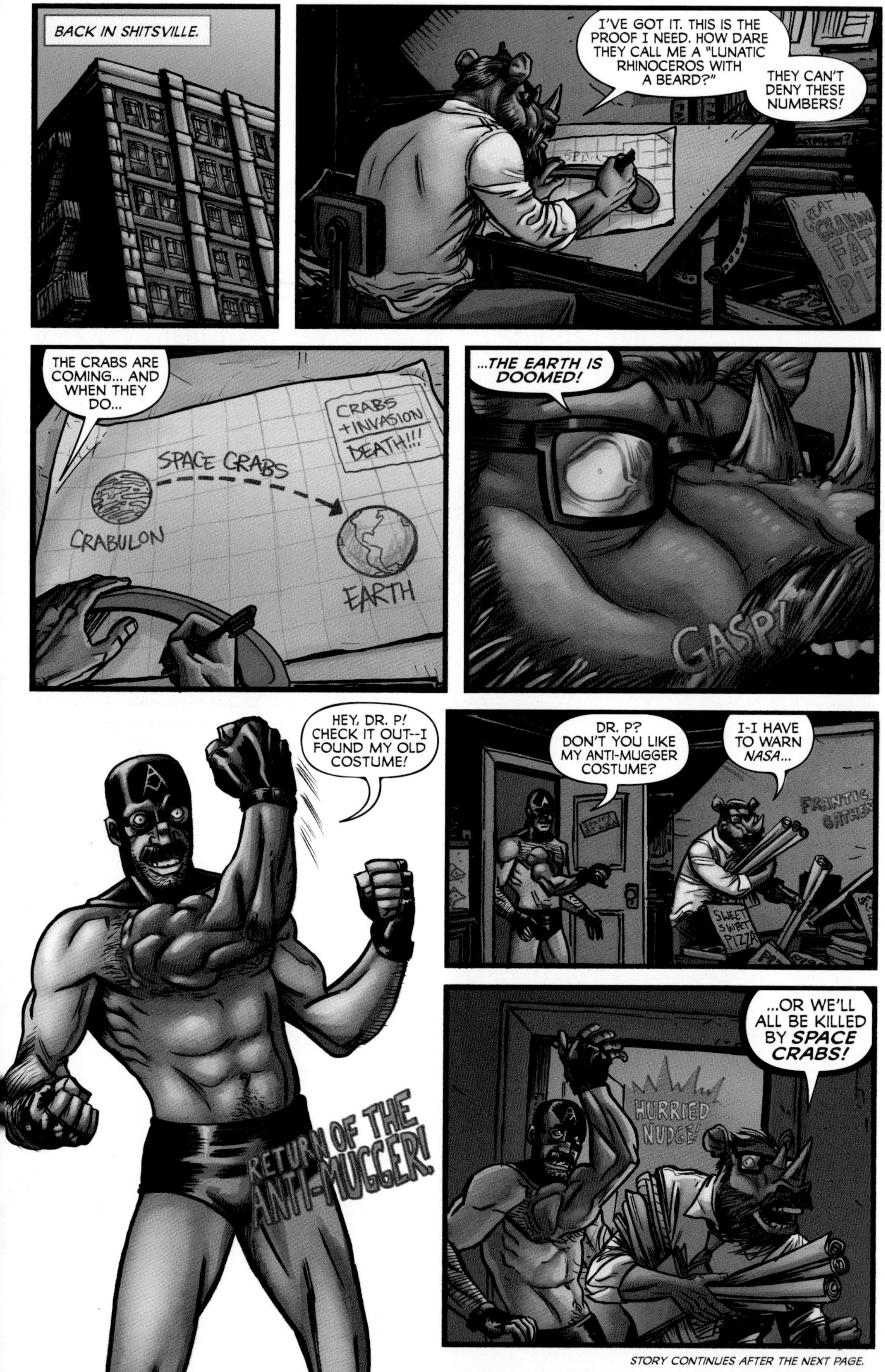
BACK IN SHITSVILLE.
I'VE GOT IT. THIS IS THE PROOF I NEED. HOW DARE THEY CALL ME A "LUNATIC RHINOCEROS WITH A BEARD?"
THEY CAN'T DENY THESE NUMBERS!
THE CRABS ARE COMING... AND WHEN THEY DO...
CRABS + INVASION DEATH!!!
SPACE CRABS
CRABULON
EARTH
...THE EARTH IS DOOMED!
GASP!
HEY, DR. P! CHECK IT OUT--I FOUND MY OLD COSTUME!
RETURN OF THE ANTI-MUGGER!
DR. P? DON'T YOU LIKE MY ANTI-MUGGER COSTUME?
I-I HAVE TO WARN NASA...
FRANTIC GATHER
SWEET SWEET PIZZA
...OR WE'LL ALL BE KILLED BY SPACE CRABS!
HURRIED NUDGE!

STORY CONTINUES AFTER THE NEXT PAGE.

ADVERTISEMENT

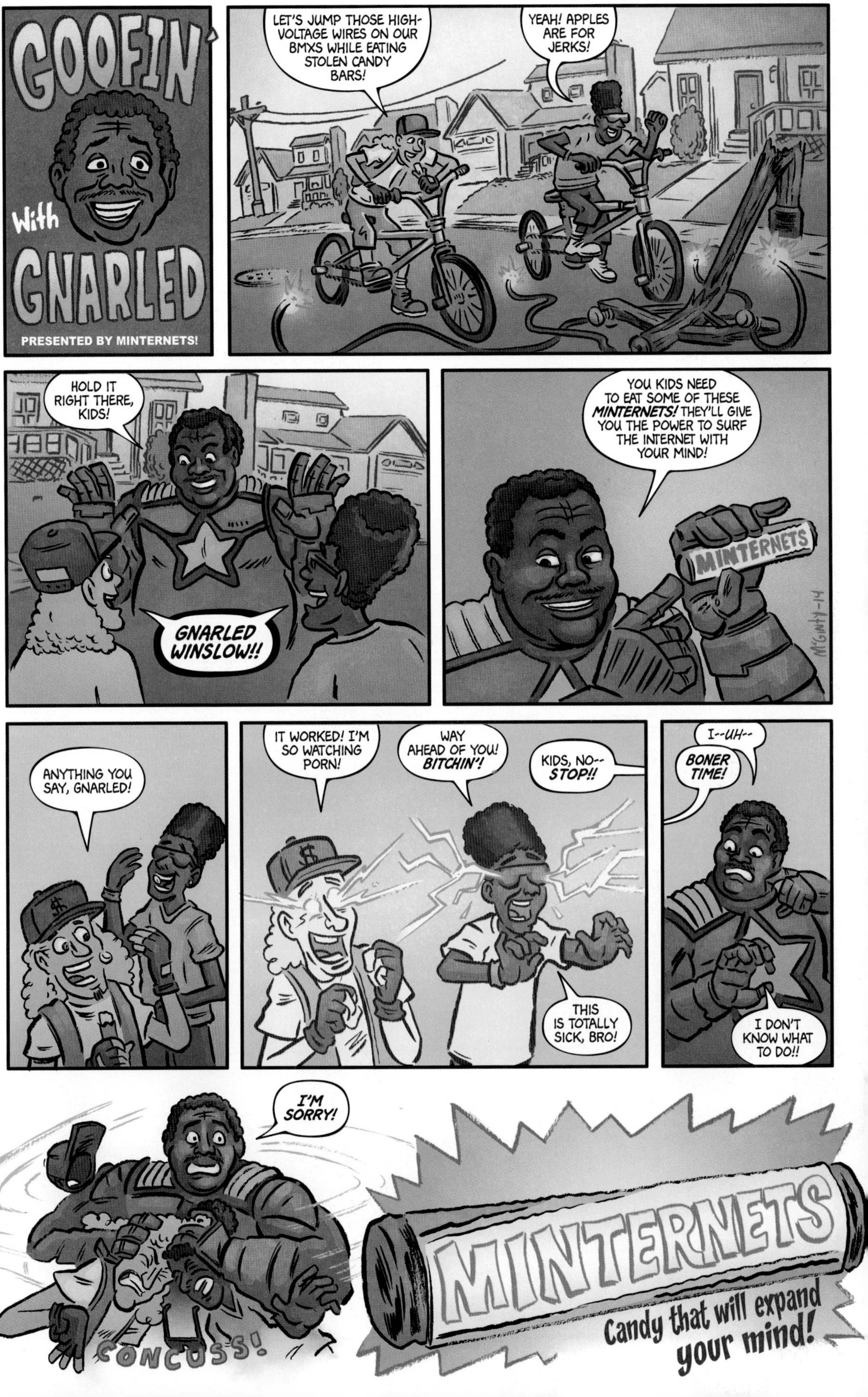
GOOFIN' With GNARLED
PRESENTED BY MINTERNETS!
LET'S JUMP THOSE HIGH-VOLTAGE WIRES ON OUR BMXS WHILE EATING STOLEN CANDY BARS!
YEAH! APPLES ARE FOR JERKS!
HOLD IT RIGHT THERE, KIDS!
GNARLED WINSLOW!!
YOU KIDS NEED TO EAT SOME OF THESE MINTERNETS! THEY'LL GIVE YOU THE POWER TO SURF THE INTERNET WITH YOUR MIND!
MINTERNETS
ANYTHING YOU SAY, GNARLED!
IT WORKED! I'M SO WATCHING PORN!
WAY AHEAD OF YOU! BITCHIN'!
KIDS, NO-- STOP!!
THIS IS TOTALLY SICK, BRO!
I--UH--
BONER TIME!
I DON'T KNOW WHAT TO DO!!
I'M SORRY!
CONCUSS!
MINTERNETS
Candy that will expand your mind!

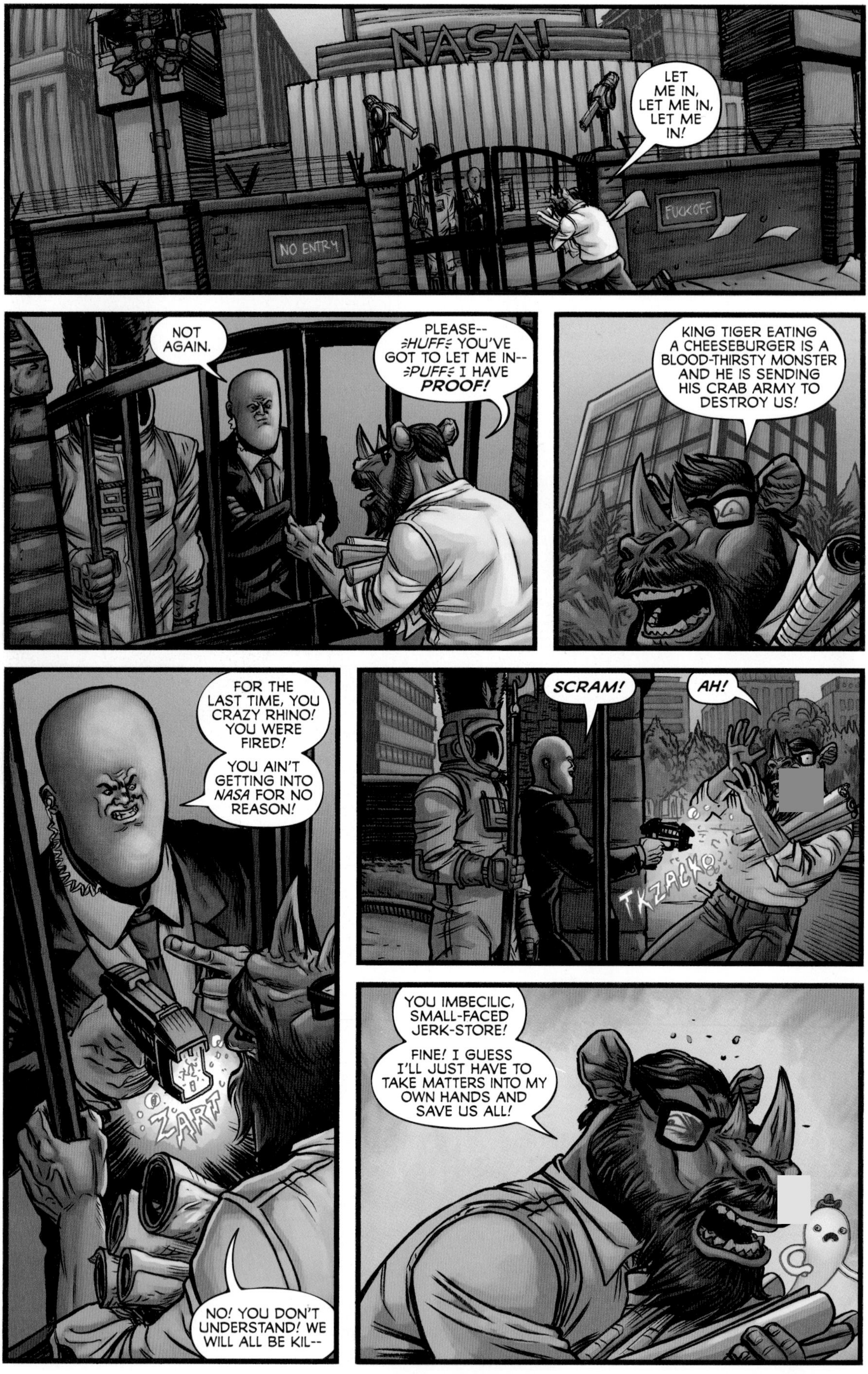
NASA!
LET ME IN, LET ME IN, LET ME IN!
NO ENTRY
FUCKOFF
NOT AGAIN.
PLEASE-- HUFF YOU'VE GOT TO LET ME IN-- PUFF I HAVE *PROOF!*
KING TIGER EATING A CHEESEBURGER IS A BLOOD-THIRSTY MONSTER AND HE IS SENDING HIS CRAB ARMY TO DESTROY US!
FOR THE LAST TIME, YOU CRAZY RHINO! YOU WERE FIRED!
YOU AIN'T GETTING INTO *NASA* FOR NO REASON!
ZART
NO! YOU DON'T UNDERSTAND! WE WILL ALL BE KIL--
SCRAM!
AH!
TKZACK
YOU IMBECILIC, SMALL-FACED JERK-STORE!
FINE! I GUESS I'LL JUST HAVE TO TAKE MATTERS INTO MY OWN HANDS AND SAVE US ALL!

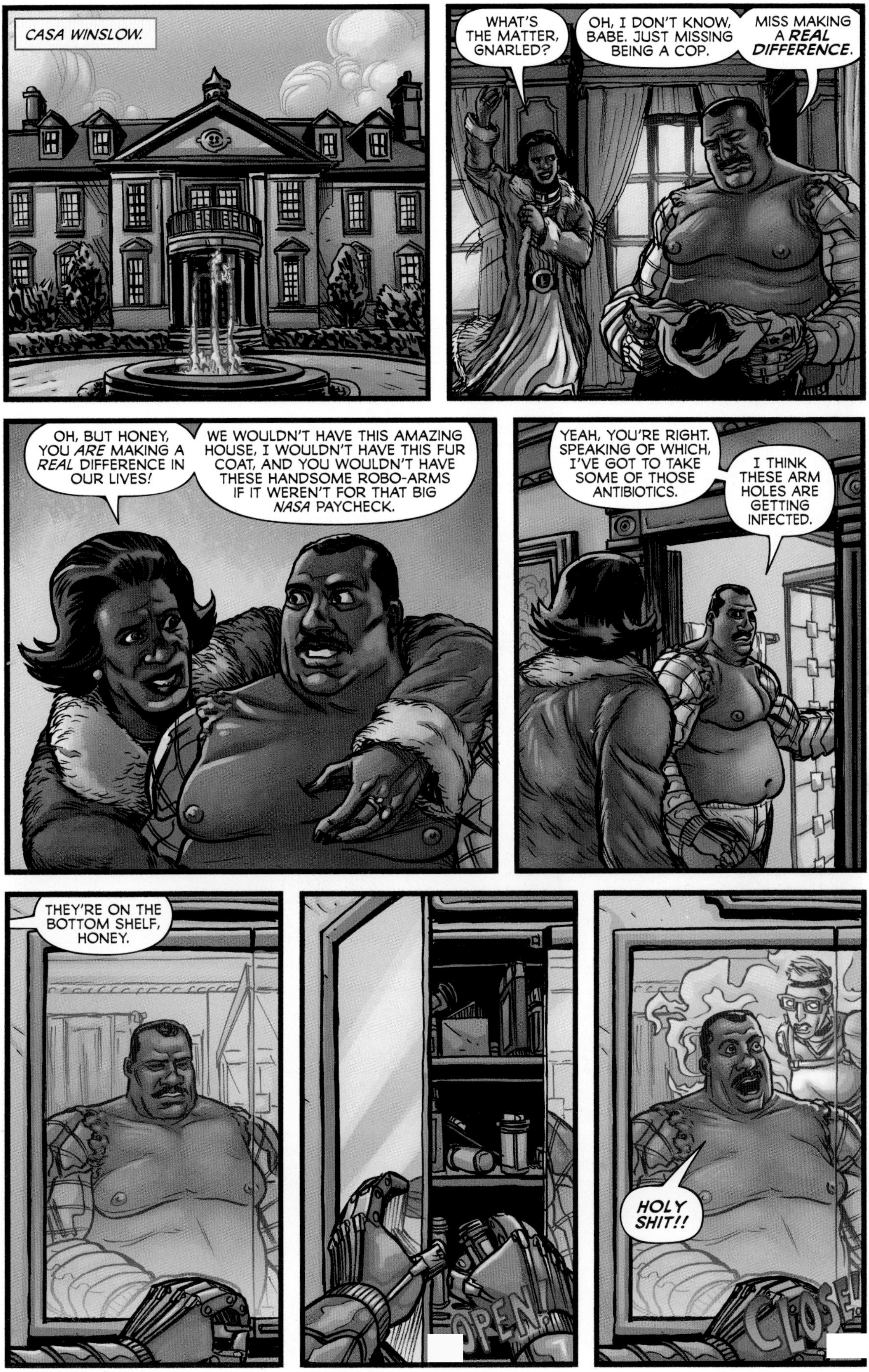
CASA WINSLOW.
WHAT'S THE MATTER, GNARLED?
OH, I DON'T KNOW, BABE. JUST MISSING BEING A COP.
MISS MAKING A REAL DIFFERENCE.
OH, BUT HONEY, YOU ARE MAKING A REAL DIFFERENCE IN OUR LIVES!
WE WOULDN'T HAVE THIS AMAZING HOUSE, I WOULDN'T HAVE THIS FUR COAT, AND YOU WOULDN'T HAVE THESE HANDSOME ROBO-ARMS IF IT WEREN'T FOR THAT BIG NASA PAYCHECK.
YEAH, YOU'RE RIGHT. SPEAKING OF WHICH, I'VE GOT TO TAKE SOME OF THOSE ANTIBIOTICS.
I THINK THESE ARM HOLES ARE GETTING INFECTED.
THEY'RE ON THE BOTTOM SHELF, HONEY.
OPEN!
HOLY SHIT!!
CLOSE!

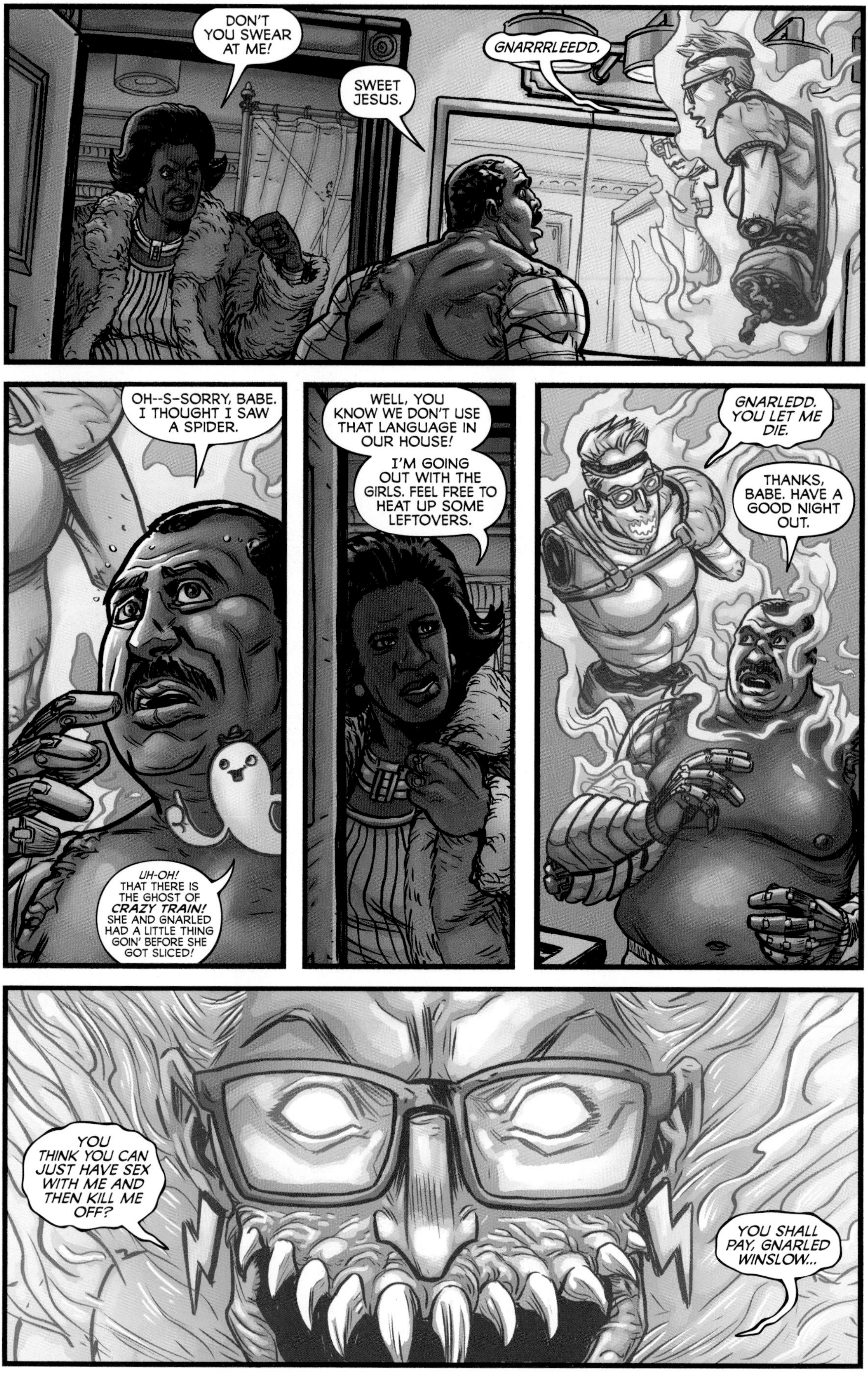
DON'T YOU SWEAR AT ME!
SWEET JESUS.
GNARRRLEEDD.
OH--S-SORRY, BABE. I THOUGHT I SAW A SPIDER.
UH-OH! THAT THERE IS THE GHOST OF CRAZY TRAIN! SHE AND GNARLED HAD A LITTLE THING GOIN' BEFORE SHE GOT SLICED!
WELL, YOU KNOW WE DON'T USE THAT LANGUAGE IN OUR HOUSE!
I'M GOING OUT WITH THE GIRLS. FEEL FREE TO HEAT UP SOME LEFTOVERS.
GNARLEDD. YOU LET ME DIE.
THANKS, BABE. HAVE A GOOD NIGHT OUT.
YOU THINK YOU CAN JUST HAVE SEX WITH ME AND THEN KILL ME OFF?
YOU SHALL PAY, GNARLED WINSLOW...

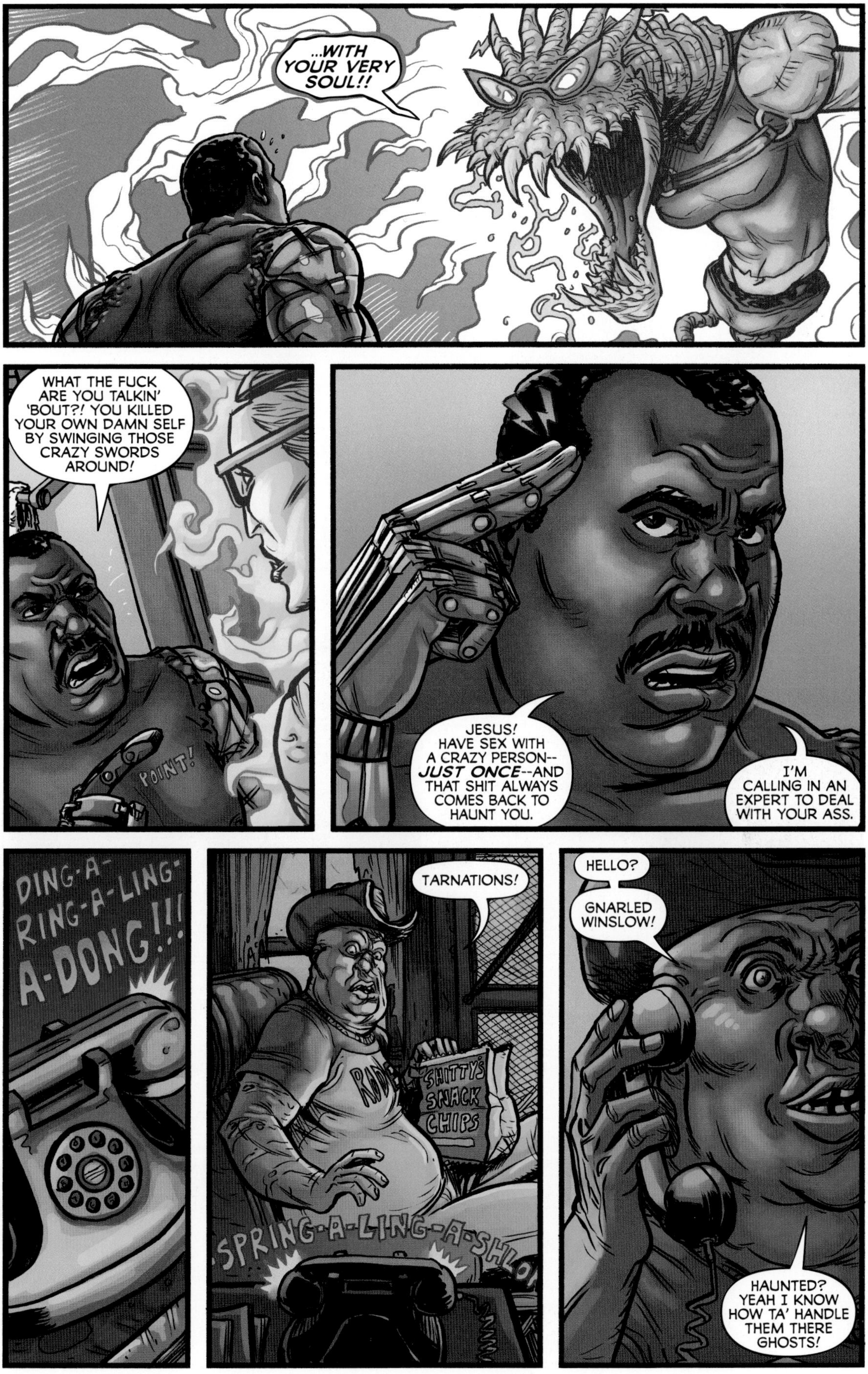
...WITH YOUR VERY SOUL!!
WHAT THE FUCK ARE YOU TALKIN' 'BOUT?! YOU KILLED YOUR OWN DAMN SELF BY SWINGING THOSE CRAZY SWORDS AROUND!
POINT!
JESUS! HAVE SEX WITH A CRAZY PERSON-- JUST ONCE--AND THAT SHIT ALWAYS COMES BACK TO HAUNT YOU.
I'M CALLING IN AN EXPERT TO DEAL WITH YOUR ASS.
DING-A-RING-A-LING-A-DONG!!!
TARNATIONS!
SHITTY'S SNACK CHIPS
HELLO?
GNARLED WINSLOW!
HAUNTED? YEAH I KNOW HOW TA' HANDLE THEM THERE GHOSTS!

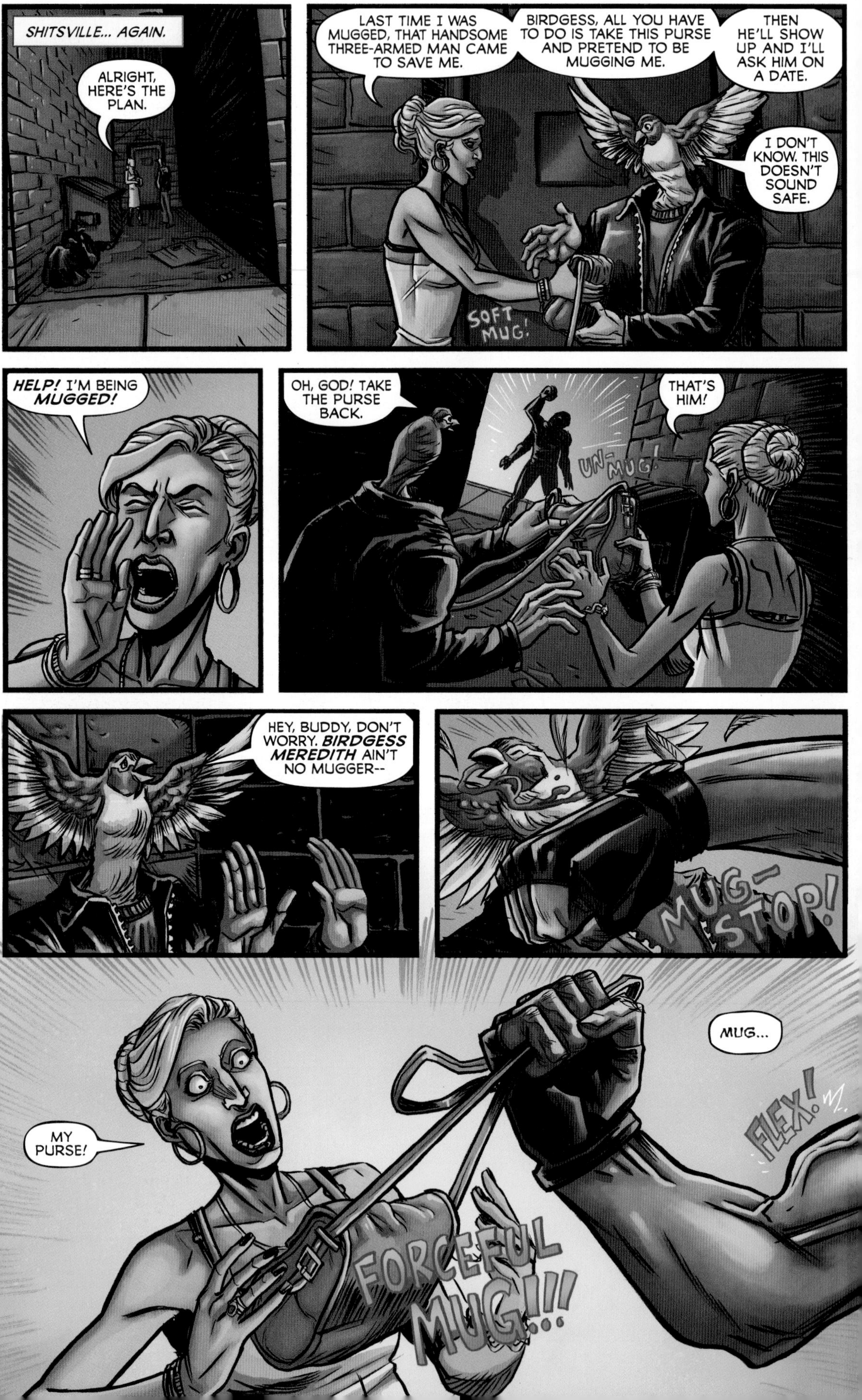
SHITSVILLE... AGAIN.
ALRIGHT, HERE'S THE PLAN.
LAST TIME I WAS MUGGED, THAT HANDSOME THREE-ARMED MAN CAME TO SAVE ME.
BIRDGESS, ALL YOU HAVE TO DO IS TAKE THIS PURSE AND PRETEND TO BE MUGGING ME.
THEN HE'LL SHOW UP AND I'LL ASK HIM ON A DATE.
I DON'T KNOW. THIS DOESN'T SOUND SAFE.
SOFT MUG!
HELP! I'M BEING MUGGED!
OH, GOD! TAKE THE PURSE BACK.
THAT'S HIM!
UN-MUG!
HEY, BUDDY, DON'T WORRY. BIRDGESS MEREDITH AIN'T NO MUGGER--
MUG-STOP!
MUG...
MY PURSE!
FLEX!
FORCEFUL MUG!!!

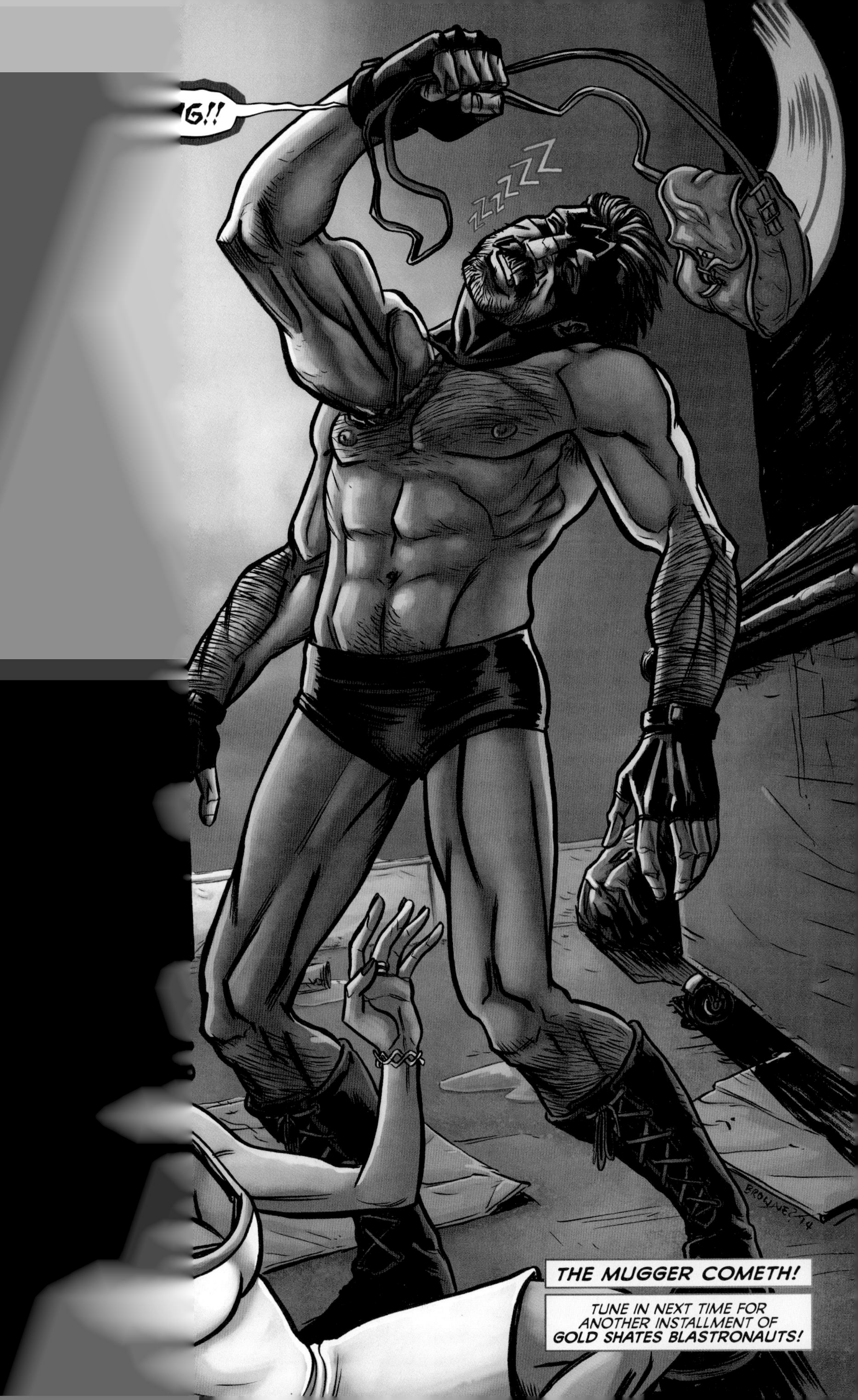

G!!
ZZZZZZ
BROWNE '14
THE MUGGER COMETH!
TUNE IN NEXT TIME FOR ANOTHER INSTALLMENT OF GOLD SHATES BLASTRONAUTS!

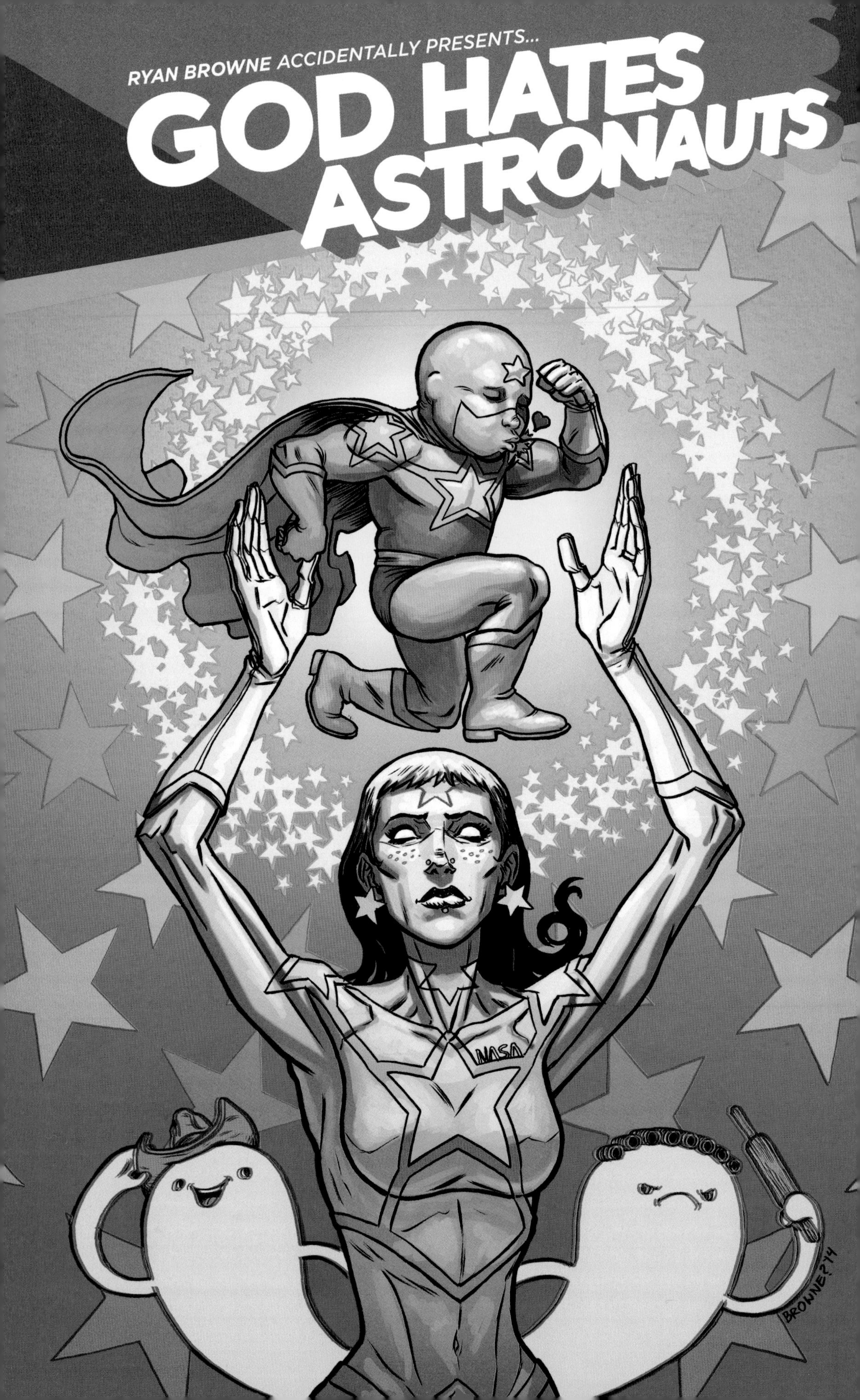
RYAN BROWNE ACCIDENTALLY PRESENTS...
GOD HATES ASTRONAUTS
NASA
BROWNE?'14

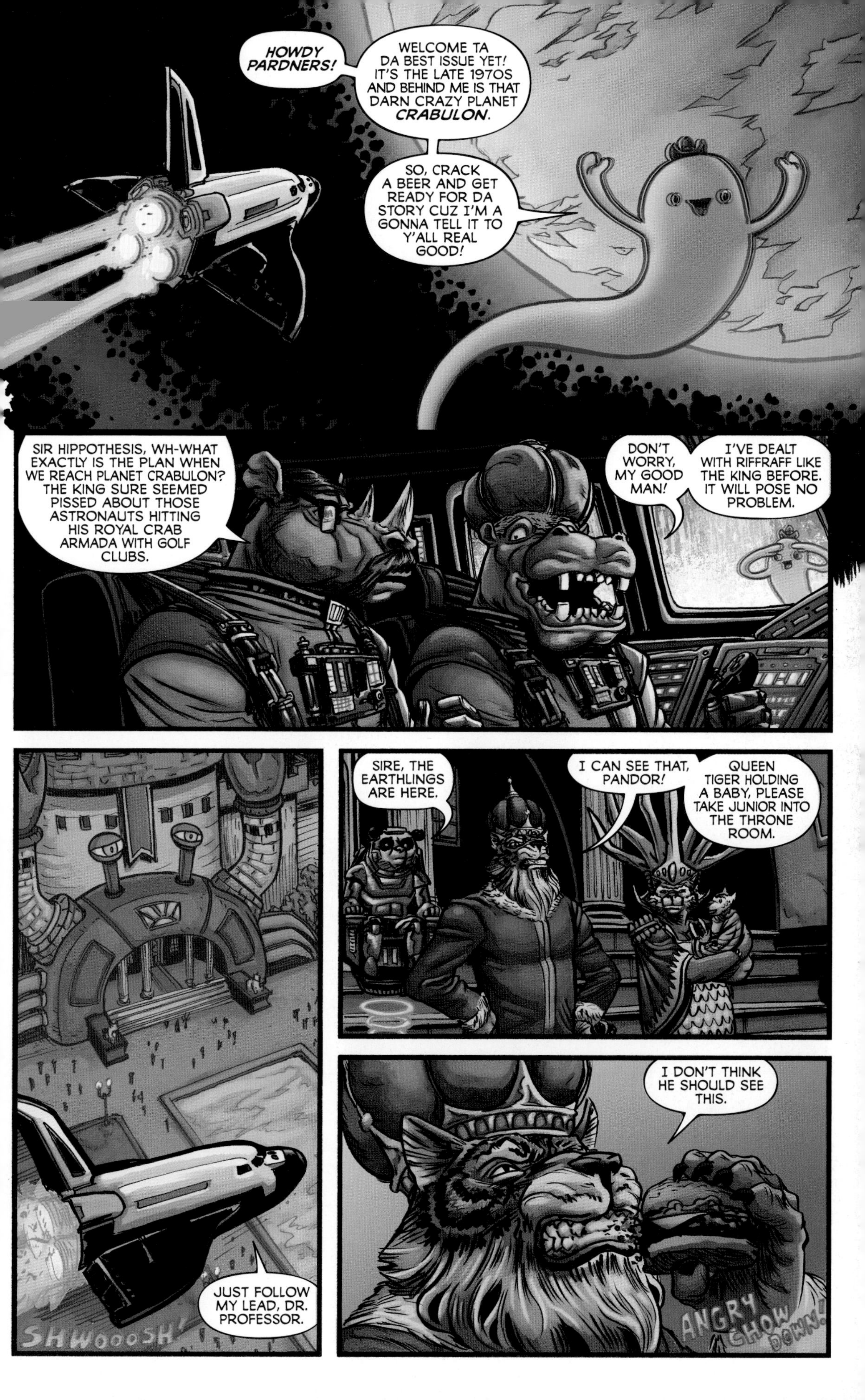
HOWDY PARDNERS!
WELCOME TA DA BEST ISSUE YET! IT'S THE LATE 1970S AND BEHIND ME IS THAT DARN CRAZY PLANET CRABULON.
SO, CRACK A BEER AND GET READY FOR DA STORY CUZ I'M A GONNA TELL IT TO Y'ALL REAL GOOD!
SIR HIPPOTHESIS, WH-WHAT EXACTLY IS THE PLAN WHEN WE REACH PLANET CRABULON? THE KING SURE SEEMED PISSED ABOUT THOSE ASTRONAUTS HITTING HIS ROYAL CRAB ARMADA WITH GOLF CLUBS.
DON'T WORRY, MY GOOD MAN!
I'VE DEALT WITH RIFFRAFF LIKE THE KING BEFORE. IT WILL POSE NO PROBLEM.
JUST FOLLOW MY LEAD, DR. PROFESSOR.
SHWOOOSH!
SIRE, THE EARTHLINGS ARE HERE.
I CAN SEE THAT, PANDOR!
QUEEN TIGER HOLDING A BABY, PLEASE TAKE JUNIOR INTO THE THRONE ROOM.
I DON'T THINK HE SHOULD SEE THIS.
ANGRY CHOW DOWN!

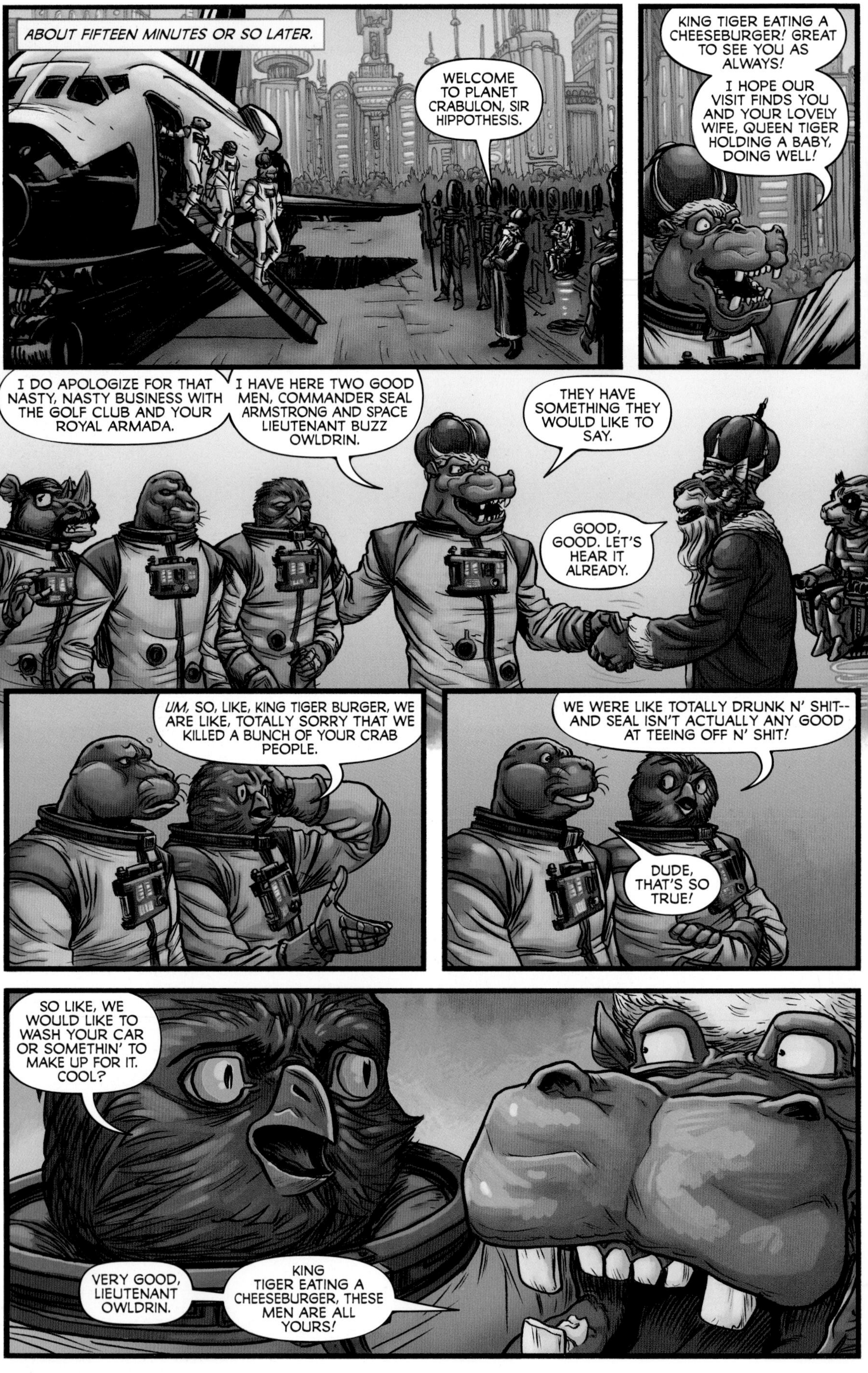
ABOUT FIFTEEN MINUTES OR SO LATER.
WELCOME TO PLANET CRABULON, SIR HIPPOTHESIS.
KING TIGER EATING A CHEESEBURGER! GREAT TO SEE YOU AS ALWAYS!
I HOPE OUR VISIT FINDS YOU AND YOUR LOVELY WIFE, QUEEN TIGER HOLDING A BABY, DOING WELL!
I DO APOLOGIZE FOR THAT NASTY, NASTY BUSINESS WITH THE GOLF CLUB AND YOUR ROYAL ARMADA.
I HAVE HERE TWO GOOD MEN, COMMANDER SEAL ARMSTRONG AND SPACE LIEUTENANT BUZZ OWLDRIN.
THEY HAVE SOMETHING THEY WOULD LIKE TO SAY.
GOOD, GOOD. LET'S HEAR IT ALREADY.
UM, SO, LIKE, KING TIGER BURGER, WE ARE LIKE, TOTALLY SORRY THAT WE KILLED A BUNCH OF YOUR CRAB PEOPLE.
WE WERE LIKE TOTALLY DRUNK N' SHIT-- AND SEAL ISN'T ACTUALLY ANY GOOD AT TEEING OFF N' SHIT!
DUDE, THAT'S SO TRUE!
SO LIKE, WE WOULD LIKE TO WASH YOUR CAR OR SOMETHIN' TO MAKE UP FOR IT. COOL?
VERY GOOD, LIEUTENANT OWLDRIN.
KING TIGER EATING A CHEESEBURGER, THESE MEN ARE ALL YOURS!

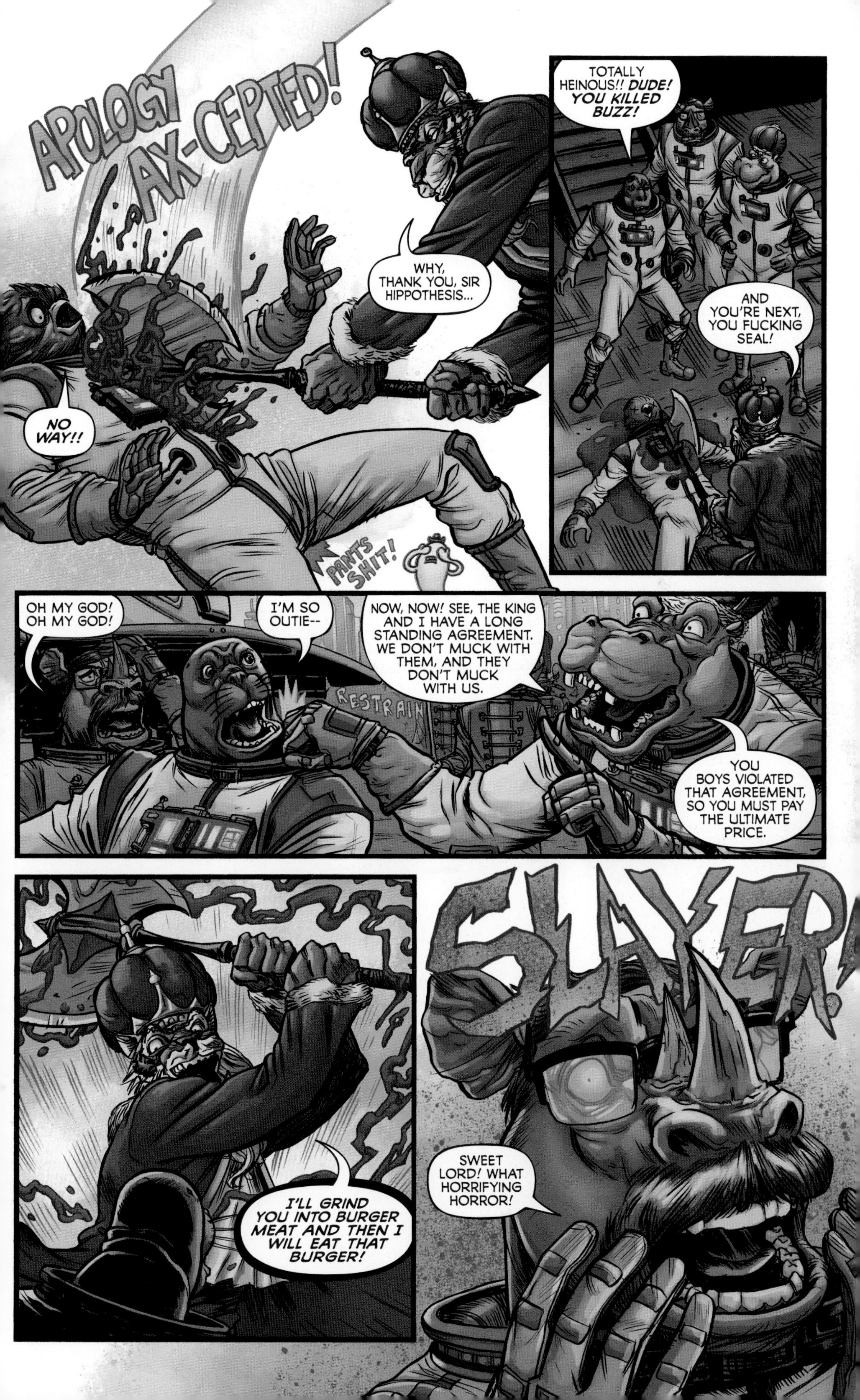
APOLOGY AX-CEPTED!
WHY, THANK YOU, SIR HIPPOTHESIS...
NO WAY!!
PANTS SHIT!
TOTALLY HEINOUS!! DUDE! YOU KILLED BUZZ!
AND YOU'RE NEXT, YOU FUCKING SEAL!
OH MY GOD! OH MY GOD!
I'M SO OUTIE--
NOW, NOW! SEE, THE KING AND I HAVE A LONG STANDING AGREEMENT. WE DON'T MUCK WITH THEM, AND THEY DON'T MUCK WITH US.
RESTRAIN
YOU BOYS VIOLATED THAT AGREEMENT, SO YOU MUST PAY THE ULTIMATE PRICE.
I'LL GRIND YOU INTO BURGER MEAT AND THEN I WILL EAT THAT BURGER!
SLAYER!
SWEET LORD! WHAT HORRIFYING HORROR!

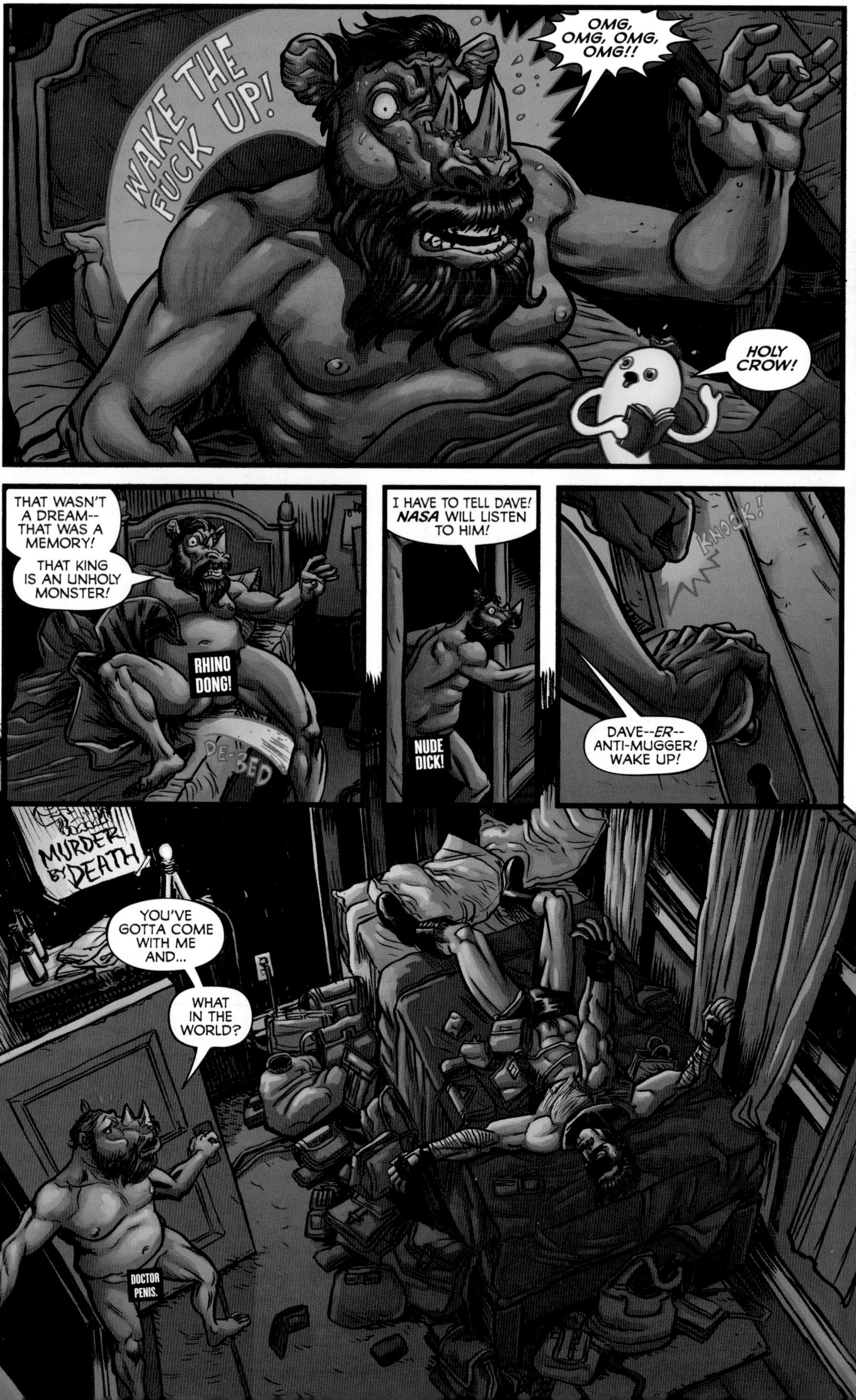
WAKE THE FUCK UP!
OMG, OMG, OMG, OMG!!
HOLY CROW!
THAT WASN'T A DREAM-- THAT WAS A MEMORY!
THAT KING IS AN UNHOLY MONSTER!
RHINO DONG!
DE-BED
I HAVE TO TELL DAVE! NASA WILL LISTEN TO HIM!
NUDE DICK!
KNOCK!
DAVE--ER-- ANTI-MUGGER! WAKE UP!
MURDER BY DEATH
YOU'VE GOTTA COME WITH ME AND...
WHAT IN THE WORLD?
DOCTOR PENIS.

PRESENTING

GOD HATES ASTRONAUTS

No3 A STAR IS BORN

You are entering part three of an epic tale of greed, lust, murder, vengeance, warm embraces, ghostly apparitions, misjudged distances, horse-manure-controlling devices, drastically under-weighed heavy freight, limp-wristed complex-tool-using, light and creamy spreadable cream cheese substitute...

PRESS START
WITH YOUR
MIND-FINGER
TO CONTINUE

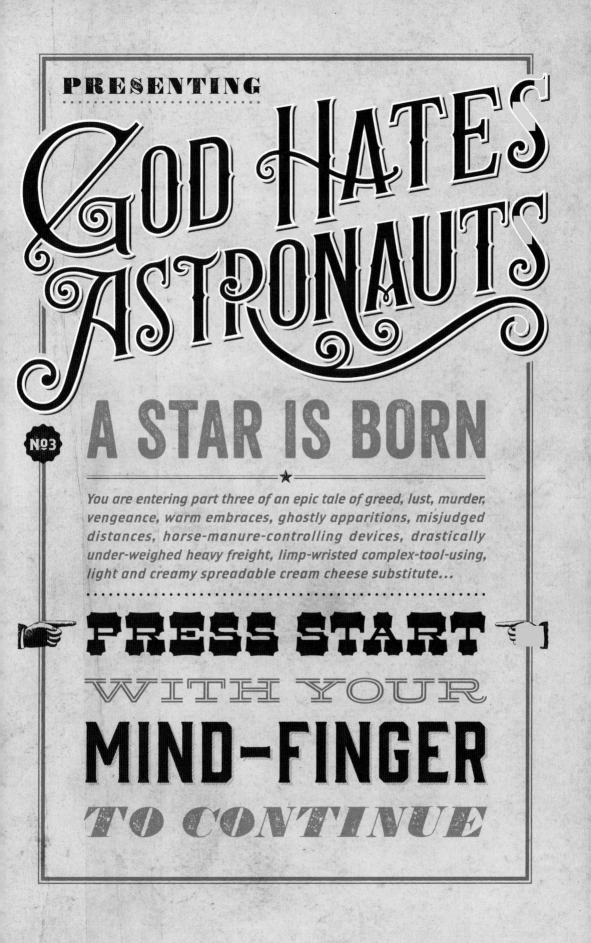

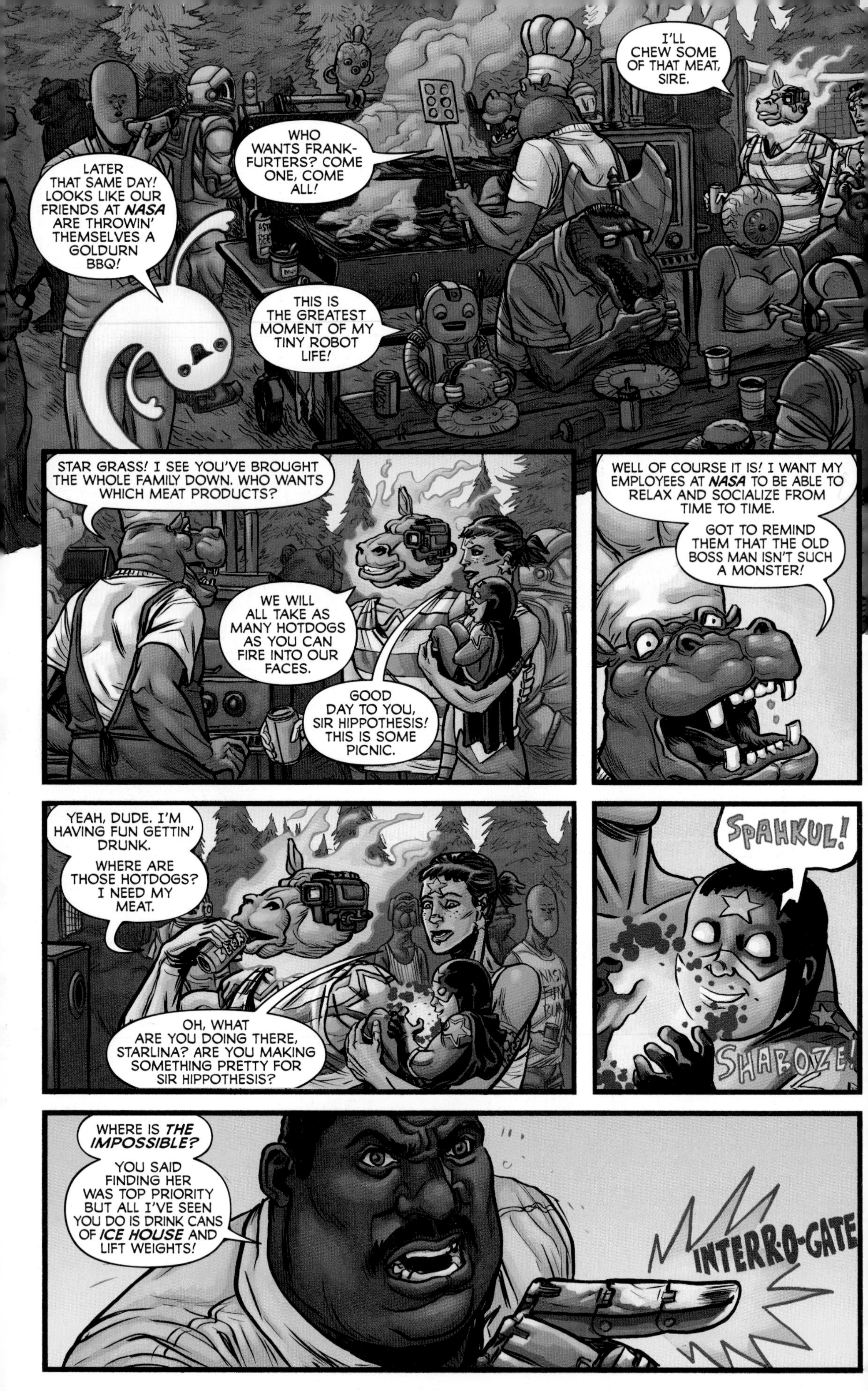
LATER THAT SAME DAY! LOOKS LIKE OUR FRIENDS AT NASA ARE THROWIN' THEMSELVES A GOLDURN BBQ!
WHO WANTS FRANK-FURTERS? COME ONE, COME ALL!
I'LL CHEW SOME OF THAT MEAT, SIRE.
THIS IS THE GREATEST MOMENT OF MY TINY ROBOT LIFE!
STAR GRASS! I SEE YOU'VE BROUGHT THE WHOLE FAMILY DOWN. WHO WANTS WHICH MEAT PRODUCTS?
WE WILL ALL TAKE AS MANY HOTDOGS AS YOU CAN FIRE INTO OUR FACES.
GOOD DAY TO YOU, SIR HIPPOTHESIS! THIS IS SOME PICNIC.
WELL OF COURSE IT IS! I WANT MY EMPLOYEES AT NASA TO BE ABLE TO RELAX AND SOCIALIZE FROM TIME TO TIME.
GOT TO REMIND THEM THAT THE OLD BOSS MAN ISN'T SUCH A MONSTER!
YEAH, DUDE. I'M HAVING FUN GETTIN' DRUNK.
WHERE ARE THOSE HOTDOGS? I NEED MY MEAT.
OH, WHAT ARE YOU DOING THERE, STARLINA? ARE YOU MAKING SOMETHING PRETTY FOR SIR HIPPOTHESIS?
SPAHKUL!
SHABOZE!
WHERE IS THE IMPOSSIBLE?
YOU SAID FINDING HER WAS TOP PRIORITY BUT ALL I'VE SEEN YOU DO IS DRINK CANS OF ICE HOUSE AND LIFT WEIGHTS!
INTERR-O-GATE

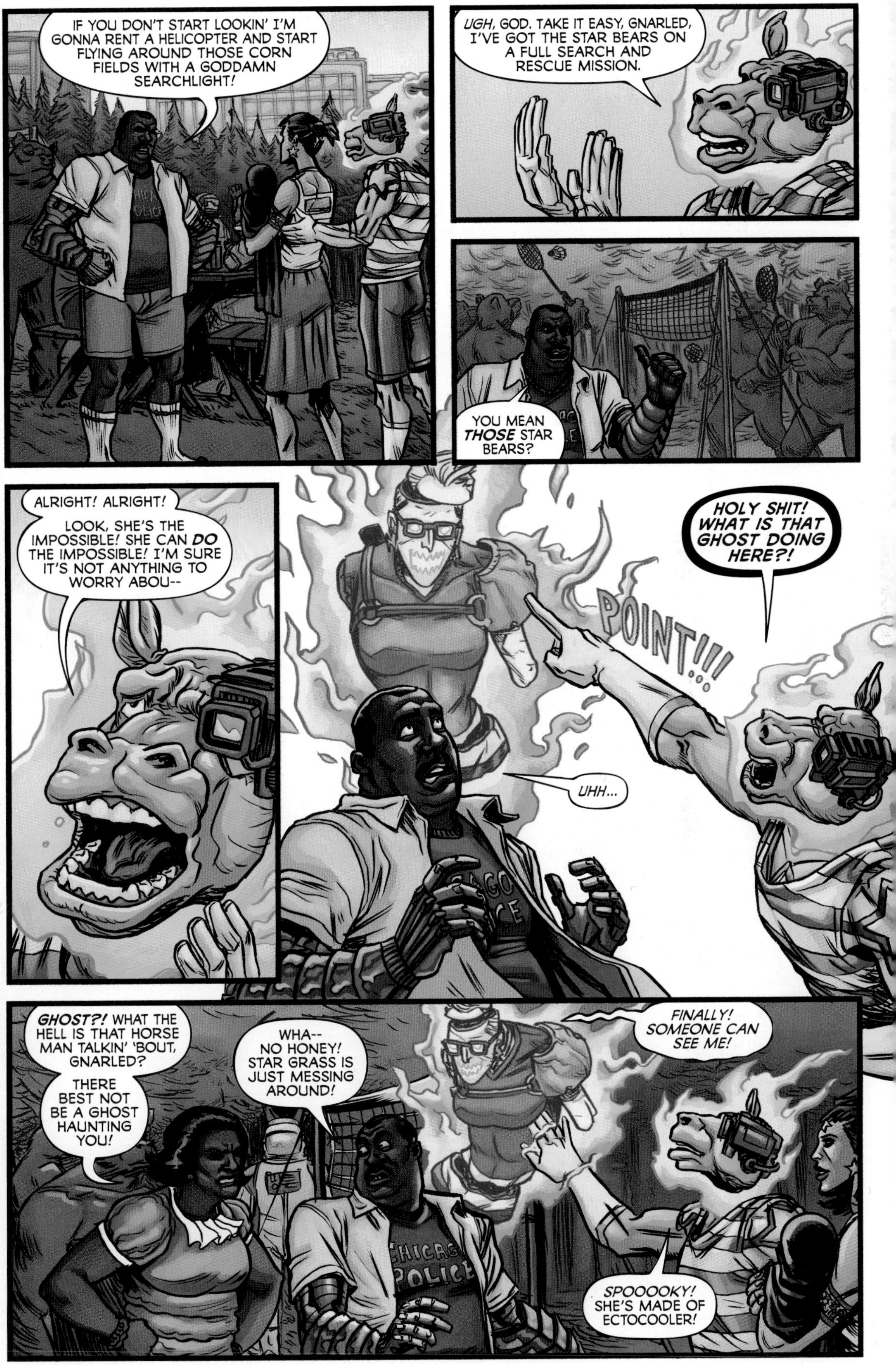
IF YOU DON'T START LOOKIN' I'M GONNA RENT A HELICOPTER AND START FLYING AROUND THOSE CORN FIELDS WITH A GODDAMN SEARCHLIGHT!
UGH, GOD. TAKE IT EASY, GNARLED, I'VE GOT THE STAR BEARS ON A FULL SEARCH AND RESCUE MISSION.
YOU MEAN THOSE STAR BEARS?
ALRIGHT! ALRIGHT!
LOOK, SHE'S THE IMPOSSIBLE! SHE CAN DO THE IMPOSSIBLE! I'M SURE IT'S NOT ANYTHING TO WORRY ABOU--
HOLY SHIT! WHAT IS THAT GHOST DOING HERE?!
POINT!!!
UHH...
GHOST?! WHAT THE HELL IS THAT HORSE MAN TALKIN' 'BOUT, GNARLED?
THERE BEST NOT BE A GHOST HAUNTING YOU!
WHA-- NO HONEY! STAR GRASS IS JUST MESSING AROUND!
FINALLY! SOMEONE CAN SEE ME!
SPOOOOKY! SHE'S MADE OF ECTOCOOLER!

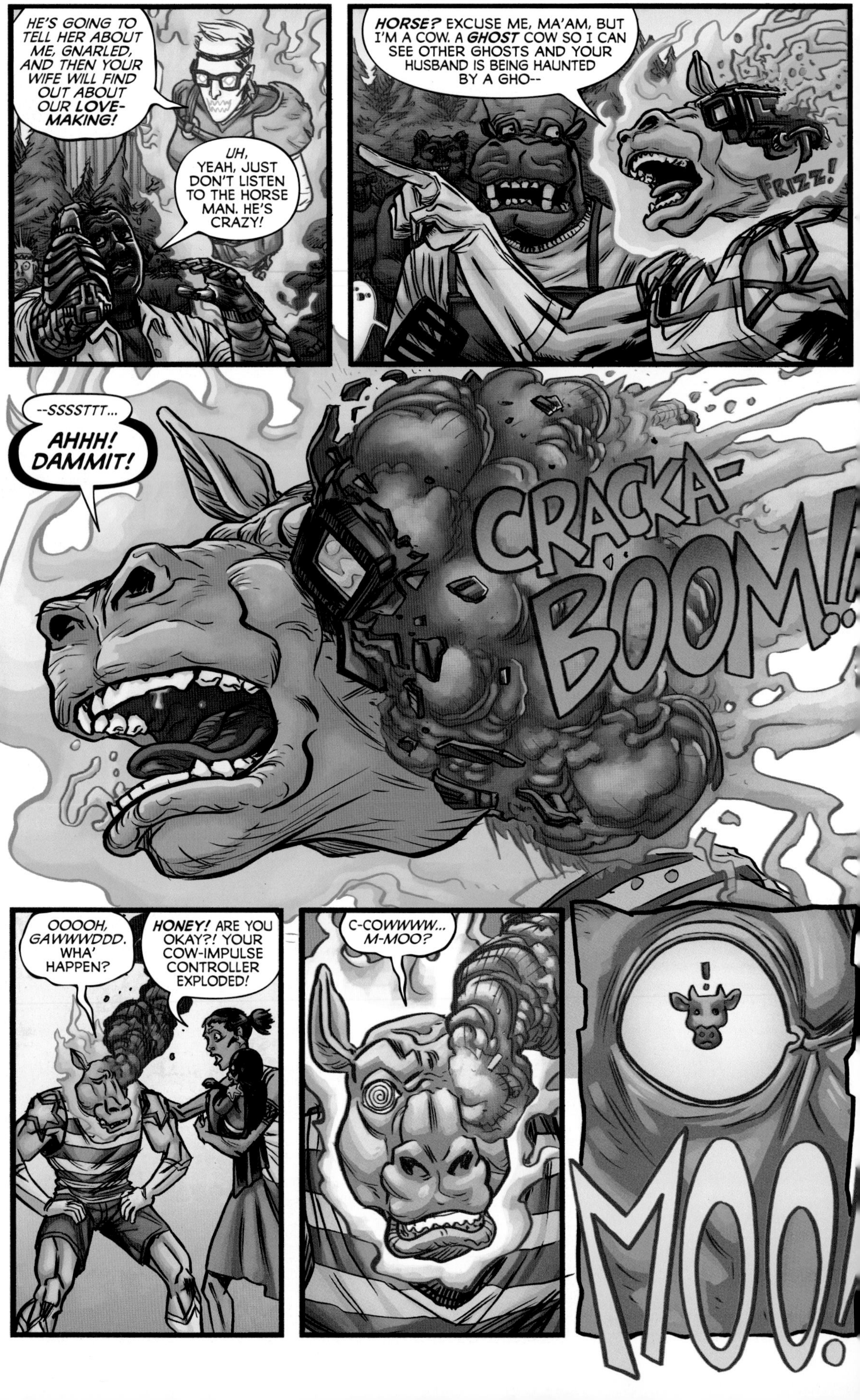
HE'S GOING TO TELL HER ABOUT ME, GNARLED, AND THEN YOUR WIFE WILL FIND OUT ABOUT OUR LOVE-MAKING!
UH, YEAH, JUST DON'T LISTEN TO THE HORSE MAN. HE'S CRAZY!
HORSE? EXCUSE ME, MA'AM, BUT I'M A COW. A GHOST COW SO I CAN SEE OTHER GHOSTS AND YOUR HUSBAND IS BEING HAUNTED BY A GHO--
FRIZZ!
--SSSSTTT...
AHHH! DAMMIT!
CRACKA-BOOM!!
OOOOH, GAWWWDDD. WHA' HAPPEN?
HONEY! ARE YOU OKAY?! YOUR COW-IMPULSE CONTROLLER EXPLODED!
C-COWWWW... M-MOO?
!
MOO!

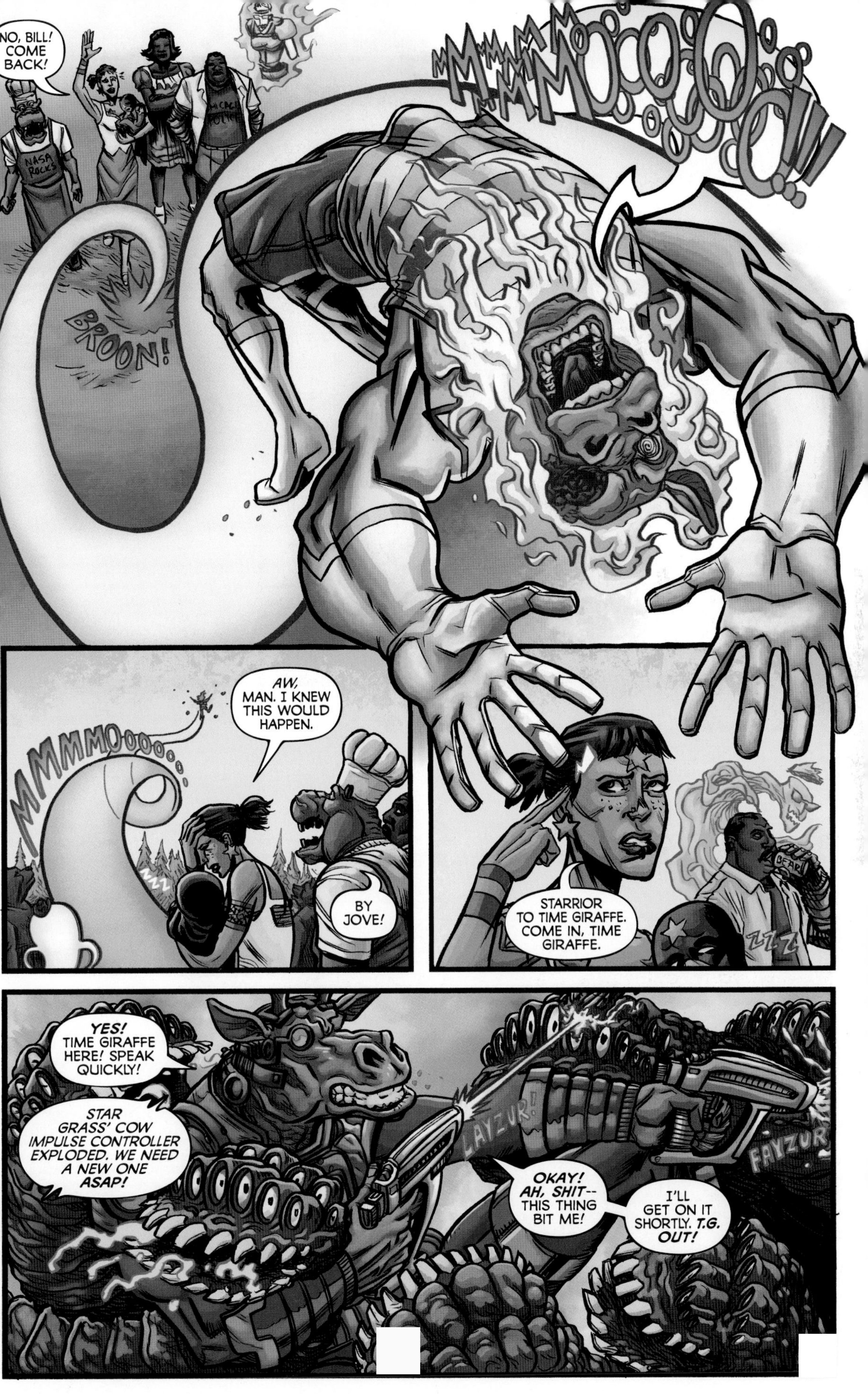
NO, BILL! COME BACK!
NASA ROCKS
MMMMMMMMOOOOOOOOOO!!!
BROON!
MMMMOoooo...
AW, MAN. I KNEW THIS WOULD HAPPEN.
ZZZ
BY JOVE!
STARRIOR TO TIME GIRAFFE. COME IN, TIME GIRAFFE.
BEAR
ZZZ
YES! TIME GIRAFFE HERE! SPEAK QUICKLY!
STAR GRASS' COW IMPULSE CONTROLLER EXPLODED. WE NEED A NEW ONE ASAP!
LAYZUR!
FAYZUR
OKAY! AH, SHIT-- THIS THING BIT ME!
I'LL GET ON IT SHORTLY. T.G. OUT!

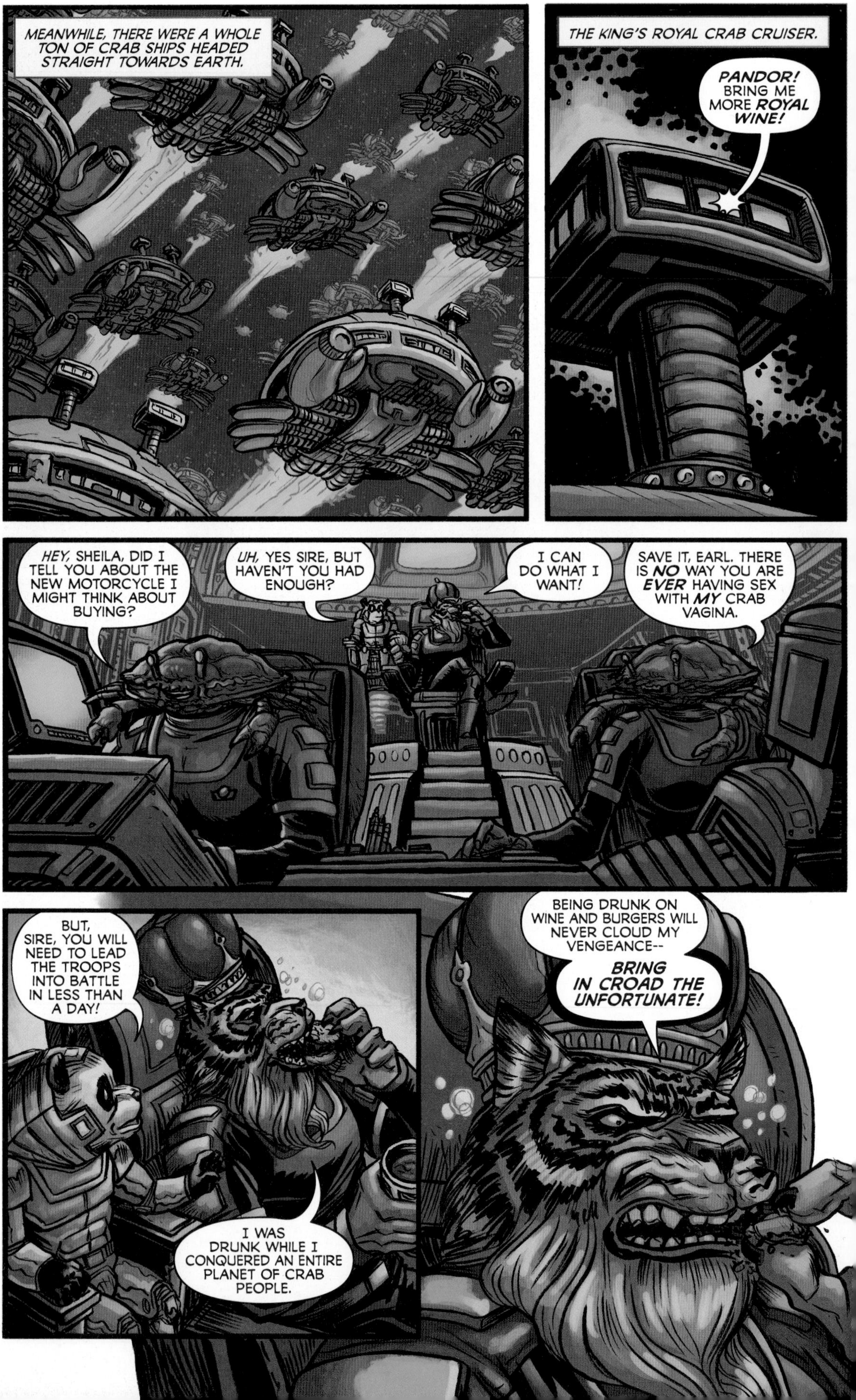
MEANWHILE, THERE WERE A WHOLE TON OF CRAB SHIPS HEADED STRAIGHT TOWARDS EARTH.
THE KING'S ROYAL CRAB CRUISER.
PANDOR! BRING ME MORE ROYAL WINE!
HEY, SHEILA, DID I TELL YOU ABOUT THE NEW MOTORCYCLE I MIGHT THINK ABOUT BUYING?
UH, YES SIRE, BUT HAVEN'T YOU HAD ENOUGH?
I CAN DO WHAT I WANT!
SAVE IT, EARL. THERE IS NO WAY YOU ARE EVER HAVING SEX WITH MY CRAB VAGINA.
BUT, SIRE, YOU WILL NEED TO LEAD THE TROOPS INTO BATTLE IN LESS THAN A DAY!
I WAS DRUNK WHILE I CONQUERED AN ENTIRE PLANET OF CRAB PEOPLE.
BEING DRUNK ON WINE AND BURGERS WILL NEVER CLOUD MY VENGEANCE--
BRING IN CROAD THE UNFORTUNATE!

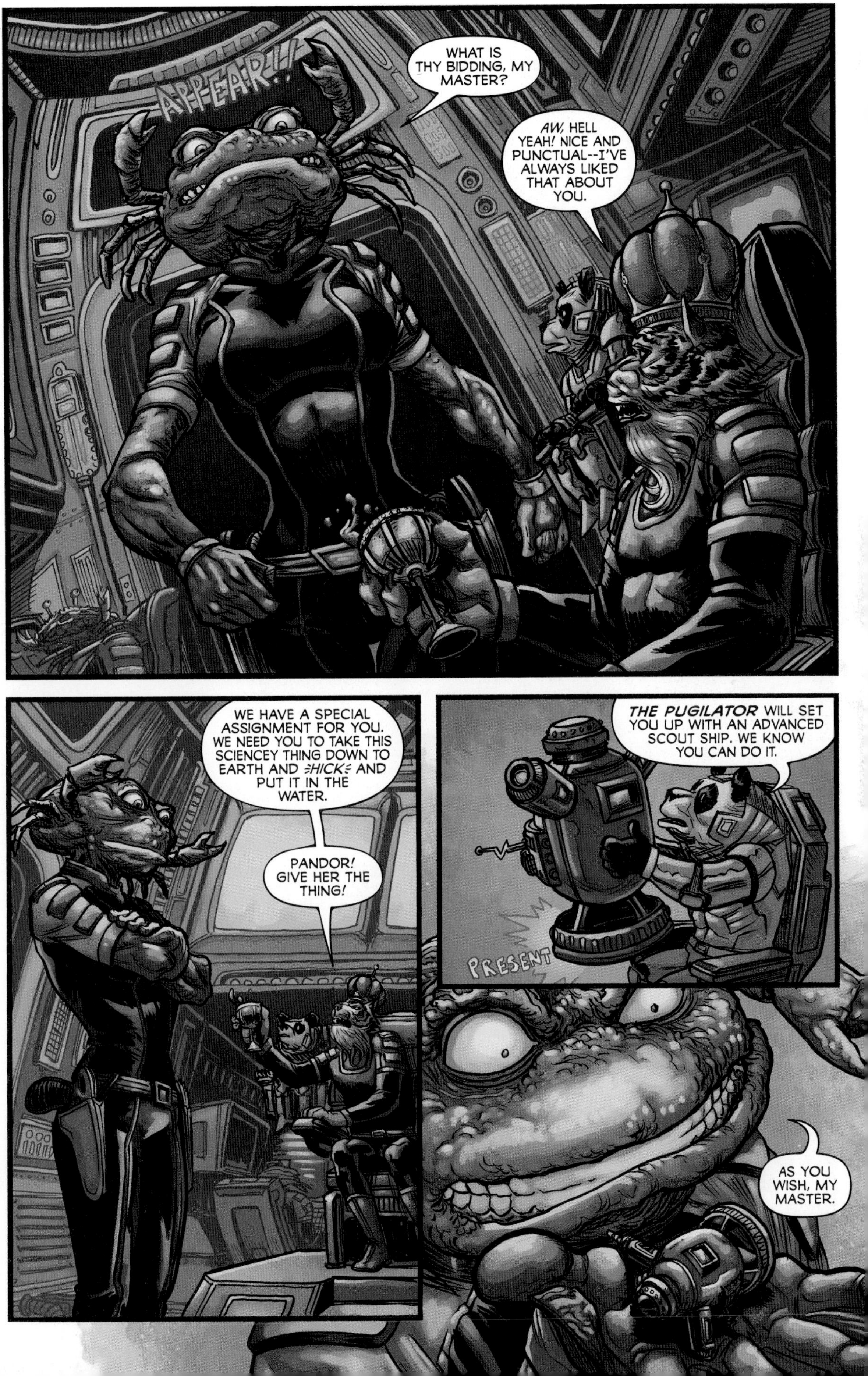
APPEAR!!
WHAT IS THY BIDDING, MY MASTER?
AW, HELL YEAH! NICE AND PUNCTUAL--I'VE ALWAYS LIKED THAT ABOUT YOU.
WE HAVE A SPECIAL ASSIGNMENT FOR YOU. WE NEED YOU TO TAKE THIS SCIENCEY THING DOWN TO EARTH AND *HICK* AND PUT IT IN THE WATER.
PANDOR! GIVE HER THE THING!
THE PUGILATOR WILL SET YOU UP WITH AN ADVANCED SCOUT SHIP. WE KNOW YOU CAN DO IT.
PRESENT
AS YOU WISH, MY MASTER.

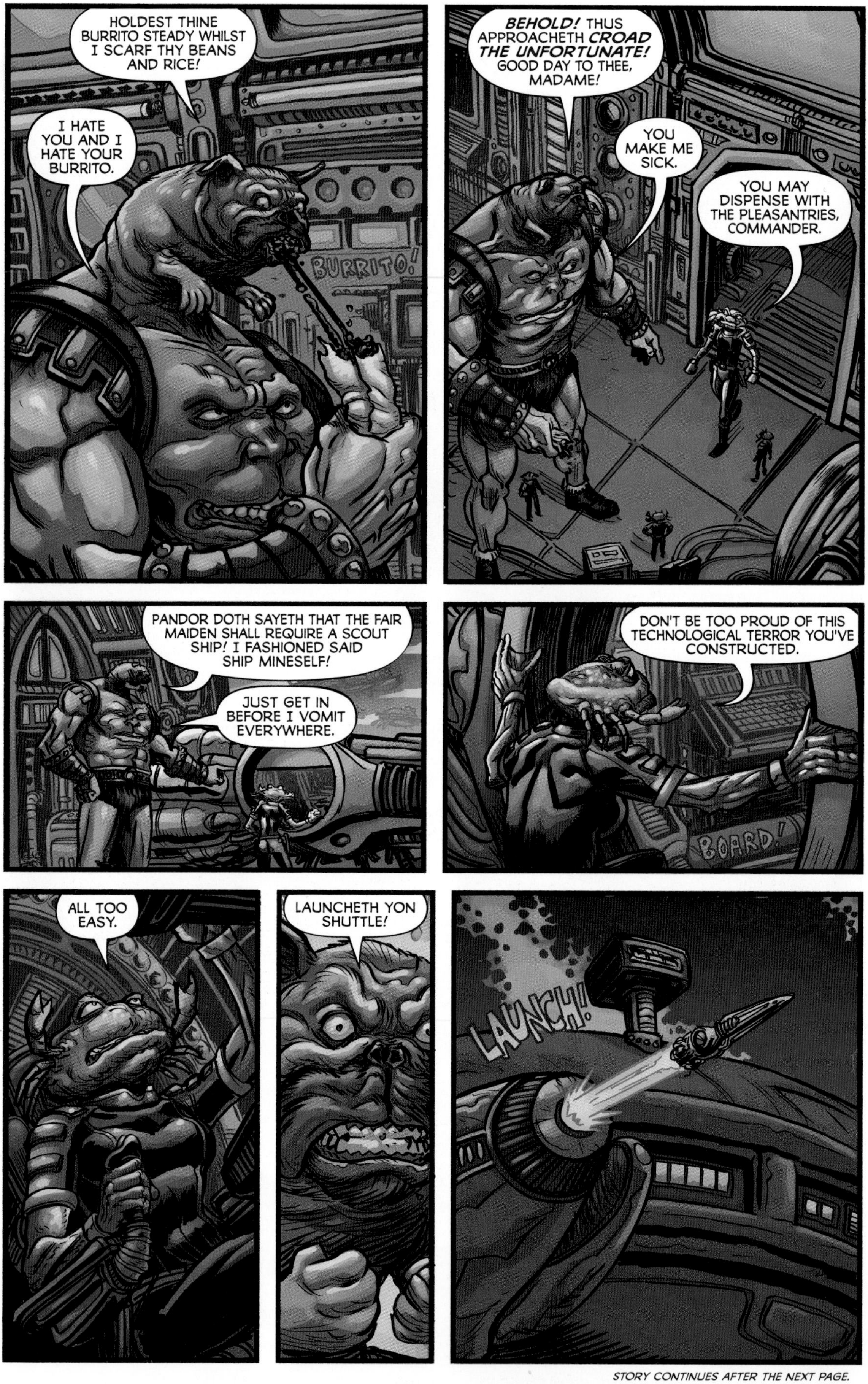
HOLDEST THINE BURRITO STEADY WHILST I SCARF THY BEANS AND RICE!
I HATE YOU AND I HATE YOUR BURRITO.
BURRITO!
BEHOLD! THUS APPROACHETH CROAD THE UNFORTUNATE! GOOD DAY TO THEE, MADAME!
YOU MAKE ME SICK.
YOU MAY DISPENSE WITH THE PLEASANTRIES, COMMANDER.
PANDOR DOTH SAYETH THAT THE FAIR MAIDEN SHALL REQUIRE A SCOUT SHIP! I FASHIONED SAID SHIP MINESELF!
JUST GET IN BEFORE I VOMIT EVERYWHERE.
DON'T BE TOO PROUD OF THIS TECHNOLOGICAL TERROR YOU'VE CONSTRUCTED.
BOARD!
ALL TOO EASY.
LAUNCHETH YON SHUTTLE!
LAUNCH!

STORY CONTINUES AFTER THE NEXT PAGE.

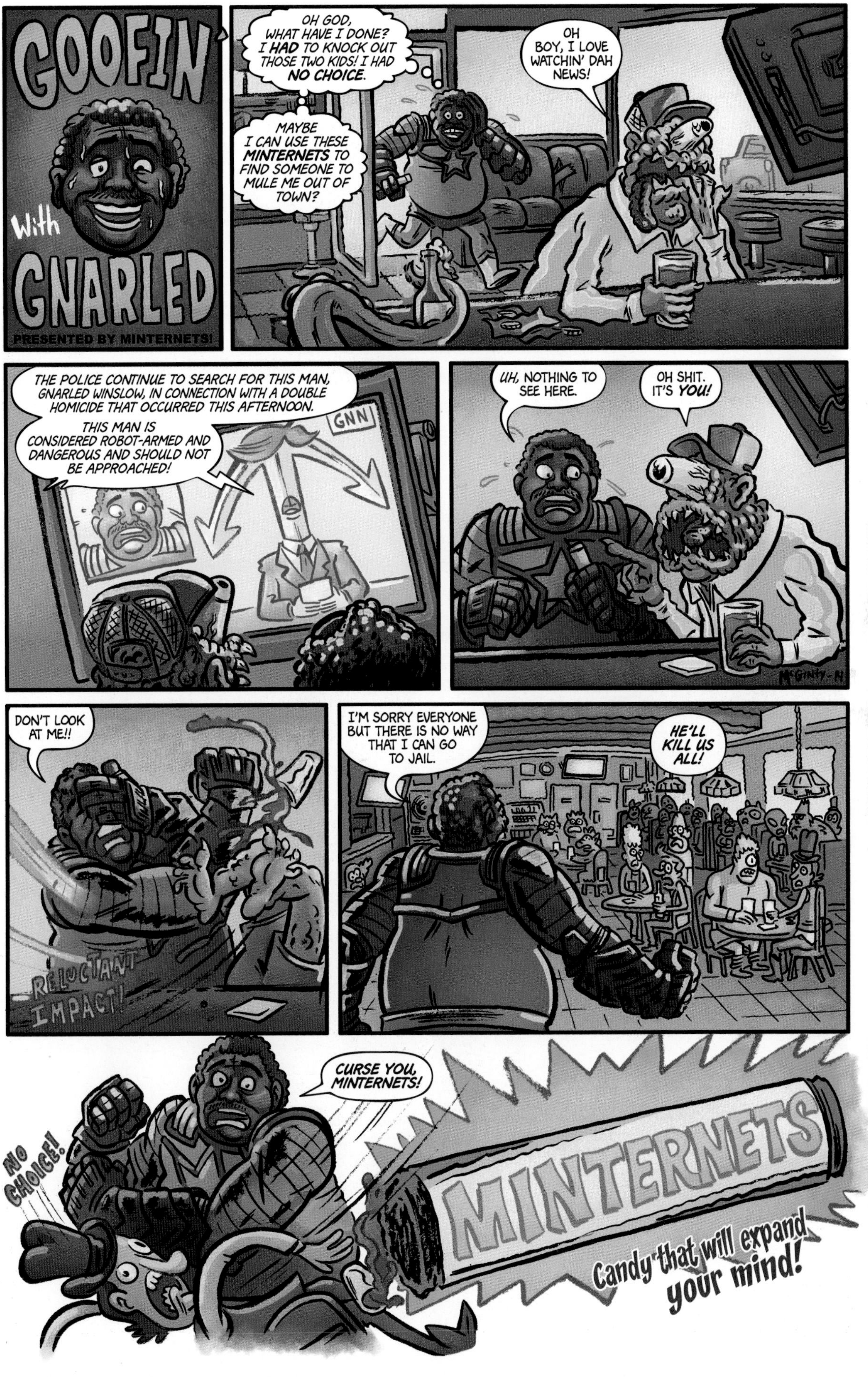
GOOFIN With GNARLED
PRESENTED BY MINTERNETS!
OH GOD, WHAT HAVE I DONE? I HAD TO KNOCK OUT THOSE TWO KIDS! I HAD NO CHOICE.
MAYBE I CAN USE THESE MINTERNETS TO FIND SOMEONE TO MULE ME OUT OF TOWN?
OH BOY, I LOVE WATCHIN' DAH NEWS!
THE POLICE CONTINUE TO SEARCH FOR THIS MAN, GNARLED WINSLOW, IN CONNECTION WITH A DOUBLE HOMICIDE THAT OCCURRED THIS AFTERNOON.
THIS MAN IS CONSIDERED ROBOT-ARMED AND DANGEROUS AND SHOULD NOT BE APPROACHED!
GNN
UH, NOTHING TO SEE HERE.
OH SHIT. IT'S YOU!
McGINTY-14
DON'T LOOK AT ME!!
RELUCTANT IMPACT!
I'M SORRY EVERYONE BUT THERE IS NO WAY THAT I CAN GO TO JAIL.
HE'LL KILL US ALL!
CURSE YOU, MINTERNETS!
NO CHOICE!
MINTERNETS
Candy that will expand your mind!

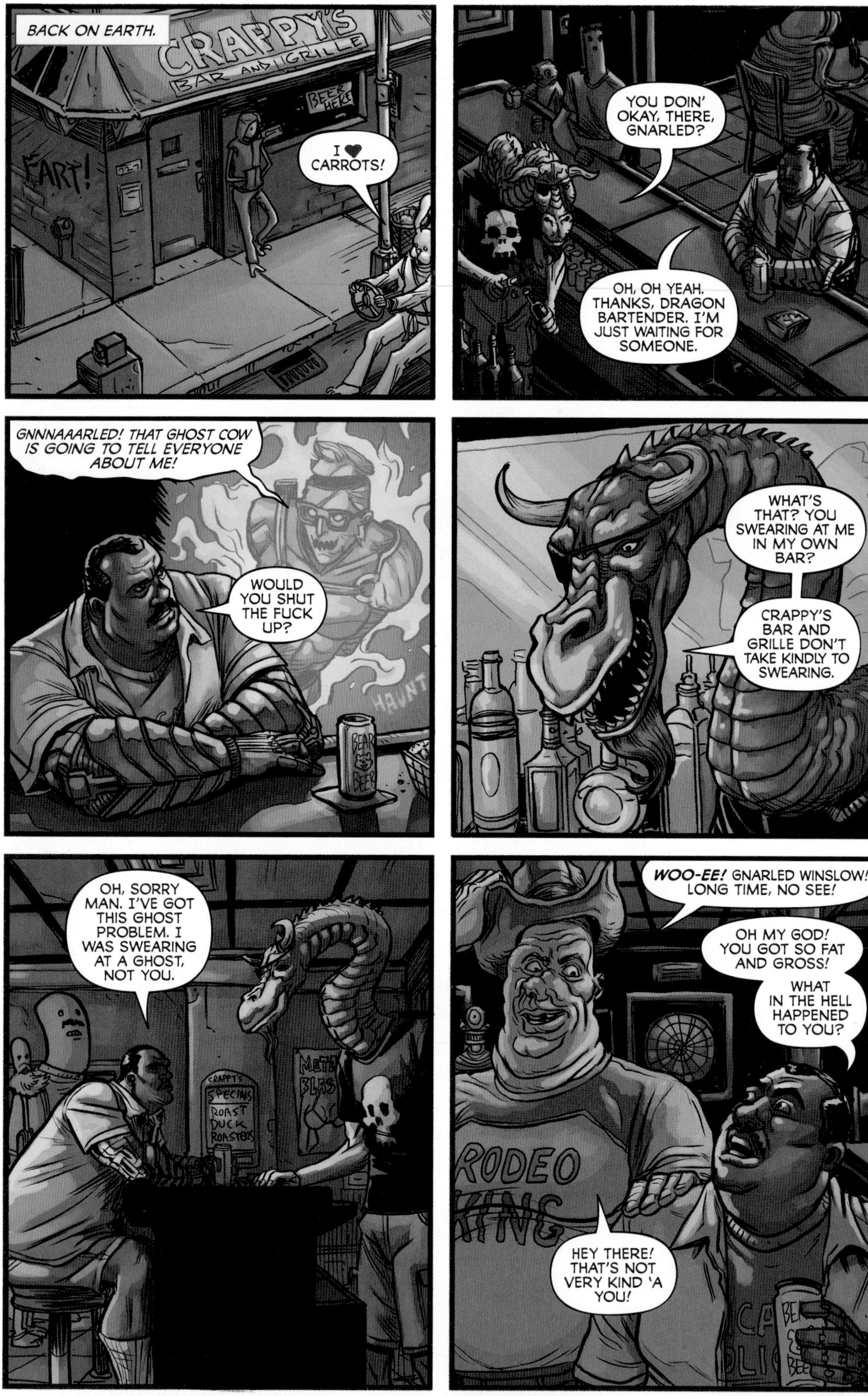
BACK ON EARTH.
CRAPPY'S
BAR AND GRILLE
BEER HERE
FART!
I ♥ CARROTS!
YOU DOIN' OKAY, THERE, GNARLED?
OH, OH YEAH. THANKS, DRAGON BARTENDER. I'M JUST WAITING FOR SOMEONE.
GNNNAAARLED! THAT GHOST COW IS GOING TO TELL EVERYONE ABOUT ME!
WOULD YOU SHUT THE FUCK UP?
HAUNT
BEAR BEER
WHAT'S THAT? YOU SWEARING AT ME IN MY OWN BAR?
CRAPPY'S BAR AND GRILLE DON'T TAKE KINDLY TO SWEARING.
OH, SORRY MAN. I'VE GOT THIS GHOST PROBLEM. I WAS SWEARING AT A GHOST, NOT YOU.
WOO-EE! GNARLED WINSLOW! LONG TIME, NO SEE!
OH MY GOD! YOU GOT SO FAT AND GROSS!
WHAT IN THE HELL HAPPENED TO YOU?
RODEO
HEY THERE! THAT'S NOT VERY KIND 'A YOU!

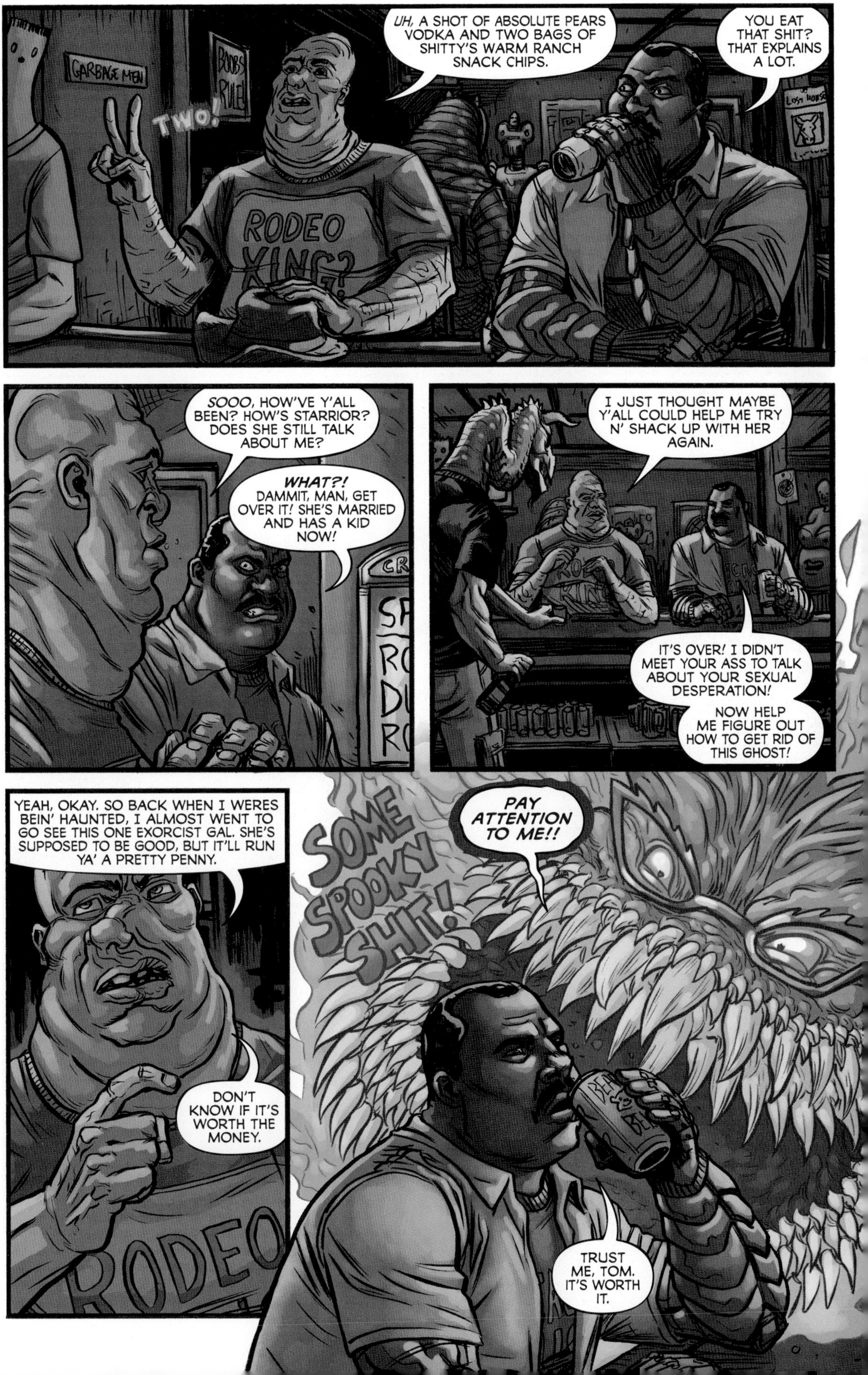

GARBAGE MEN
BOOBS RULE!
TWO!
UH, A SHOT OF ABSOLUTE PEARS VODKA AND TWO BAGS OF SHITTY'S WARM RANCH SNACK CHIPS.
YOU EAT THAT SHIT? THAT EXPLAINS A LOT.
RODEO KING?
SOOO, HOW'VE Y'ALL BEEN? HOW'S STARRIOR? DOES SHE STILL TALK ABOUT ME?
WHAT?! DAMMIT, MAN, GET OVER IT! SHE'S MARRIED AND HAS A KID NOW!
I JUST THOUGHT MAYBE Y'ALL COULD HELP ME TRY N' SHACK UP WITH HER AGAIN.
IT'S OVER! I DIDN'T MEET YOUR ASS TO TALK ABOUT YOUR SEXUAL DESPERATION!
NOW HELP ME FIGURE OUT HOW TO GET RID OF THIS GHOST!
YEAH, OKAY. SO BACK WHEN I WERES BEIN' HAUNTED, I ALMOST WENT TO GO SEE THIS ONE EXORCIST GAL. SHE'S SUPPOSED TO BE GOOD, BUT IT'LL RUN YA' A PRETTY PENNY.
DON'T KNOW IF IT'S WORTH THE MONEY.
RODEO
SOME SPOOKY SHIT!
PAY ATTENTION TO ME!!
TRUST ME, TOM. IT'S WORTH IT.

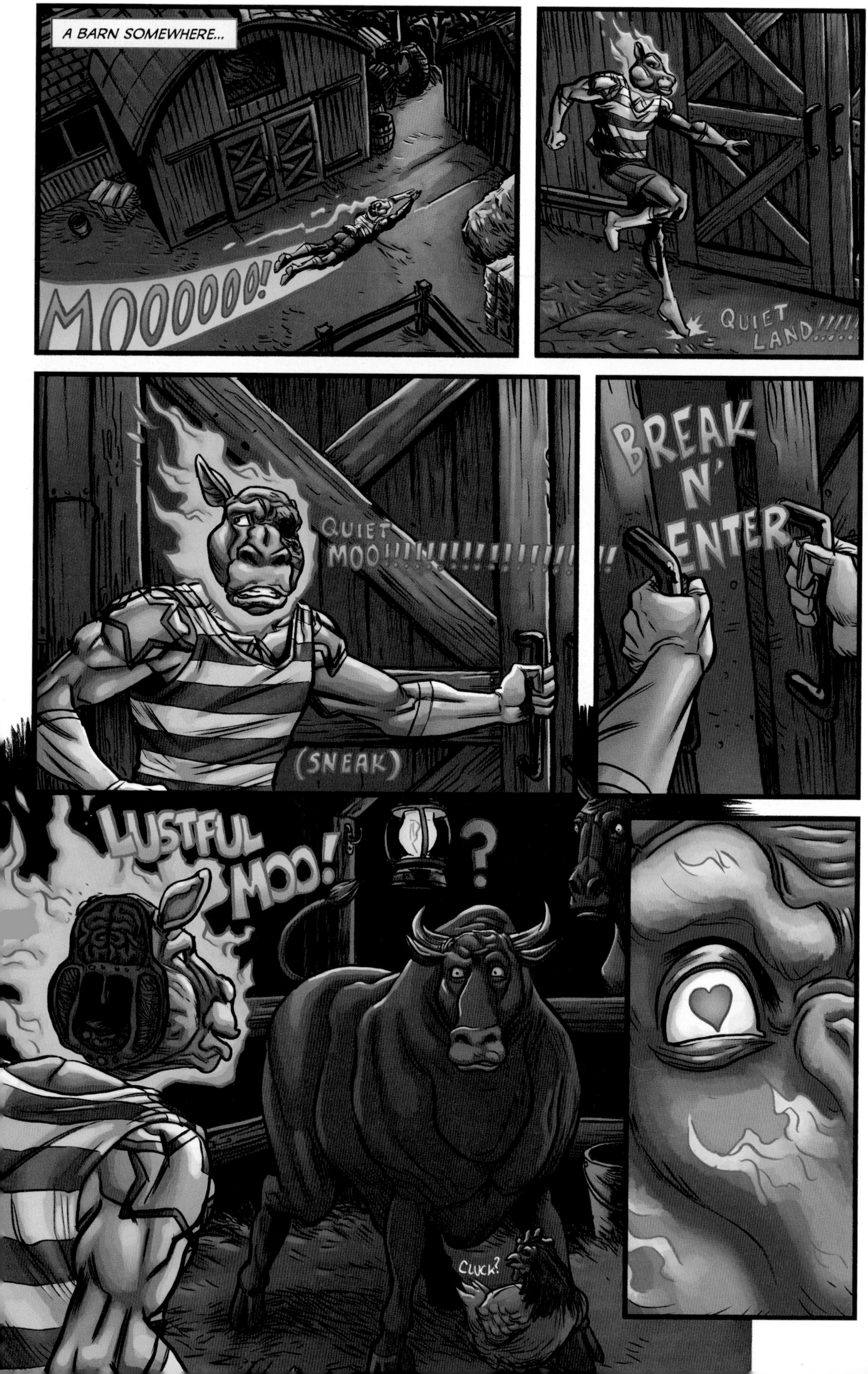
A BARN SOMEWHERE...
MOOOOOO!
QUIET LAND!!!!!
QUIET MOO!!!!!!!!!!!!!!!!!!
(SNEAK)
BREAK N' ENTER
LUSTFUL MOO!
?
CLUCK?

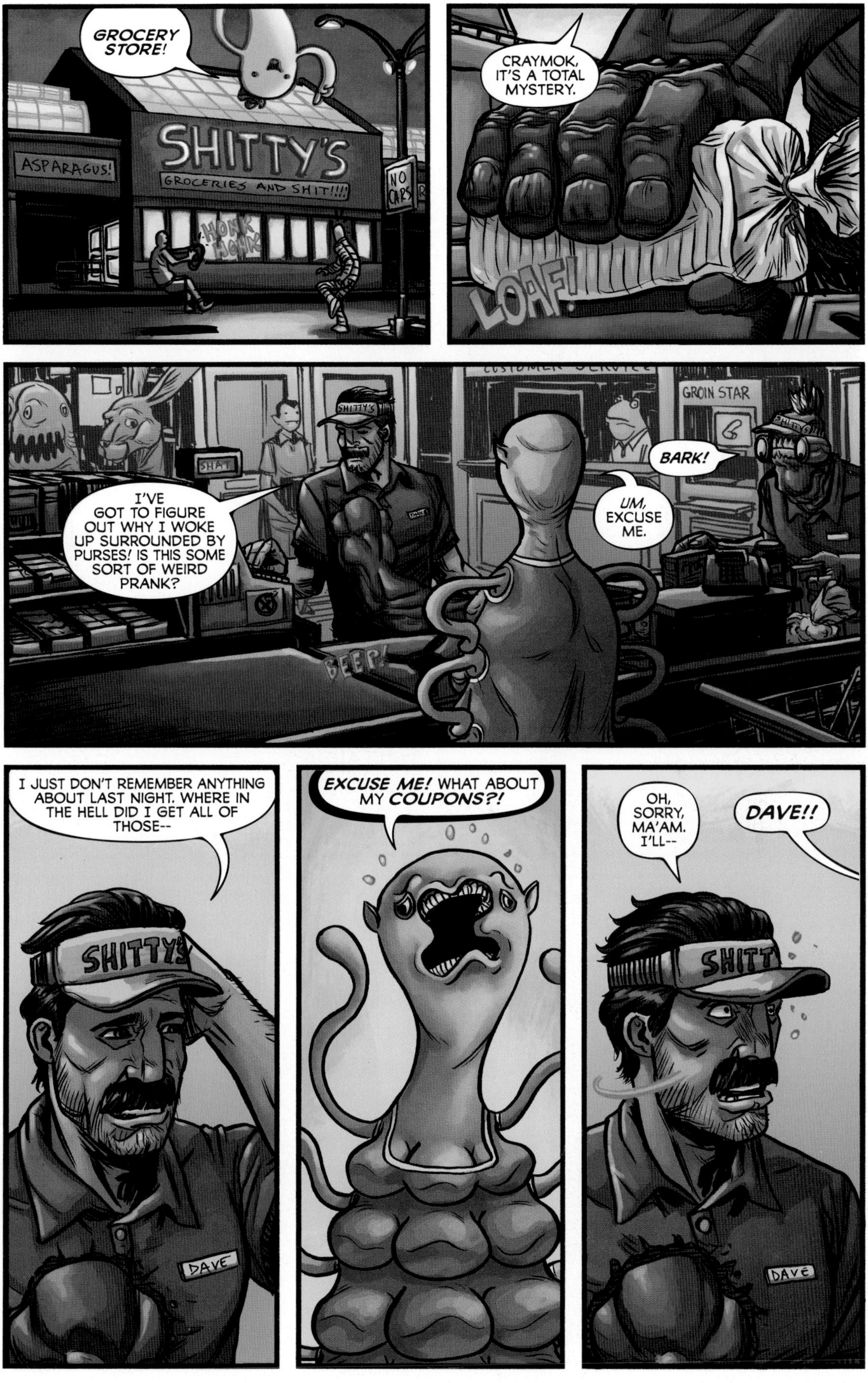
GROCERY STORE!
SHITTY'S
GROCERIES AND SHIT!!!!
ASPARAGUS!
NO CARS
HONK HONK
CRAYMOK, IT'S A TOTAL MYSTERY.
LOAF!
GROIN STAR
SHAT
I'VE GOT TO FIGURE OUT WHY I WOKE UP SURROUNDED BY PURSES! IS THIS SOME SORT OF WEIRD PRANK?
UM, EXCUSE ME.
BARK!
BEEP!
I JUST DON'T REMEMBER ANYTHING ABOUT LAST NIGHT. WHERE IN THE HELL DID I GET ALL OF THOSE--
SHITTY'S
DAVE
EXCUSE ME! WHAT ABOUT MY COUPONS?!
OH, SORRY, MA'AM. I'LL--
DAVE!!
DAVE

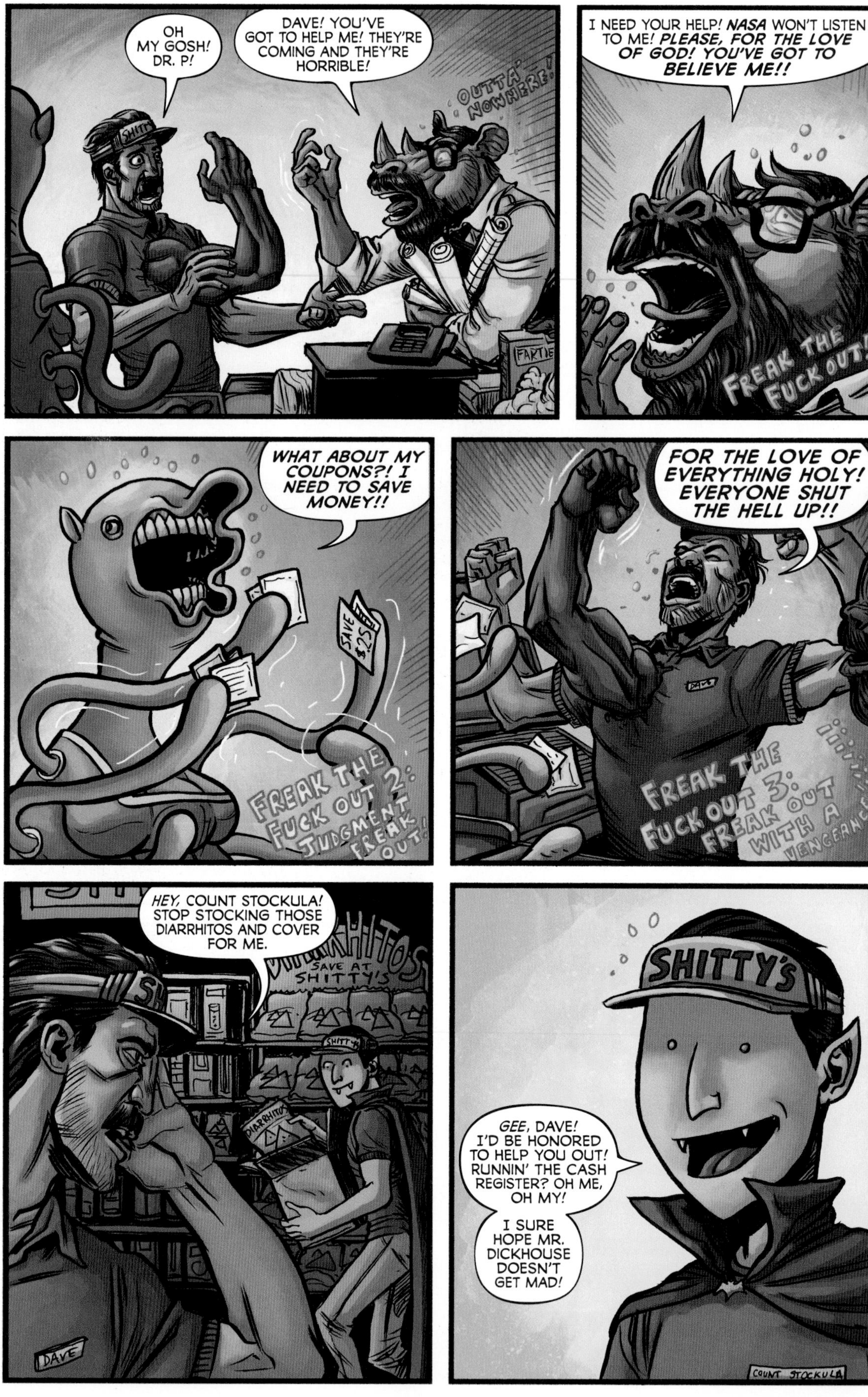
OH MY GOSH! DR. P!
DAVE! YOU'VE GOT TO HELP ME! THEY'RE COMING AND THEY'RE HORRIBLE!
OUTTA' NOWHERE!
SHITTY
FARTIE
I NEED YOUR HELP! NASA WON'T LISTEN TO ME! PLEASE, FOR THE LOVE OF GOD! YOU'VE GOT TO BELIEVE ME!!
FREAK THE FUCK OUT!
WHAT ABOUT MY COUPONS?! I NEED TO SAVE MONEY!!
SAVE $.25
FREAK THE FUCK OUT 2: JUDGMENT FREAK OUT
FOR THE LOVE OF EVERYTHING HOLY! EVERYONE SHUT THE HELL UP!!
DAVE
FREAK THE FUCK OUT 3: FREAK OUT WITH A VENGEANCE!!!
HEY, COUNT STOCKULA! STOP STOCKING THOSE DIARRHITOS AND COVER FOR ME.
SAVE AT SHITTY'S
DIARRHITOS
DAVE
SHITTY'S
GEE, DAVE! I'D BE HONORED TO HELP YOU OUT! RUNNIN' THE CASH REGISTER? OH ME, OH MY!
I SURE HOPE MR. DICKHOUSE DOESN'T GET MAD!
COUNT STOCKULA

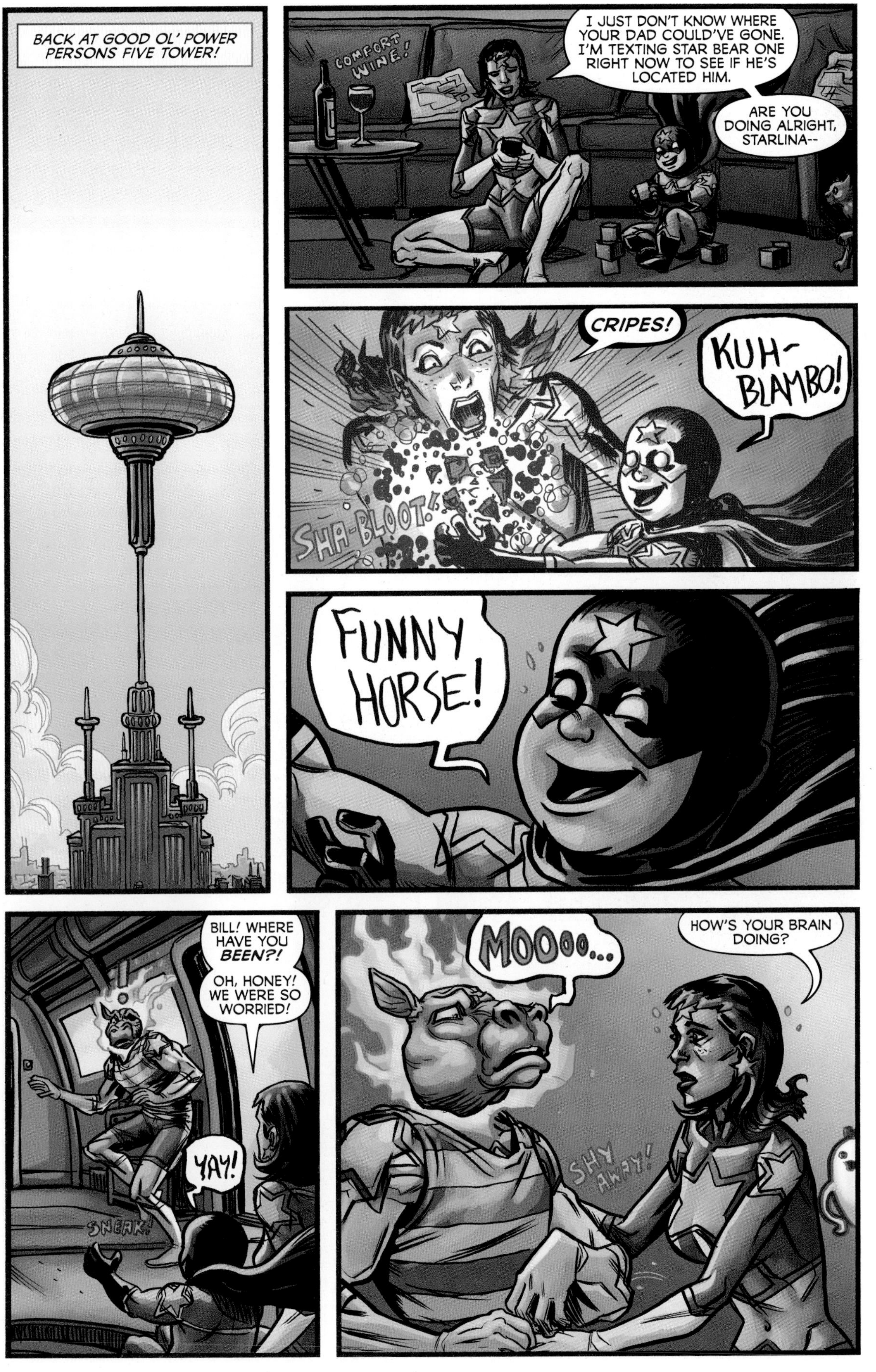
BACK AT GOOD OL' POWER PERSONS FIVE TOWER!
COMFORT WINE!
I JUST DON'T KNOW WHERE YOUR DAD COULD'VE GONE. I'M TEXTING STAR BEAR ONE RIGHT NOW TO SEE IF HE'S LOCATED HIM.
ARE YOU DOING ALRIGHT, STARLINA--
CRIPES!
KUH-BLAMBO!
SHA-BLOOT!
FUNNY HORSE!
BILL! WHERE HAVE YOU BEEN?!
OH, HONEY! WE WERE SO WORRIED!
YAY!
SNEAK!
MOOoo...
HOW'S YOUR BRAIN DOING?
SHY AWAY!

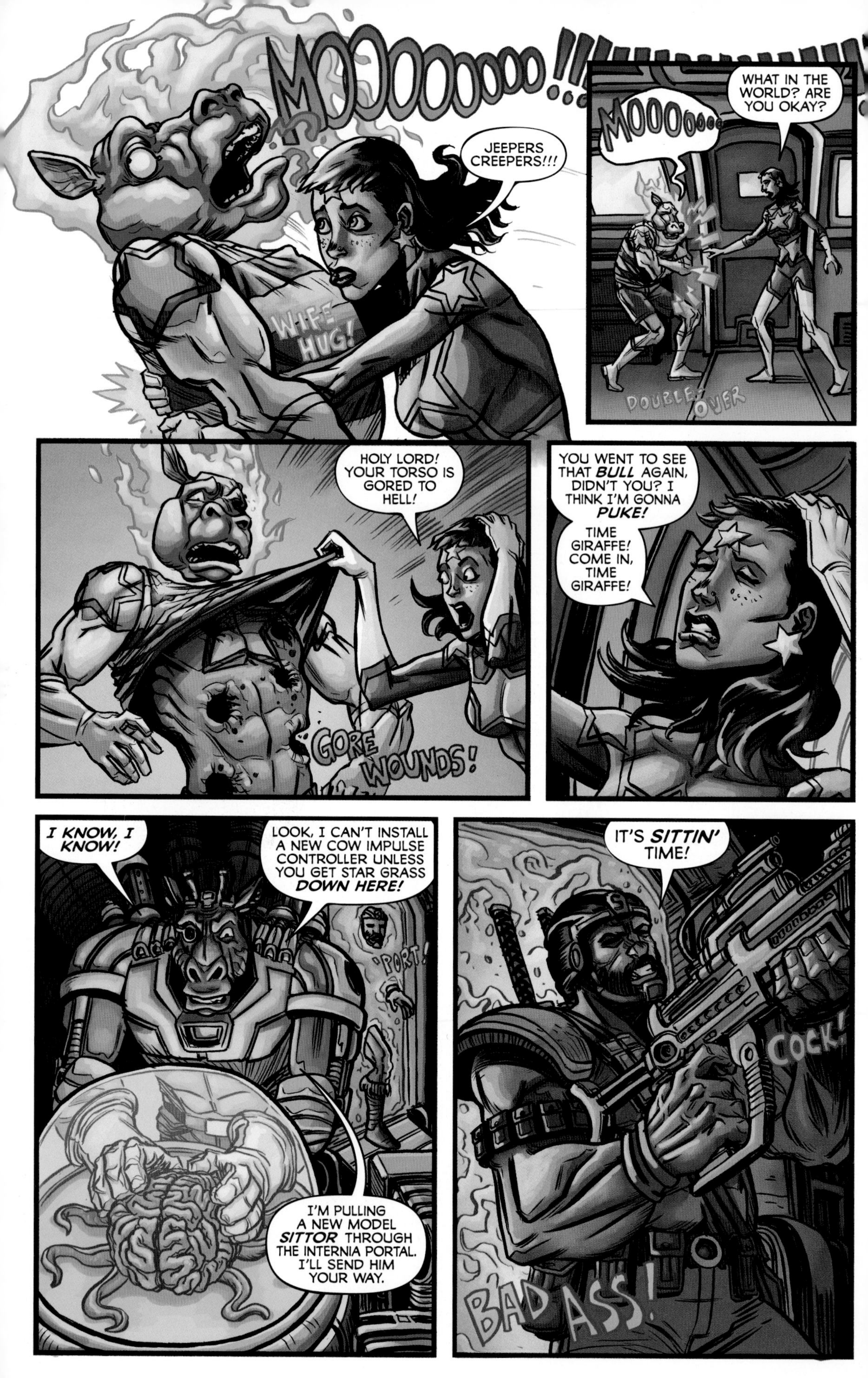
MOOOOOOOO!!!!!!!!!!!!!!!!
JEEPERS CREEPERS!!!
WIFE HUG!
WHAT IN THE WORLD? ARE YOU OKAY?
MOOOOooo
DOUBLE OVER
HOLY LORD! YOUR TORSO IS GORED TO HELL!
GORE WOUNDS!
YOU WENT TO SEE THAT BULL AGAIN, DIDN'T YOU? I THINK I'M GONNA PUKE!
TIME GIRAFFE! COME IN, TIME GIRAFFE!
I KNOW, I KNOW!
LOOK, I CAN'T INSTALL A NEW COW IMPULSE CONTROLLER UNLESS YOU GET STAR GRASS DOWN HERE!
'PORT!
I'M PULLING A NEW MODEL SITTOR THROUGH THE INTERNIA PORTAL. I'LL SEND HIM YOUR WAY.
IT'S SITTIN' TIME!
COCK!
BAD ASS!

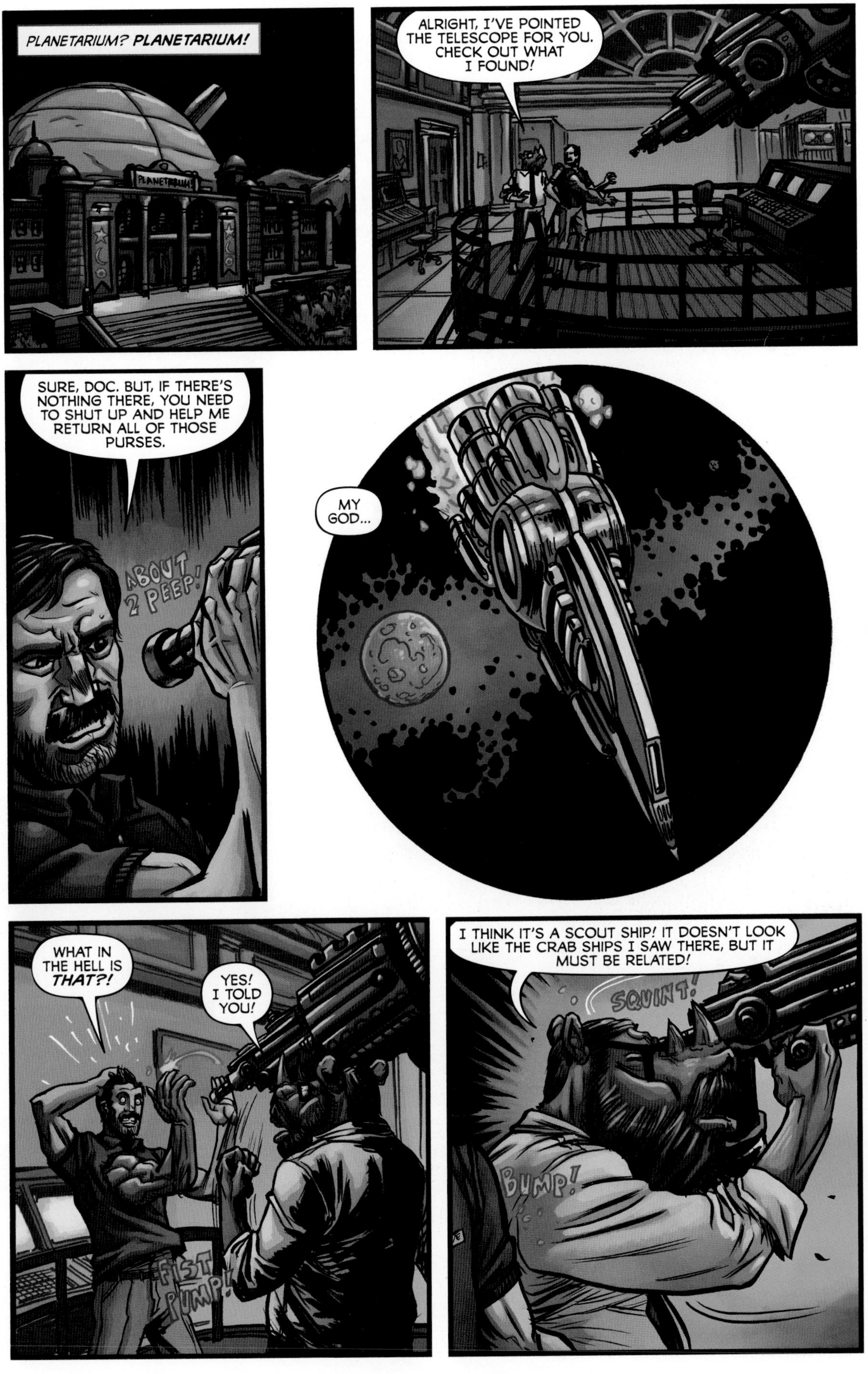
PLANETARIUM? **PLANETARIUM!**
PLANETARIUM
ALRIGHT, I'VE POINTED THE TELESCOPE FOR YOU. CHECK OUT WHAT I FOUND!
SURE, DOC. BUT, IF THERE'S NOTHING THERE, YOU NEED TO SHUT UP AND HELP ME RETURN ALL OF THOSE PURSES.
ABOUT 2 PEEP!
MY GOD...
WHAT IN THE HELL IS *THAT?!*
YES! I TOLD YOU!
FIST PUMP!
I THINK IT'S A SCOUT SHIP! IT DOESN'T LOOK LIKE THE CRAB SHIPS I SAW THERE, BUT IT MUST BE RELATED!
SQUINT!
BUMP!

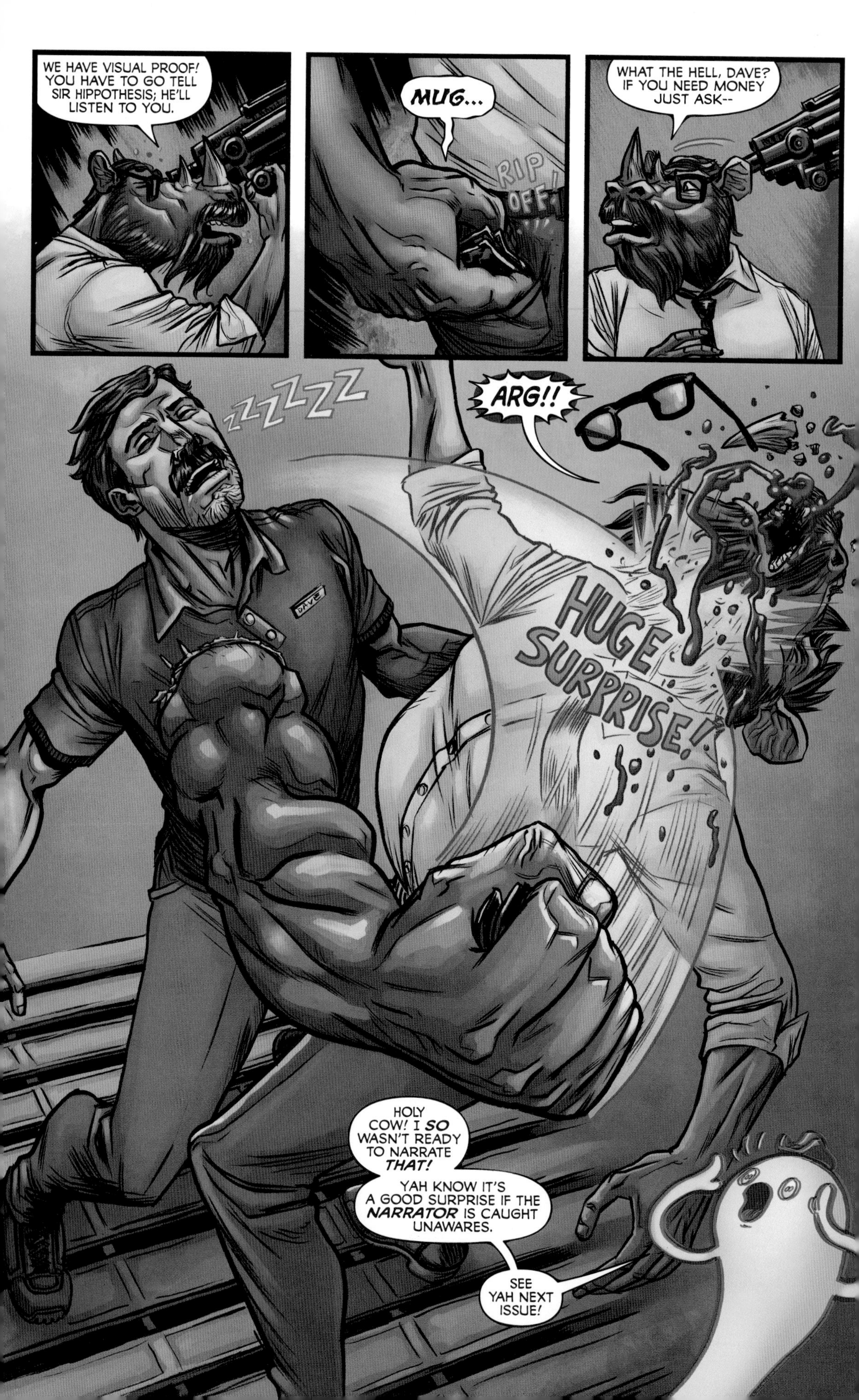
WE HAVE VISUAL PROOF! YOU HAVE TO GO TELL SIR HIPPOTHESIS; HE'LL LISTEN TO YOU.
MUG...
RIP OFF!
WHAT THE HELL, DAVE? IF YOU NEED MONEY JUST ASK--
ZZZZZZZ
ARG!!
DAVE
HUGE SURPRISE!
HOLY COW! I SO WASN'T READY TO NARRATE THAT!
YAH KNOW IT'S A GOOD SURPRISE IF THE NARRATOR IS CAUGHT UNAWARES.
SEE YAH NEXT ISSUE!

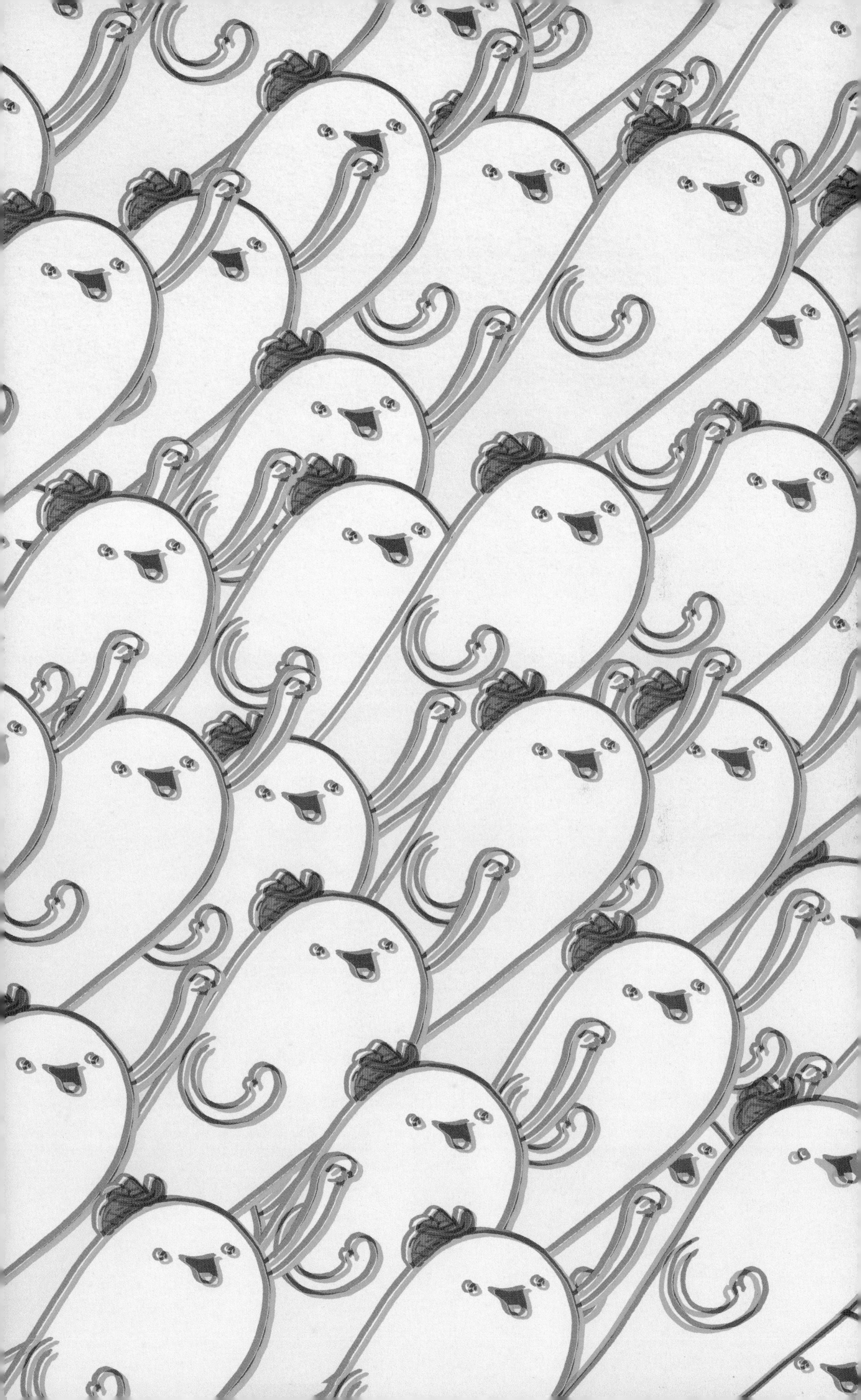

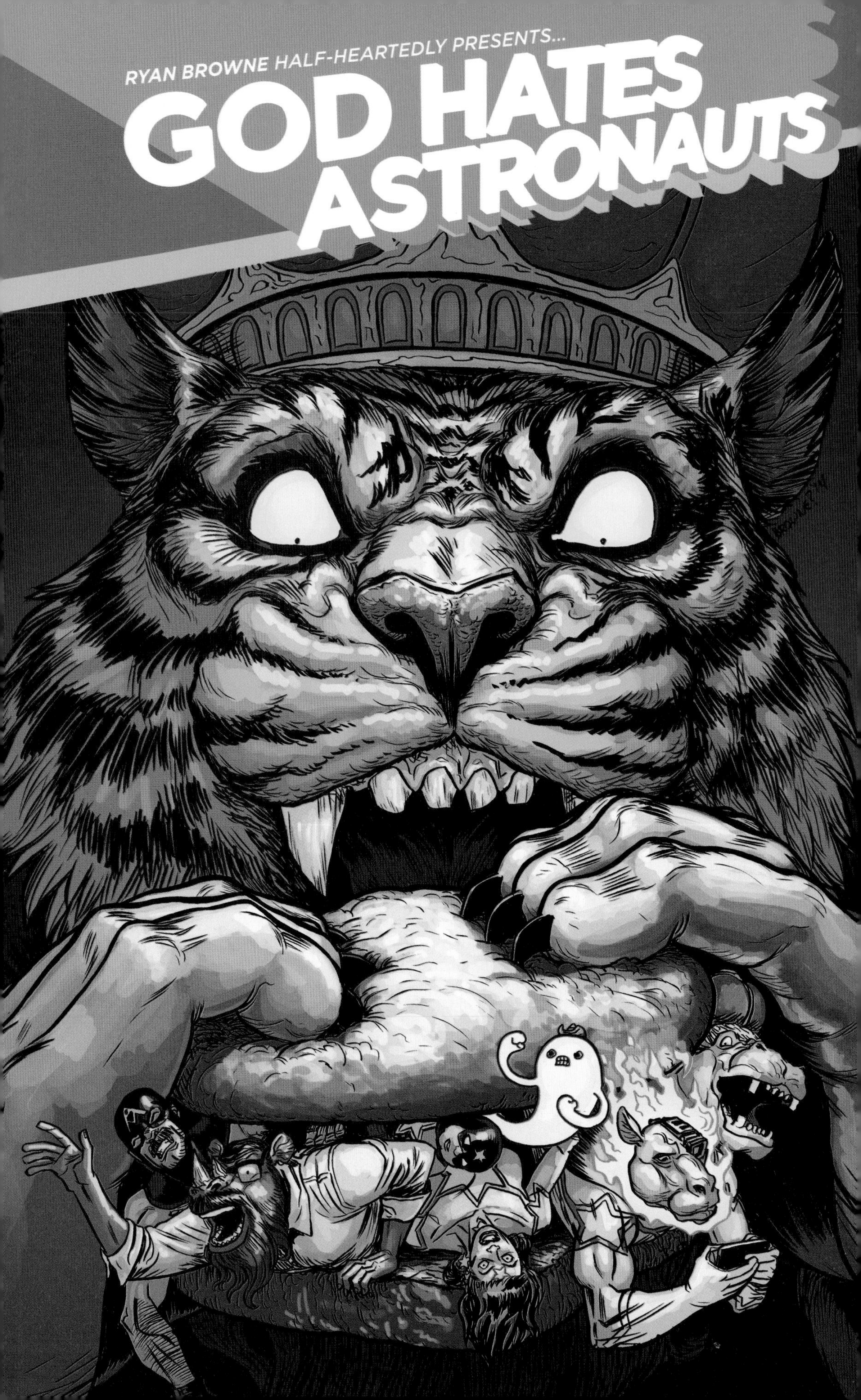
RYAN BROWNE HALF-HEARTEDLY PRESENTS...
GOD HATES ASTRONAUTS

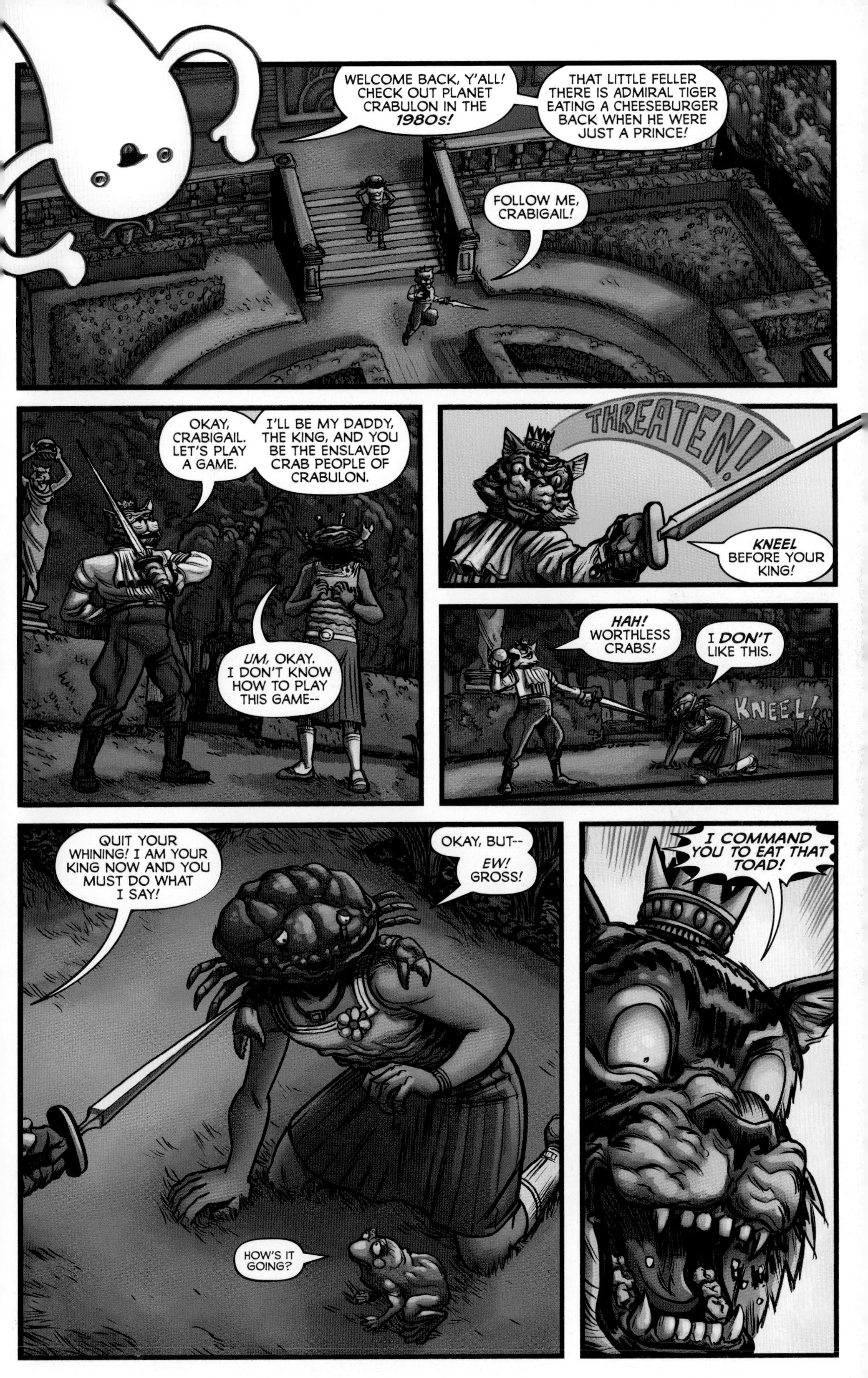
WELCOME BACK, Y'ALL! CHECK OUT PLANET CRABULON IN THE *1980s!*
THAT LITTLE FELLER THERE IS ADMIRAL TIGER EATING A CHEESEBURGER BACK WHEN HE WERE JUST A PRINCE!
FOLLOW ME, CRABIGAIL!
OKAY, CRABIGAIL. LET'S PLAY A GAME.
I'LL BE MY DADDY, THE KING, AND YOU BE THE ENSLAVED CRAB PEOPLE OF CRABULON.
UM, OKAY. I DON'T KNOW HOW TO PLAY THIS GAME--
THREATEN!
KNEEL BEFORE YOUR KING!
HAH! WORTHLESS CRABS!
I *DON'T* LIKE THIS.
KNEEL!
QUIT YOUR WHINING! I AM YOUR KING NOW AND YOU MUST DO WHAT I SAY!
OKAY, BUT--
EW! GROSS!
HOW'S IT GOING?
I COMMAND YOU TO EAT THAT TOAD!

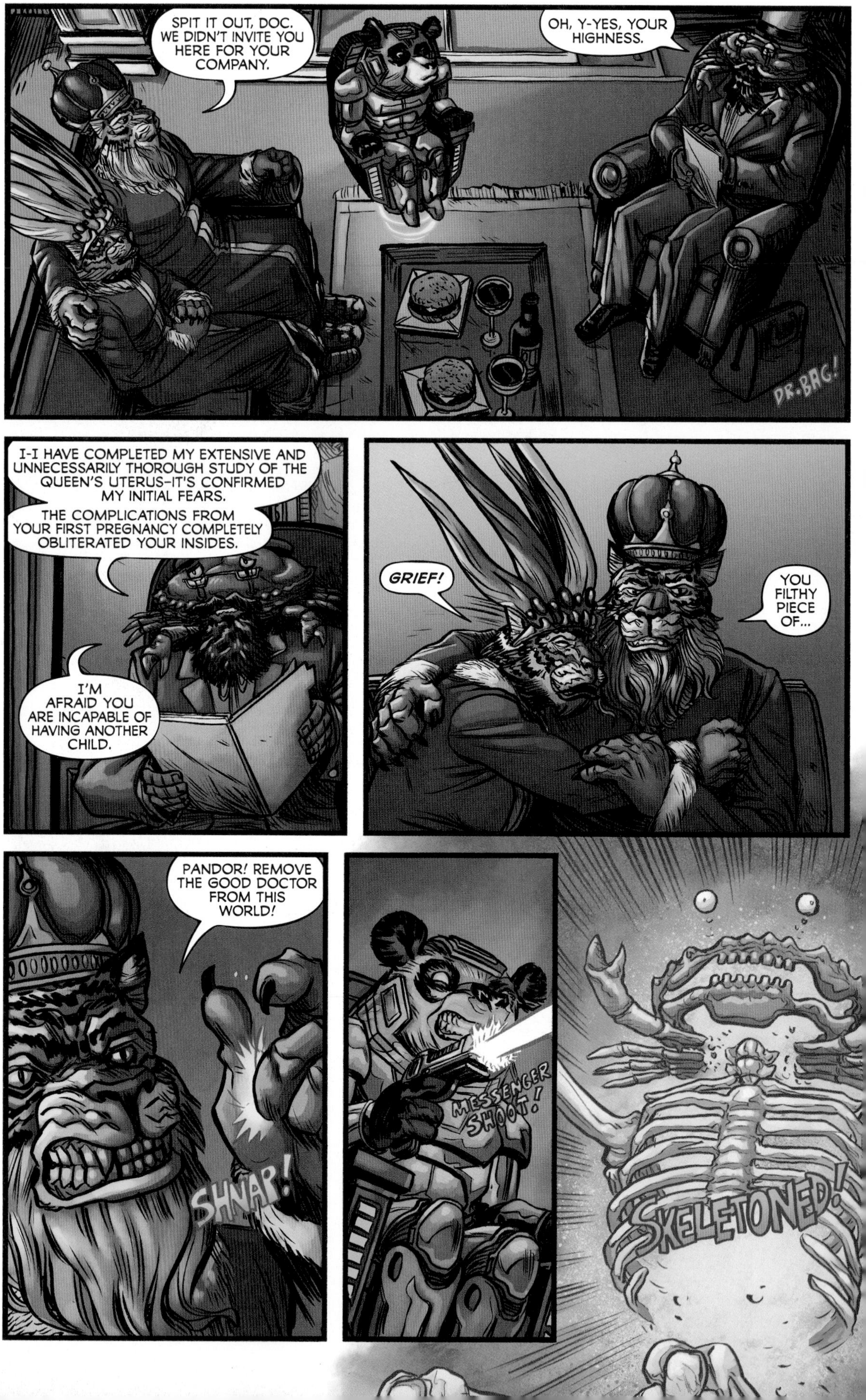
SPIT IT OUT, DOC. WE DIDN'T INVITE YOU HERE FOR YOUR COMPANY.
OH, Y-YES, YOUR HIGHNESS.
DR. BAG!
I-I HAVE COMPLETED MY EXTENSIVE AND UNNECESSARILY THOROUGH STUDY OF THE QUEEN'S UTERUS–IT'S CONFIRMED MY INITIAL FEARS.
THE COMPLICATIONS FROM YOUR FIRST PREGNANCY COMPLETELY OBLITERATED YOUR INSIDES.
I'M AFRAID YOU ARE INCAPABLE OF HAVING ANOTHER CHILD.
GRIEF!
YOU FILTHY PIECE OF...
PANDOR! REMOVE THE GOOD DOCTOR FROM THIS WORLD!
SHNAP!
MESSENGER SHOOT!
SKELETONED!

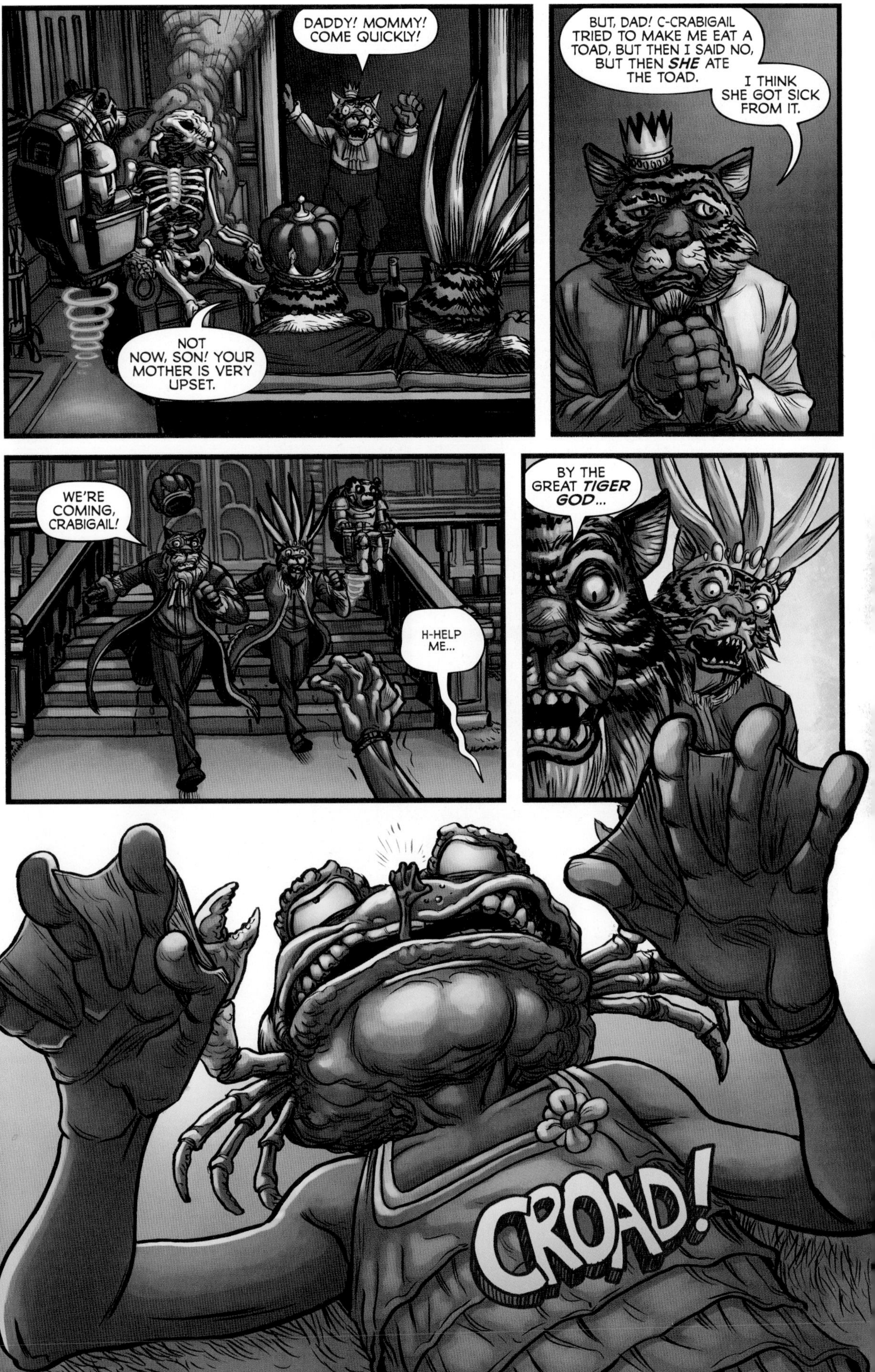
DADDY! MOMMY! COME QUICKLY!
NOT NOW, SON! YOUR MOTHER IS VERY UPSET.
BUT, DAD! C-CRABIGAIL TRIED TO MAKE ME EAT A TOAD, BUT THEN I SAID NO, BUT THEN SHE ATE THE TOAD.
I THINK SHE GOT SICK FROM IT.
WE'RE COMING, CRABIGAIL!
H-HELP ME...
BY THE GREAT TIGER GOD...
CROAD!

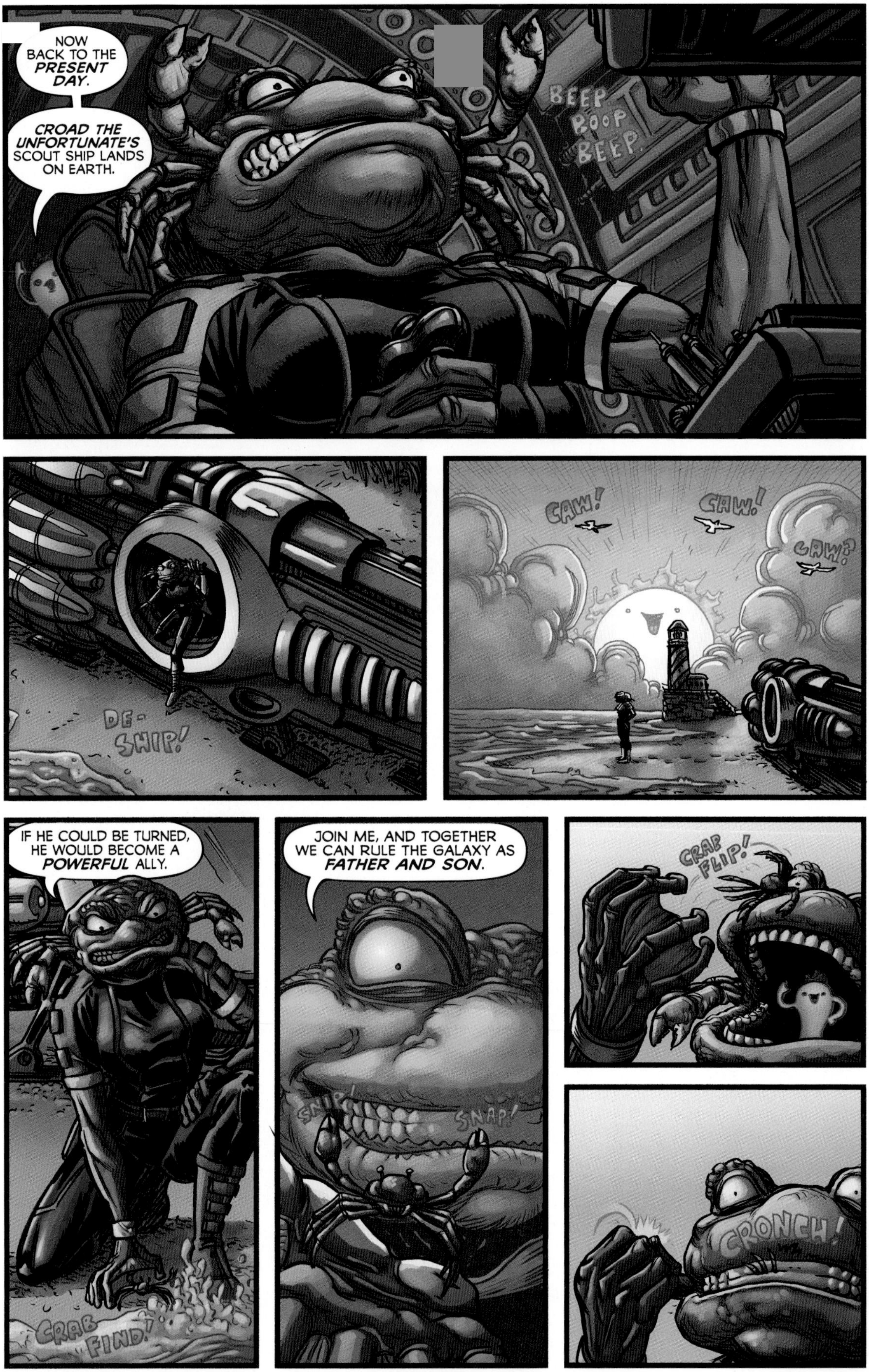
NOW BACK TO THE PRESENT DAY.
CROAD THE UNFORTUNATE'S SCOUT SHIP LANDS ON EARTH.
BEEP. BOOP BEEP.
DE-SHIP!
CAW!
CAW!
CAW?
IF HE COULD BE TURNED, HE WOULD BECOME A POWERFUL ALLY.
CRAB FIND!
JOIN ME, AND TOGETHER WE CAN RULE THE GALAXY AS FATHER AND SON.
SNIP!
SNAP!
CRAB FLIP!
CRONCH!

PRESENTING

GOD HATES ASTRONAUTS

Nº4

A STAR IS BORN

...rage-induced diarrhea, impossible math equations about bees, fluffy fat-guy undercarriages, poorly run non-government elections, hate, soft-served eye scream, Bruce Boxleitner "films," golf caddies "Gone Wild," unprecedented tooth decay, Carry the Label Guy stand-up comedy disasters...

PRESS START

WITH YOUR

MIND-FINGER

TO CONTINUE

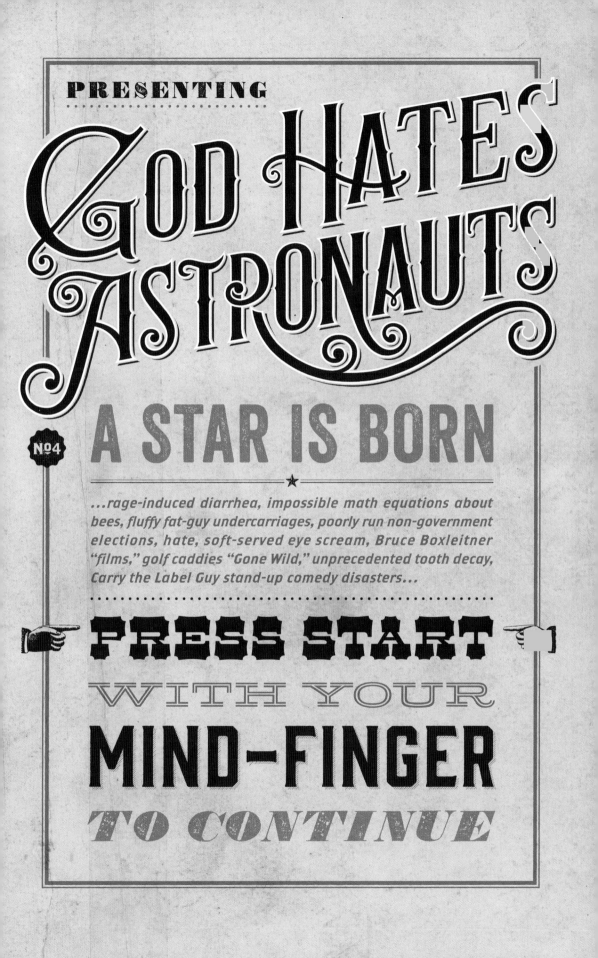

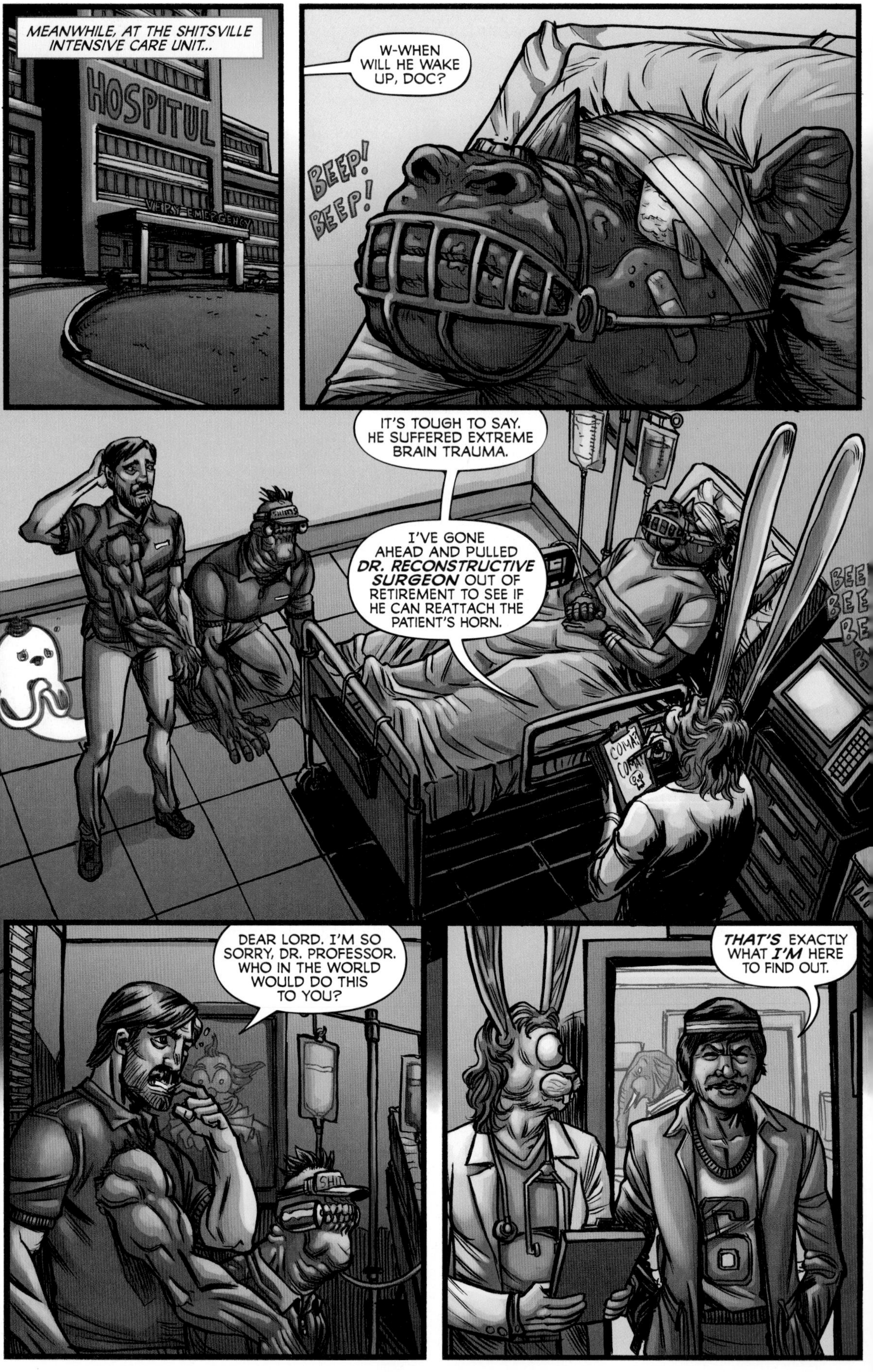
MEANWHILE, AT THE SHITSVILLE INTENSIVE CARE UNIT...
HOSPITUL
VERY EMERGENCY
W-WHEN WILL HE WAKE UP, DOC?
BEEP! BEEP!
IT'S TOUGH TO SAY. HE SUFFERED EXTREME BRAIN TRAUMA.
I'VE GONE AHEAD AND PULLED ***DR. RECONSTRUCTIVE SURGEON*** OUT OF RETIREMENT TO SEE IF HE CAN REATTACH THE PATIENT'S HORN.
COMA? COMA?
DEAR LORD. I'M SO SORRY, DR. PROFESSOR. WHO IN THE WORLD WOULD DO THIS TO YOU?
THAT'S EXACTLY WHAT ***I'M*** HERE TO FIND OUT.

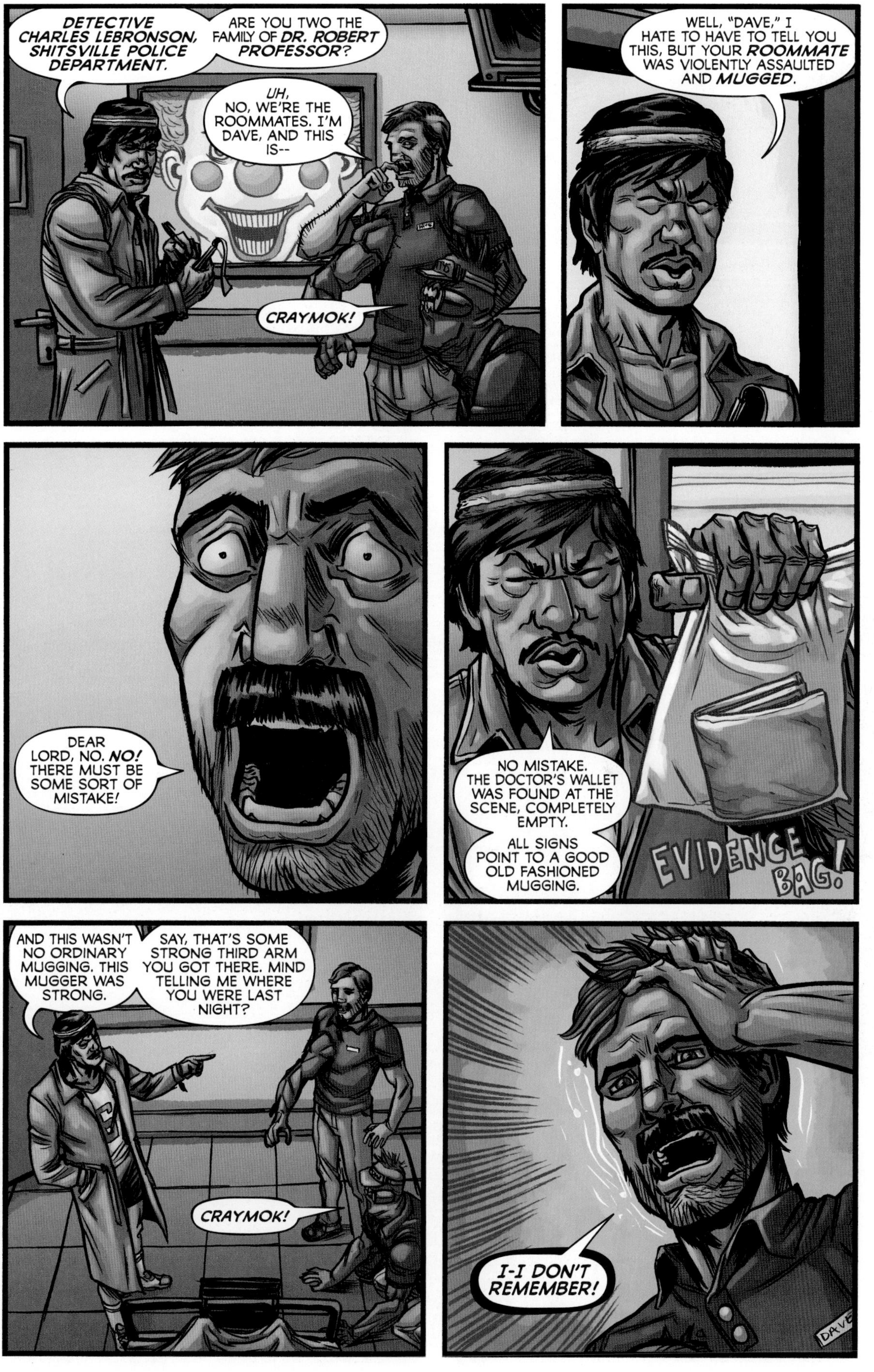
DETECTIVE CHARLES LEBRONSON, SHITSVILLE POLICE DEPARTMENT.
ARE YOU TWO THE FAMILY OF DR. ROBERT PROFESSOR?
UH, NO, WE'RE THE ROOMMATES. I'M DAVE, AND THIS IS--
CRAYMOK!
DAVE
WELL, "DAVE," I HATE TO HAVE TO TELL YOU THIS, BUT YOUR ROOMMATE WAS VIOLENTLY ASSAULTED AND MUGGED.
DEAR LORD, NO. NO! THERE MUST BE SOME SORT OF MISTAKE!
NO MISTAKE. THE DOCTOR'S WALLET WAS FOUND AT THE SCENE, COMPLETELY EMPTY.
ALL SIGNS POINT TO A GOOD OLD FASHIONED MUGGING.
EVIDENCE BAG!
AND THIS WASN'T NO ORDINARY MUGGING. THIS MUGGER WAS STRONG.
SAY, THAT'S SOME STRONG THIRD ARM YOU GOT THERE. MIND TELLING ME WHERE YOU WERE LAST NIGHT?
CRAYMOK!
I-I DON'T REMEMBER!
DAVE

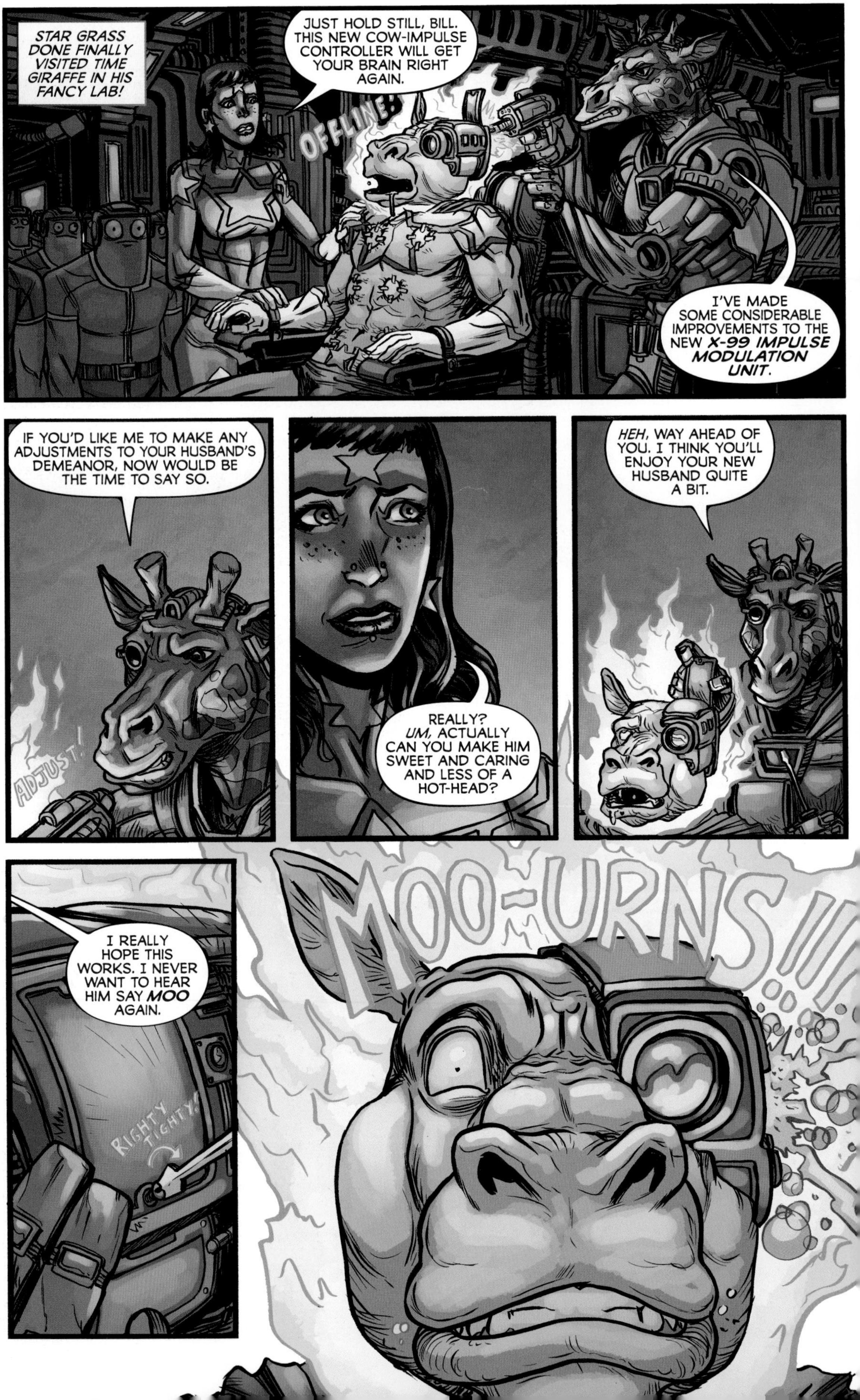
STAR GRASS DONE FINALLY VISITED TIME GIRAFFE IN HIS FANCY LAB!
JUST HOLD STILL, BILL. THIS NEW COW-IMPULSE CONTROLLER WILL GET YOUR BRAIN RIGHT AGAIN.
OFFLINE!
I'VE MADE SOME CONSIDERABLE IMPROVEMENTS TO THE NEW X-99 IMPULSE MODULATION UNIT.
IF YOU'D LIKE ME TO MAKE ANY ADJUSTMENTS TO YOUR HUSBAND'S DEMEANOR, NOW WOULD BE THE TIME TO SAY SO.
ADJUST!
REALLY? UM, ACTUALLY CAN YOU MAKE HIM SWEET AND CARING AND LESS OF A HOT-HEAD?
HEH, WAY AHEAD OF YOU. I THINK YOU'LL ENJOY YOUR NEW HUSBAND QUITE A BIT.
I REALLY HOPE THIS WORKS. I NEVER WANT TO HEAR HIM SAY MOO AGAIN.
RIGHTY TIGHTY!
MOO-URNS!!!

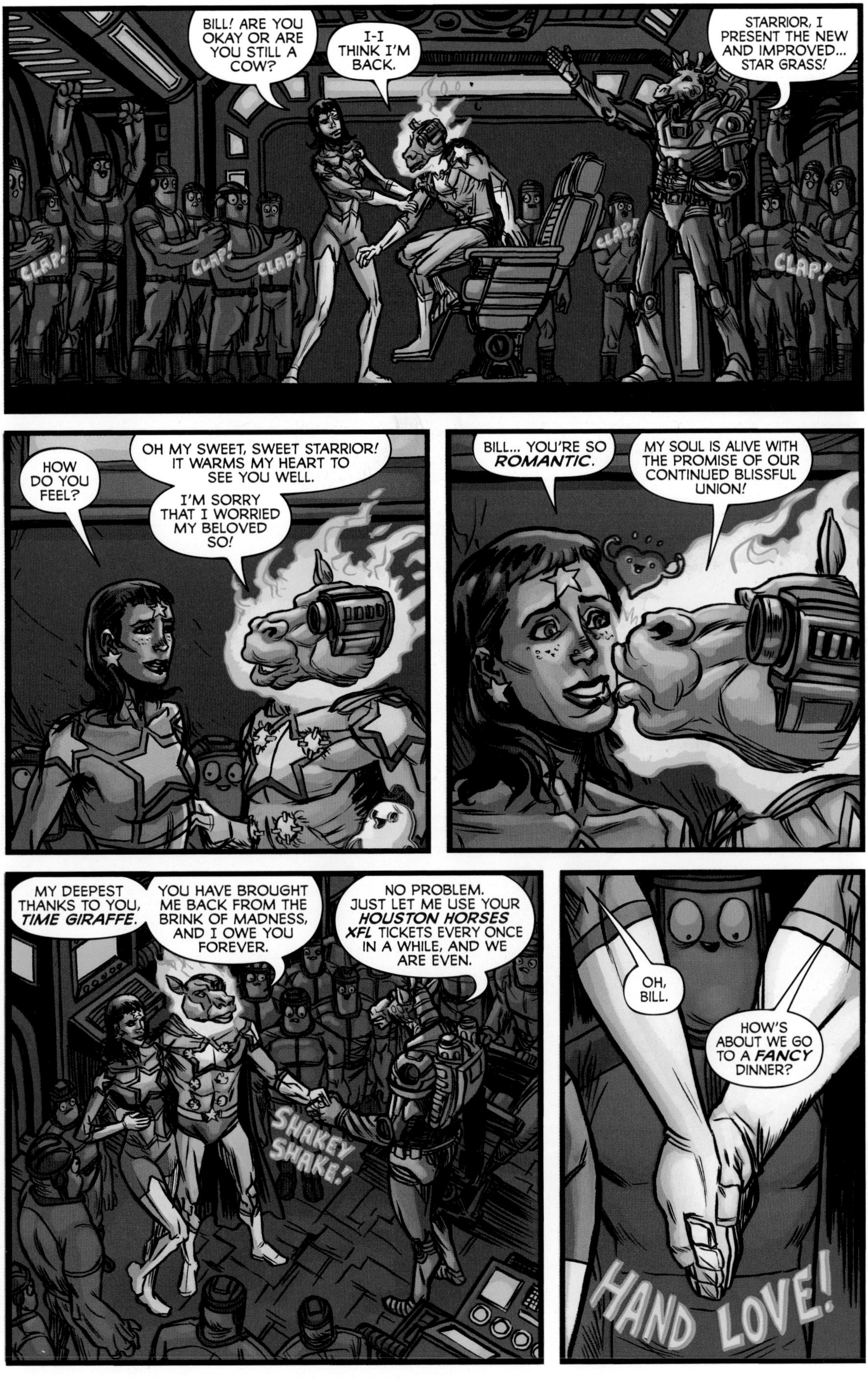
BILL! ARE YOU OKAY OR ARE YOU STILL A COW?
I-I THINK I'M BACK.
STARRIOR, I PRESENT THE NEW AND IMPROVED... STAR GRASS!
CLAP!
CLAP!
CLAP!
CLAP!
CLAP!
HOW DO YOU FEEL?
OH MY SWEET, SWEET STARRIOR! IT WARMS MY HEART TO SEE YOU WELL.
I'M SORRY THAT I WORRIED MY BELOVED SO!
BILL... YOU'RE SO *ROMANTIC*.
MY SOUL IS ALIVE WITH THE PROMISE OF OUR CONTINUED BLISSFUL UNION!
MY DEEPEST THANKS TO YOU, *TIME GIRAFFE*.
YOU HAVE BROUGHT ME BACK FROM THE BRINK OF MADNESS, AND I OWE YOU FOREVER.
NO PROBLEM. JUST LET ME USE YOUR ***HOUSTON HORSES XFL*** TICKETS EVERY ONCE IN A WHILE, AND WE ARE EVEN.
SHAKEY SHAKE!
OH, BILL.
HOW'S ABOUT WE GO TO A *FANCY* DINNER?
HAND LOVE!

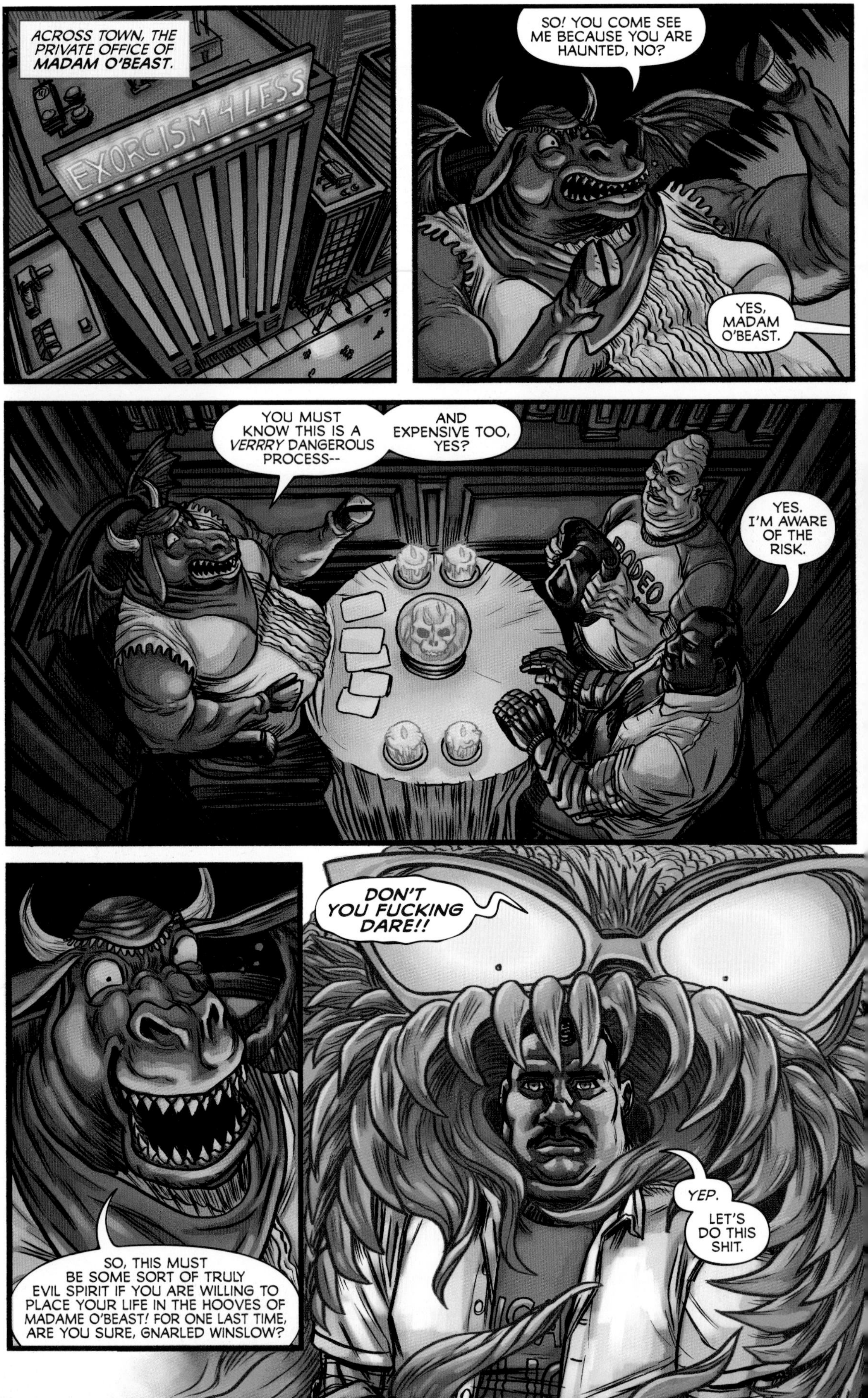
ACROSS TOWN, THE PRIVATE OFFICE OF MADAM O'BEAST.
EXORCISM 4 LESS
SO! YOU COME SEE ME BECAUSE YOU ARE HAUNTED, NO?
YES, MADAM O'BEAST.
YOU MUST KNOW THIS IS A VERRRY DANGEROUS PROCESS--
AND EXPENSIVE TOO, YES?
YES. I'M AWARE OF THE RISK.
RODEO
SO, THIS MUST BE SOME SORT OF TRULY EVIL SPIRIT IF YOU ARE WILLING TO PLACE YOUR LIFE IN THE HOOVES OF MADAME O'BEAST! FOR ONE LAST TIME, ARE YOU SURE, GNARLED WINSLOW?
DON'T YOU FUCKING DARE!!
YEP.
LET'S DO THIS SHIT.

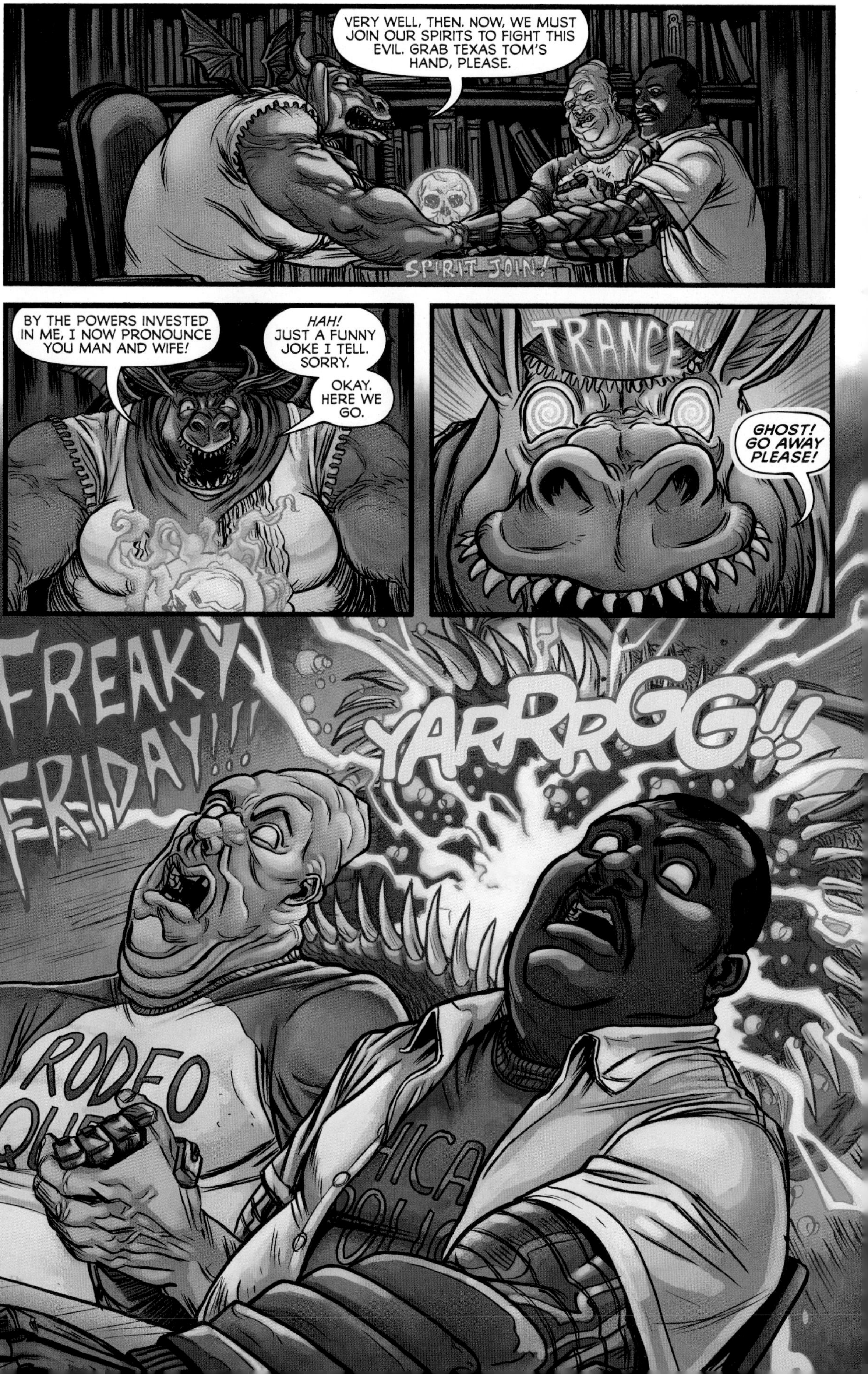
VERY WELL, THEN. NOW, WE MUST JOIN OUR SPIRITS TO FIGHT THIS EVIL. GRAB TEXAS TOM'S HAND, PLEASE.
SPIRIT JOIN!
BY THE POWERS INVESTED IN ME, I NOW PRONOUNCE YOU MAN AND WIFE!
HAH! JUST A FUNNY JOKE I TELL. SORRY.
OKAY. HERE WE GO.
TRANCE
GHOST! GO AWAY PLEASE!
FREAKY FRIDAY!!!
YARRRGG!!
RODEO QUE
HICA POLIC

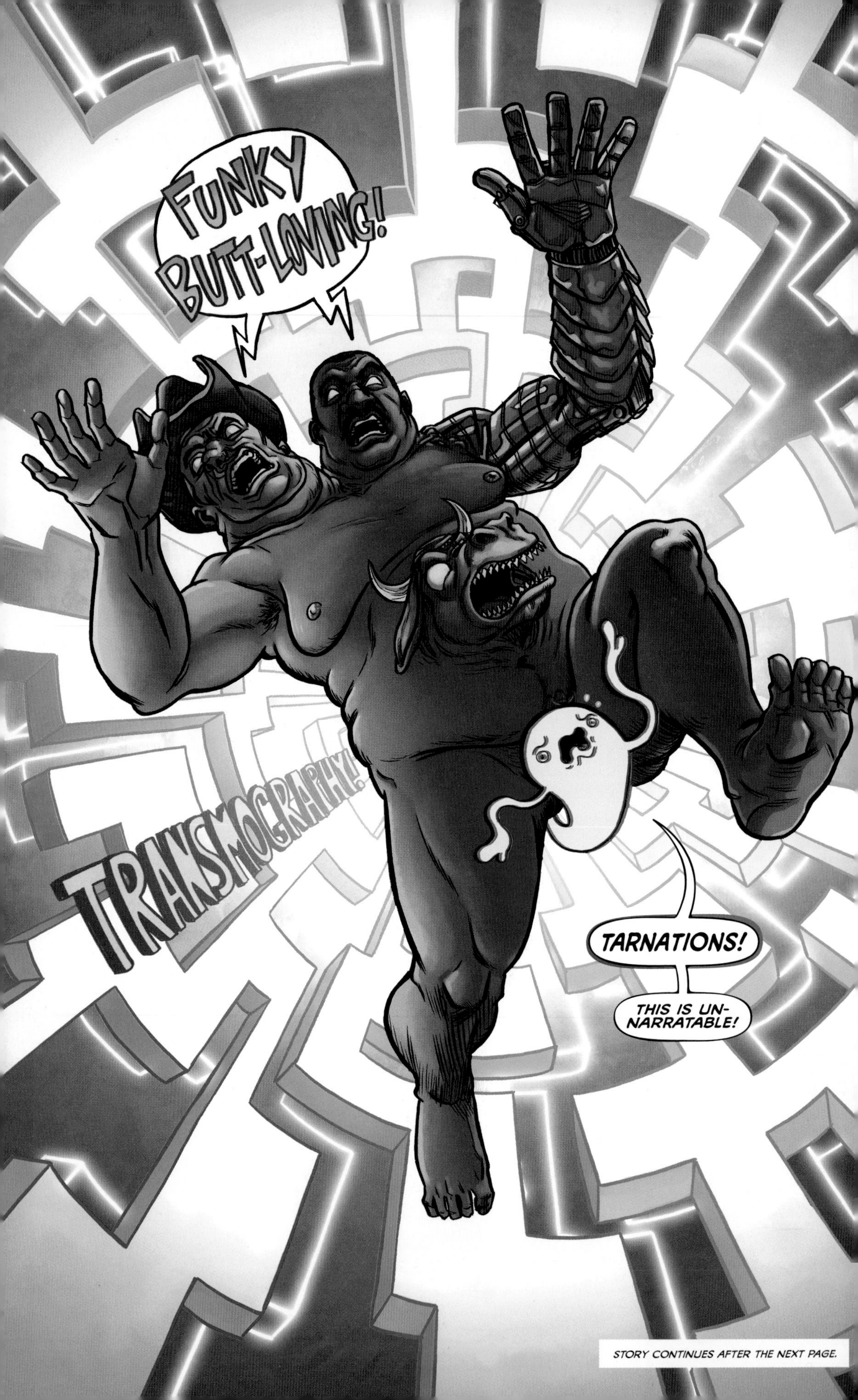
FUNKY BUTT-LOVING!
TRANSMOGRAPHY!
TARNATIONS!
THIS IS UN-NARRATABLE!

STORY CONTINUES AFTER THE NEXT PAGE.

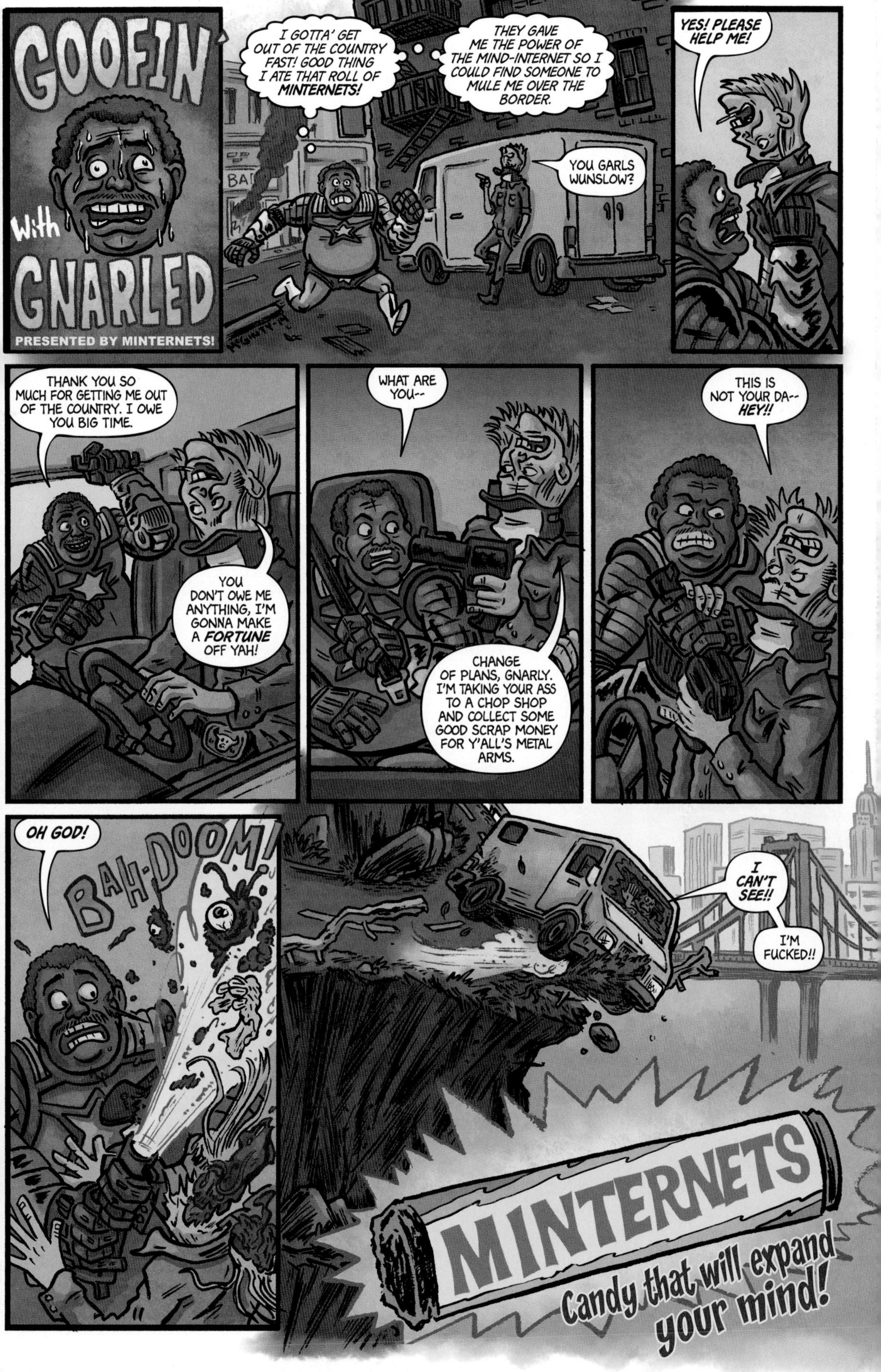

GOOFIN with GNARLED
PRESENTED BY MINTERNETS!
I GOTTA' GET OUT OF THE COUNTRY FAST! GOOD THING I ATE THAT ROLL OF MINTERNETS!
THEY GAVE ME THE POWER OF THE MIND-INTERNET SO I COULD FIND SOMEONE TO MULE ME OVER THE BORDER.
YOU GARLS WUNSLOW?
YES! PLEASE HELP ME!
THANK YOU SO MUCH FOR GETTING ME OUT OF THE COUNTRY. I OWE YOU BIG TIME.
YOU DON'T OWE ME ANYTHING, I'M GONNA MAKE A FORTUNE OFF YAH!
WHAT ARE YOU--
CHANGE OF PLANS, GNARLY. I'M TAKING YOUR ASS TO A CHOP SHOP AND COLLECT SOME GOOD SCRAP MONEY FOR Y'ALL'S METAL ARMS.
THIS IS NOT YOUR DA-- HEY!!
OH GOD!
BAH-DOOM!
I CAN'T SEE!!
I'M FUCKED!!
MINTERNETS
Candy that will expand your mind!

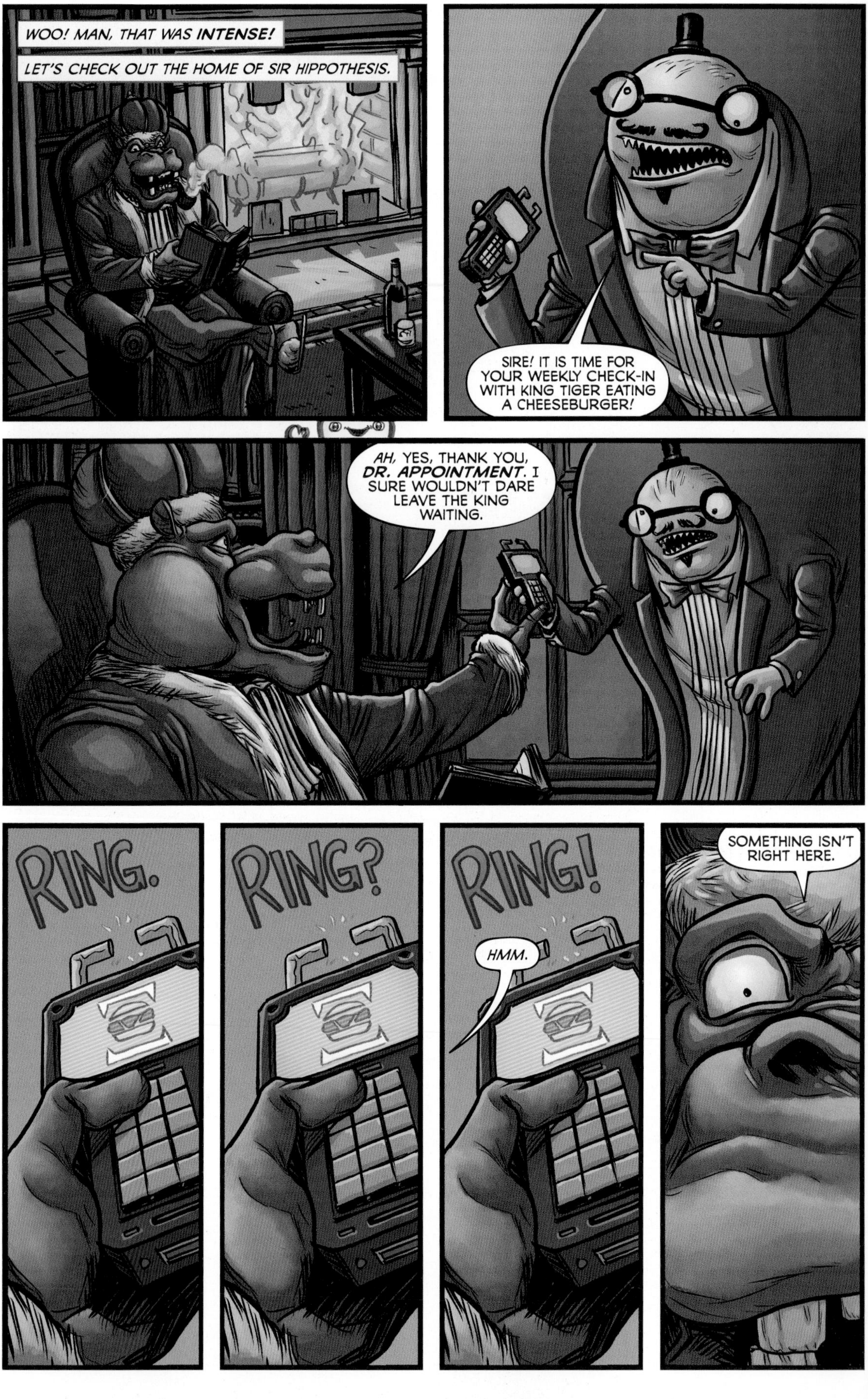
WOO! MAN, THAT WAS **INTENSE!**
LET'S CHECK OUT THE HOME OF SIR HIPPOTHESIS.
SIRE! IT IS TIME FOR YOUR WEEKLY CHECK-IN WITH KING TIGER EATING A CHEESEBURGER!
AH, YES, THANK YOU, **DR. APPOINTMENT**. I SURE WOULDN'T DARE LEAVE THE KING WAITING.
RING.
RING?
RING!
HMM.
SOMETHING ISN'T RIGHT HERE.

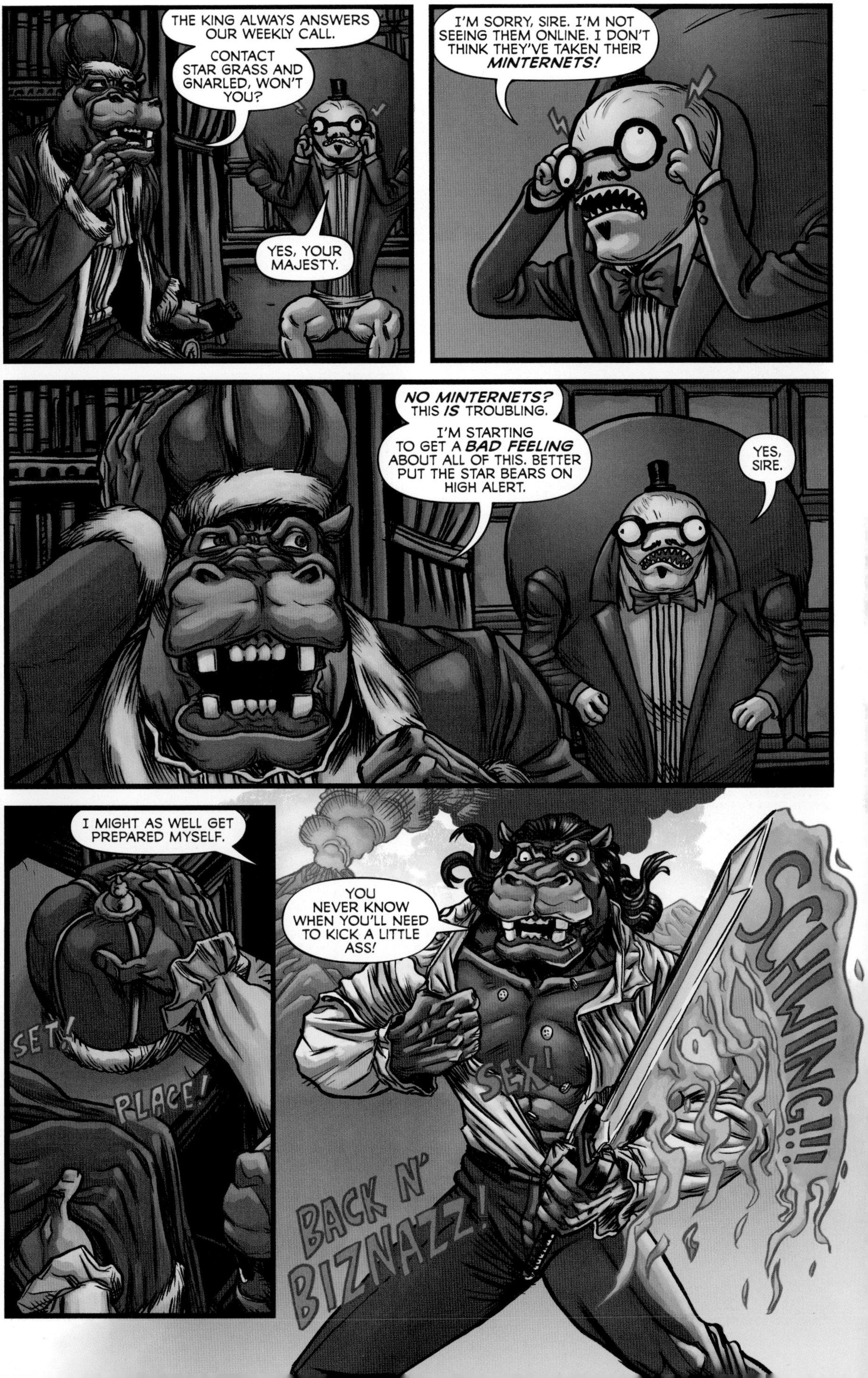

THE KING ALWAYS ANSWERS OUR WEEKLY CALL.
CONTACT STAR GRASS AND GNARLED, WON'T YOU?
YES, YOUR MAJESTY.
I'M SORRY, SIRE. I'M NOT SEEING THEM ONLINE. I DON'T THINK THEY'VE TAKEN THEIR MINTERNETS!
NO MINTERNETS? THIS IS TROUBLING.
I'M STARTING TO GET A BAD FEELING ABOUT ALL OF THIS. BETTER PUT THE STAR BEARS ON HIGH ALERT.
YES, SIRE.
I MIGHT AS WELL GET PREPARED MYSELF.
SET!
PLACE!
YOU NEVER KNOW WHEN YOU'LL NEED TO KICK A LITTLE ASS!
SEX!
SCHWING!!!
BACK N' BIZNAZZ!

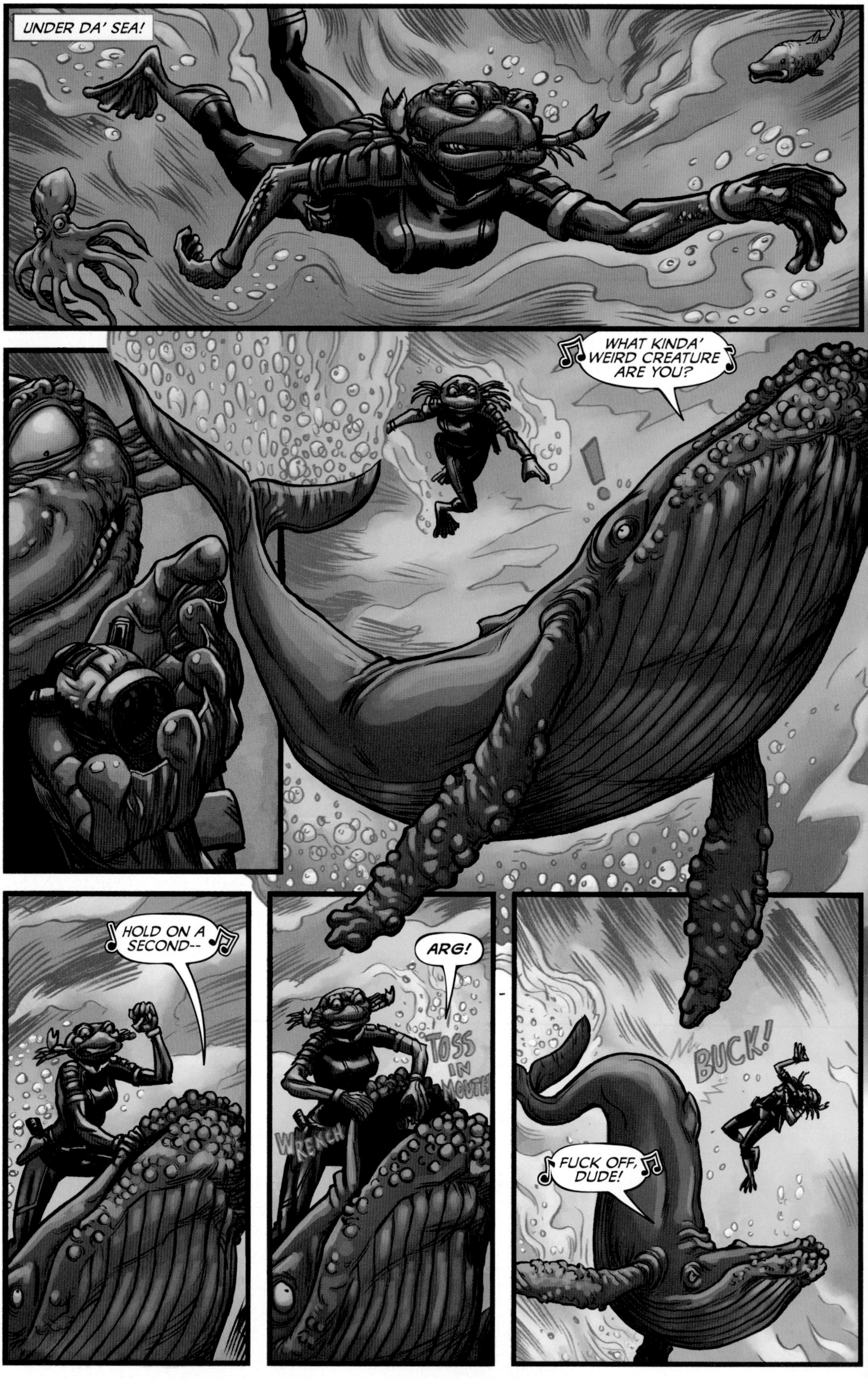
UNDER DA' SEA!
WHAT KINDA' WEIRD CREATURE ARE YOU?
!
HOLD ON A SECOND--
ARG!
TOSS IN MOUTH
WRENCH
BUCK!
FUCK OFF, DUDE!

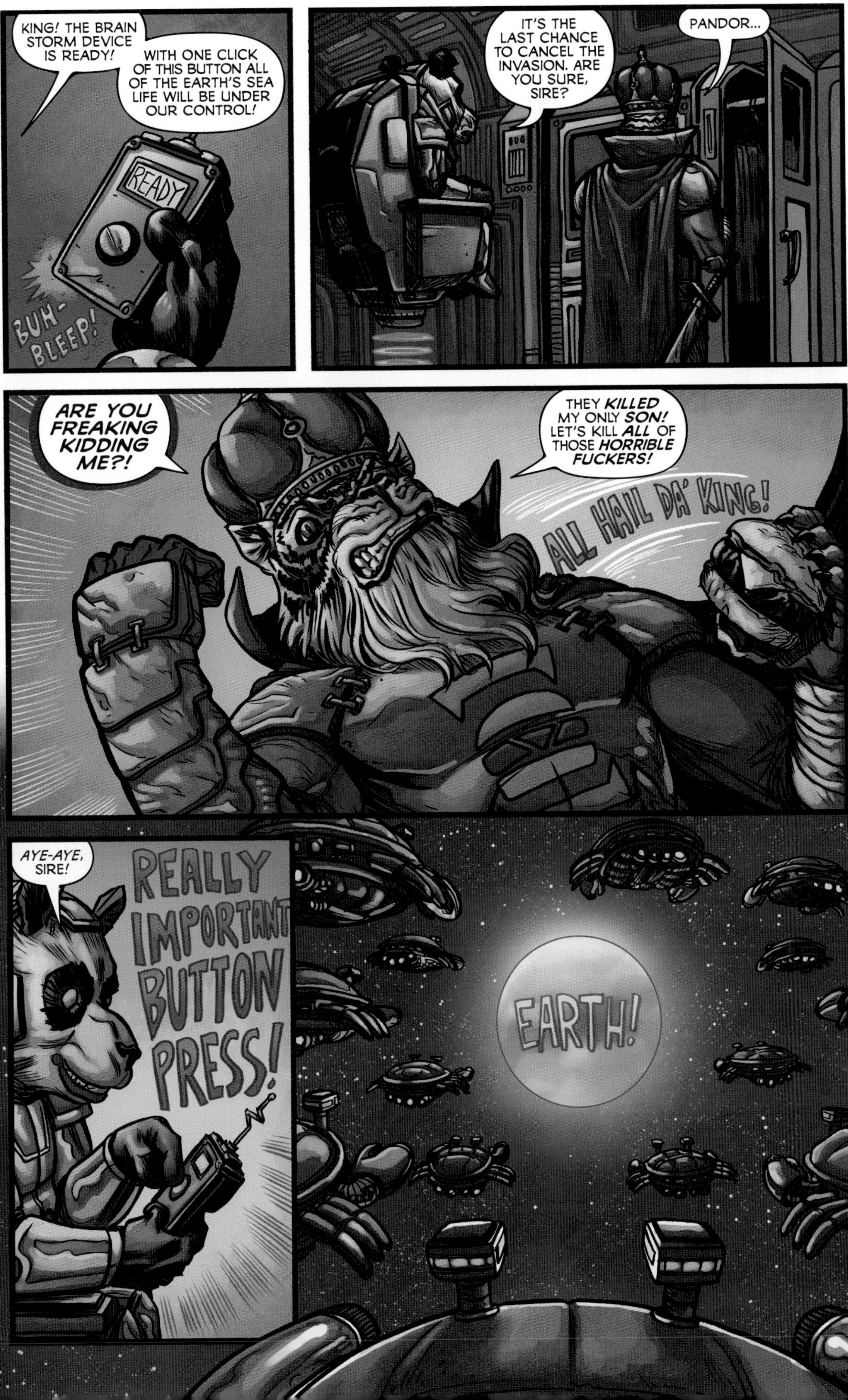
KING! THE BRAIN STORM DEVICE IS READY!
WITH ONE CLICK OF THIS BUTTON ALL OF THE EARTH'S SEA LIFE WILL BE UNDER OUR CONTROL!
READY
BUH-BLEEP!
IT'S THE LAST CHANCE TO CANCEL THE INVASION. ARE YOU SURE, SIRE?
PANDOR...
ARE YOU FREAKING KIDDING ME?!
THEY KILLED MY ONLY SON! LET'S KILL ALL OF THOSE HORRIBLE FUCKERS!
ALL HAIL DA' KING!
AYE-AYE, SIRE!
REALLY IMPORTANT BUTTON PRESS!
EARTH!

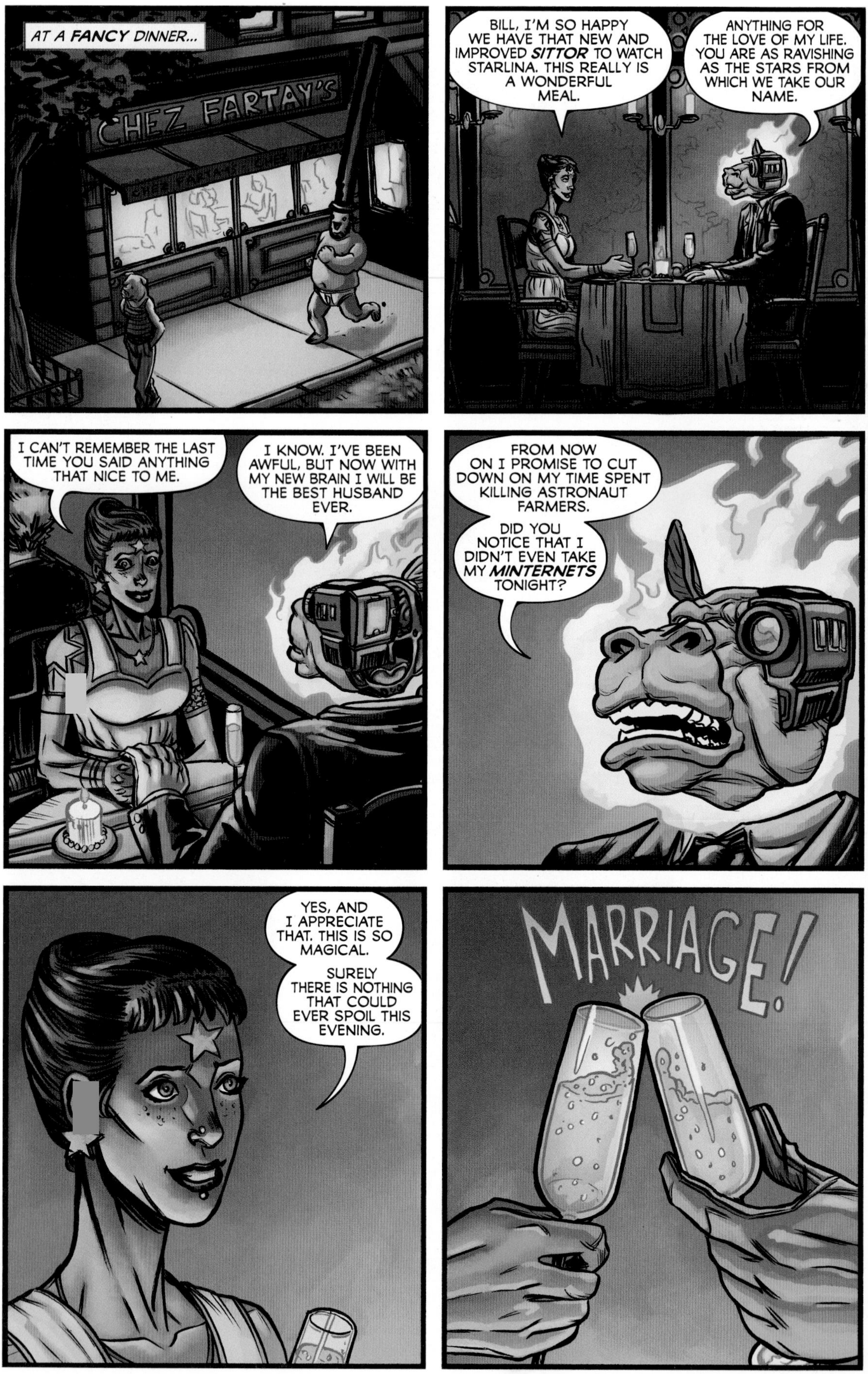
AT A FANCY DINNER...
CHEZ FARTAY'S
BILL, I'M SO HAPPY WE HAVE THAT NEW AND IMPROVED SITTOR TO WATCH STARLINA. THIS REALLY IS A WONDERFUL MEAL.
ANYTHING FOR THE LOVE OF MY LIFE. YOU ARE AS RAVISHING AS THE STARS FROM WHICH WE TAKE OUR NAME.
I CAN'T REMEMBER THE LAST TIME YOU SAID ANYTHING THAT NICE TO ME.
I KNOW. I'VE BEEN AWFUL, BUT NOW WITH MY NEW BRAIN I WILL BE THE BEST HUSBAND EVER.
FROM NOW ON I PROMISE TO CUT DOWN ON MY TIME SPENT KILLING ASTRONAUT FARMERS.
DID YOU NOTICE THAT I DIDN'T EVEN TAKE MY MINTERNETS TONIGHT?
YES, AND I APPRECIATE THAT. THIS IS SO MAGICAL.
SURELY THERE IS NOTHING THAT COULD EVER SPOIL THIS EVENING.
MARRIAGE!

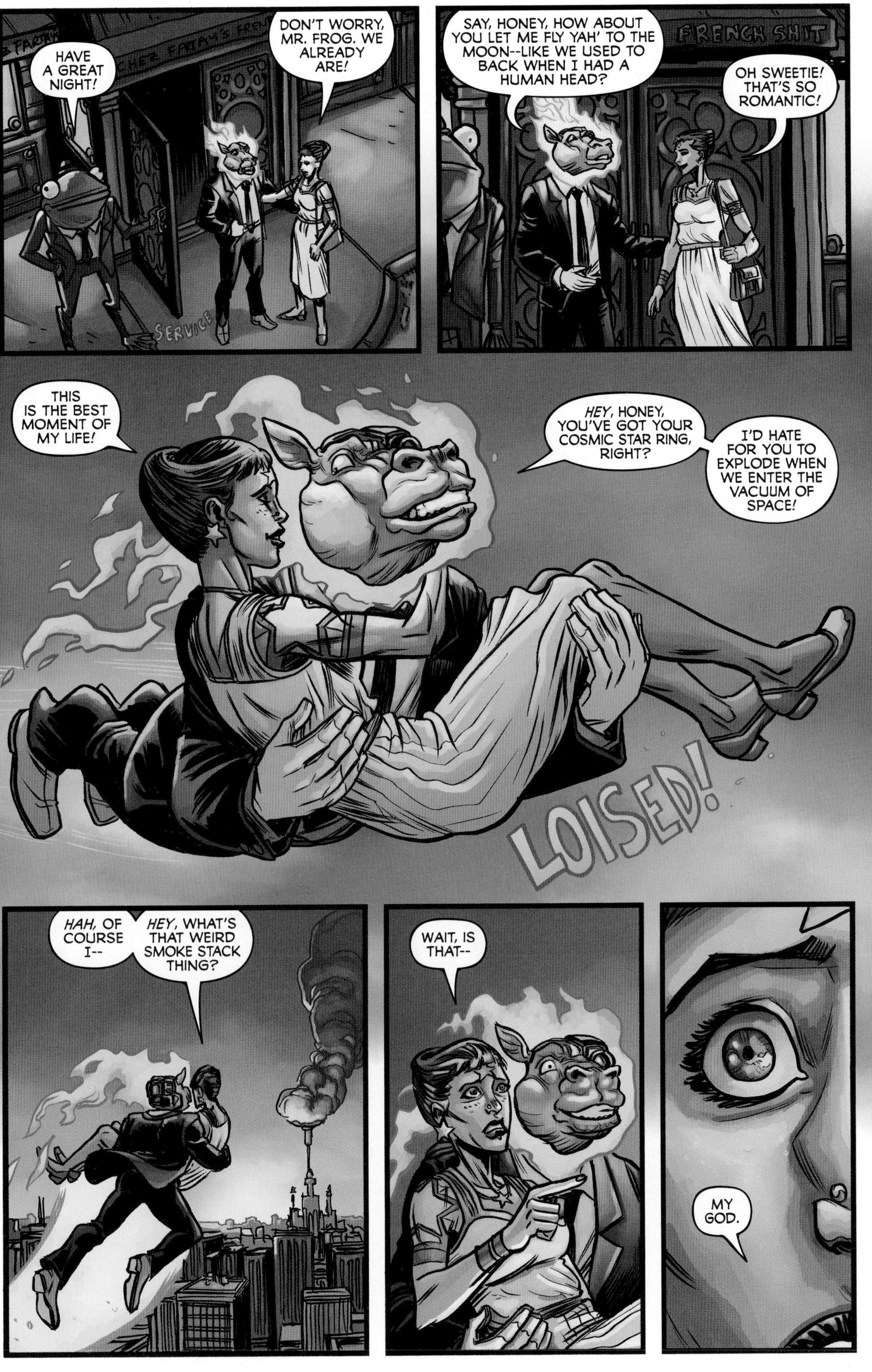
HAVE A GREAT NIGHT!
DON'T WORRY, MR. FROG. WE ALREADY ARE!
SERVICE
FRENCH SHIT
SAY, HONEY, HOW ABOUT YOU LET ME FLY YAH' TO THE MOON--LIKE WE USED TO BACK WHEN I HAD A HUMAN HEAD?
OH SWEETIE! THAT'S SO ROMANTIC!
THIS IS THE BEST MOMENT OF MY LIFE!
HEY, HONEY, YOU'VE GOT YOUR COSMIC STAR RING, RIGHT?
I'D HATE FOR YOU TO EXPLODE WHEN WE ENTER THE VACUUM OF SPACE!
LOISED!
HAH, OF COURSE I--
HEY, WHAT'S THAT WEIRD SMOKE STACK THING?
WAIT, IS THAT--
MY GOD.

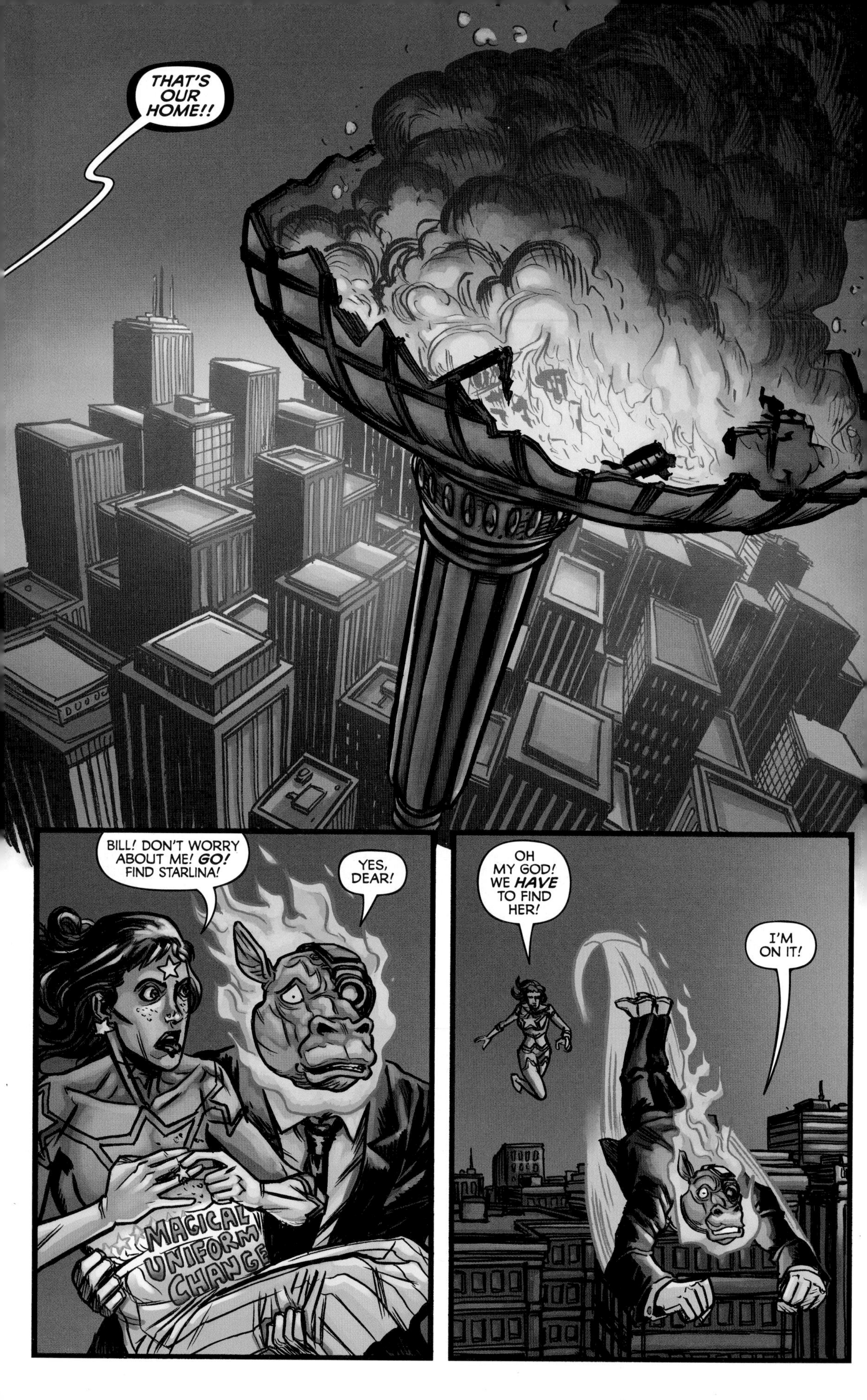
THAT'S OUR HOME!!
BILL! DON'T WORRY ABOUT ME! GO! FIND STARLINA!
YES, DEAR!
MAGICAL UNIFORM CHANGE
OH MY GOD! WE HAVE TO FIND HER!
I'M ON IT!

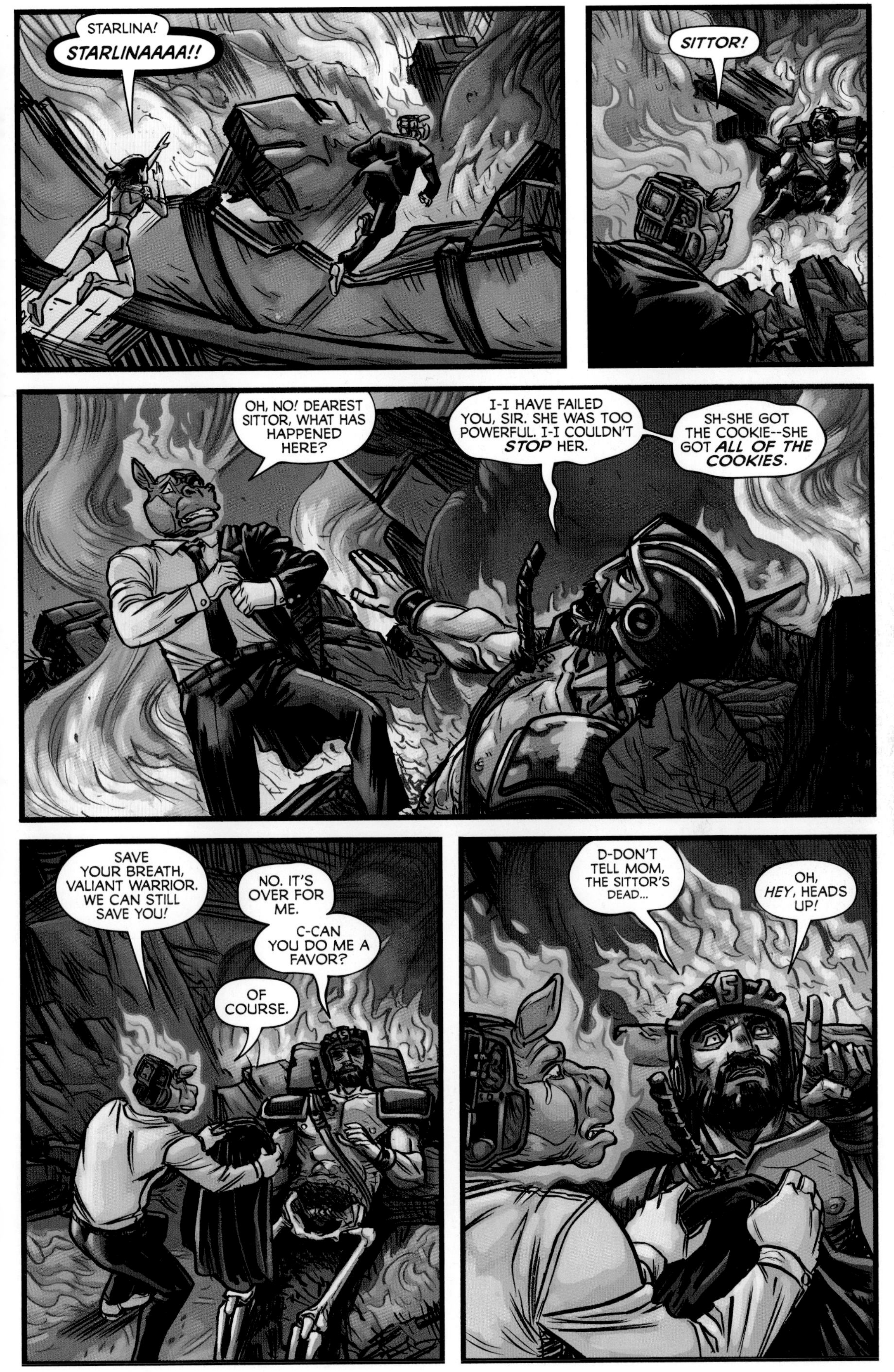
STARLINA! STARLINAAAA!!
SITTOR!
OH, NO! DEAREST SITTOR, WHAT HAS HAPPENED HERE?
I-I HAVE FAILED YOU, SIR. SHE WAS TOO POWERFUL. I-I COULDN'T STOP HER.
SH-SHE GOT THE COOKIE--SHE GOT ALL OF THE COOKIES.
SAVE YOUR BREATH, VALIANT WARRIOR. WE CAN STILL SAVE YOU!
NO. IT'S OVER FOR ME.
C-CAN YOU DO ME A FAVOR?
OF COURSE.
D-DON'T TELL MOM, THE SITTOR'S DEAD...
OH, HEY, HEADS UP!

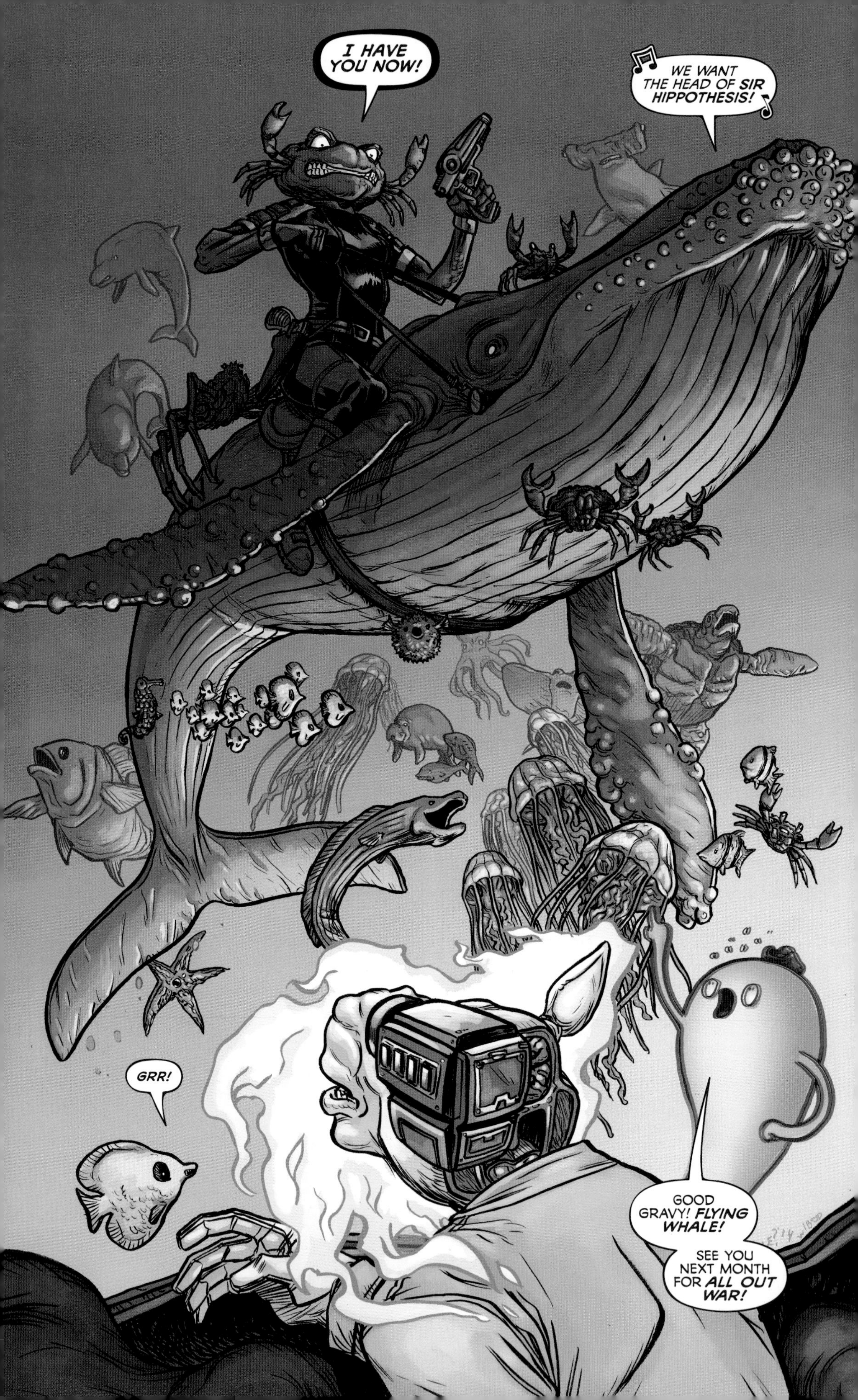
I HAVE YOU NOW!
WE WANT THE HEAD OF SIR HIPPOTHESIS!
GRR!
GOOD GRAVY! FLYING WHALE!
SEE YOU NEXT MONTH FOR ALL OUT WAR!

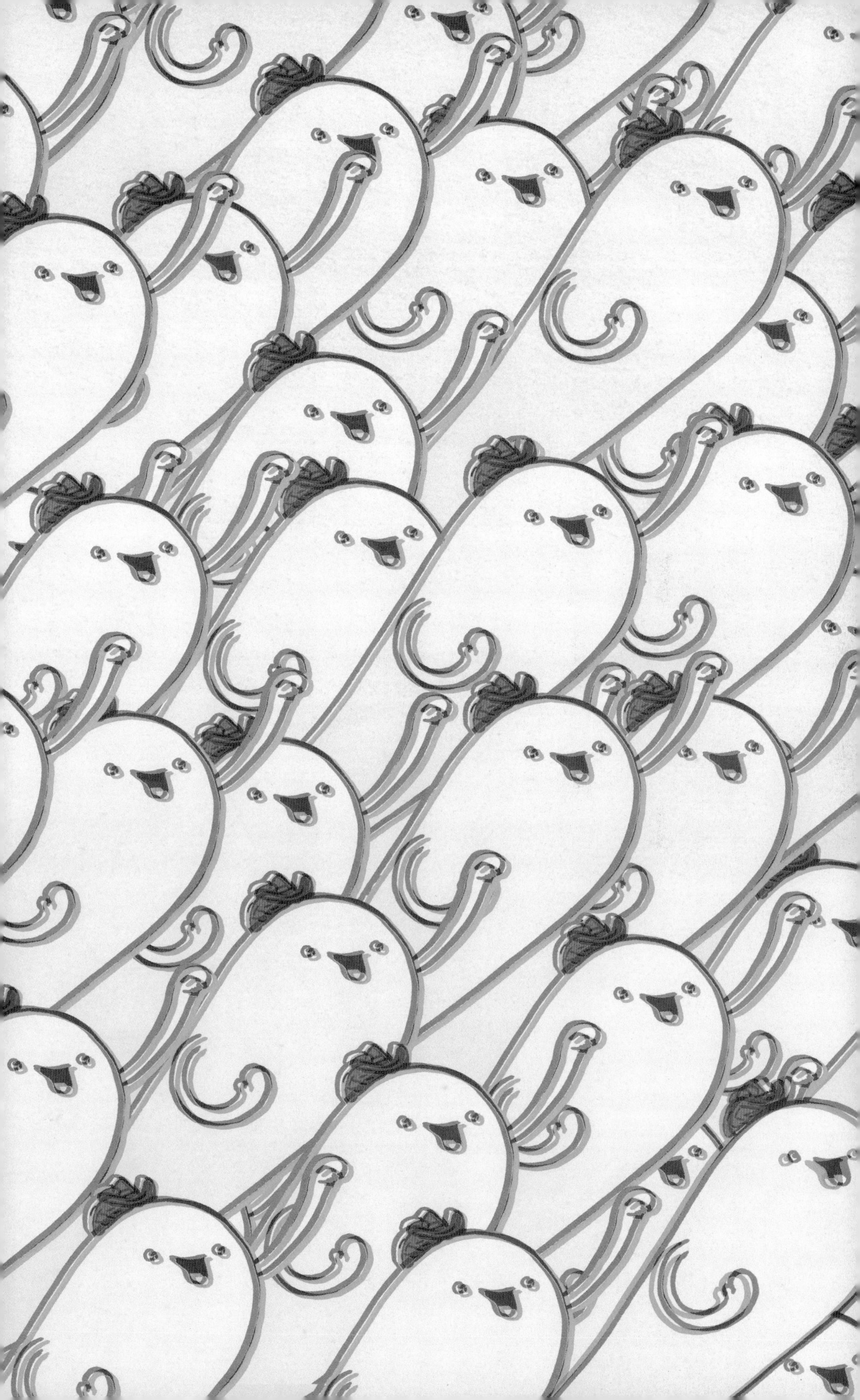

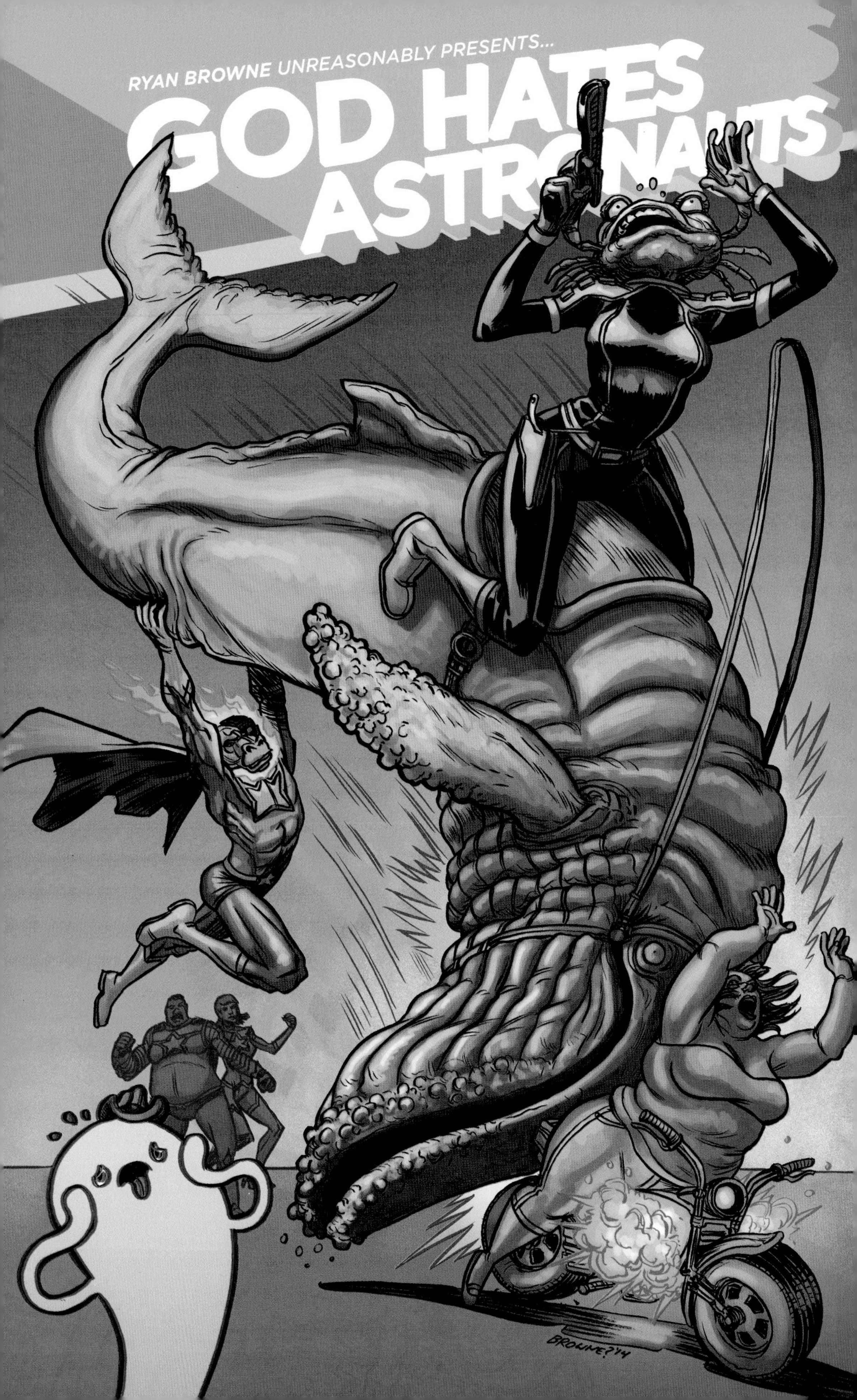
RYAN BROWNE UNREASONABLY PRESENTS...
GOD HATES ASTRONAUTS
BROWNE?'14

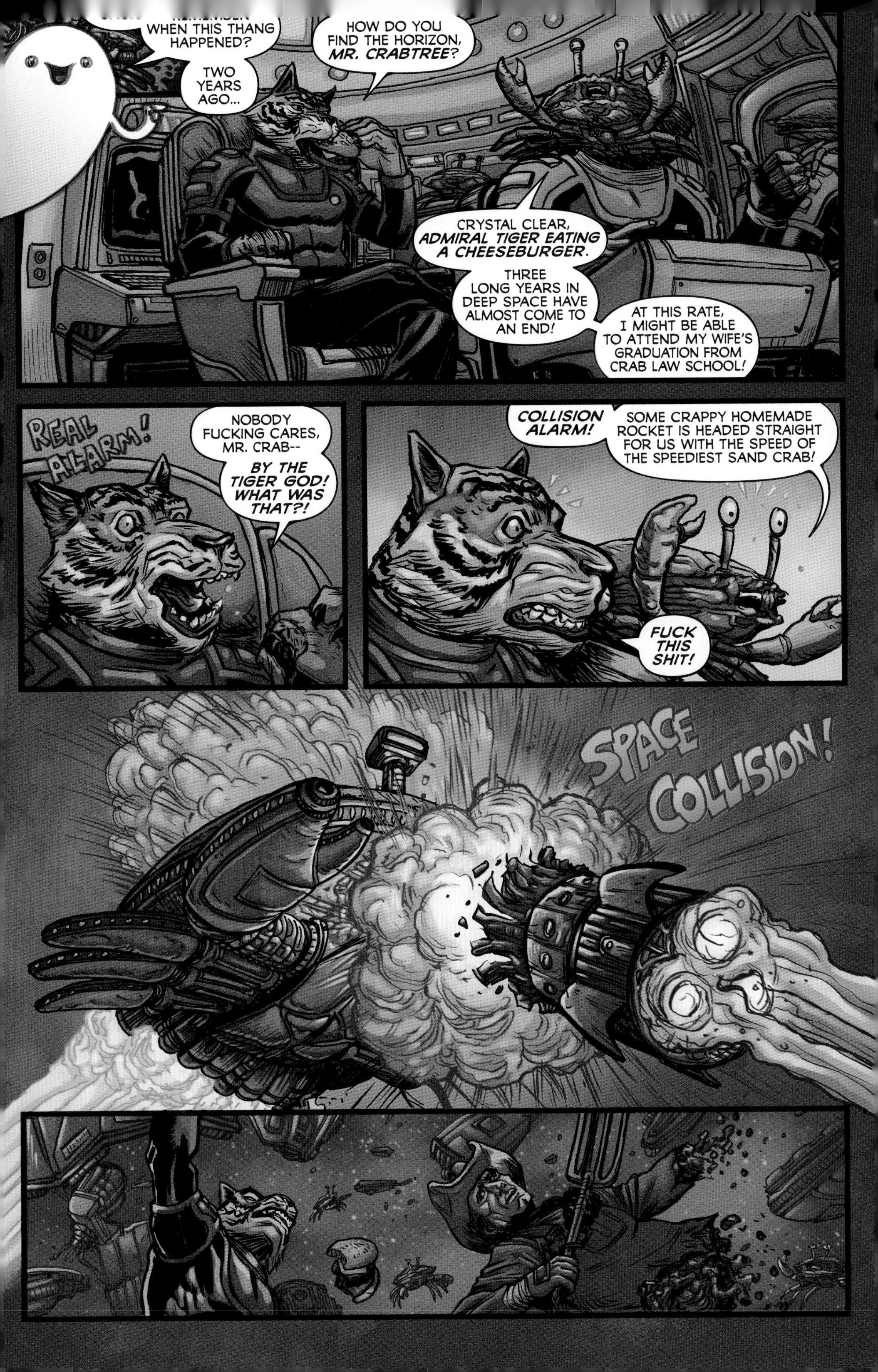
WHEN THIS THANG HAPPENED?
TWO YEARS AGO...
HOW DO YOU FIND THE HORIZON, *MR. CRABTREE*?
CRYSTAL CLEAR, *ADMIRAL TIGER EATING A CHEESEBURGER*.
THREE LONG YEARS IN DEEP SPACE HAVE ALMOST COME TO AN END!
AT THIS RATE, I MIGHT BE ABLE TO ATTEND MY WIFE'S GRADUATION FROM CRAB LAW SCHOOL!
REAL ALARM!
NOBODY FUCKING CARES, MR. CRAB--
BY THE TIGER GOD! WHAT WAS THAT?!
COLLISION ALARM!
SOME CRAPPY HOMEMADE ROCKET IS HEADED STRAIGHT FOR US WITH THE SPEED OF THE SPEEDIEST SAND CRAB!
FUCK THIS SHIT!
SPACE COLLISION!

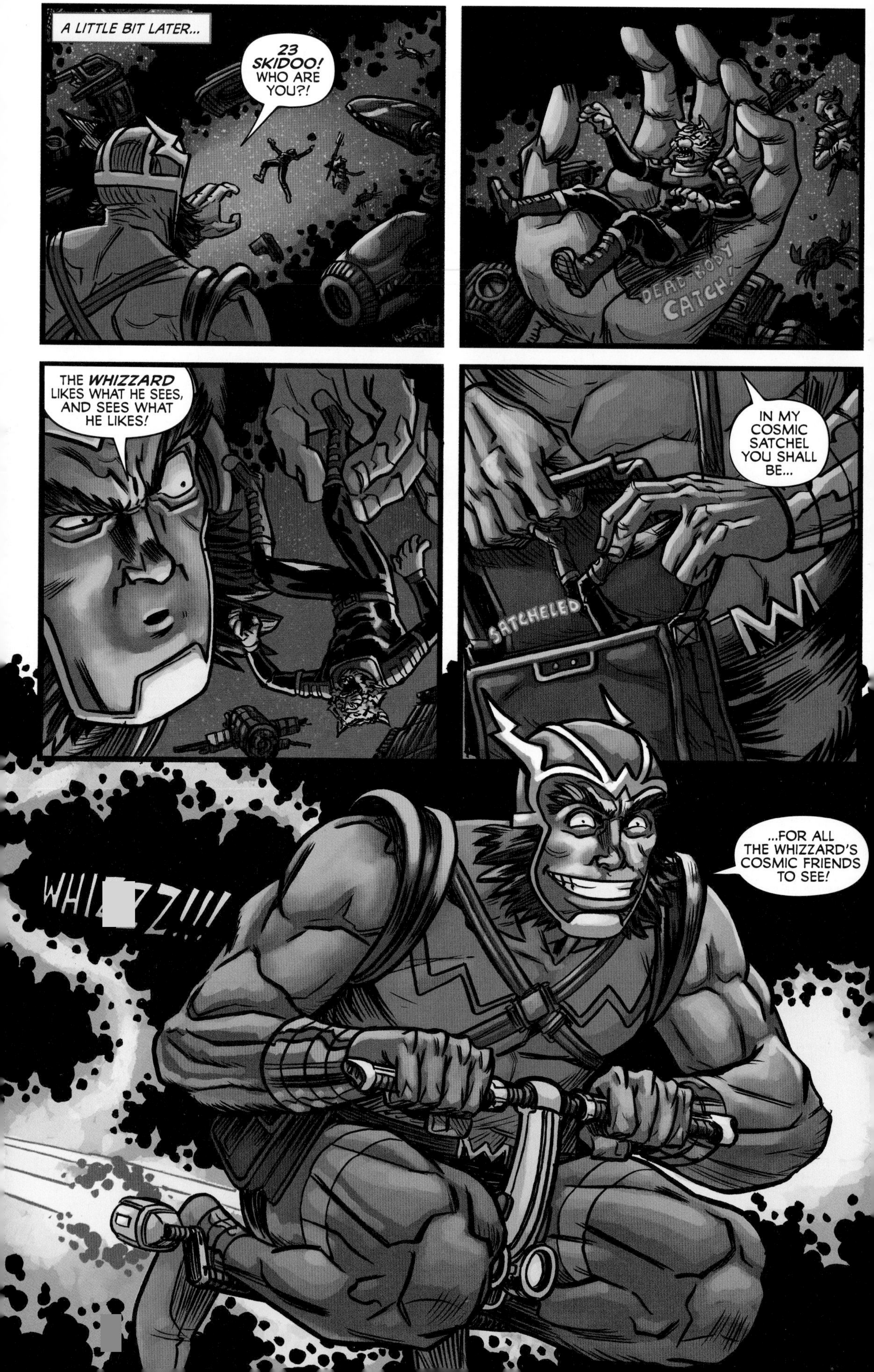
A LITTLE BIT LATER...
23 SKIDOO! WHO ARE YOU?!
DEAD-BODY CATCH!
THE WHIZZARD LIKES WHAT HE SEES, AND SEES WHAT HE LIKES!
IN MY COSMIC SATCHEL YOU SHALL BE...
SATCHELED
...FOR ALL THE WHIZZARD'S COSMIC FRIENDS TO SEE!

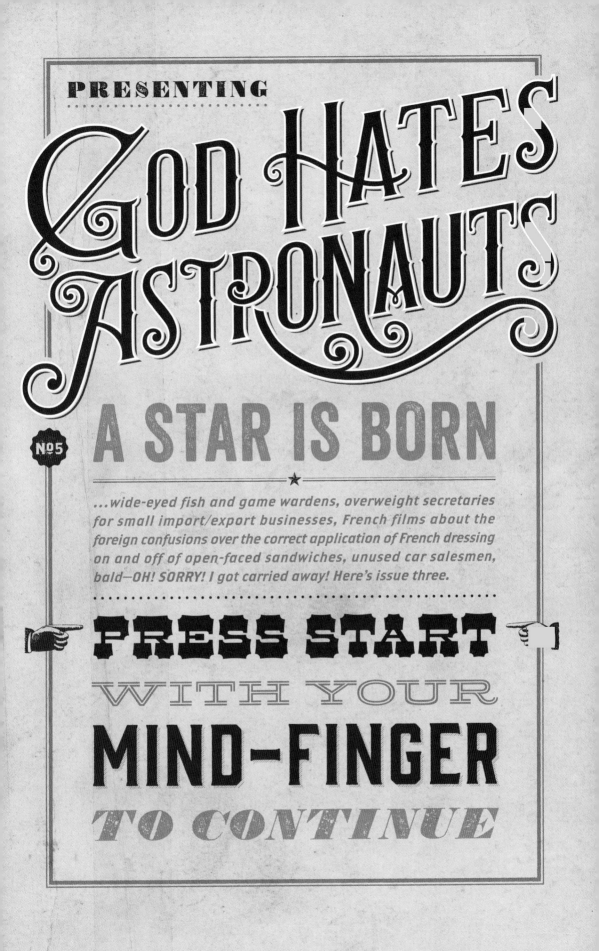

PRESENTING

GOD HATES ASTRONAUTS

№5

A STAR IS BORN

★

...wide-eyed fish and game wardens, overweight secretaries for small import/export businesses, French films about the foreign confusions over the correct application of French dressing on and off of open-faced sandwiches, unused car salesmen, bald—OH! SORRY! I got carried away! Here's issue three.

PRESS START

WITH YOUR

MIND-FINGER

TO CONTINUE

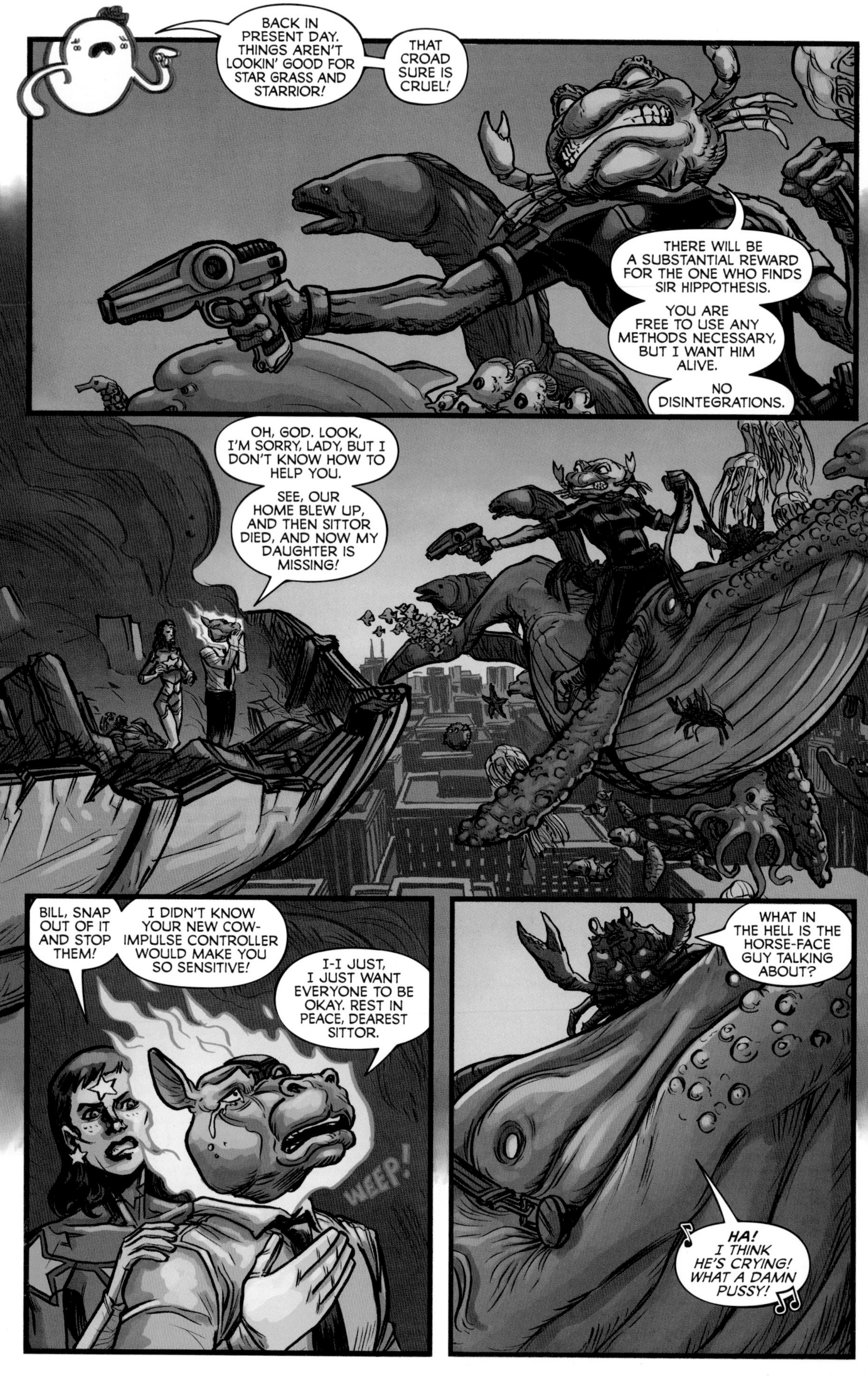
BACK IN PRESENT DAY. THINGS AREN'T LOOKIN' GOOD FOR STAR GRASS AND STARRIOR!
THAT CROAD SURE IS CRUEL!
THERE WILL BE A SUBSTANTIAL REWARD FOR THE ONE WHO FINDS SIR HIPPOTHESIS.
YOU ARE FREE TO USE ANY METHODS NECESSARY, BUT I WANT HIM ALIVE.
NO DISINTEGRATIONS.
OH, GOD. LOOK, I'M SORRY, LADY, BUT I DON'T KNOW HOW TO HELP YOU.
SEE, OUR HOME BLEW UP, AND THEN SITTOR DIED, AND NOW MY DAUGHTER IS MISSING!
BILL, SNAP OUT OF IT AND STOP THEM!
I DIDN'T KNOW YOUR NEW COW-IMPULSE CONTROLLER WOULD MAKE YOU SO SENSITIVE!
I-I JUST, I JUST WANT EVERYONE TO BE OKAY. REST IN PEACE, DEAREST SITTOR.
WEEP!
WHAT IN THE HELL IS THE HORSE-FACE GUY TALKING ABOUT?
HA! I THINK HE'S CRYING! WHAT A DAMN PUSSY!

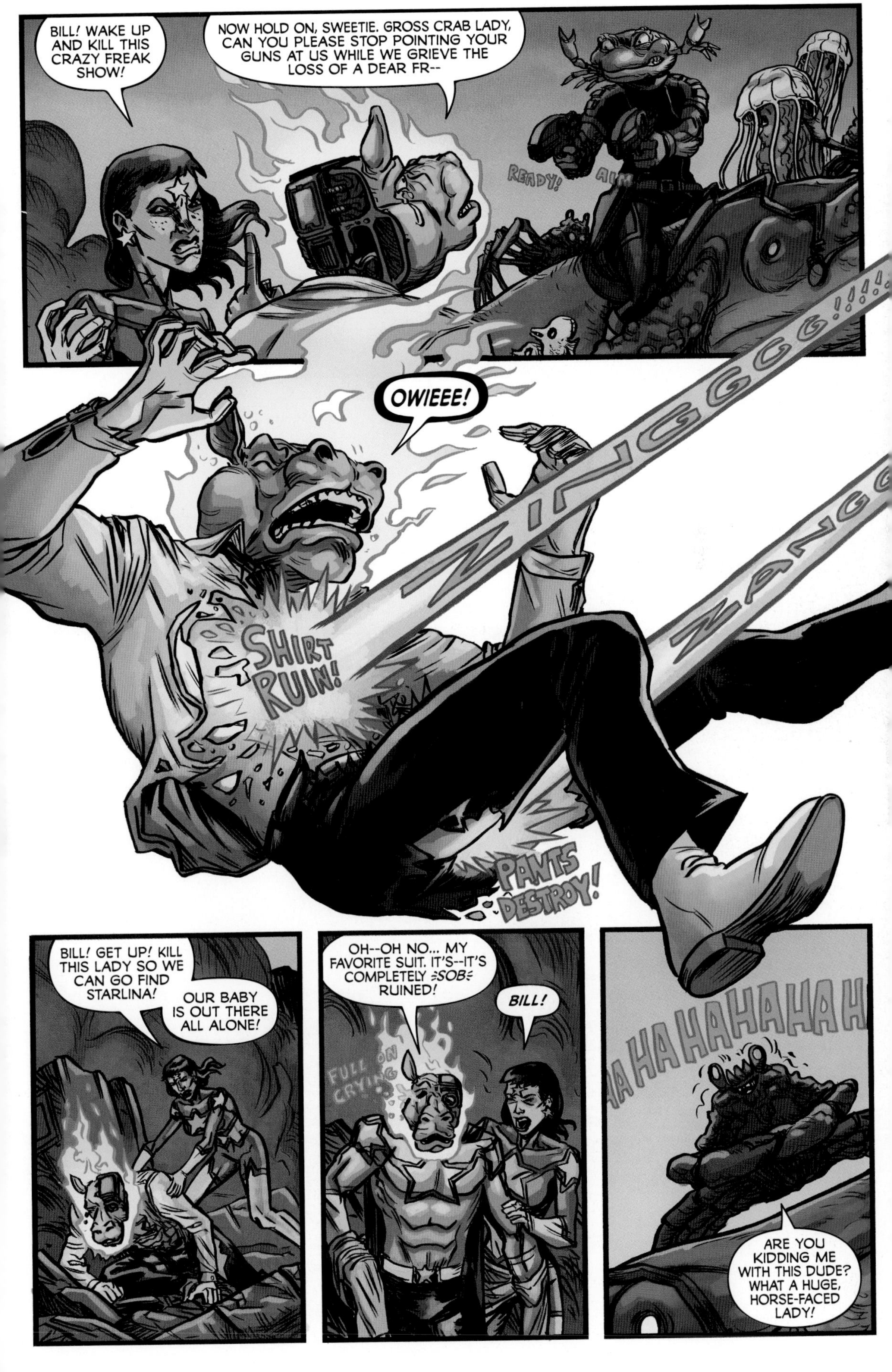
BILL! WAKE UP AND KILL THIS CRAZY FREAK SHOW!
NOW HOLD ON, SWEETIE. GROSS CRAB LADY, CAN YOU PLEASE STOP POINTING YOUR GUNS AT US WHILE WE GRIEVE THE LOSS OF A DEAR FR--
READY!
AIM
OWIEEE!
ZINGGGG!!!!!
ZANGG
SHIRT RUIN!
PANTS DESTROY!
BILL! GET UP! KILL THIS LADY SO WE CAN GO FIND STARLINA!
OUR BABY IS OUT THERE ALL ALONE!
OH--OH NO... MY FAVORITE SUIT. IT'S--IT'S COMPLETELY *SOB* RUINED!
BILL!
FULL ON CRYING
HAHAHAHAHAHAH
ARE YOU KIDDING ME WITH THIS DUDE? WHAT A HUGE, HORSE-FACED LADY!

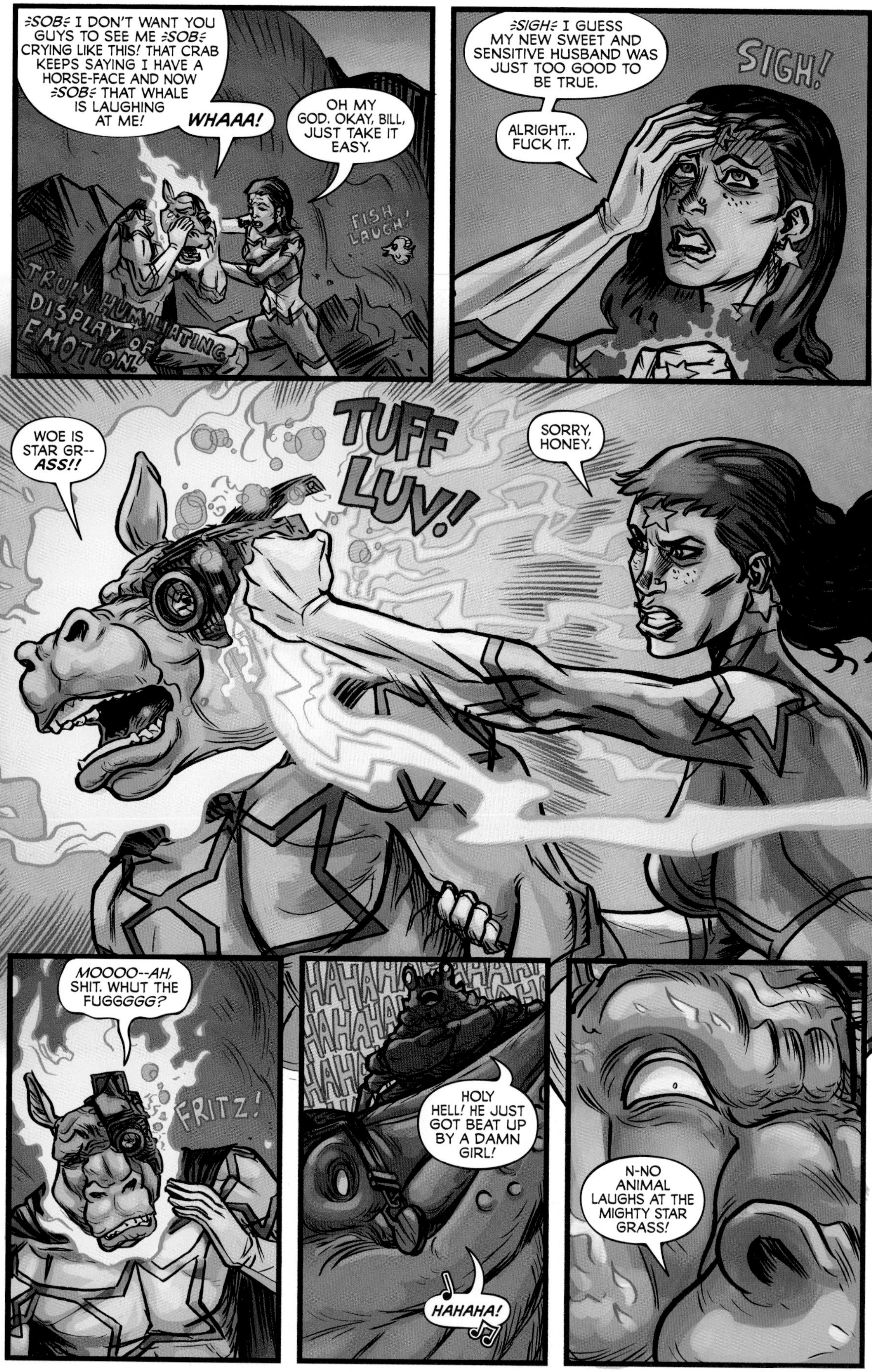

≶SOB≶ I DON'T WANT YOU GUYS TO SEE ME ≶SOB≶ CRYING LIKE THIS! THAT CRAB KEEPS SAYING I HAVE A HORSE-FACE AND NOW ≶SOB≶ THAT WHALE IS LAUGHING AT ME!
WHAAA!
OH MY GOD. OKAY, BILL, JUST TAKE IT EASY.
FISH LAUGH!
TRULY HUMILIATING DISPLAY OF EMOTION!
≶SIGH≶ I GUESS MY NEW SWEET AND SENSITIVE HUSBAND WAS JUST TOO GOOD TO BE TRUE.
SIGH!
ALRIGHT... FUCK IT.
WOE IS STAR GR-- ASS!!
TUFF LUV!
SORRY, HONEY.
MOOOO--AH, SHIT. WHUT THE FUGGGGG?
FRITZ!
HAHAHAHAHAHA
HOLY HELL! HE JUST GOT BEAT UP BY A DAMN GIRL!
HAHAHA!
N-NO ANIMAL LAUGHS AT THE MIGHTY STAR GRASS!

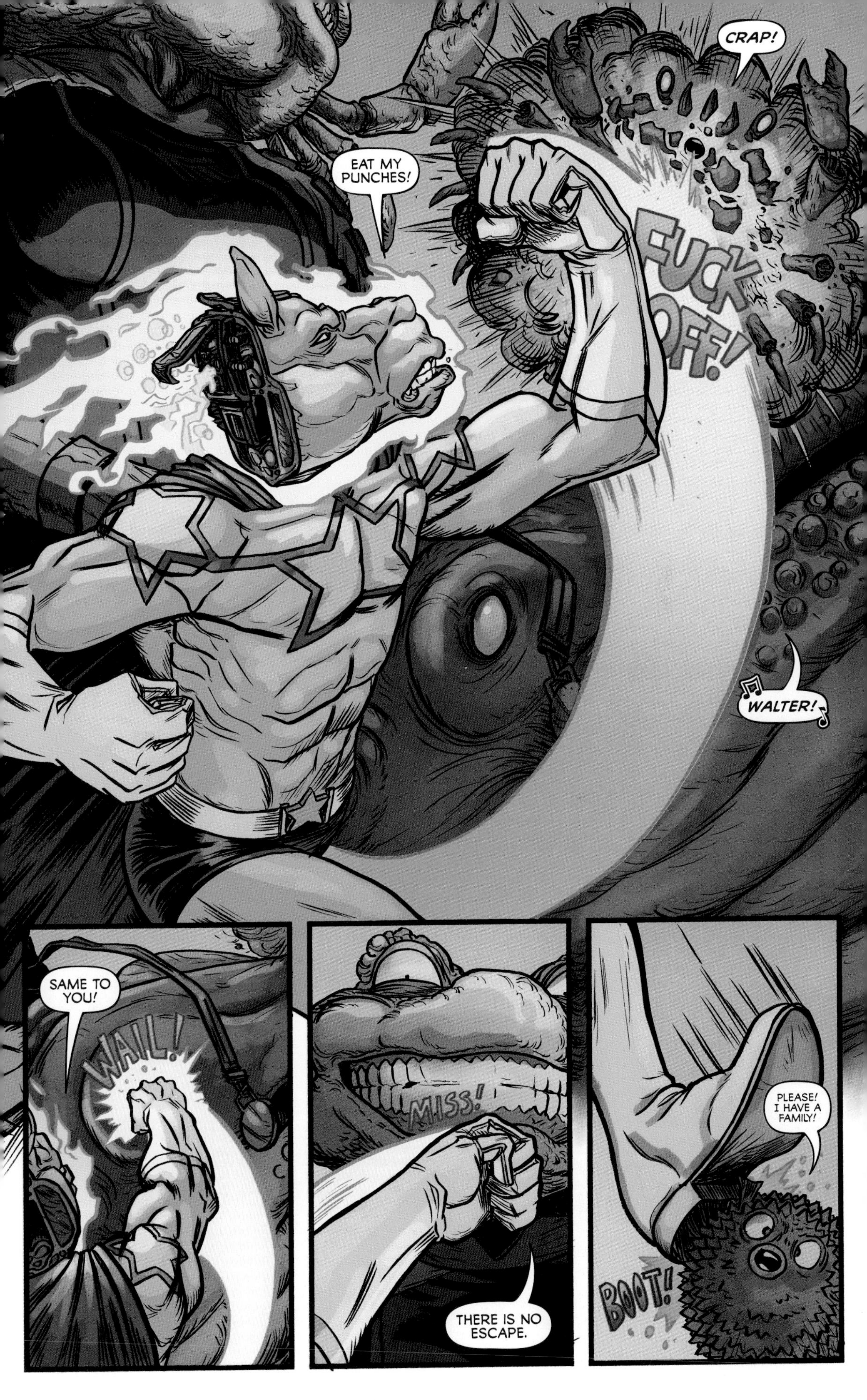
CRAP!
EAT MY PUNCHES!
FUCK OFF!
WALTER!
SAME TO YOU!
WAIL!
MISS!
THERE IS NO ESCAPE.
PLEASE! I HAVE A FAMILY!
BOOT!

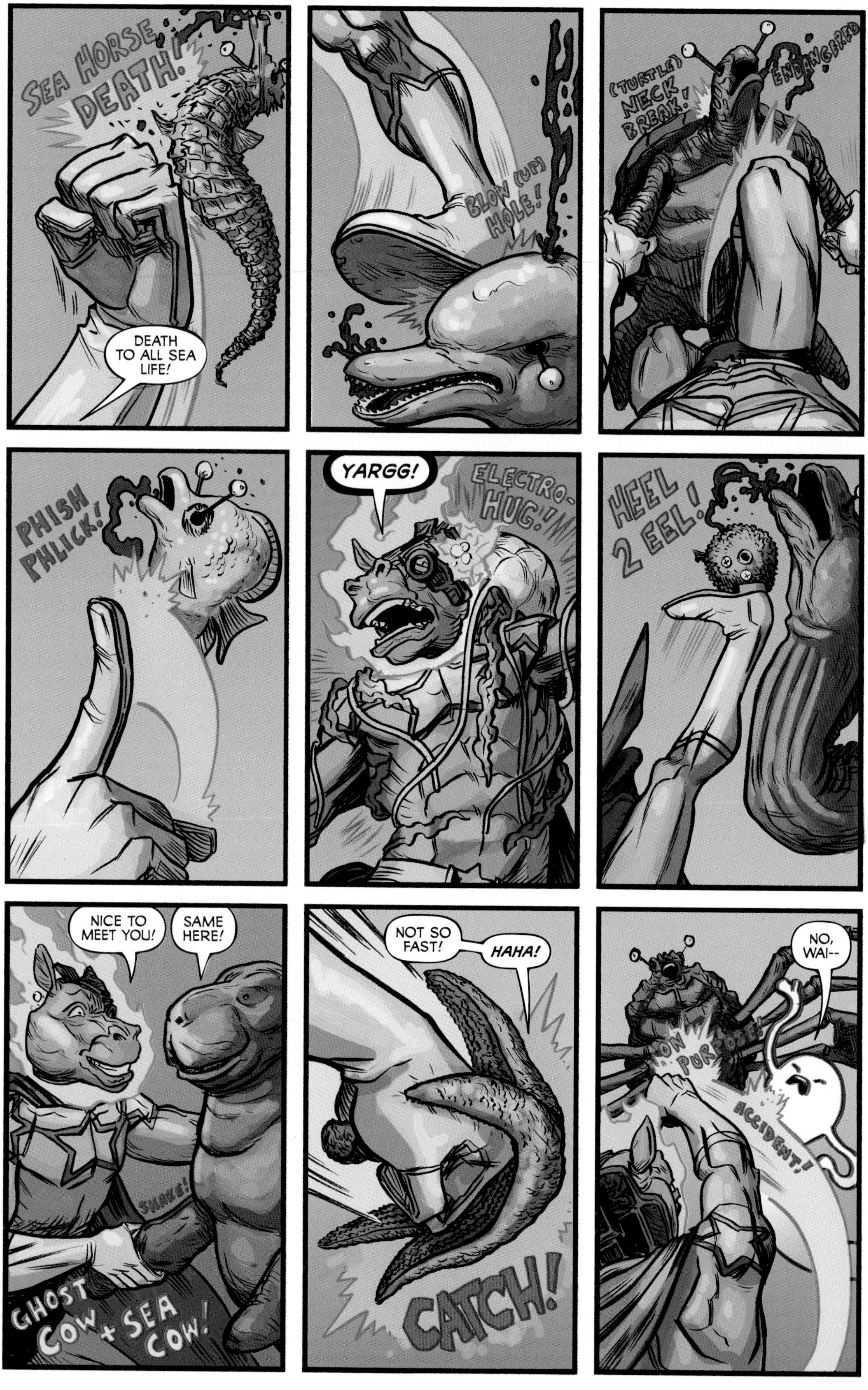
SEA HORSE DEATH!
DEATH TO ALL SEA LIFE!
BLOW (UP) HOLE!
(TURTLE) NECK BREAK!
ENDANGERED
PHISH PHLICK!
YARGG!
ELECTRO-HUG!
HEEL 2 EEL!
NICE TO MEET YOU!
SAME HERE!
SHAKE!
GHOST COW + SEA COW!
NOT SO FAST!
HAHA!
CATCH!
NO, WAI--
ON PURPOSE!
ACCIDENT!

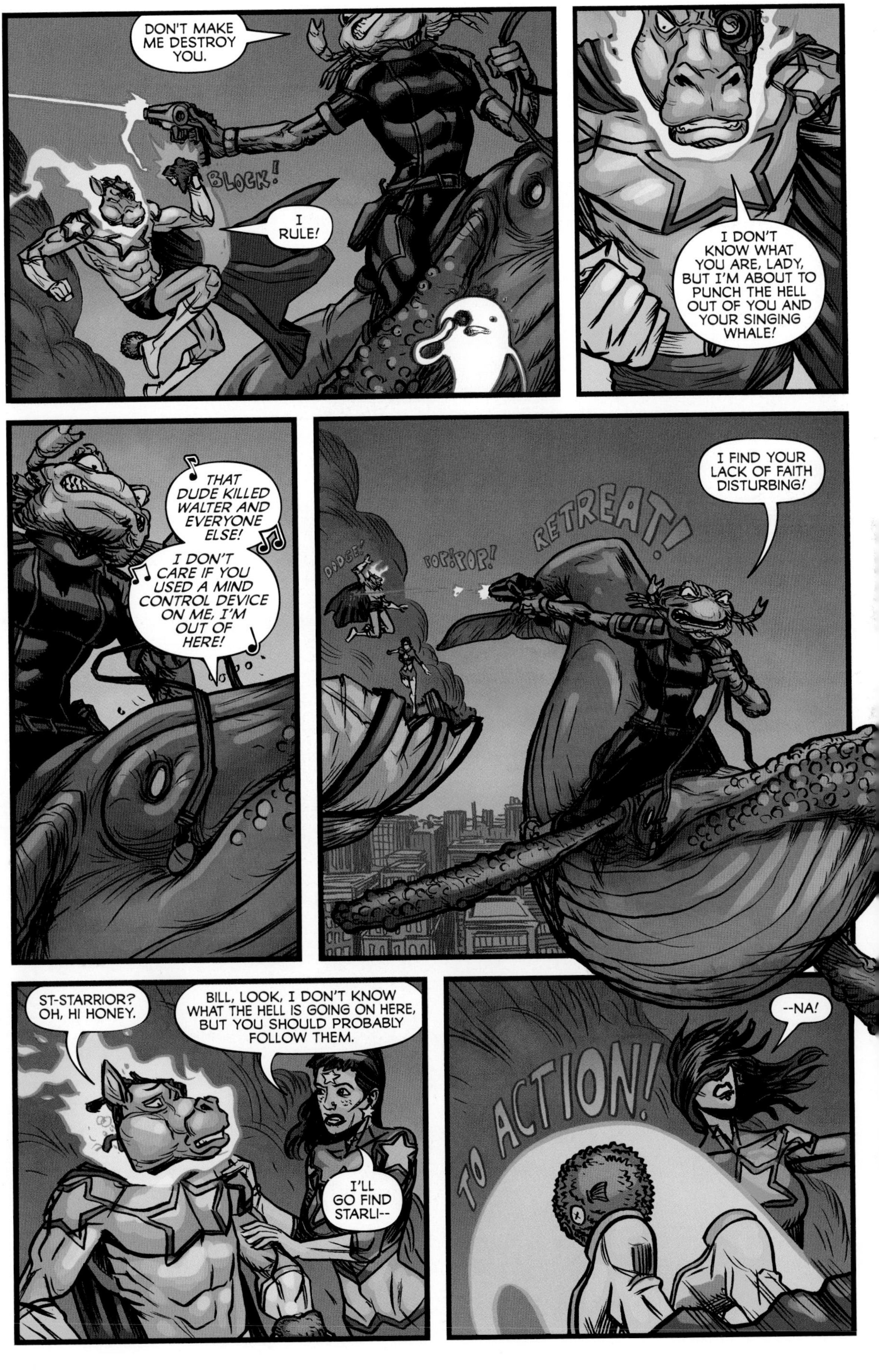
DON'T MAKE ME DESTROY YOU.
BLOCK!
I RULE!
I DON'T KNOW WHAT YOU ARE, LADY, BUT I'M ABOUT TO PUNCH THE HELL OUT OF YOU AND YOUR SINGING WHALE!
THAT DUDE KILLED WALTER AND EVERYONE ELSE!
I DON'T CARE IF YOU USED A MIND CONTROL DEVICE ON ME, I'M OUT OF HERE!
I FIND YOUR LACK OF FAITH DISTURBING!
RETREAT!
DODGE!
POP! POP!
ST-STARRIOR? OH, HI HONEY.
BILL, LOOK, I DON'T KNOW WHAT THE HELL IS GOING ON HERE, BUT YOU SHOULD PROBABLY FOLLOW THEM.
I'LL GO FIND STARLI--
--NA!
TO ACTION!

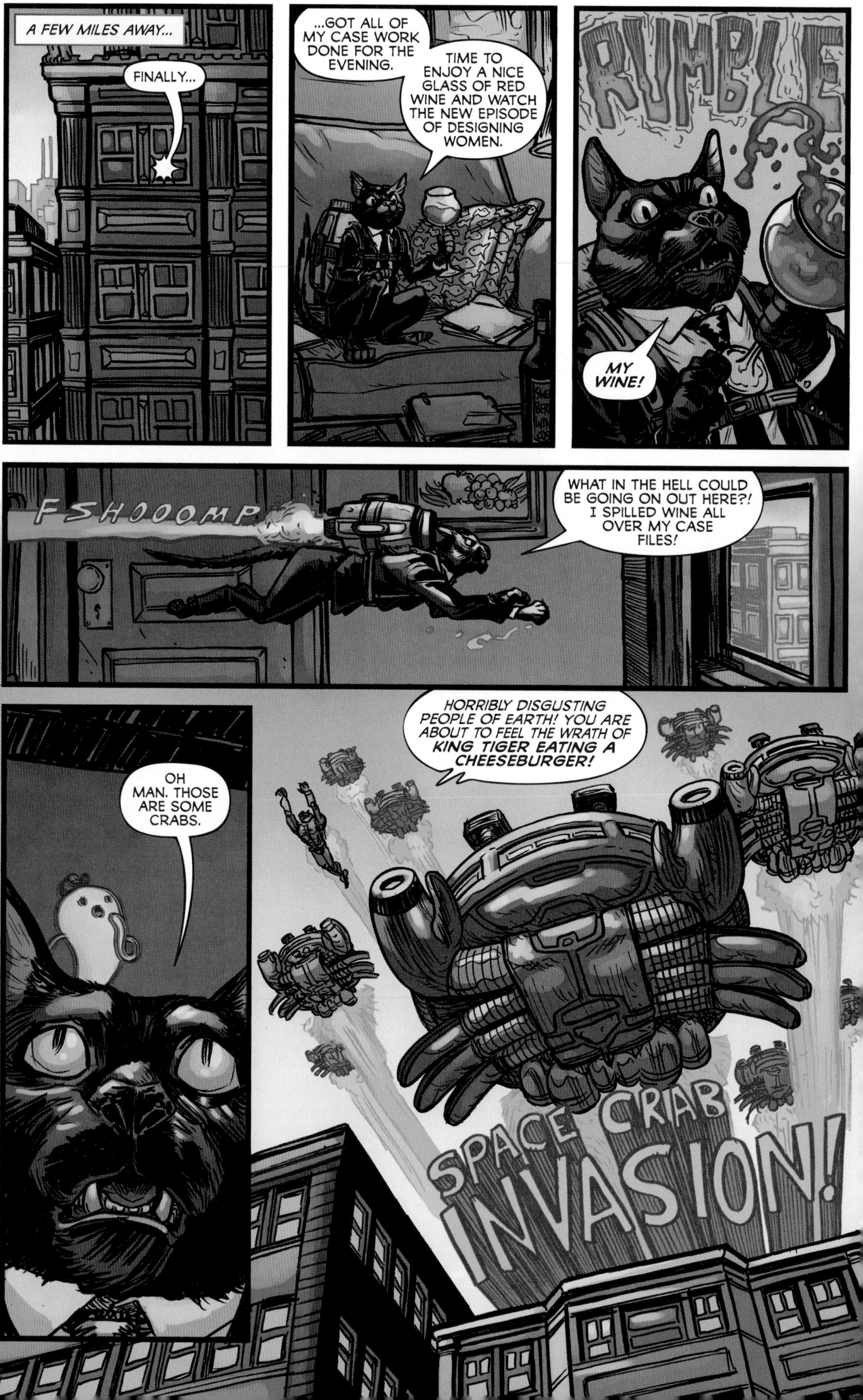
A FEW MILES AWAY...
FINALLY...
...GOT ALL OF MY CASE WORK DONE FOR THE EVENING.
TIME TO ENJOY A NICE GLASS OF RED WINE AND WATCH THE NEW EPISODE OF DESIGNING WOMEN.
RUMBLE
MY WINE!
FSHOOOMP
WHAT IN THE HELL COULD BE GOING ON OUT HERE?! I SPILLED WINE ALL OVER MY CASE FILES!
OH MAN. THOSE ARE SOME CRABS.
HORRIBLY DISGUSTING PEOPLE OF EARTH! YOU ARE ABOUT TO FEEL THE WRATH OF KING TIGER EATING A CHEESEBURGER!
SPACE CRAB INVASION!

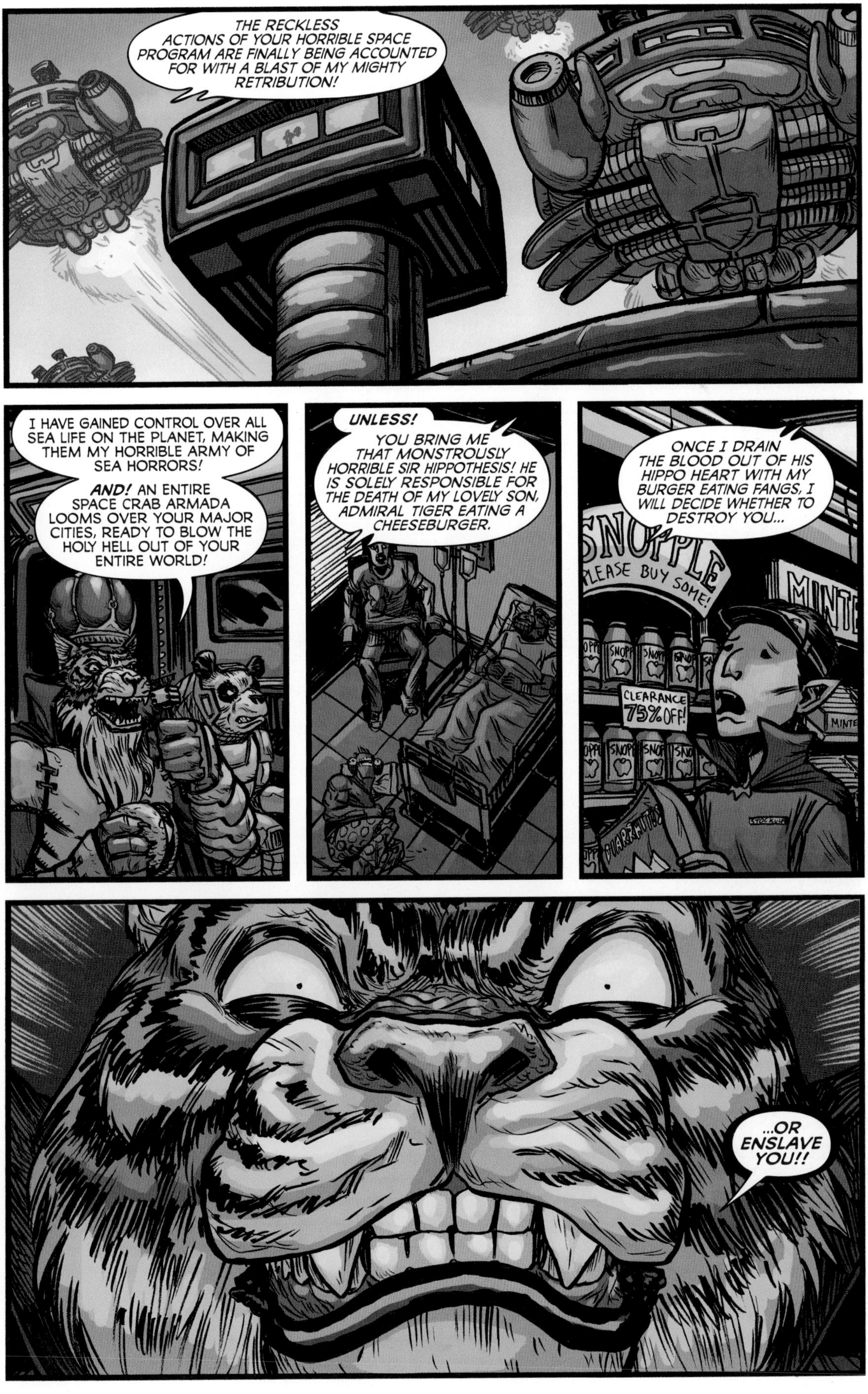
THE RECKLESS ACTIONS OF YOUR HORRIBLE SPACE PROGRAM ARE FINALLY BEING ACCOUNTED FOR WITH A BLAST OF MY MIGHTY RETRIBUTION!
I HAVE GAINED CONTROL OVER ALL SEA LIFE ON THE PLANET, MAKING THEM MY HORRIBLE ARMY OF SEA HORRORS!
AND! AN ENTIRE SPACE CRAB ARMADA LOOMS OVER YOUR MAJOR CITIES, READY TO BLOW THE HOLY HELL OUT OF YOUR ENTIRE WORLD!
UNLESS!
YOU BRING ME THAT MONSTROUSLY HORRIBLE SIR HIPPOTHESIS! HE IS SOLELY RESPONSIBLE FOR THE DEATH OF MY LOVELY SON, ADMIRAL TIGER EATING A CHEESEBURGER.
ONCE I DRAIN THE BLOOD OUT OF HIS HIPPO HEART WITH MY BURGER EATING FANGS, I WILL DECIDE WHETHER TO DESTROY YOU...
PLEASE BUY SOME!
CLEARANCE 75% OFF!
...OR ENSLAVE YOU!!

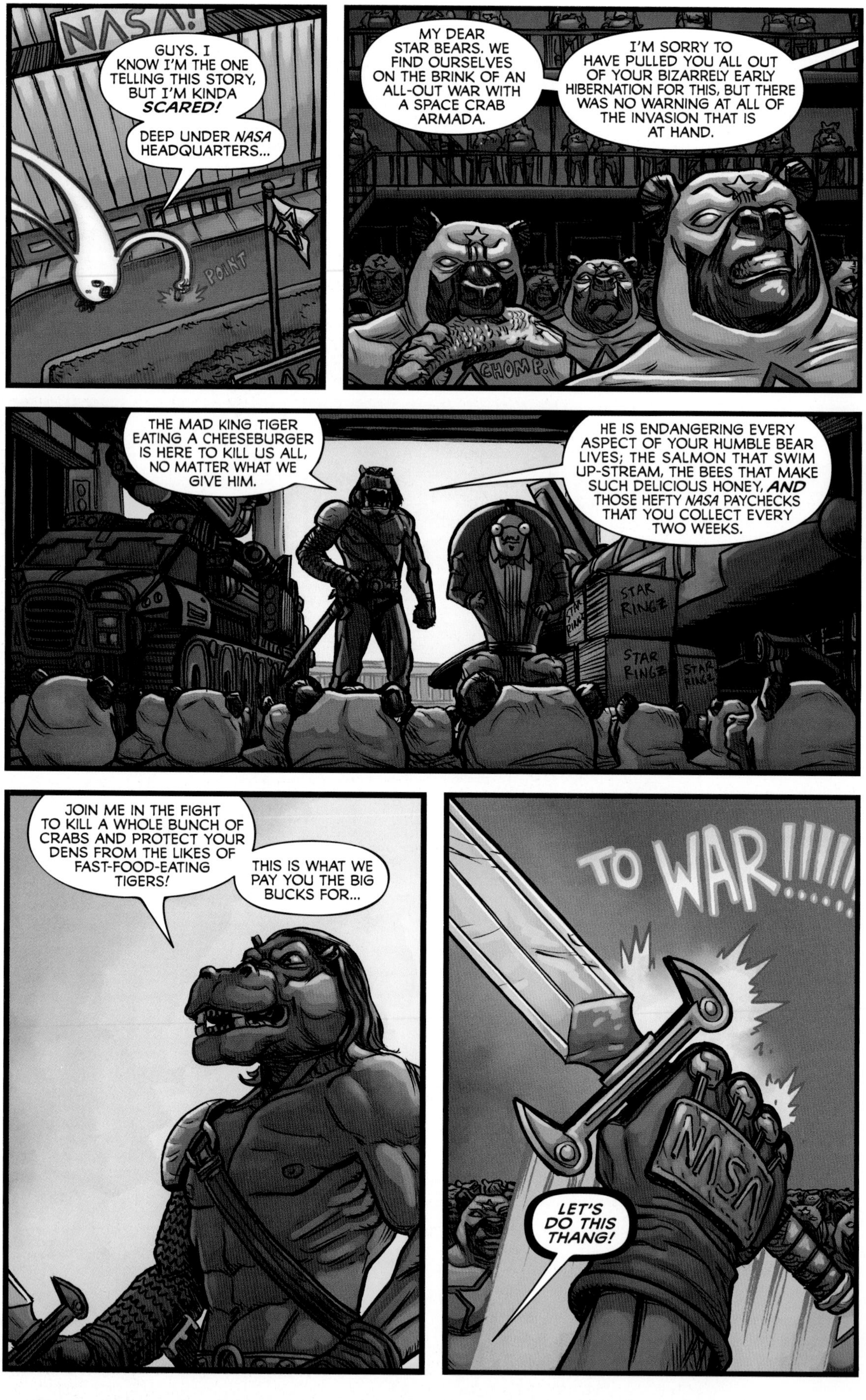
NASA!
GUYS. I KNOW I'M THE ONE TELLING THIS STORY, BUT I'M KINDA *SCARED!*
DEEP UNDER *NASA* HEADQUARTERS...
POINT
MY DEAR STAR BEARS. WE FIND OURSELVES ON THE BRINK OF AN ALL-OUT WAR WITH A SPACE CRAB ARMADA.
I'M SORRY TO HAVE PULLED YOU ALL OUT OF YOUR BIZARRELY EARLY HIBERNATION FOR THIS, BUT THERE WAS NO WARNING AT ALL OF THE INVASION THAT IS AT HAND.
CHOMP.
THE MAD KING TIGER EATING A CHEESEBURGER IS HERE TO KILL US ALL, NO MATTER WHAT WE GIVE HIM.
HE IS ENDANGERING EVERY ASPECT OF YOUR HUMBLE BEAR LIVES; THE SALMON THAT SWIM UP-STREAM, THE BEES THAT MAKE SUCH DELICIOUS HONEY, ***AND*** THOSE HEFTY *NASA* PAYCHECKS THAT YOU COLLECT EVERY TWO WEEKS.
STAR RINGZ
STAR RINGZ
STAR RINGZ
STAR RINGZ
JOIN ME IN THE FIGHT TO KILL A WHOLE BUNCH OF CRABS AND PROTECT YOUR DENS FROM THE LIKES OF FAST-FOOD-EATING TIGERS!
THIS IS WHAT WE PAY YOU THE BIG BUCKS FOR...
TO WAR!!!!!......
NASA
LET'S DO THIS THANG!

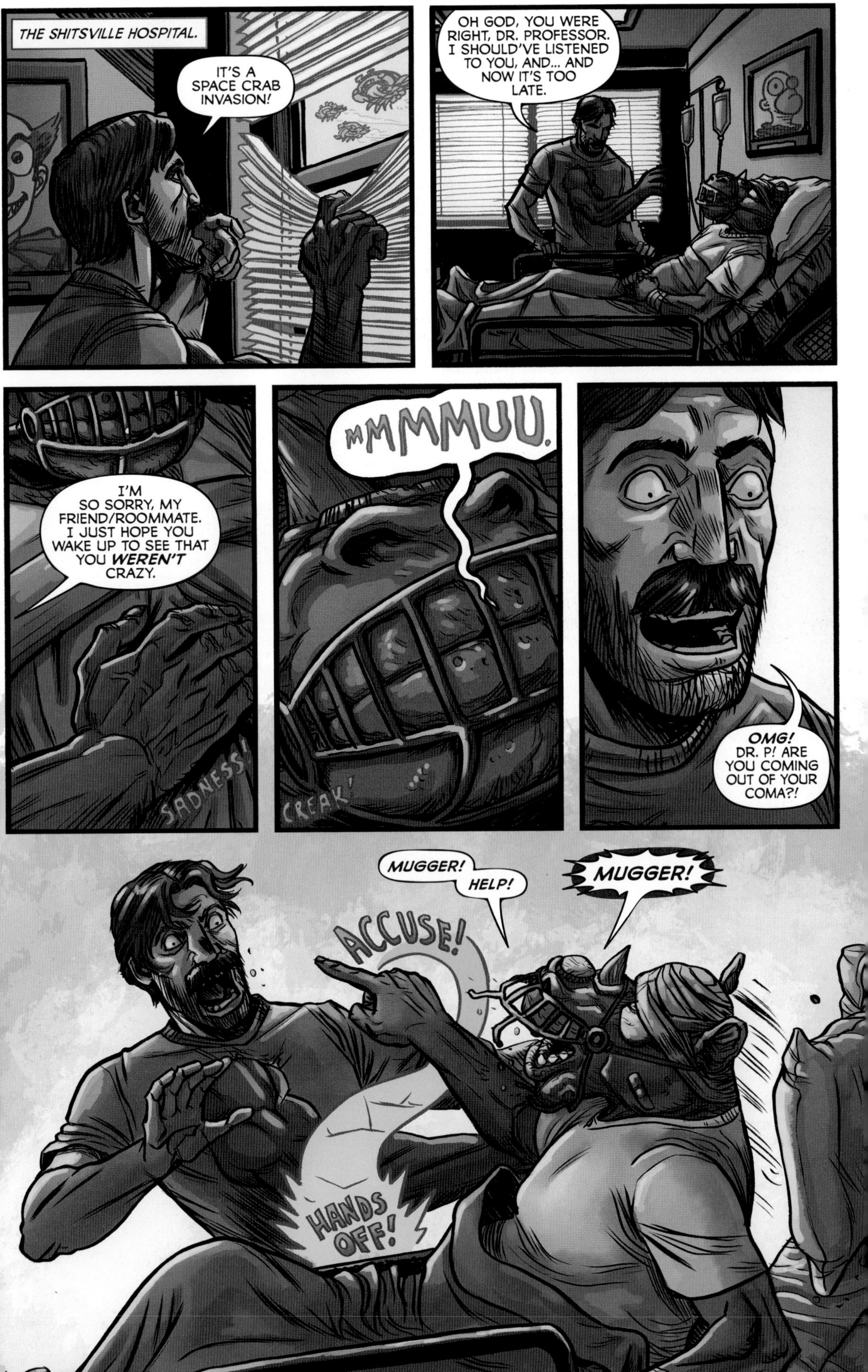
THE SHITSVILLE HOSPITAL.
IT'S A SPACE CRAB INVASION!
OH GOD, YOU WERE RIGHT, DR. PROFESSOR. I SHOULD'VE LISTENED TO YOU, AND... AND NOW IT'S TOO LATE.
I'M SO SORRY, MY FRIEND/ROOMMATE. I JUST HOPE YOU WAKE UP TO SEE THAT YOU *WEREN'T* CRAZY.
SADNESS!
MMMMUU.
CREAK!
OMG! DR. P! ARE YOU COMING OUT OF YOUR COMA?!
ACCUSE!
MUGGER! HELP!
MUGGER!
HANDS OFF!

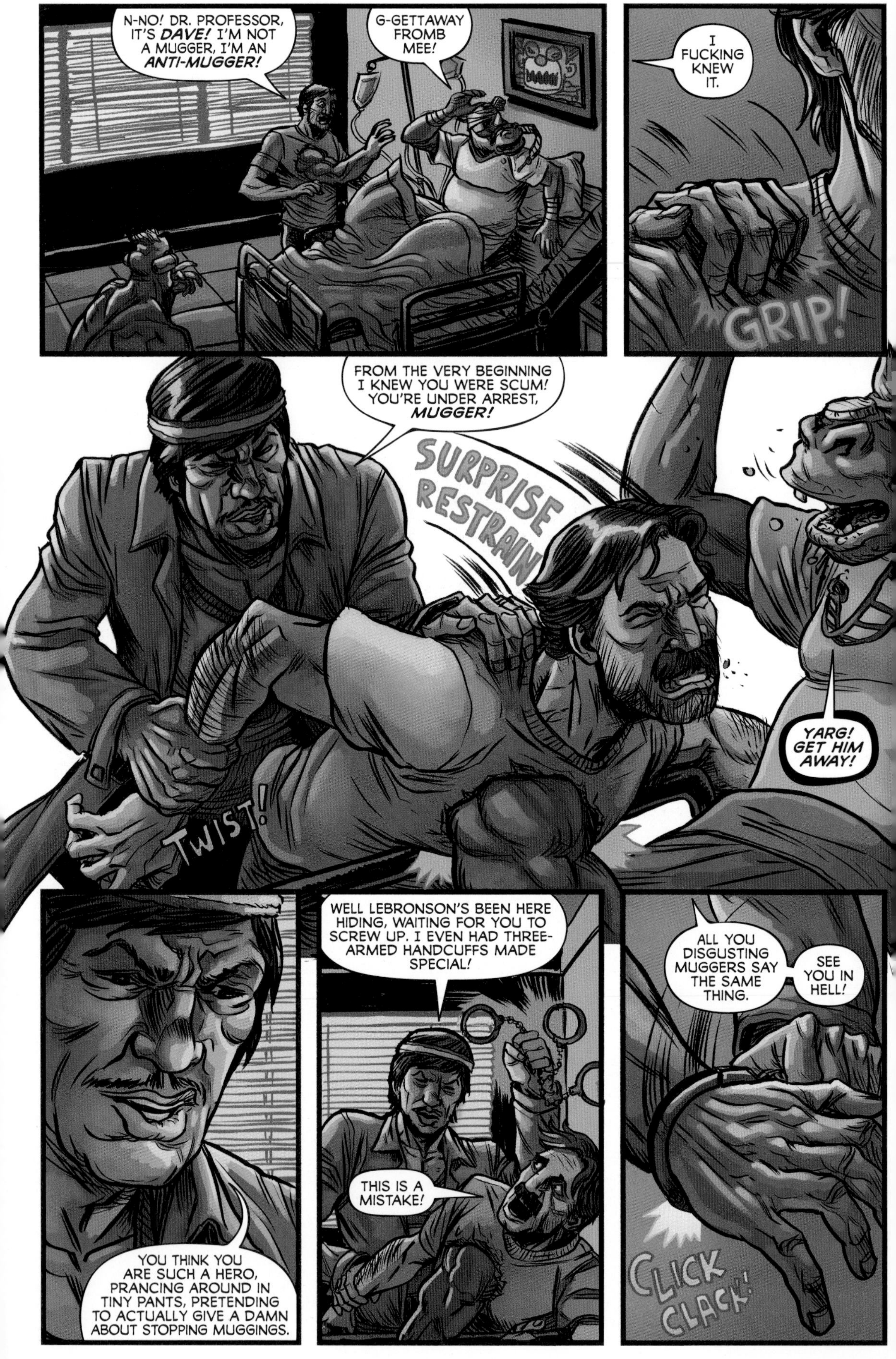
N-NO! DR. PROFESSOR, IT'S DAVE! I'M NOT A MUGGER, I'M AN ANTI-MUGGER!
G-GETTAWAY FROMB MEE!
I FUCKING KNEW IT.
GRIP!
FROM THE VERY BEGINNING I KNEW YOU WERE SCUM! YOU'RE UNDER ARREST, MUGGER!
SURPRISE RESTRAIN
YARG! GET HIM AWAY!
TWIST!
YOU THINK YOU ARE SUCH A HERO, PRANCING AROUND IN TINY PANTS, PRETENDING TO ACTUALLY GIVE A DAMN ABOUT STOPPING MUGGINGS.
WELL LEBRONSON'S BEEN HERE HIDING, WAITING FOR YOU TO SCREW UP. I EVEN HAD THREE-ARMED HANDCUFFS MADE SPECIAL!
THIS IS A MISTAKE!
ALL YOU DISGUSTING MUGGERS SAY THE SAME THING.
SEE YOU IN HELL!
CLICK CLACK!

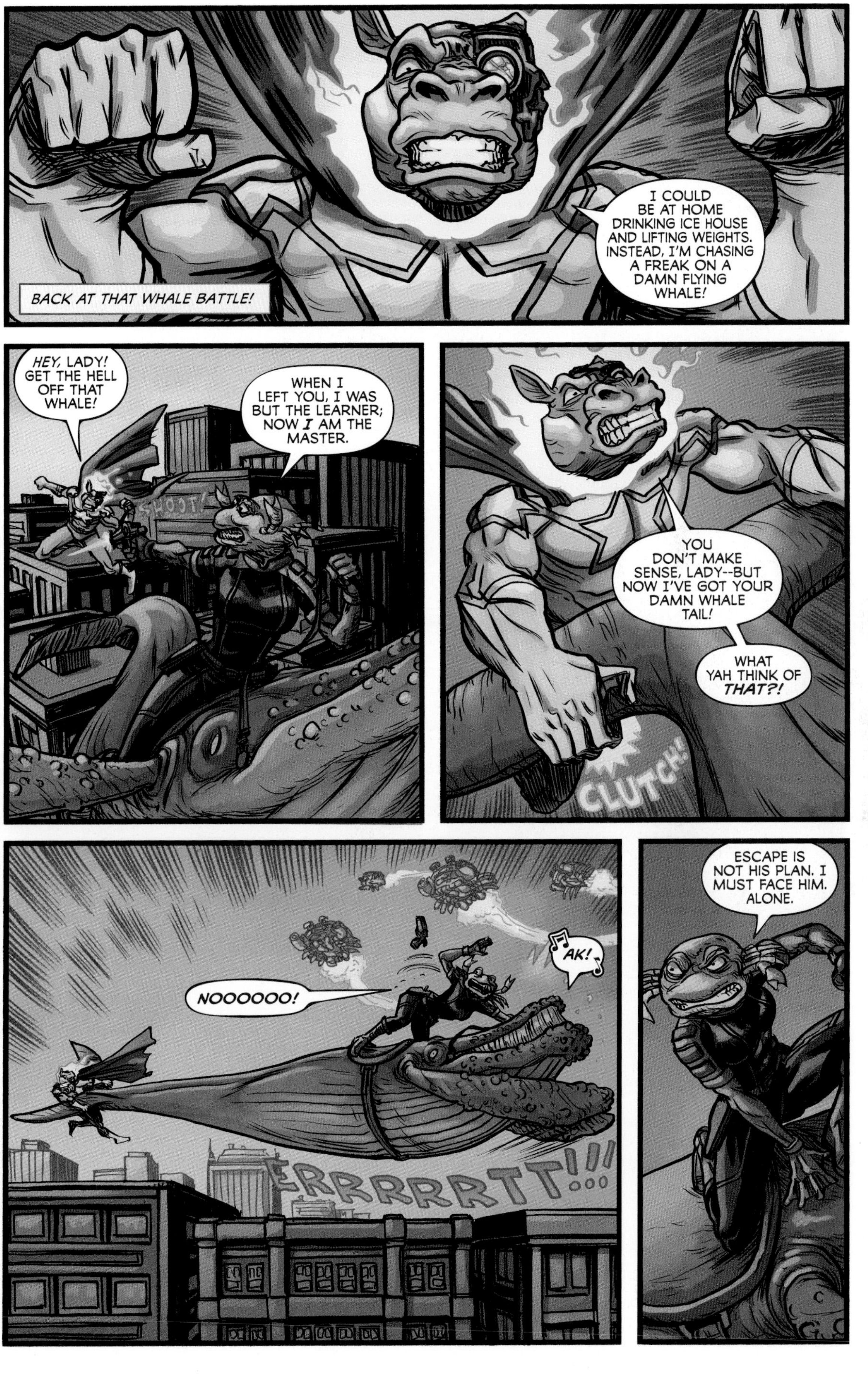
BACK AT THAT WHALE BATTLE!
I COULD BE AT HOME DRINKING ICE HOUSE AND LIFTING WEIGHTS. INSTEAD, I'M CHASING A FREAK ON A DAMN FLYING WHALE!
HEY, LADY! GET THE HELL OFF THAT WHALE!
WHEN I LEFT YOU, I WAS BUT THE LEARNER; NOW I AM THE MASTER.
SHOOT!
YOU DON'T MAKE SENSE, LADY--BUT NOW I'VE GOT YOUR DAMN WHALE TAIL!
WHAT YAH THINK OF THAT?!
CLUTCH!
AK!
NOOOOOO!
ERRRRRTT!!!
ESCAPE IS NOT HIS PLAN. I MUST FACE HIM. ALONE.

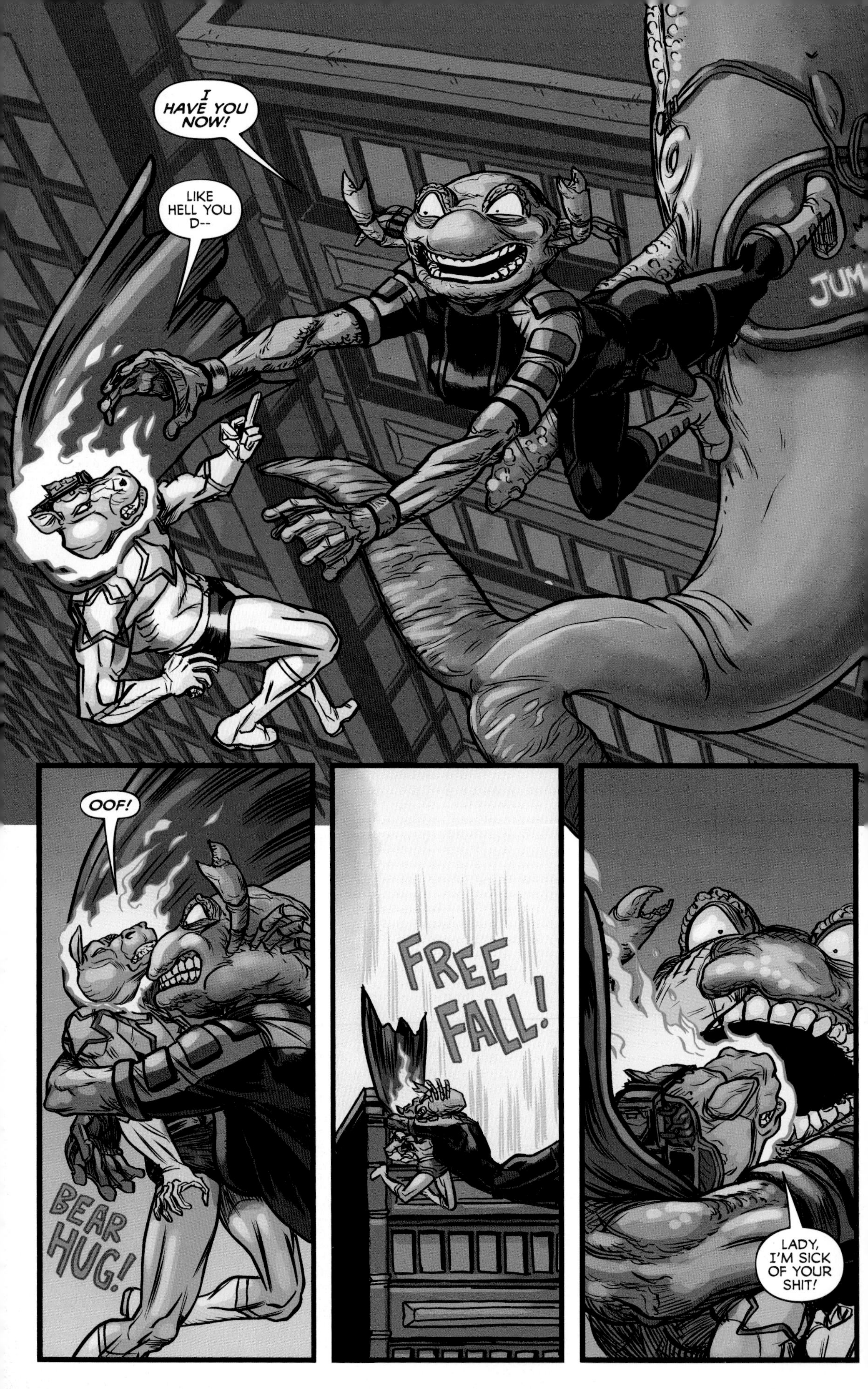
I HAVE YOU NOW!
LIKE HELL YOU D--
JUM
OOF!
BEAR HUG!
FREE FALL!
LADY, I'M SICK OF YOUR SHIT!

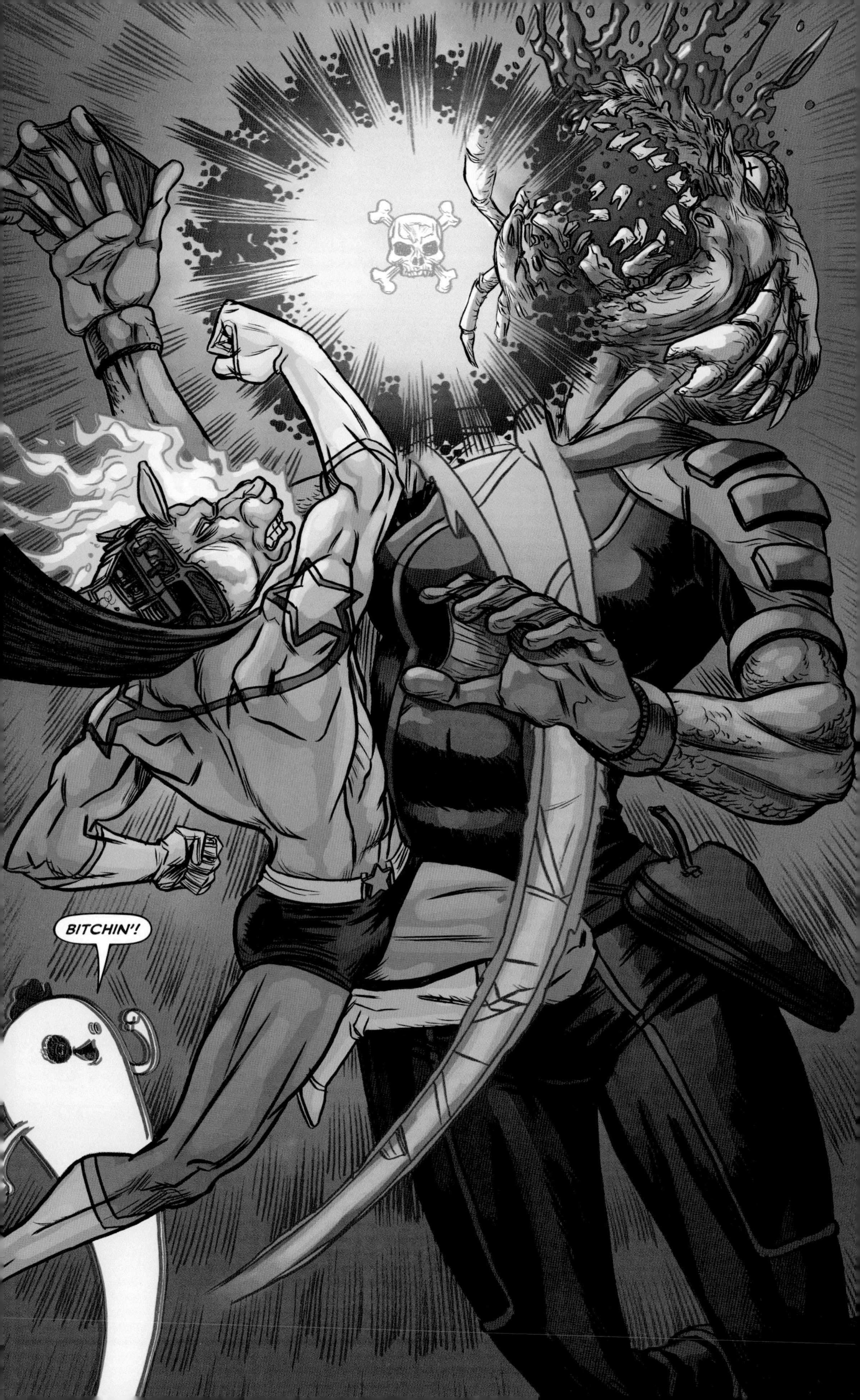
BITCHIN'!

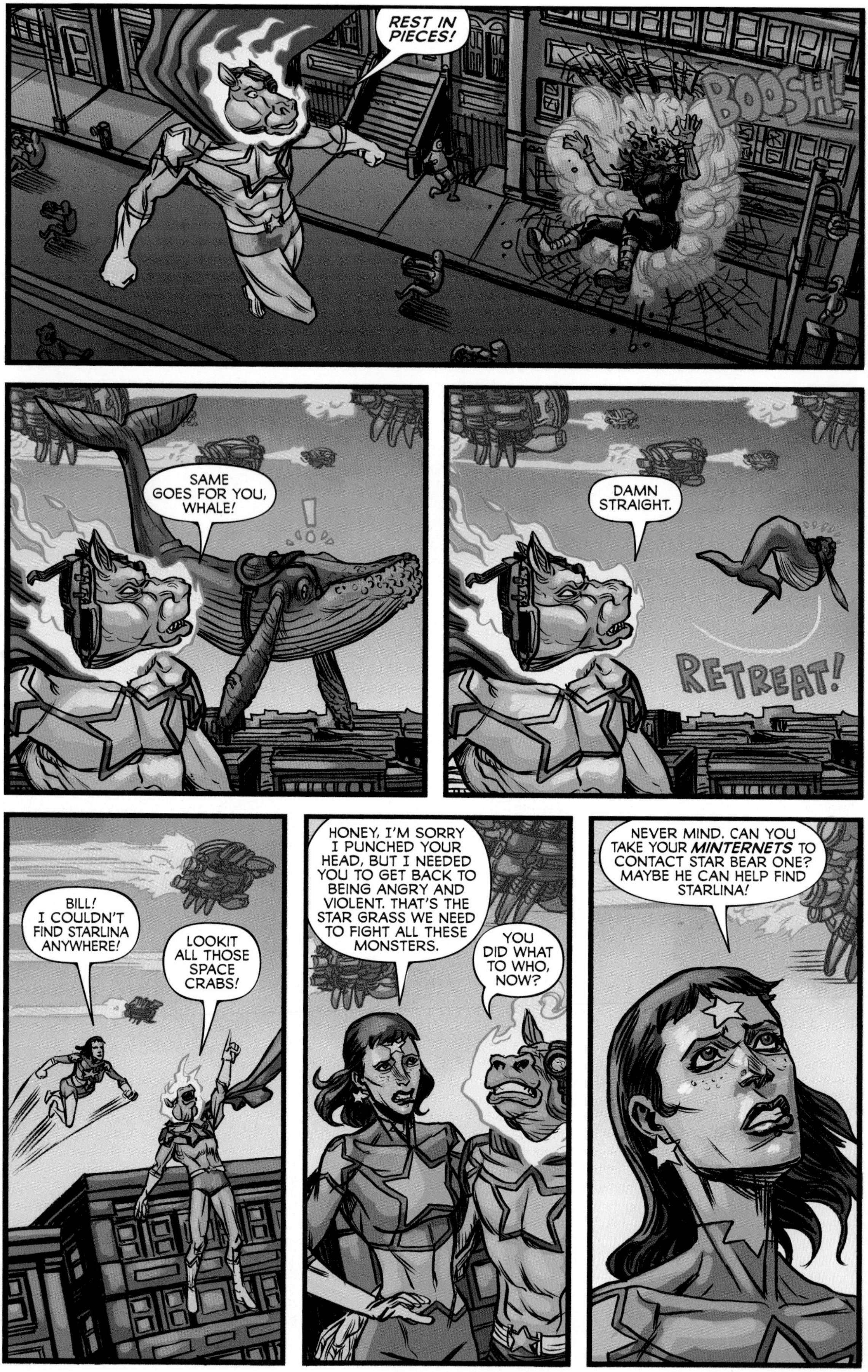
REST IN PIECES!
BOOSH!
SAME GOES FOR YOU, WHALE!
!
DAMN STRAIGHT.
RETREAT!
BILL! I COULDN'T FIND STARLINA ANYWHERE!
LOOKIT ALL THOSE SPACE CRABS!
HONEY, I'M SORRY I PUNCHED YOUR HEAD, BUT I NEEDED YOU TO GET BACK TO BEING ANGRY AND VIOLENT. THAT'S THE STAR GRASS WE NEED TO FIGHT ALL THESE MONSTERS.
YOU DID WHAT TO WHO, NOW?
NEVER MIND. CAN YOU TAKE YOUR *MINTERNETS* TO CONTACT STAR BEAR ONE? MAYBE HE CAN HELP FIND STARLINA!

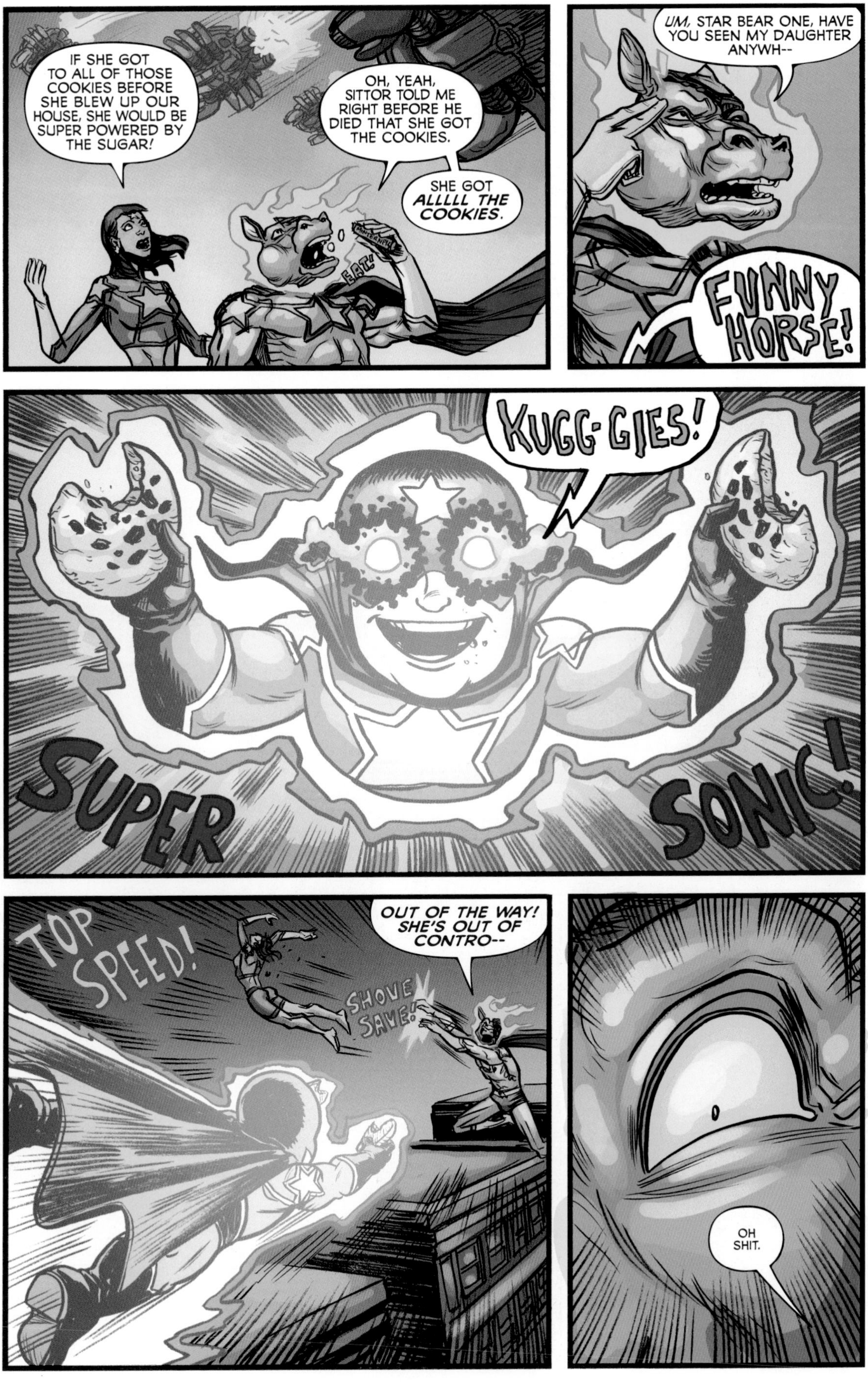
IF SHE GOT TO ALL OF THOSE COOKIES BEFORE SHE BLEW UP OUR HOUSE, SHE WOULD BE SUPER POWERED BY THE SUGAR!
OH, YEAH, SITTOR TOLD ME RIGHT BEFORE HE DIED THAT SHE GOT THE COOKIES.
SHE GOT *ALLLLL THE COOKIES*.
EAT!
UM, STAR BEAR ONE, HAVE YOU SEEN MY DAUGHTER ANYWH--
FUNNY HORSE!
KUGG-GIES!
SUPER
SONIC!
TOP SPEED!
OUT OF THE WAY! SHE'S OUT OF CONTRO--
SHOVE SAVE!
OH SHIT.

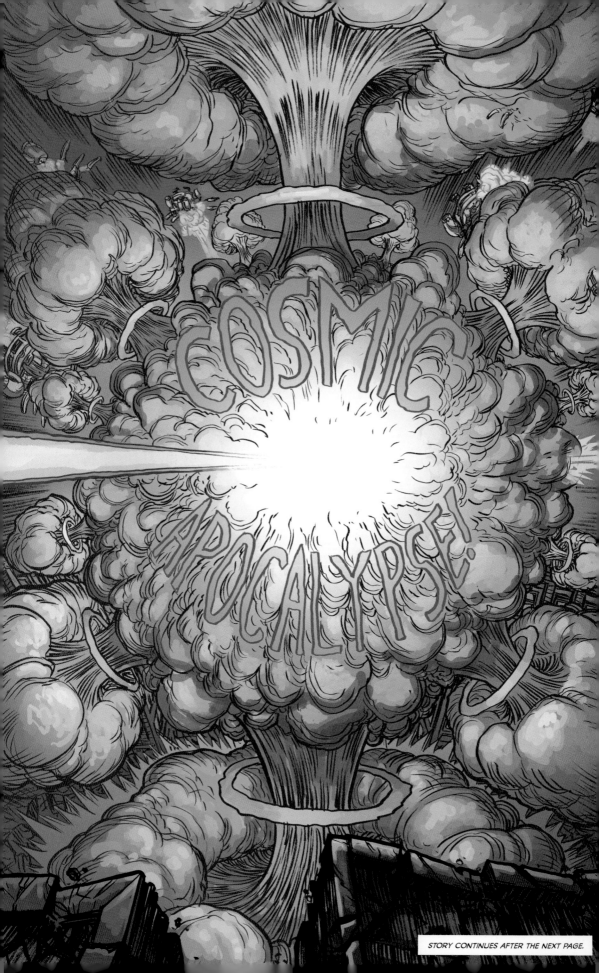

STORY CONTINUES AFTER THE NEXT PAGE.

ADVERTISEMENT

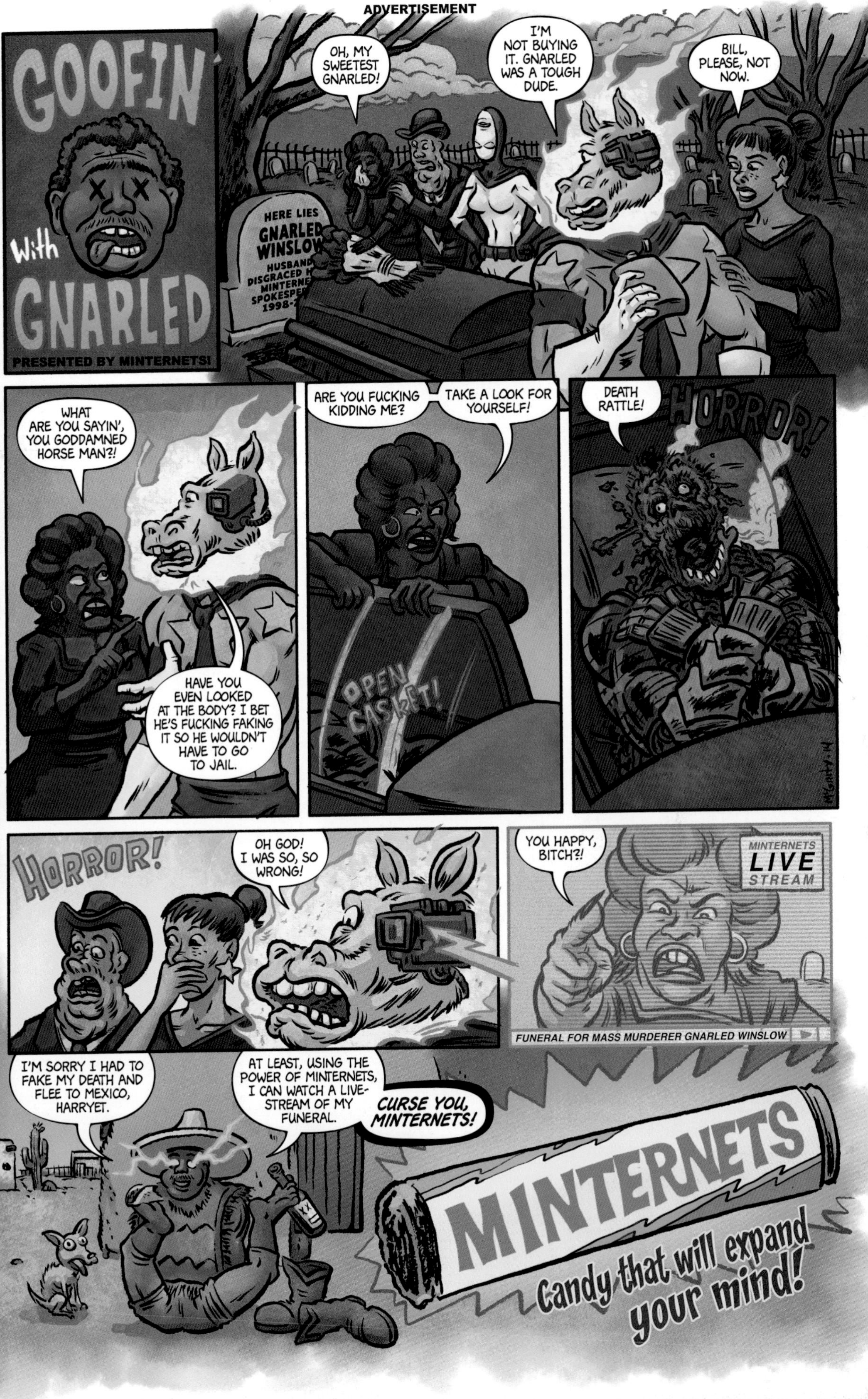

GOOFIN With GNARLED
PRESENTED BY MINTERNETS!
OH, MY SWEETEST GNARLED!
I'M NOT BUYING IT. GNARLED WAS A TOUGH DUDE.
BILL, PLEASE, NOT NOW.
HERE LIES
GNARLED WINSLOW
HUSBAND
WHAT ARE YOU SAYIN', YOU GODDAMNED HORSE MAN?!
HAVE YOU EVEN LOOKED AT THE BODY? I BET HE'S FUCKING FAKING IT SO HE WOULDN'T HAVE TO GO TO JAIL.
ARE YOU FUCKING KIDDING ME?
TAKE A LOOK FOR YOURSELF!
OPEN CASKET!
DEATH RATTLE!
HORROR!
HORROR!
OH GOD! I WAS SO, SO WRONG!
YOU HAPPY, BITCH?!
MINTERNETS LIVE STREAM
FUNERAL FOR MASS MURDERER GNARLED WINSLOW
I'M SORRY I HAD TO FAKE MY DEATH AND FLEE TO MEXICO, HARRYET.
AT LEAST, USING THE POWER OF MINTERNETS, I CAN WATCH A LIVE-STREAM OF MY FUNERAL.
CURSE YOU, MINTERNETS!
MINTERNETS
Candy that will expand your mind!

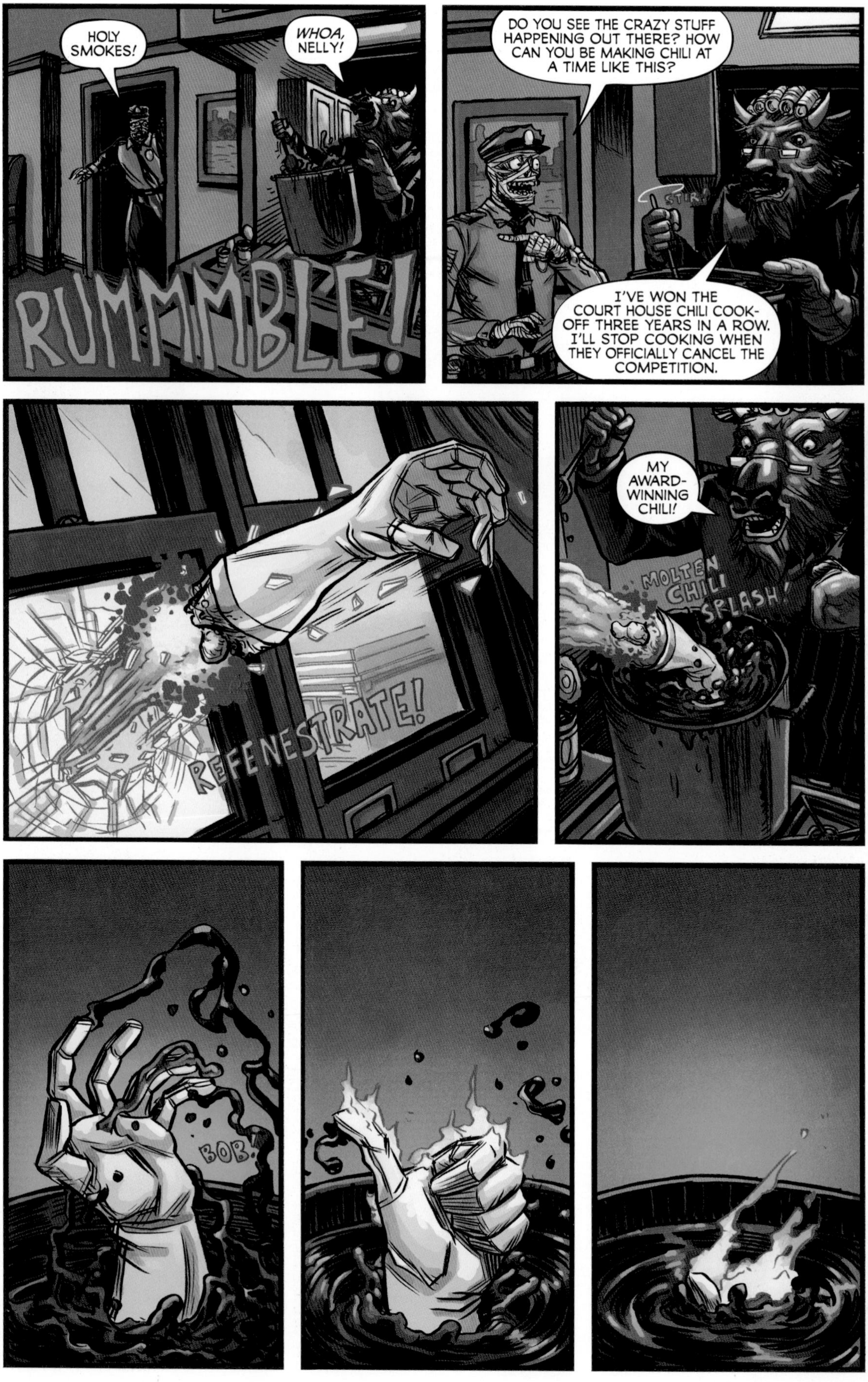
HOLY SMOKES!
WHOA, NELLY!
RUMMMBLE!
DO YOU SEE THE CRAZY STUFF HAPPENING OUT THERE? HOW CAN YOU BE MAKING CHILI AT A TIME LIKE THIS?
STIR
I'VE WON THE COURT HOUSE CHILI COOK-OFF THREE YEARS IN A ROW. I'LL STOP COOKING WHEN THEY OFFICIALLY CANCEL THE COMPETITION.
REFENESTRATE!
MY AWARD-WINNING CHILI!
MOLTEN CHILI SPLASH!
BOB!

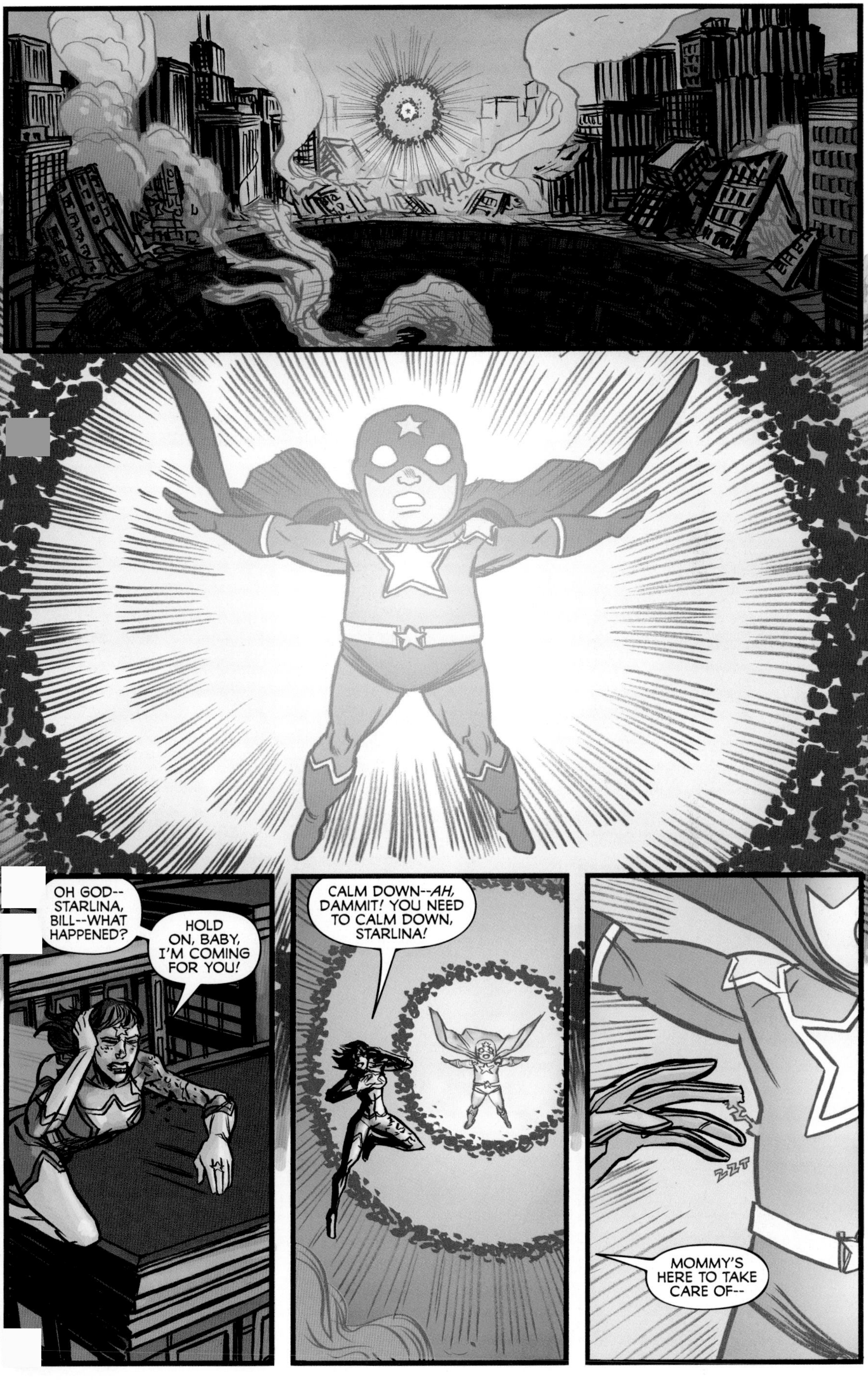
OH GOD--STARLINA, BILL--WHAT HAPPENED?
HOLD ON, BABY, I'M COMING FOR YOU!
CALM DOWN--*AH,* DAMMIT! YOU NEED TO CALM DOWN, STARLINA!
ZZT
MOMMY'S HERE TO TAKE CARE OF--

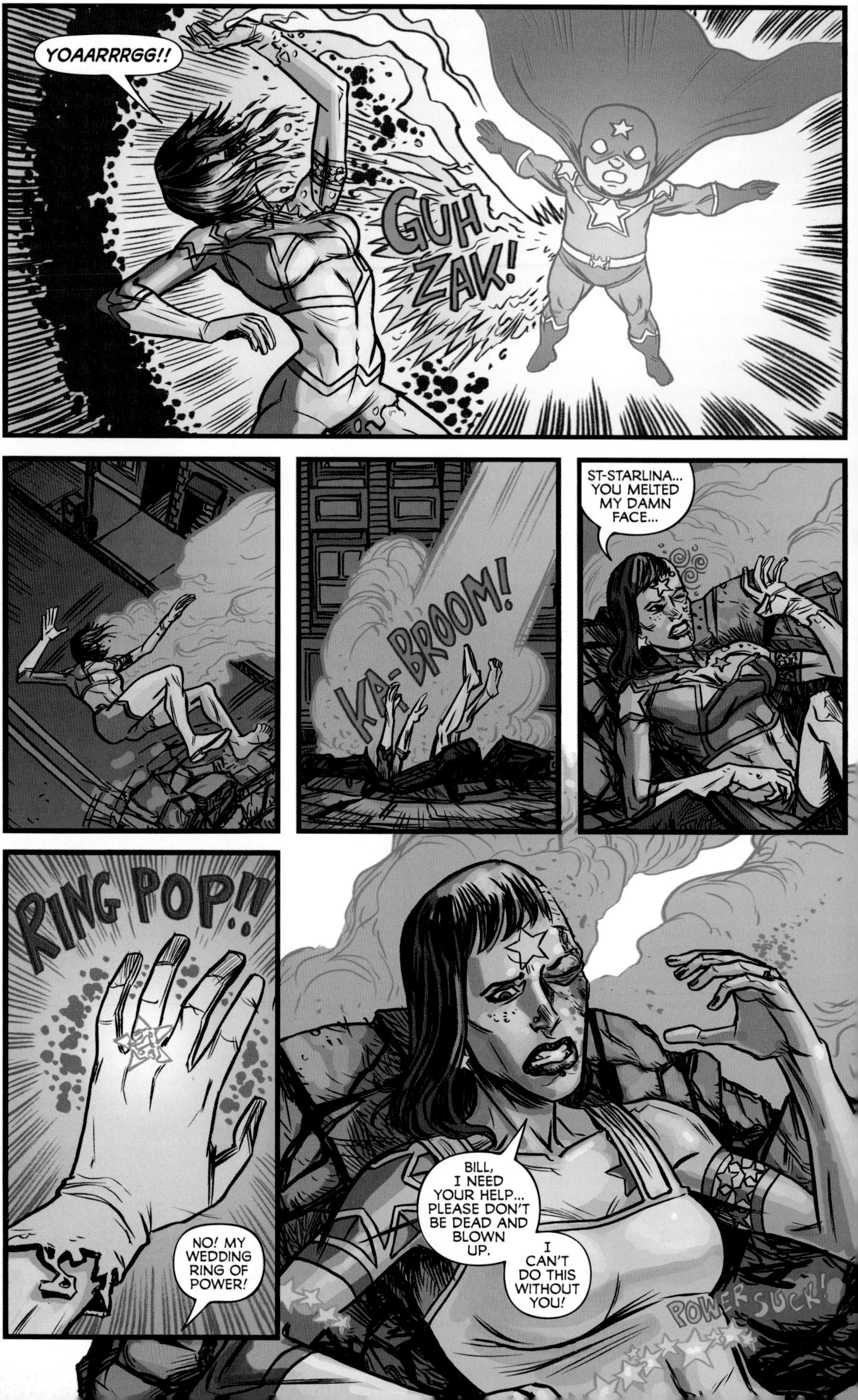
YOAARRRGG!!
GUH ZAK!
KA-BROOM!
ST-STARLINA... YOU MELTED MY DAMN FACE...
RING POP!!
NO! MY WEDDING RING OF POWER!
BILL, I NEED YOUR HELP... PLEASE DON'T BE DEAD AND BLOWN UP.
I CAN'T DO THIS WITHOUT YOU!
POWER SUCK!

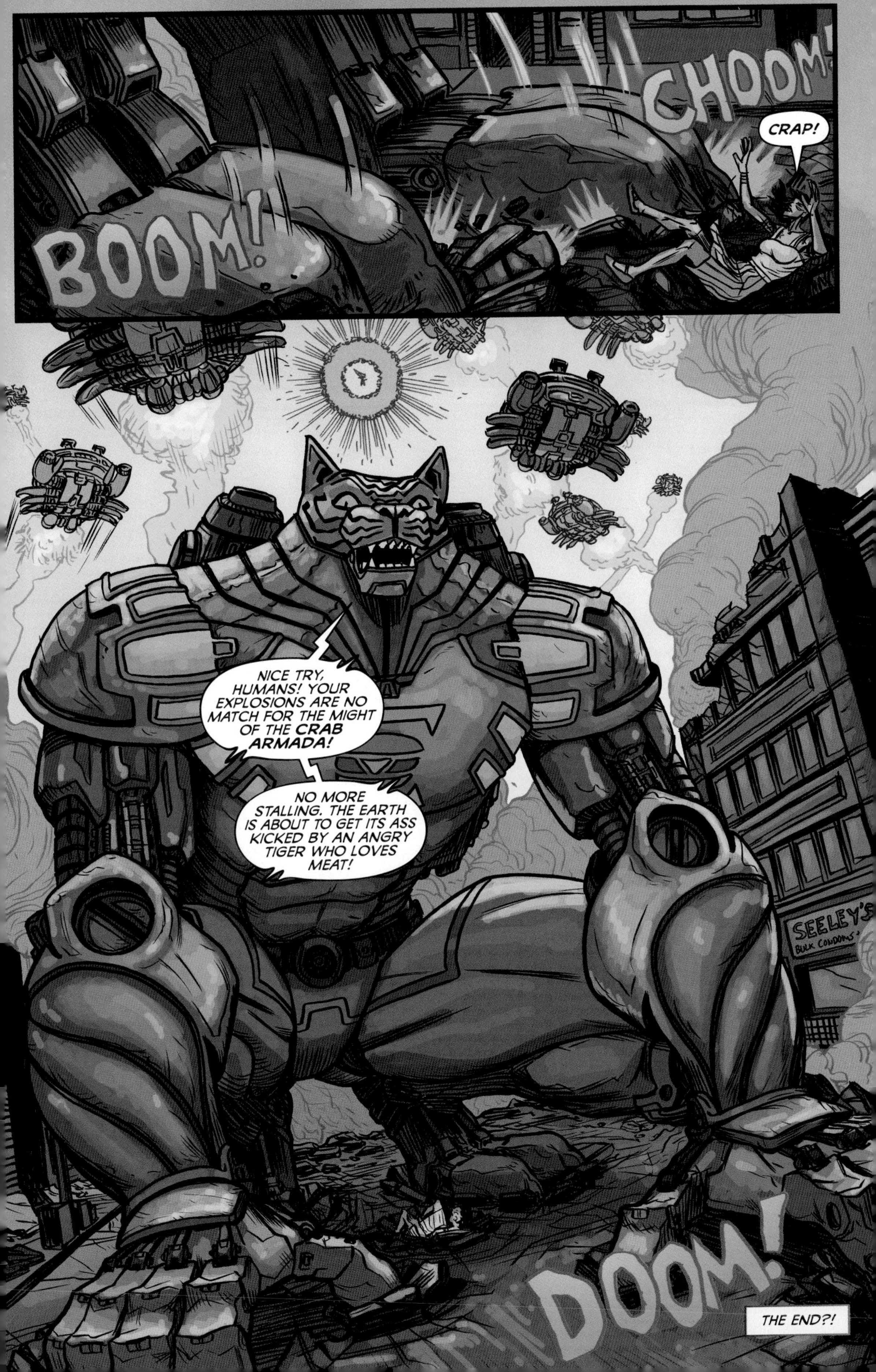
BOOM!
CHOOM!
CRAP!
NICE TRY, HUMANS! YOUR EXPLOSIONS ARE NO MATCH FOR THE MIGHT OF THE CRAB ARMADA!
NO MORE STALLING. THE EARTH IS ABOUT TO GET ITS ASS KICKED BY AN ANGRY TIGER WHO LOVES MEAT!
SEELEY'S
BULK CONDOMS
DOOM!
THE END?!

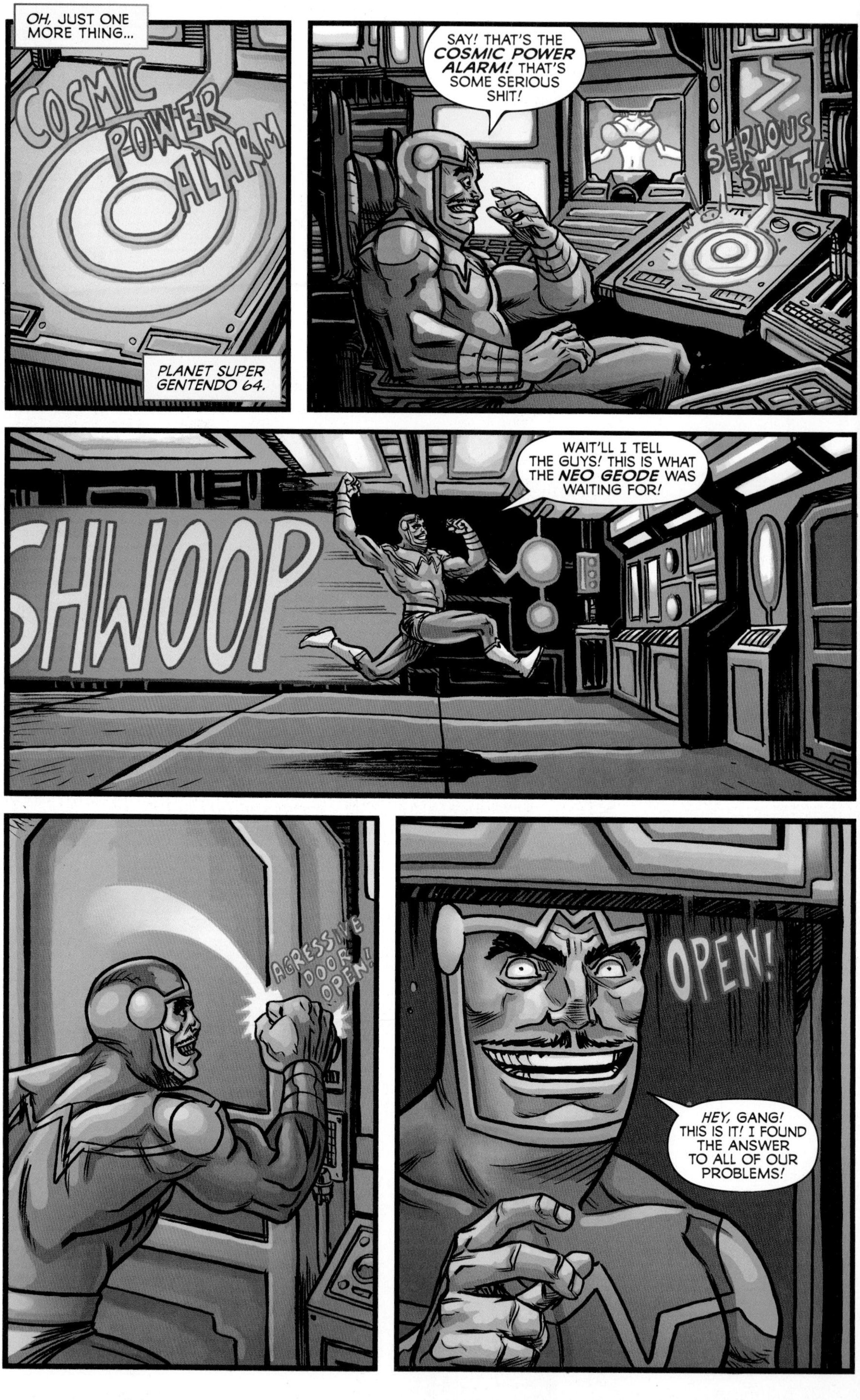
OH, JUST ONE MORE THING...
COSMIC POWER ALARM
PLANET SUPER GENTENDO 64.
SAY! THAT'S THE COSMIC POWER ALARM! THAT'S SOME SERIOUS SHIT!
SERIOUS SHIT!!
WAIT'LL I TELL THE GUYS! THIS IS WHAT THE NEO GEODE WAS WAITING FOR!
SHWOOP
AGRESSIVE DOOR OPEN!
OPEN!
HEY, GANG! THIS IS IT! I FOUND THE ANSWER TO ALL OF OUR PROBLEMS!

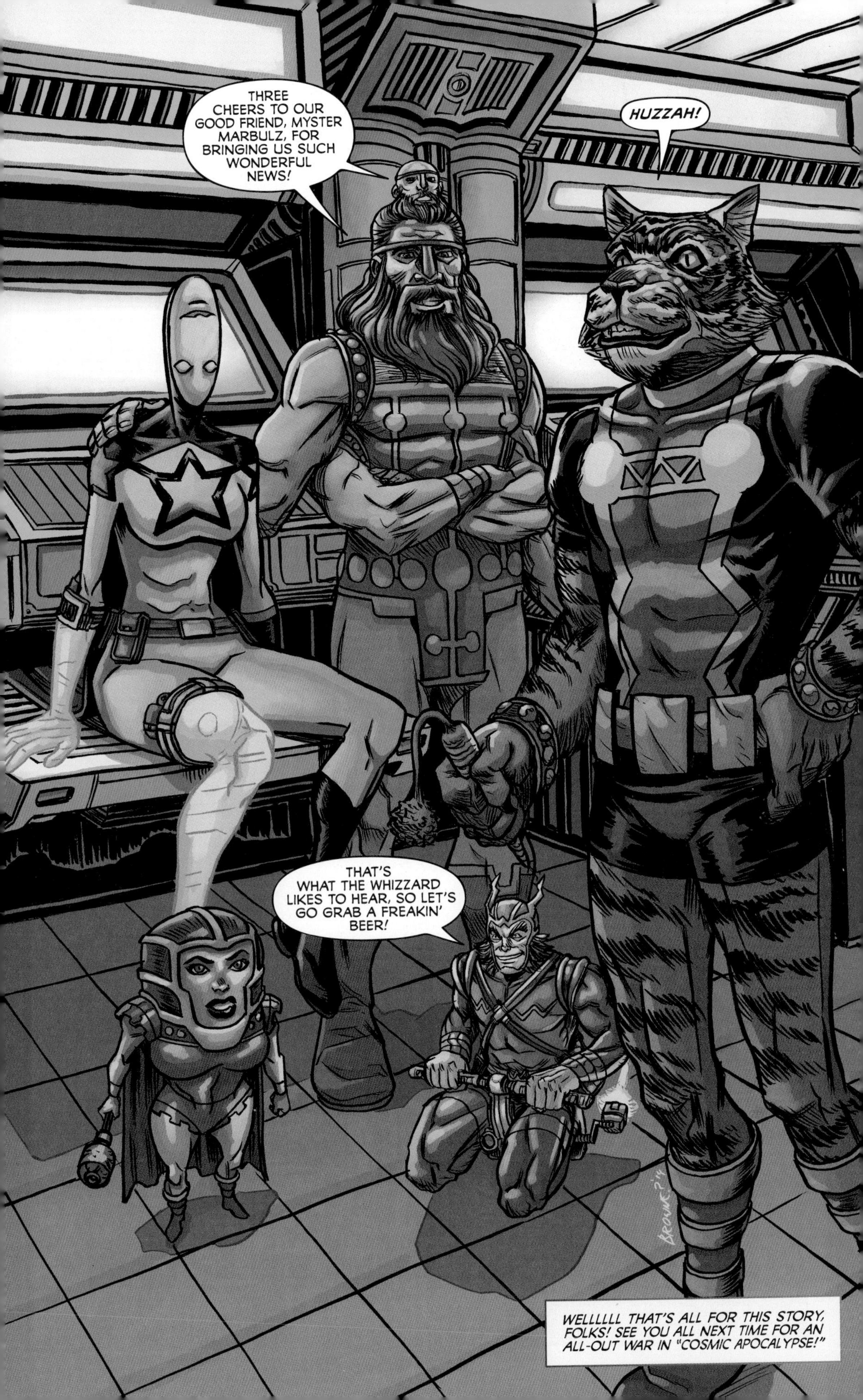
THREE CHEERS TO OUR GOOD FRIEND, MYSTER MARBULZ, FOR BRINGING US SUCH WONDERFUL NEWS!
HUZZAH!
THAT'S WHAT THE WHIZZARD LIKES TO HEAR, SO LET'S GO GRAB A FREAKIN' BEER!
WELLLLLL THAT'S ALL FOR THIS STORY, FOLKS! SEE YOU ALL NEXT TIME FOR AN ALL-OUT WAR IN "COSMIC APOCALYPSE!"

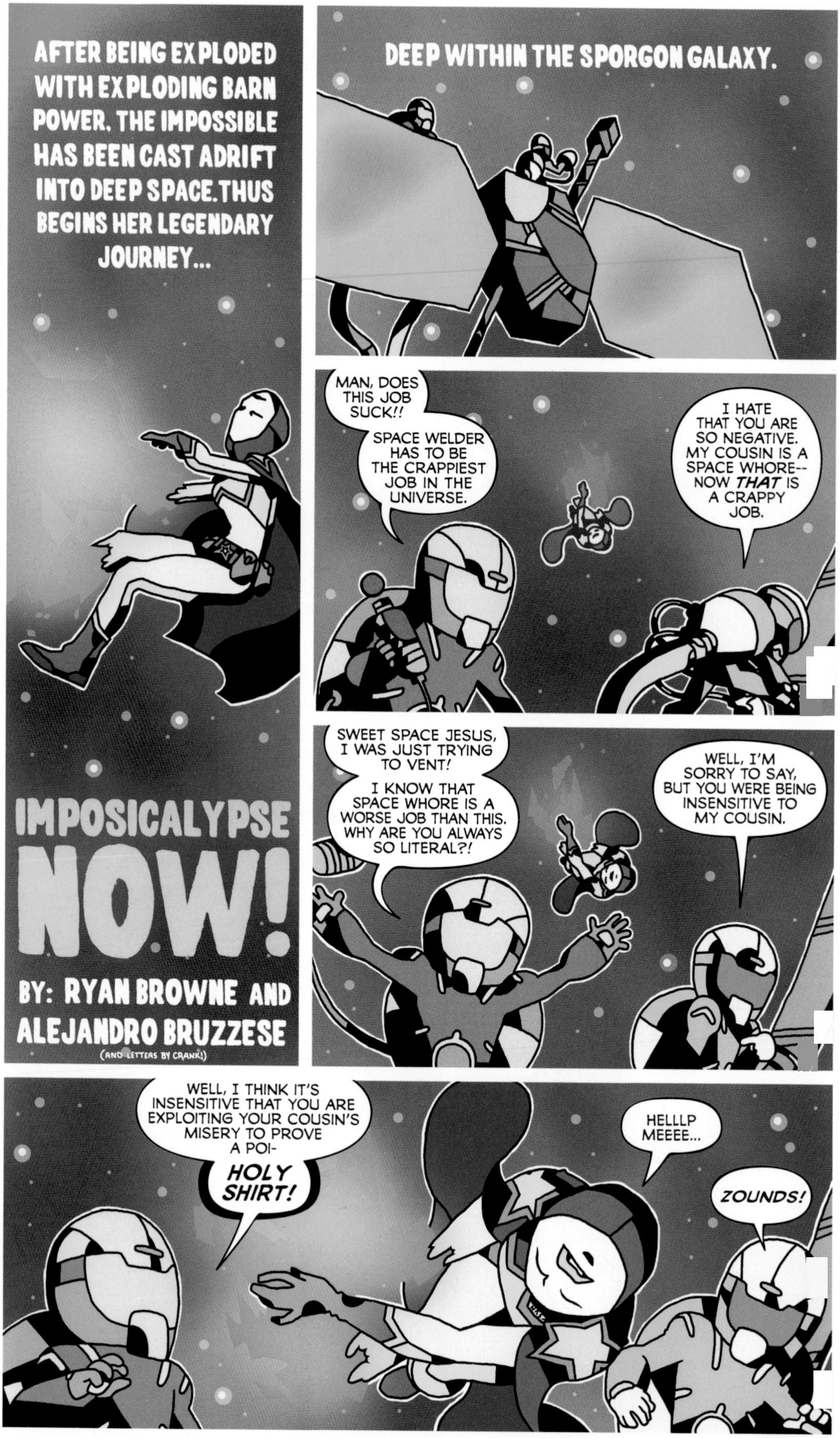
AFTER BEING EXPLODED WITH EXPLODING BARN POWER, THE IMPOSSIBLE HAS BEEN CAST ADRIFT INTO DEEP SPACE. THUS BEGINS HER LEGENDARY JOURNEY...
IMPOSICALYPSE NOW!
BY: RYAN BROWNE AND ALEJANDRO BRUZZESE
(AND LETTERS BY CRANK!)
DEEP WITHIN THE SPORGON GALAXY.
MAN, DOES THIS JOB SUCK!!
SPACE WELDER HAS TO BE THE CRAPPIEST JOB IN THE UNIVERSE.
I HATE THAT YOU ARE SO NEGATIVE. MY COUSIN IS A SPACE WHORE-- NOW THAT IS A CRAPPY JOB.
SWEET SPACE JESUS, I WAS JUST TRYING TO VENT!
I KNOW THAT SPACE WHORE IS A WORSE JOB THAN THIS. WHY ARE YOU ALWAYS SO LITERAL?!
WELL, I'M SORRY TO SAY, BUT YOU WERE BEING INSENSITIVE TO MY COUSIN.
WELL, I THINK IT'S INSENSITIVE THAT YOU ARE EXPLOITING YOUR COUSIN'S MISERY TO PROVE A POI-
HOLY SHIRT!
HELLLP MEEEE...
ZOUNDS!

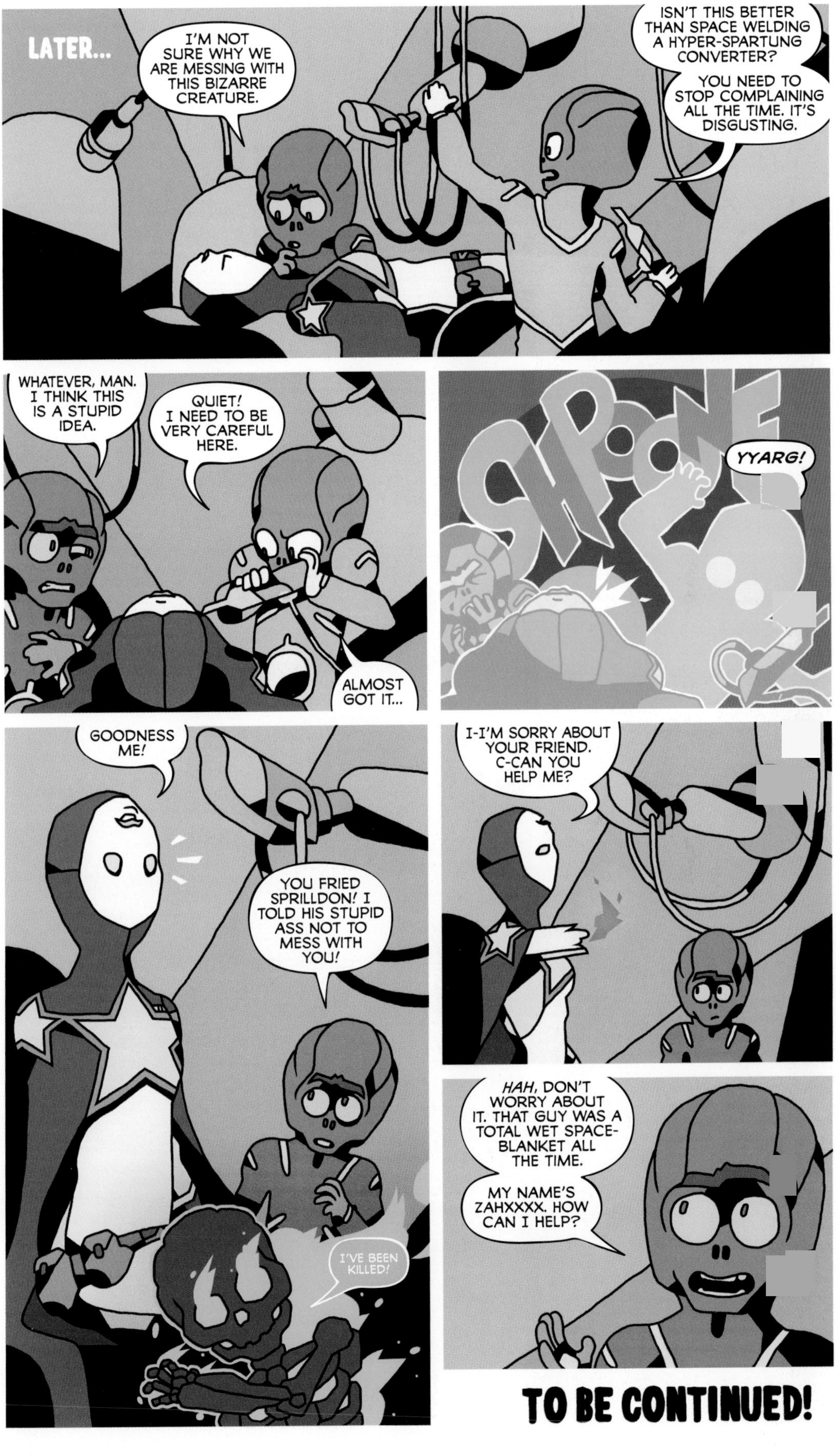
LATER...
I'M NOT SURE WHY WE ARE MESSING WITH THIS BIZARRE CREATURE.
ISN'T THIS BETTER THAN SPACE WELDING A HYPER-SPARTUNG CONVERTER?
YOU NEED TO STOP COMPLAINING ALL THE TIME. IT'S DISGUSTING.
WHATEVER, MAN. I THINK THIS IS A STUPID IDEA.
QUIET! I NEED TO BE VERY CAREFUL HERE.
ALMOST GOT IT...
SHPOONE
YYARG!
GOODNESS ME!
YOU FRIED SPRILLDON! I TOLD HIS STUPID ASS NOT TO MESS WITH YOU!
I'VE BEEN KILLED!
I-I'M SORRY ABOUT YOUR FRIEND. C-CAN YOU HELP ME?
HAH, DON'T WORRY ABOUT IT. THAT GUY WAS A TOTAL WET SPACE-BLANKET ALL THE TIME.
MY NAME'S ZAHXXXX. HOW CAN I HELP?
TO BE CONTINUED!

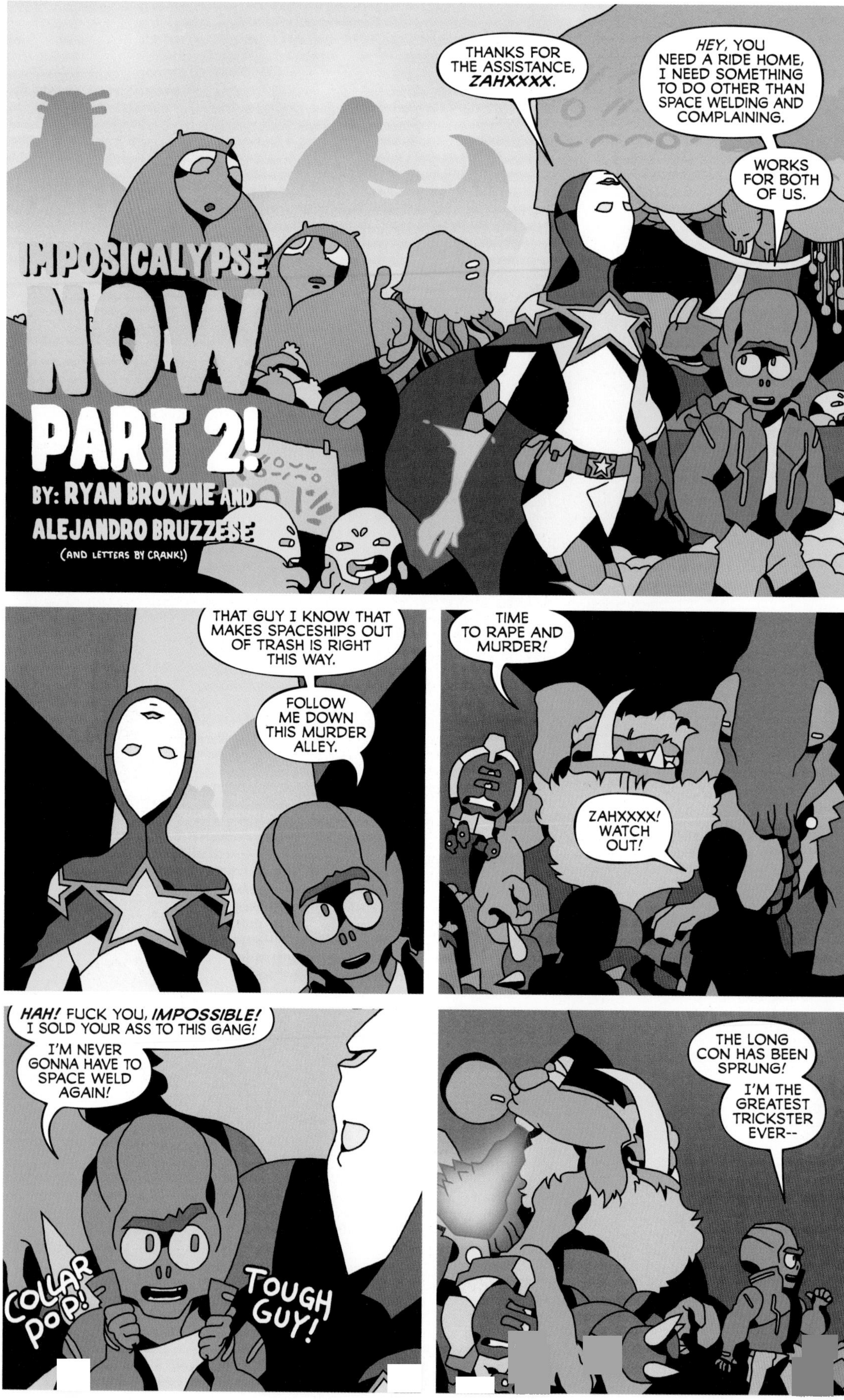
IMPOSICALYPSE NOW PART 2!
BY: RYAN BROWNE AND ALEJANDRO BRUZZESE
(AND LETTERS BY CRANK!)
THANKS FOR THE ASSISTANCE, ZAHXXXX.
HEY, YOU NEED A RIDE HOME, I NEED SOMETHING TO DO OTHER THAN SPACE WELDING AND COMPLAINING.
WORKS FOR BOTH OF US.
THAT GUY I KNOW THAT MAKES SPACESHIPS OUT OF TRASH IS RIGHT THIS WAY.
FOLLOW ME DOWN THIS MURDER ALLEY.
TIME TO RAPE AND MURDER!
ZAHXXXX! WATCH OUT!
HAH! FUCK YOU, IMPOSSIBLE! I SOLD YOUR ASS TO THIS GANG!
I'M NEVER GONNA HAVE TO SPACE WELD AGAIN!
COLLAR POP!
TOUGH GUY!
THE LONG CON HAS BEEN SPRUNG!
I'M THE GREATEST TRICKSTER EVER--

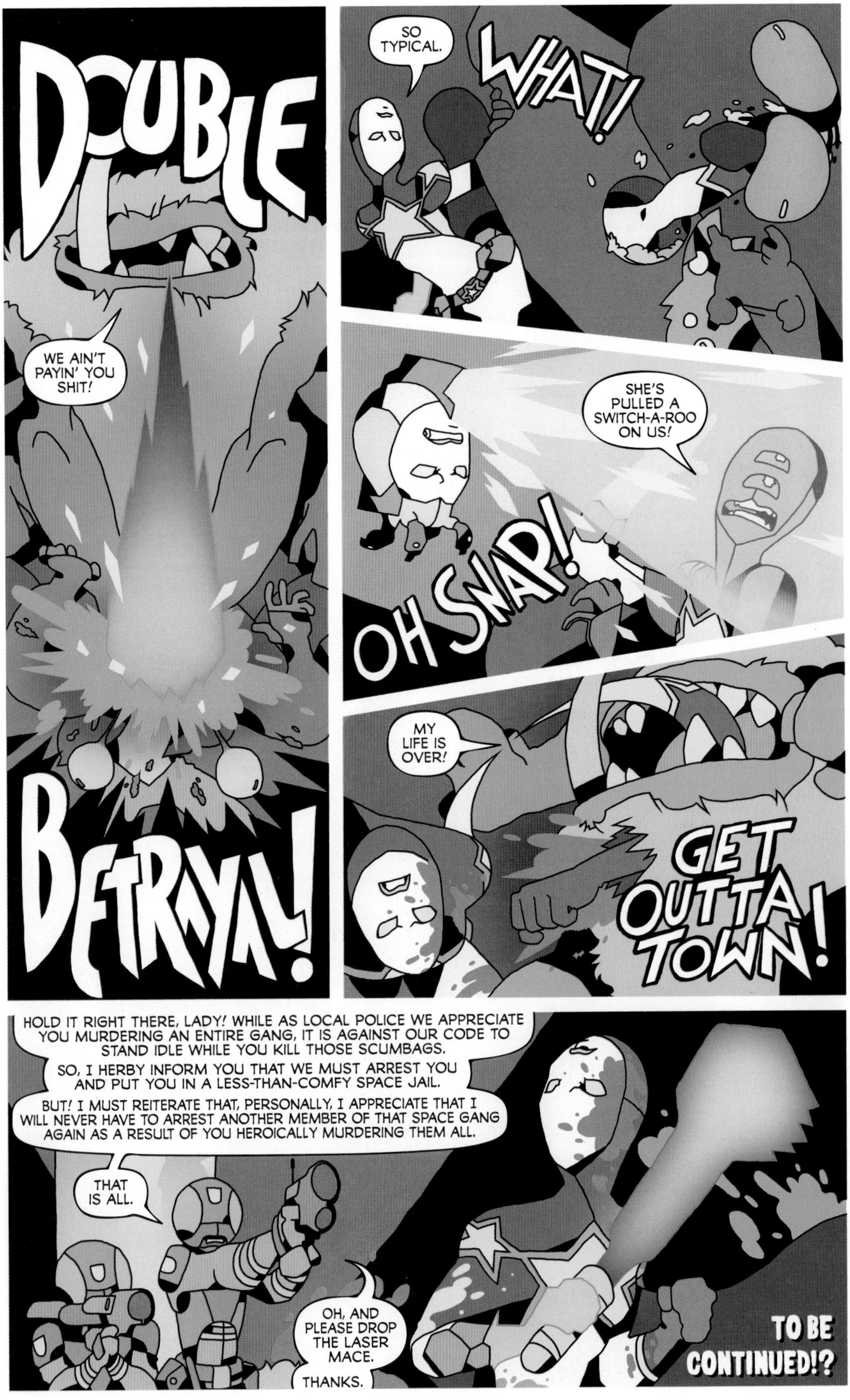
DOUBLE
WE AIN'T PAYIN' YOU SHIT!
BETRYAL!
SO TYPICAL.
WHAT!
SHE'S PULLED A SWITCH-A-ROO ON US!
OH SNAP!
MY LIFE IS OVER!
GET OUTTA TOWN!
HOLD IT RIGHT THERE, LADY! WHILE AS LOCAL POLICE WE APPRECIATE YOU MURDERING AN ENTIRE GANG, IT IS AGAINST OUR CODE TO STAND IDLE WHILE YOU KILL THOSE SCUMBAGS.
SO, I HERBY INFORM YOU THAT WE MUST ARREST YOU AND PUT YOU IN A LESS-THAN-COMFY SPACE JAIL.
BUT! I MUST REITERATE THAT, PERSONALLY, I APPRECIATE THAT I WILL NEVER HAVE TO ARREST ANOTHER MEMBER OF THAT SPACE GANG AGAIN AS A RESULT OF YOU HEROICALLY MURDERING THEM ALL.
THAT IS ALL.
OH, AND PLEASE DROP THE LASER MACE.
THANKS.
TO BE CONTINUED!?

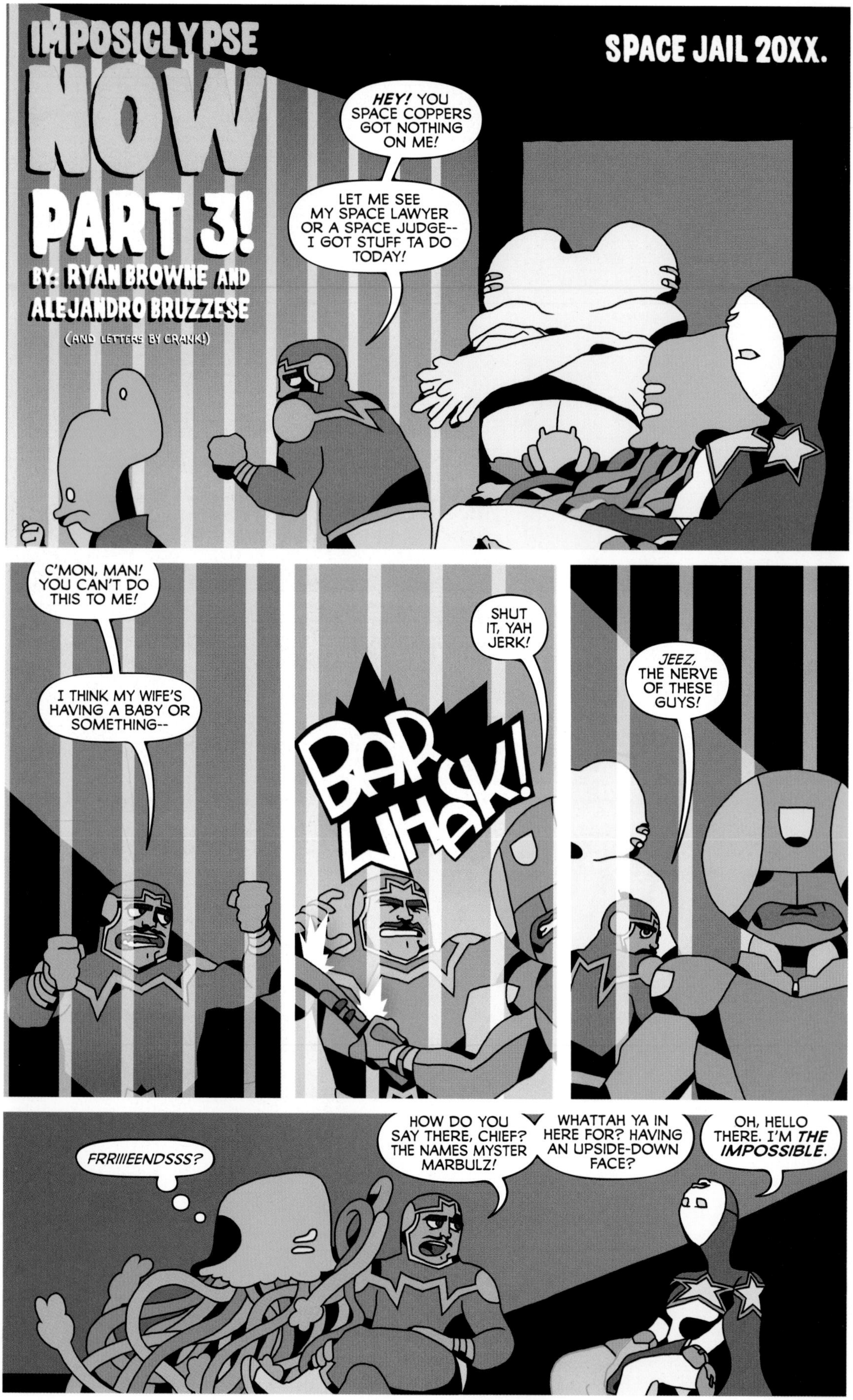
IMPOSICLYPSE NOW PART 3!
BY: RYAN BROWNE AND ALEJANDRO BRUZZESE
(AND LETTERS BY CRANK!)
SPACE JAIL 20XX.
HEY! YOU SPACE COPPERS GOT NOTHING ON ME!
LET ME SEE MY SPACE LAWYER OR A SPACE JUDGE-- I GOT STUFF TA DO TODAY!
C'MON, MAN! YOU CAN'T DO THIS TO ME!
I THINK MY WIFE'S HAVING A BABY OR SOMETHING--
SHUT IT, YAH JERK!
BAR WHACK!
JEEZ, THE NERVE OF THESE GUYS!
FRRIIIEENDSSS?
HOW DO YOU SAY THERE, CHIEF? THE NAMES MYSTER MARBULZ!
WHATTAH YA IN HERE FOR? HAVING AN UPSIDE-DOWN FACE?
OH, HELLO THERE. I'M THE IMPOSSIBLE.

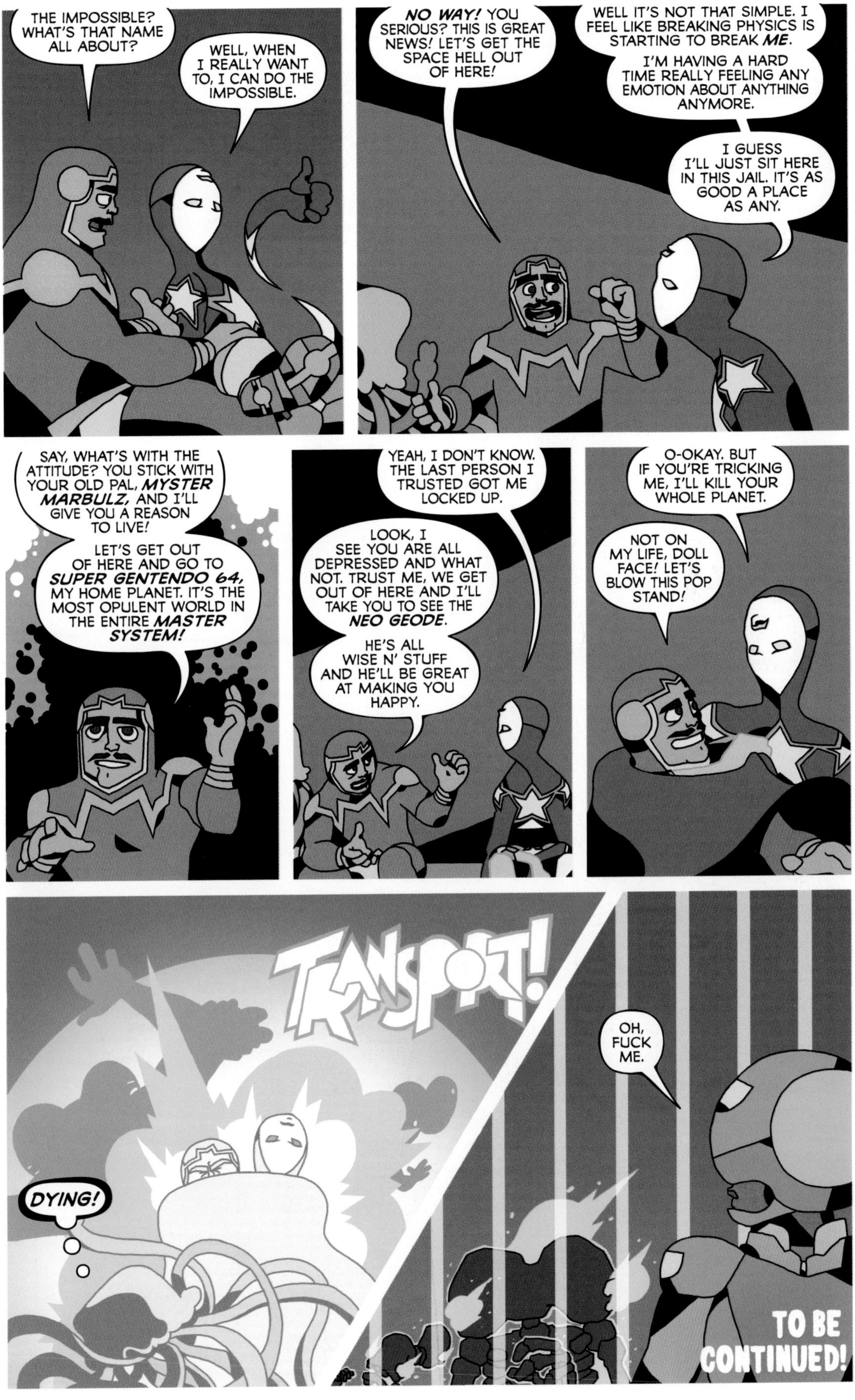
THE IMPOSSIBLE? WHAT'S THAT NAME ALL ABOUT?
WELL, WHEN I REALLY WANT TO, I CAN DO THE IMPOSSIBLE.
NO WAY! YOU SERIOUS? THIS IS GREAT NEWS! LET'S GET THE SPACE HELL OUT OF HERE!
WELL IT'S NOT THAT SIMPLE. I FEEL LIKE BREAKING PHYSICS IS STARTING TO BREAK ME.
I'M HAVING A HARD TIME REALLY FEELING ANY EMOTION ABOUT ANYTHING ANYMORE.
I GUESS I'LL JUST SIT HERE IN THIS JAIL. IT'S AS GOOD A PLACE AS ANY.
SAY, WHAT'S WITH THE ATTITUDE? YOU STICK WITH YOUR OLD PAL, MYSTER MARBULZ, AND I'LL GIVE YOU A REASON TO LIVE!
LET'S GET OUT OF HERE AND GO TO SUPER GENTENDO 64, MY HOME PLANET. IT'S THE MOST OPULENT WORLD IN THE ENTIRE MASTER SYSTEM!
YEAH, I DON'T KNOW. THE LAST PERSON I TRUSTED GOT ME LOCKED UP.
LOOK, I SEE YOU ARE ALL DEPRESSED AND WHAT NOT. TRUST ME, WE GET OUT OF HERE AND I'LL TAKE YOU TO SEE THE NEO GEODE.
HE'S ALL WISE N' STUFF AND HE'LL BE GREAT AT MAKING YOU HAPPY.
O-OKAY. BUT IF YOU'RE TRICKING ME, I'LL KILL YOUR WHOLE PLANET.
NOT ON MY LIFE, DOLL FACE! LET'S BLOW THIS POP STAND!
TRANSPORT!
DYING!
OH, FUCK ME.
TO BE CONTINUED!

IMPOSICLYPSE NOW PART 4!

BY: RYAN BROWNE AND ALEJANDRO BRUZZESE

(AND LETTERS BY CRANK!)

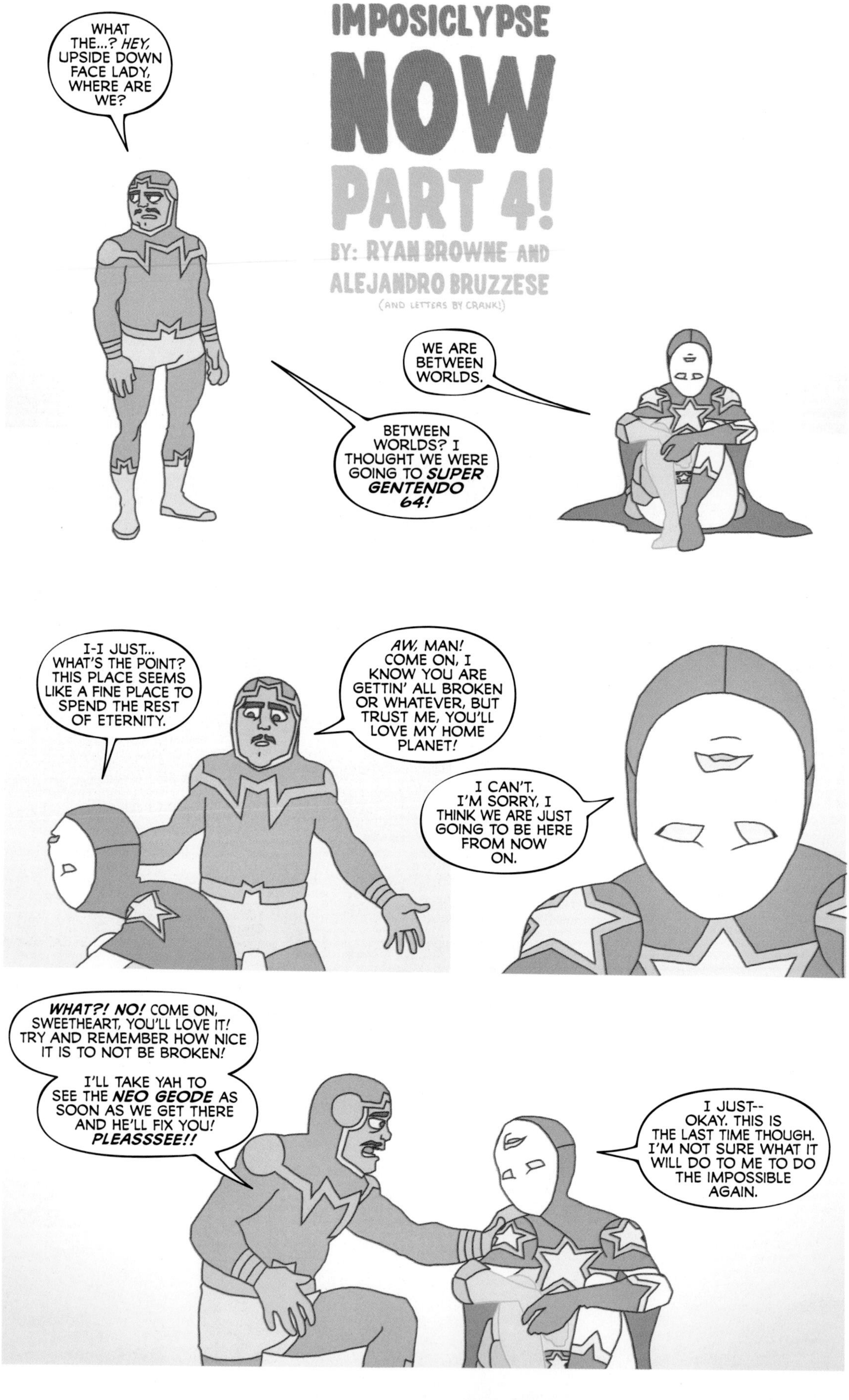

WHAT THE...? *HEY,* UPSIDE DOWN FACE LADY, WHERE ARE WE?
WE ARE BETWEEN WORLDS.
BETWEEN WORLDS? I THOUGHT WE WERE GOING TO ***SUPER GENTENDO 64!***
I-I JUST... WHAT'S THE POINT? THIS PLACE SEEMS LIKE A FINE PLACE TO SPEND THE REST OF ETERNITY.
AW, MAN! COME ON, I KNOW YOU ARE GETTIN' ALL BROKEN OR WHATEVER, BUT TRUST ME, YOU'LL LOVE MY HOME PLANET!
I CAN'T. I'M SORRY, I THINK WE ARE JUST GOING TO BE HERE FROM NOW ON.
WHAT?! NO! COME ON, SWEETHEART, YOU'LL LOVE IT! TRY AND REMEMBER HOW NICE IT IS TO NOT BE BROKEN!
I'LL TAKE YAH TO SEE THE ***NEO GEODE*** AS SOON AS WE GET THERE AND HE'LL FIX YOU! ***PLEASSSEE!!***
I JUST-- OKAY. THIS IS THE LAST TIME THOUGH. I'M NOT SURE WHAT IT WILL DO TO ME TO DO THE IMPOSSIBLE AGAIN.

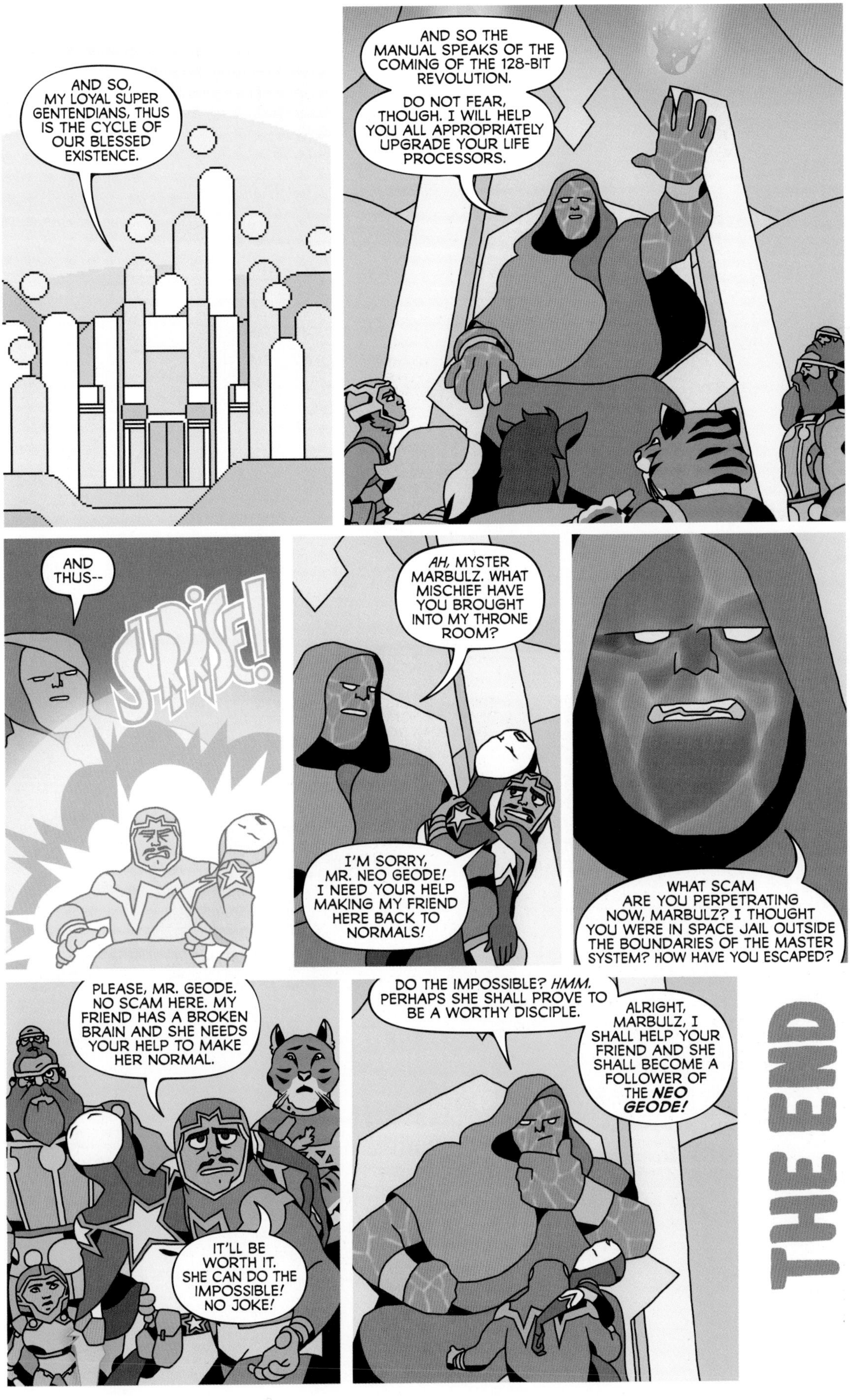
AND SO, MY LOYAL SUPER GENTENDIANS, THUS IS THE CYCLE OF OUR BLESSED EXISTENCE.
AND SO THE MANUAL SPEAKS OF THE COMING OF THE 128-BIT REVOLUTION.
DO NOT FEAR, THOUGH. I WILL HELP YOU ALL APPROPRIATELY UPGRADE YOUR LIFE PROCESSORS.
AND THUS--
SURPRISE!
AH, MYSTER MARBULZ. WHAT MISCHIEF HAVE YOU BROUGHT INTO MY THRONE ROOM?
I'M SORRY, MR. NEO GEODE! I NEED YOUR HELP MAKING MY FRIEND HERE BACK TO NORMALS!
WHAT SCAM ARE YOU PERPETRATING NOW, MARBULZ? I THOUGHT YOU WERE IN SPACE JAIL OUTSIDE THE BOUNDARIES OF THE MASTER SYSTEM? HOW HAVE YOU ESCAPED?
PLEASE, MR. GEODE. NO SCAM HERE. MY FRIEND HAS A BROKEN BRAIN AND SHE NEEDS YOUR HELP TO MAKE HER NORMAL.
IT'LL BE WORTH IT. SHE CAN DO THE IMPOSSIBLE! NO JOKE!
DO THE IMPOSSIBLE? *HMM.* PERHAPS SHE SHALL PROVE TO BE A WORTHY DISCIPLE.
ALRIGHT, MARBULZ, I SHALL HELP YOUR FRIEND AND SHE SHALL BECOME A FOLLOWER OF THE ***NEO GEODE!***
THE END

The following is an advertisement for *Gob Huts Astromen* that was produced for the back pages of *The Manhattan Projects*. It was made before issue one and has some design differences from what was actually used in the second series. Most notably, Dr. Professor is much hairier than we see here. Please enjoy, won't you?

After the advertisment is a hilarious collection of fantastic alternate covers for the series.

ISSUE ONE PHANTOM VARIANT
Cryin' Frowne

ISSUE ONE 2ND PRINTING
Bryan Rowne

ISSUE ONE ACME COMICS VARIANT
Ry-Ry Brownestein

ISSUE ONE COVER B
Geof Darrow + Ryan Braun

ISSUE TWO COVER B
Jim Rugg

ISSUE THREE COVER B
Chris Burnham + Reginald Browne

ISSUE FOUR COVER B
Paolo Rivera + Ryeanne Brown

ISSUE FIVE COVER B
Nick Pitarra + Rusty Bulldozer

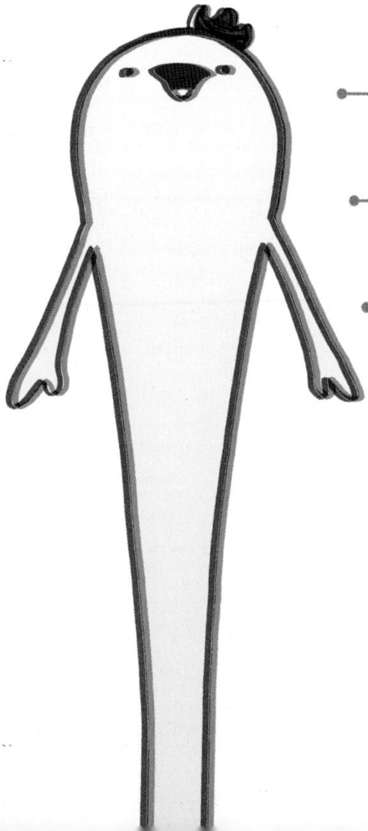

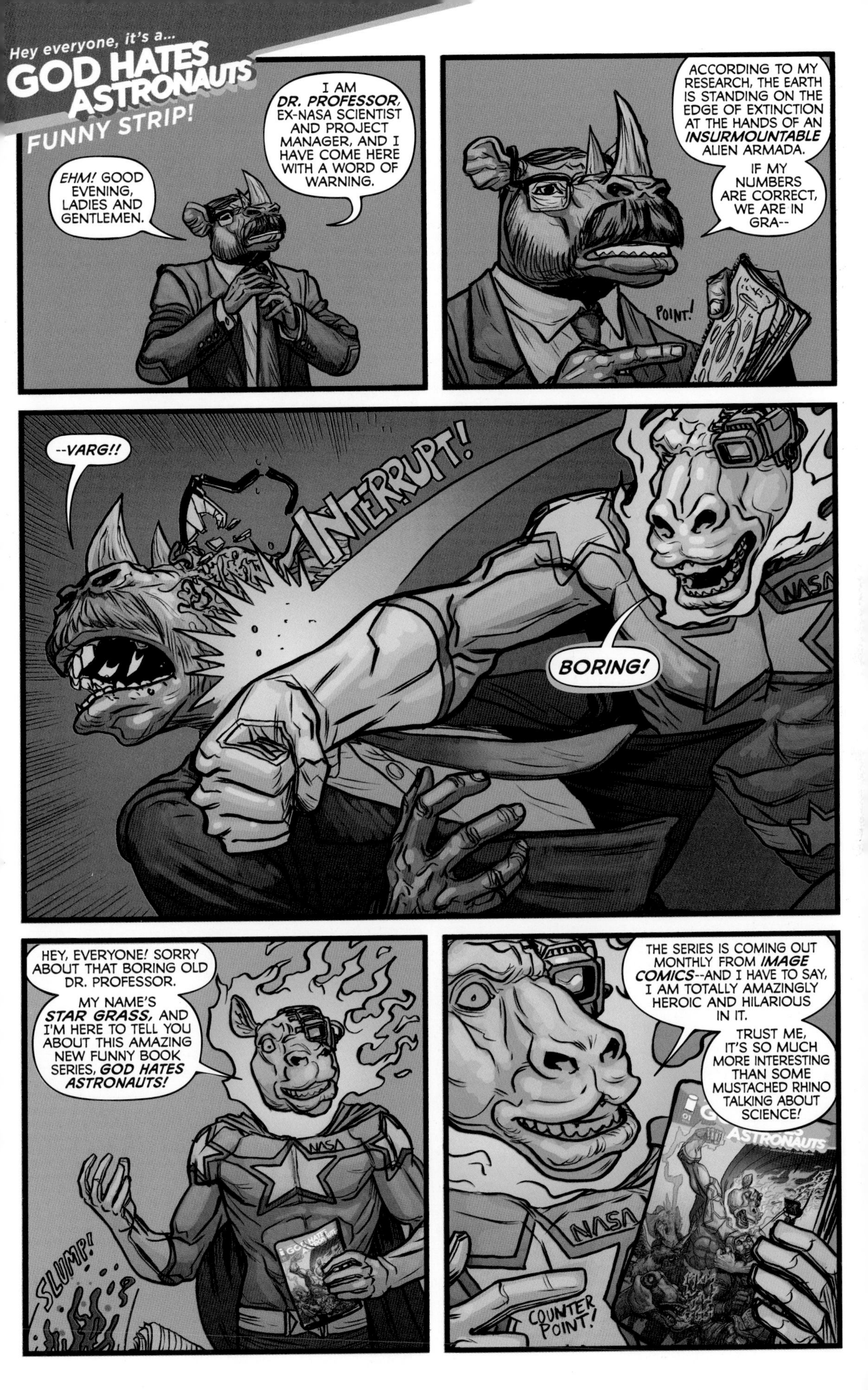
Hey everyone, it's a...
GOD HATES ASTRONAUTS
FUNNY STRIP!
EHM! GOOD EVENING, LADIES AND GENTLEMEN.
I AM DR. PROFESSOR, EX-NASA SCIENTIST AND PROJECT MANAGER, AND I HAVE COME HERE WITH A WORD OF WARNING.
ACCORDING TO MY RESEARCH, THE EARTH IS STANDING ON THE EDGE OF EXTINCTION AT THE HANDS OF AN INSURMOUNTABLE ALIEN ARMADA.
IF MY NUMBERS ARE CORRECT, WE ARE IN GRA--
POINT!
--VARG!!
INTERRUPT!
BORING!
NASA
HEY, EVERYONE! SORRY ABOUT THAT BORING OLD DR. PROFESSOR.
MY NAME'S STAR GRASS, AND I'M HERE TO TELL YOU ABOUT THIS AMAZING NEW FUNNY BOOK SERIES, GOD HATES ASTRONAUTS!
NASA
SLUMP!
THE SERIES IS COMING OUT MONTHLY FROM IMAGE COMICS--AND I HAVE TO SAY, I AM TOTALLY AMAZINGLY HEROIC AND HILARIOUS IN IT.
TRUST ME, IT'S SO MUCH MORE INTERESTING THAN SOME MUSTACHED RHINO TALKING ABOUT SCIENCE!
ASTRONAUTS
NASA
COUNTER POINT!

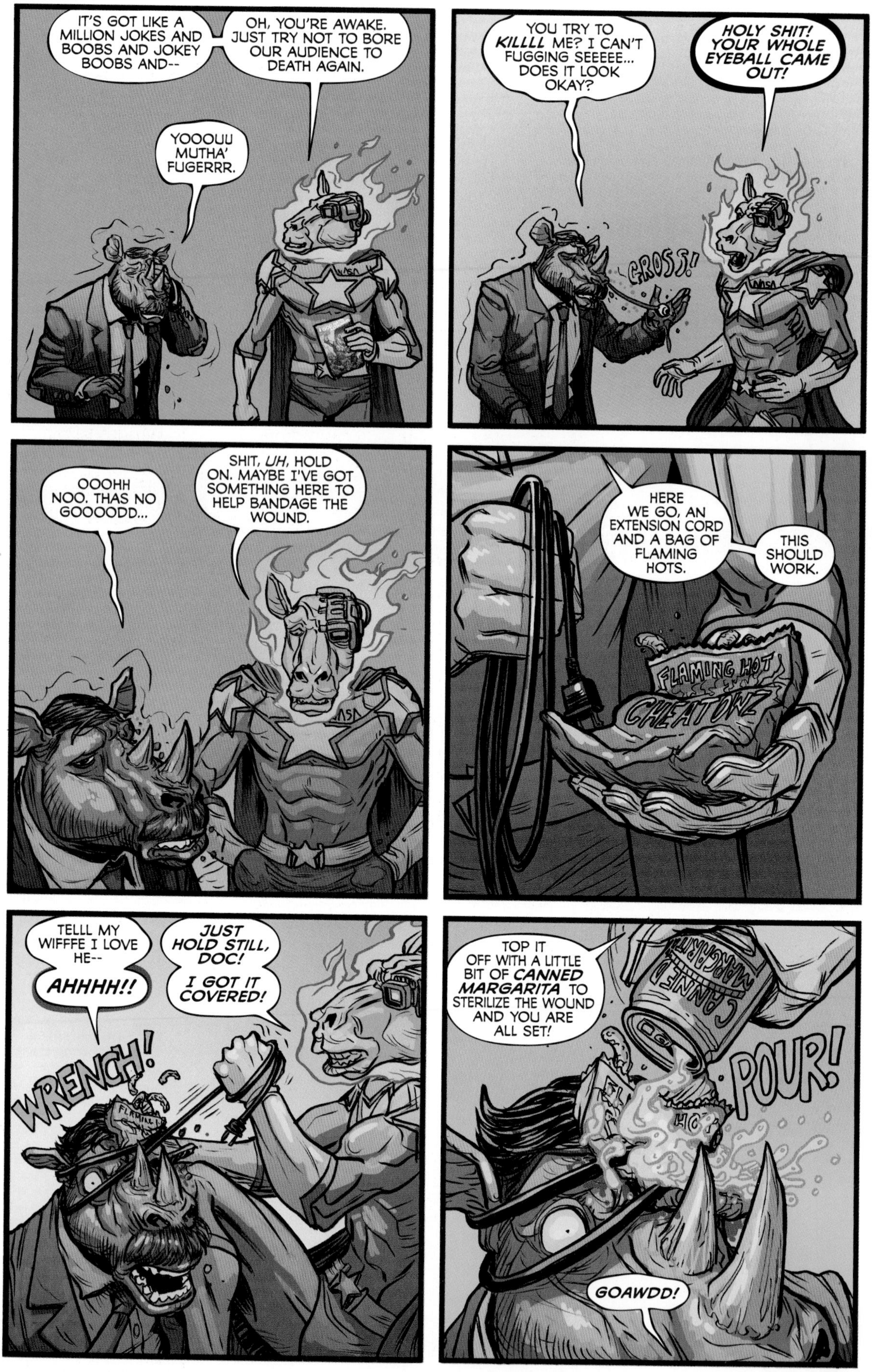
IT'S GOT LIKE A MILLION JOKES AND BOOBS AND JOKEY BOOBS AND--
OH, YOU'RE AWAKE. JUST TRY NOT TO BORE OUR AUDIENCE TO DEATH AGAIN.
YOOOUU MUTHA' FUGERRR.
YOU TRY TO KILLLL ME? I CAN'T FUGGING SEEEEE... DOES IT LOOK OKAY?
HOLY SHIT! YOUR WHOLE EYEBALL CAME OUT!
GROSS!
OOOHH NOO. THAS NO GOOOODD...
SHIT, UH, HOLD ON. MAYBE I'VE GOT SOMETHING HERE TO HELP BANDAGE THE WOUND.
HERE WE GO, AN EXTENSION CORD AND A BAG OF FLAMING HOTS.
THIS SHOULD WORK.
FLAMING HOT
CHEATOWZ
TELLL MY WIFFFE I LOVE HE--
AHHHH!!
JUST HOLD STILL, DOC!
I GOT IT COVERED!
WRENCH!
TOP IT OFF WITH A LITTLE BIT OF CANNED MARGARITA TO STERILIZE THE WOUND AND YOU ARE ALL SET!
CANNED MARGARITA
POUR!
GOAWDD!

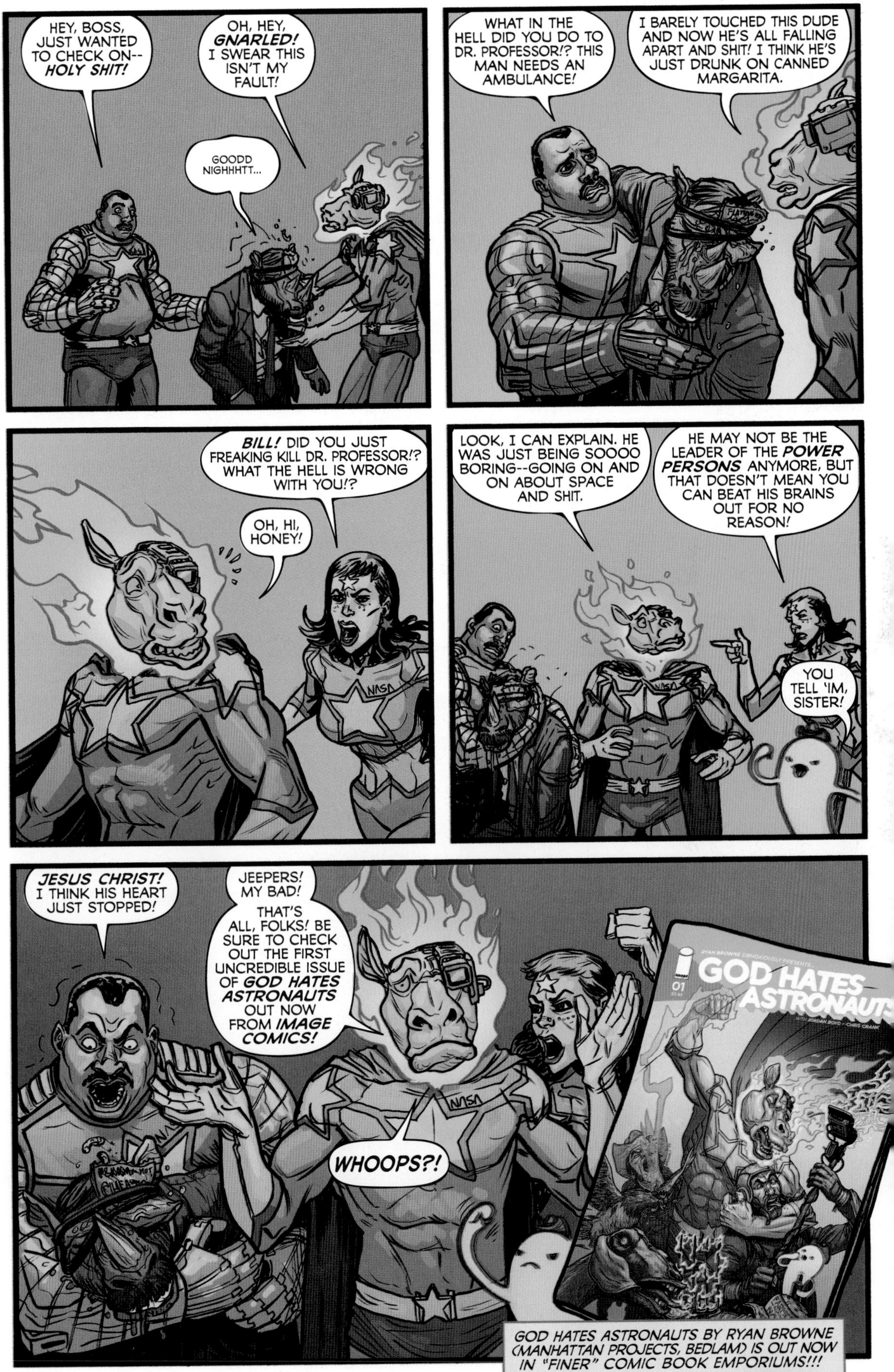

HEY, BOSS, JUST WANTED TO CHECK ON-- HOLY SHIT!
OH, HEY, GNARLED! I SWEAR THIS ISN'T MY FAULT!
GOODD NIGHHHTT...
WHAT IN THE HELL DID YOU DO TO DR. PROFESSOR!? THIS MAN NEEDS AN AMBULANCE!
I BARELY TOUCHED THIS DUDE AND NOW HE'S ALL FALLING APART AND SHIT! I THINK HE'S JUST DRUNK ON CANNED MARGARITA.
BILL! DID YOU JUST FREAKING KILL DR. PROFESSOR!? WHAT THE HELL IS WRONG WITH YOU!?
OH, HI, HONEY!
NASA
LOOK, I CAN EXPLAIN. HE WAS JUST BEING SOOOO BORING--GOING ON AND ON ABOUT SPACE AND SHIT.
HE MAY NOT BE THE LEADER OF THE POWER PERSONS ANYMORE, BUT THAT DOESN'T MEAN YOU CAN BEAT HIS BRAINS OUT FOR NO REASON!
YOU TELL 'IM, SISTER!
JESUS CHRIST! I THINK HIS HEART JUST STOPPED!
JEEPERS! MY BAD!
THAT'S ALL, FOLKS! BE SURE TO CHECK OUT THE FIRST UNCREDIBLE ISSUE OF GOD HATES ASTRONAUTS OUT NOW FROM IMAGE COMICS!
NASA
WHOOPS?!
GOD HATES ASTRONAUTS
01
GOD HATES ASTRONAUTS BY RYAN BROWNE (MANHATTAN PROJECTS, BEDLAM) IS OUT NOW IN "FINER" COMIC BOOK EMPORIUMS!!!

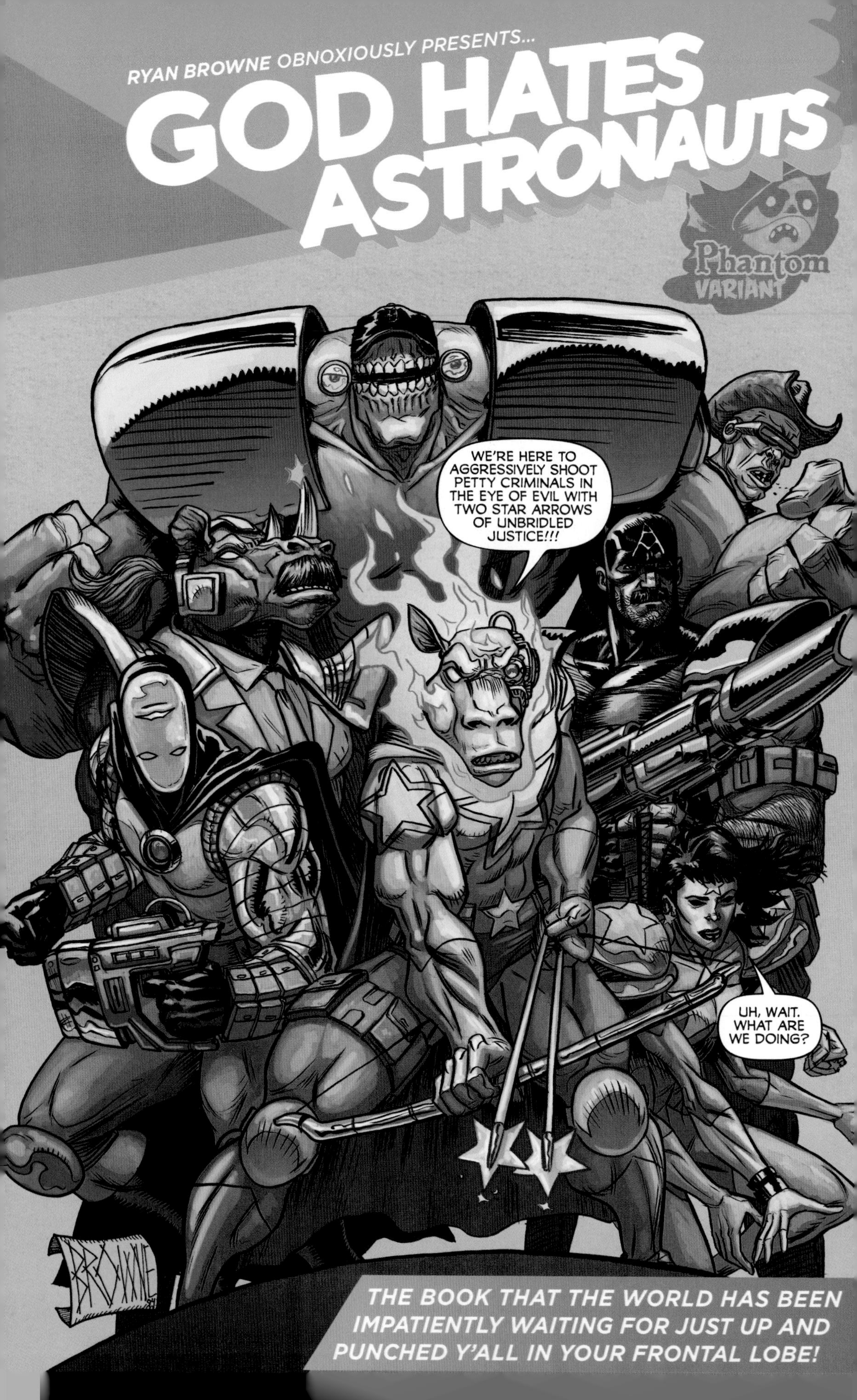
RYAN BROWNE OBNOXIOUSLY PRESENTS...
GOD HATES ASTRONAUTS
Phantom VARIANT
WE'RE HERE TO AGGRESSIVELY SHOOT PETTY CRIMINALS IN THE EYE OF EVIL WITH TWO STAR ARROWS OF UNBRIDLED JUSTICE!!!
UH, WAIT. WHAT ARE WE DOING?
THE BOOK THAT THE WORLD HAS BEEN IMPATIENTLY WAITING FOR JUST UP AND PUNCHED Y'ALL IN YOUR FRONTAL LOBE!

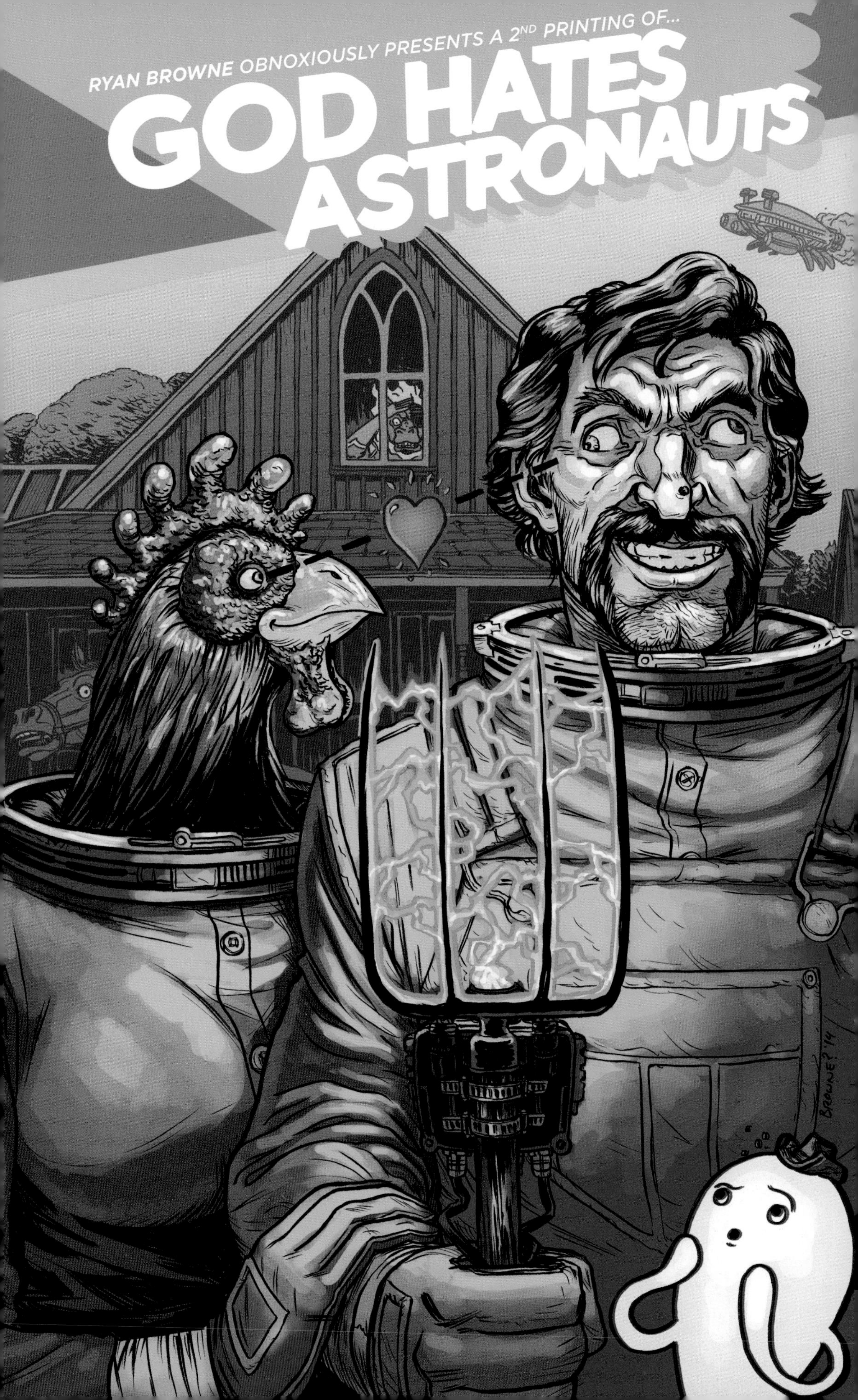
RYAN BROWNE OBNOXIOUSLY PRESENTS A 2ND PRINTING OF...
GOD HATES ASTRONAUTS
BROWNE? '14

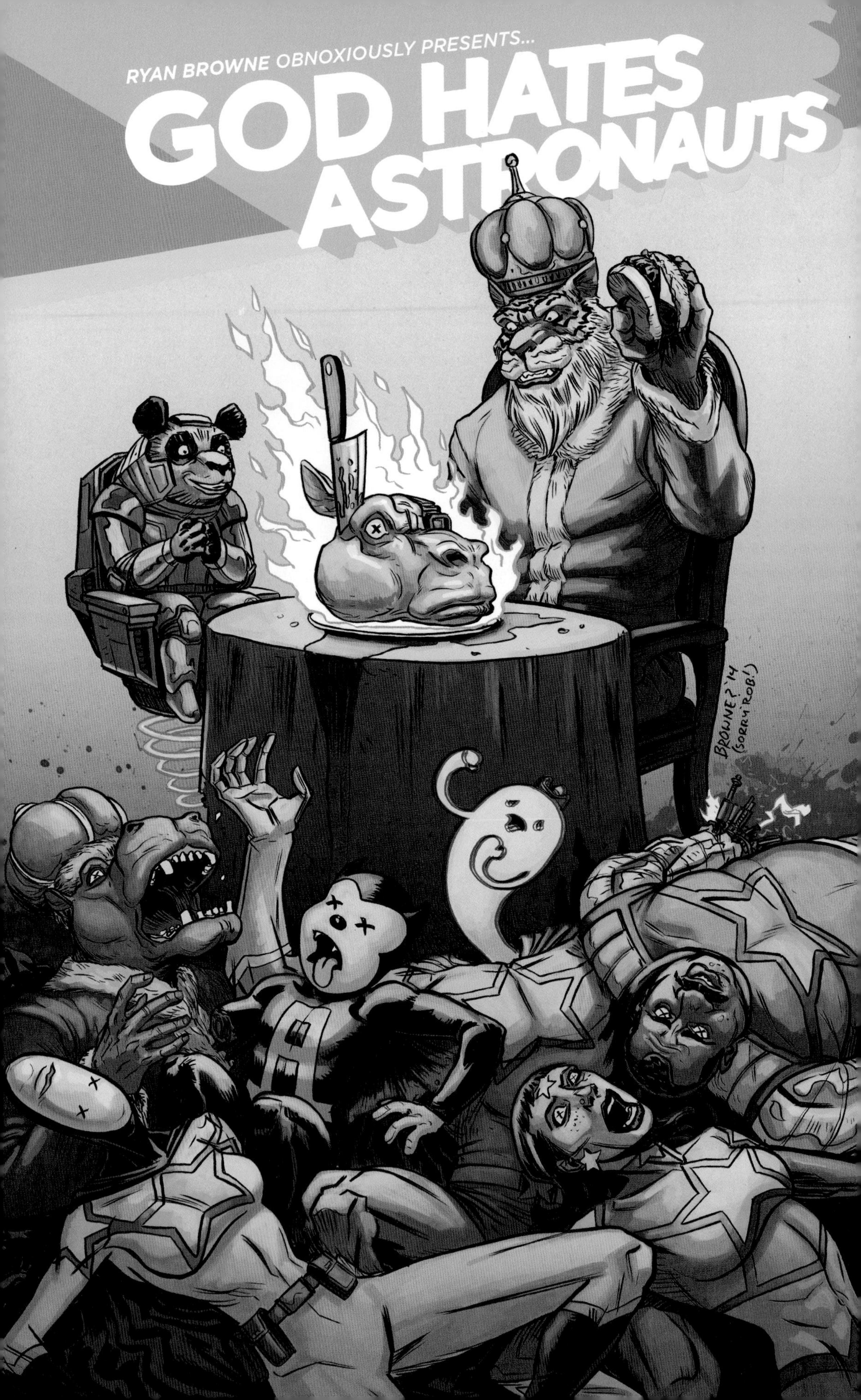
RYAN BROWNE OBNOXIOUSLY PRESENTS...
GOD HATES ASTRONAUTS
BROWNE? '14 (SORRY ROB!)

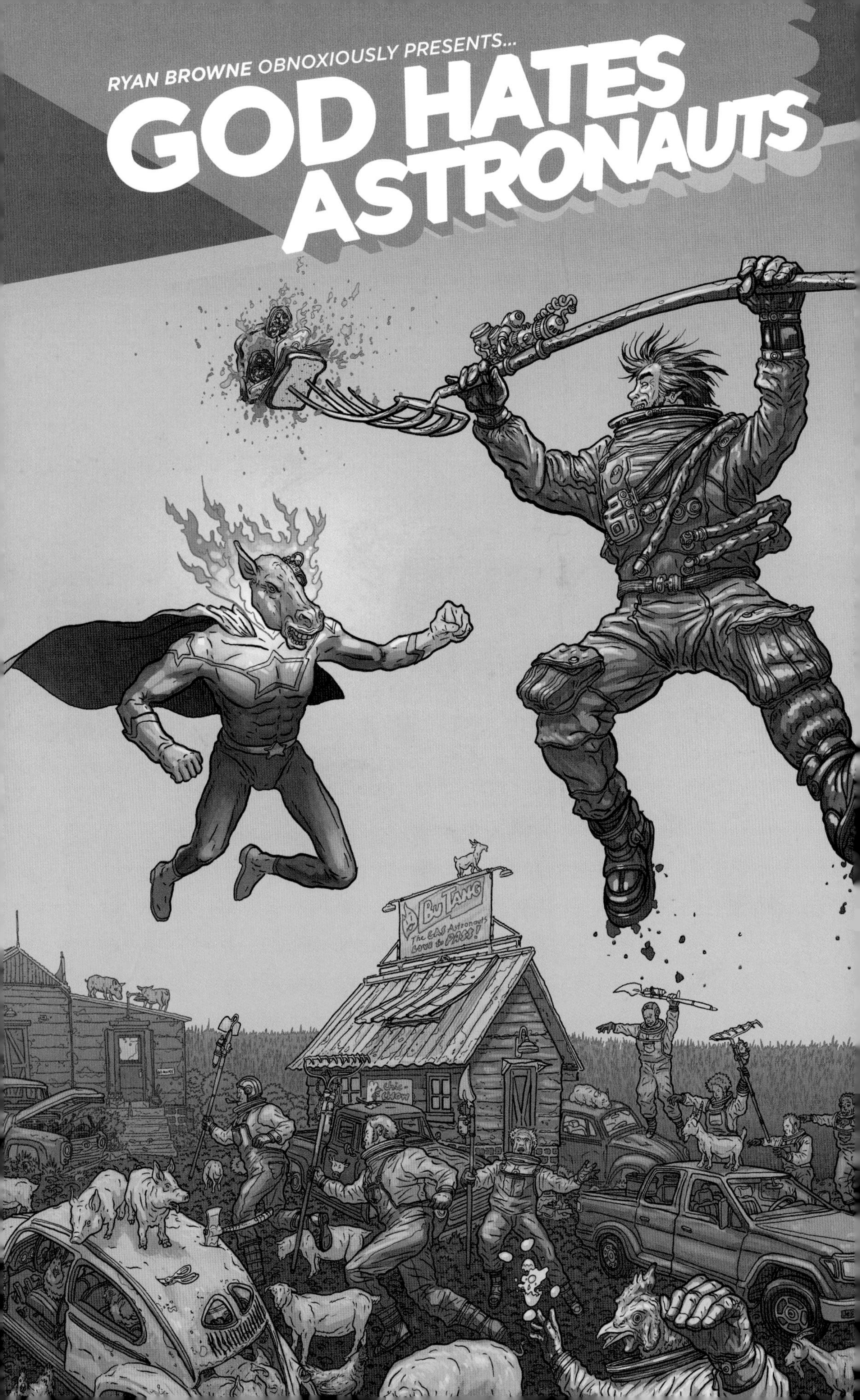
RYAN BROWNE OBNOXIOUSLY PRESENTS...
GOD HATES ASTRONAUTS
Bu Tang
The GAS Astronauts LOVE to PASS!

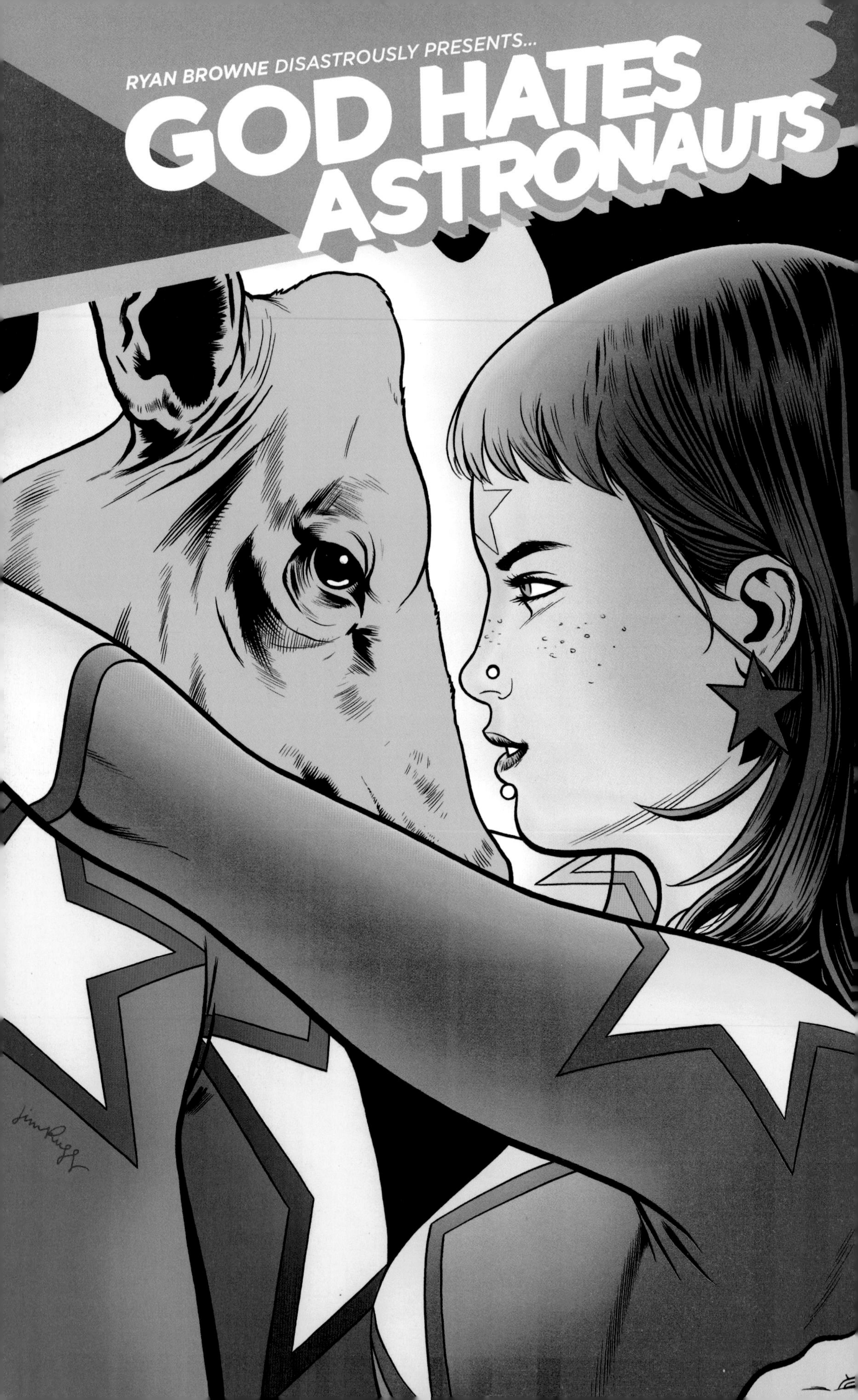
RYAN BROWNE DISASTROUSLY PRESENTS...
GOD HATES ASTRONAUTS

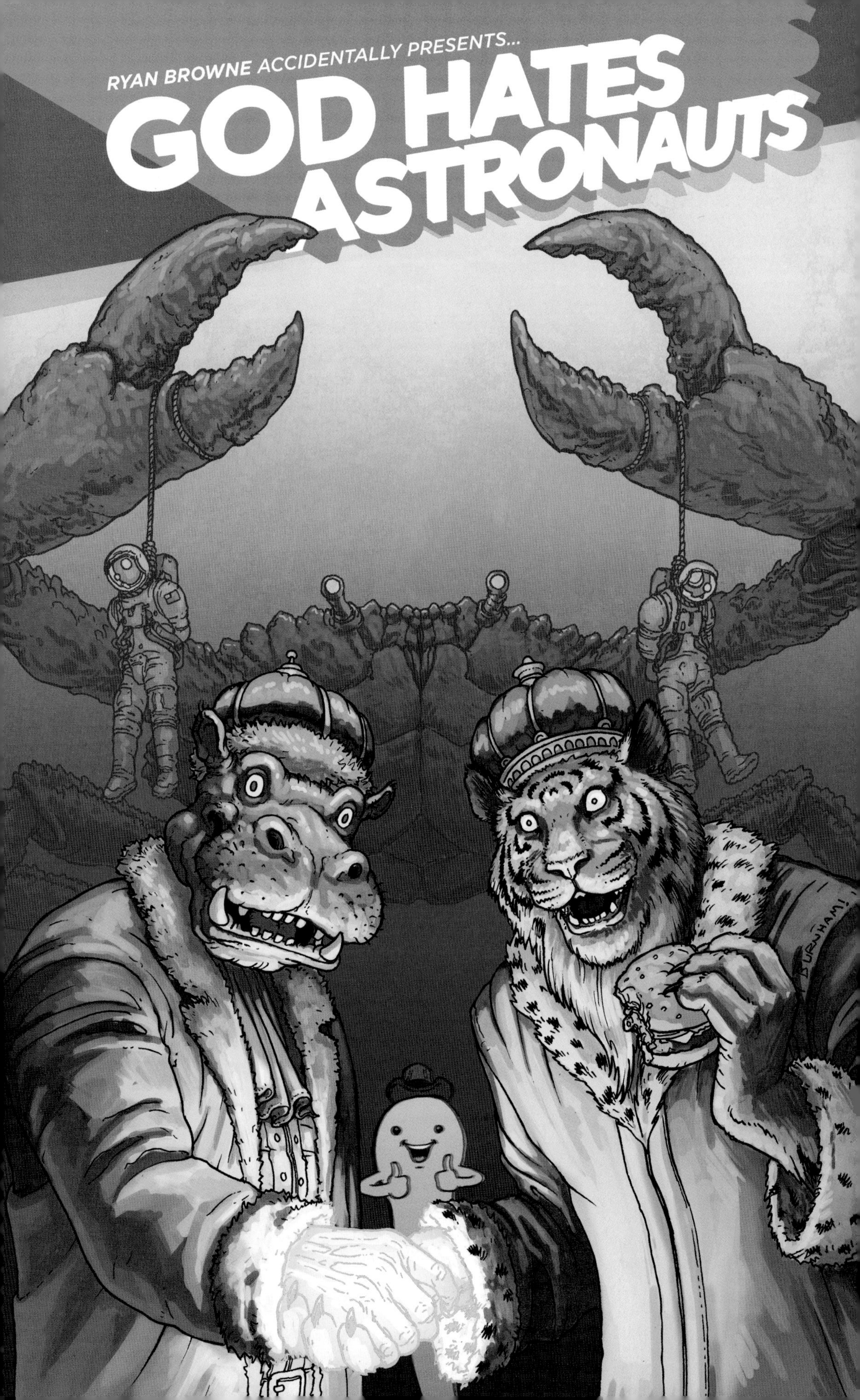
RYAN BROWNE ACCIDENTALLY PRESENTS...
GOD HATES ASTRONAUTS
BURNHAM!

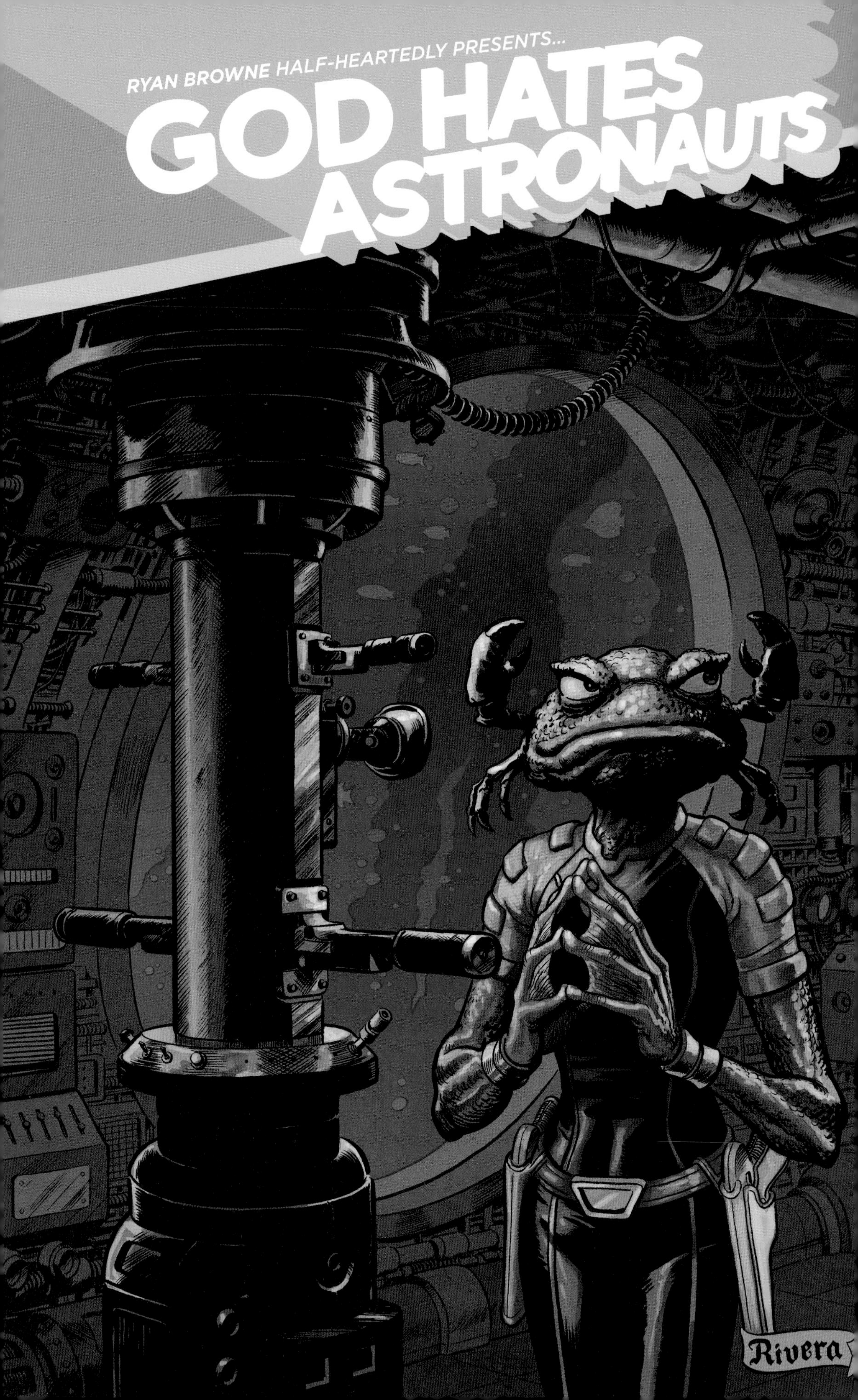
RYAN BROWNE HALF-HEARTEDLY PRESENTS...
GOD HATES ASTRONAUTS
Rivera

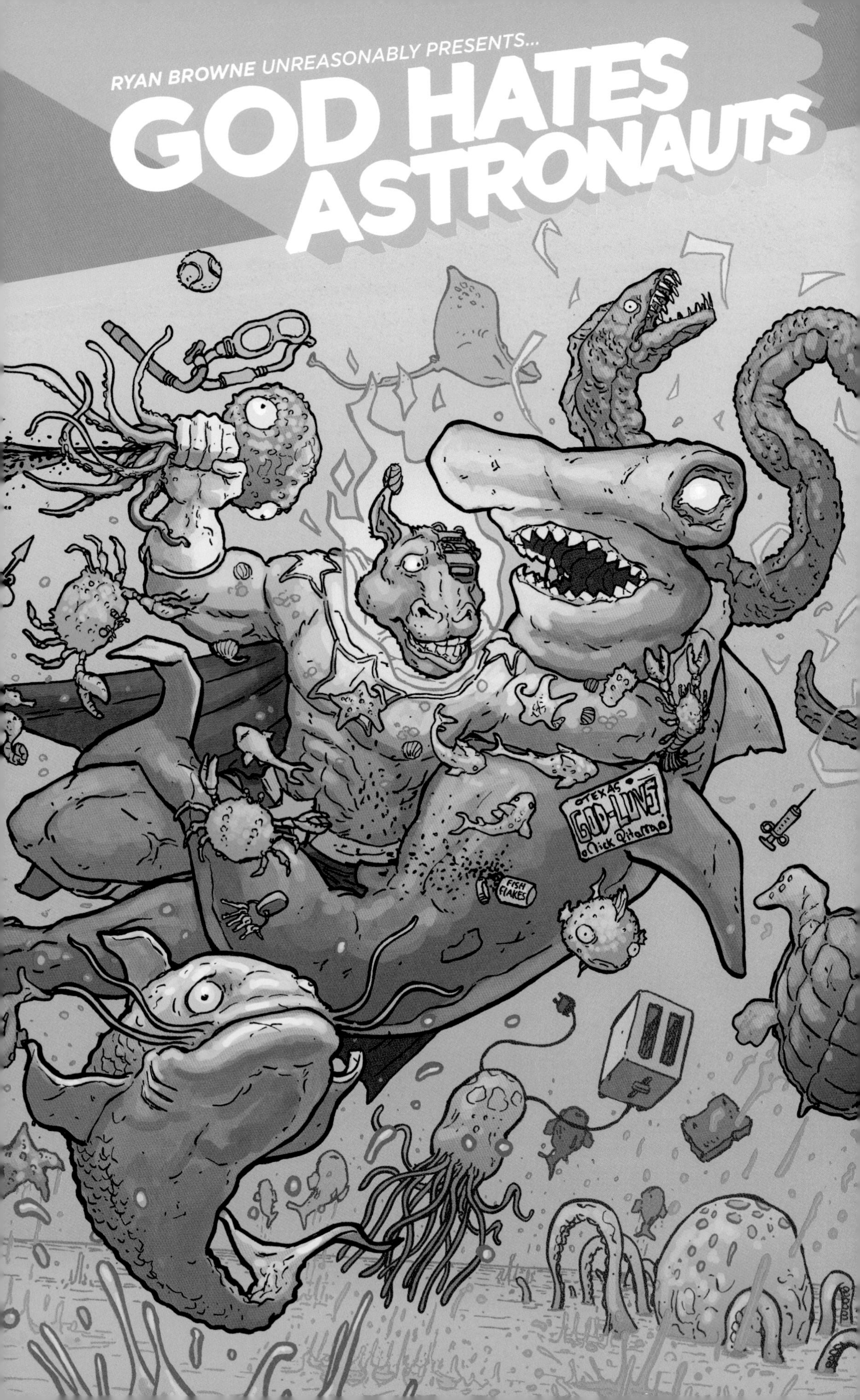
RYAN BROWNE UNREASONABLY PRESENTS...
GOD HATES ASTRONAUTS
TEXAS
FISH FLAKES

VARIOUS KIND AND UNKIND WORDS FOR

God Hats Astronuts fills me with the same diseased hate as a late night run for the border.

SEAL EVERETT KOOP
REGIONAL SHARK AND FOOD DOCTOR OF SCIENCE

Unlike refreshing Snopple, this is not made from the best stuff on Earth.

MARYWEATHER T. SNOPPLE
HEIR TO THE SNOPPLE BEVERAGE FORTUNE

It reminds me of a disgusting piece of pottery thrown on a disgusting wheel by a pair of disgustingly Swazye-like hands.

WHIPTY GOLDBURD
ACTRESS/ACTOR OF BEST PICTURE

For once in his horrific life, Ryan slightly doesn't not disappoint in refusing to make me almost not unhappy. Sort of.

CONFUSED MAN ON THE BUS

Instead of buying this book, why not refresh yourself by spending money or monies on a refreshing Snopple Beverage?

MARYWEATHER T. SNOPPLE
HEIR TO THE SNOPPLE BEVERAGE FORTUNE

Oh! Sorry, I didn't know it was my turn to order. Can I try the London Broil?

RETIRED UMPIRE OVERHEARD AT A RESTAURANT

Please, I know this is not an appropriate place to beg, but Snopple Beverages are NOT selling well. I need your help, my fortune is all but worthless!

MARYWEATHER T. SNOPPLE
HEIR TO THE SNOPPLE BEVERAGE FORTUNE

You know how gross it is when you vurp? Yeah, dude, it's like that, but with more hot sauce flavor up in your mouth.

BRO-DUDE BROSEPH
PALE(ALE)ONTOLOGIST TO THE STARS

Hey guys. Sorry about last time. I was having a bad day. Why not try our new Cran-Raspple Diet Snopple?

MARYWEATHER T. SNOPPLE
HEIR TO THE SNOPPLE BEVERAGE FORTUNE

Why would someone purposefully make a piece of trashy garbage like this?! It defies all logic and insults my family!

CORNFELLER P. PROPELLERTOP
LEADING EXPORTER OF CORN AND AIRPLANE PROPELLERS

Reading this was a worse experience than when I was trapped in a gas station bathroom with a super-powered chimpanzee.

MAN WHO DIED OF SUPER-POWERED CHIMPANZEE WOUNDS

Man! Snopple brand beverages sure are doing great! Why not invest in the company today?

MARYWEATHER T. SNOPPLE
HEIR TO THE SNOPPLE BEVERAGE FORTUNE

I actually really liked this book. No, seriously. I actually did. Not joking at all here. It was the best experience ever. Yay.

PAINFULLY SARCASTIC ZOO KEEPER

Look. I'm so sorry. Someone please help me! People refuse to buy Snopple beverages and the company owes money to some very, very bad people! I'm afraid for my life!!!

MARYWEATHER T. SNOPPLE
HEIR TO THE SNOPPLE BEVERAGE FORTUNE

Hello, may I take your order? What? No, I'm sorry sir, I don't know what Gord Hates Astronautz is. Please stop recording.

HALLEY-JOAN OSMOND
INVENTOR OF THE MODERN DOUBLE-WINDOWED DRIVE-THRU

Snopple owes a ton of money to some very scary people and I think they are coming to collect! I have to hide!

MARYWEATHER T. SNOPPLE
HEIR TO THE SNOPPLE BEVERAGE FORTUNE

I like astronauts just fine. Does that mean I hate God, or that God hates me? What about dog (which is God spelled backwards)?

CONFUSED CHARLES SOULE
WRITER OF SWAMP-HULK, SUPERWONDER MAN, AND LETTER 27

Are you kidding me? I love it! Quick, put more in my veins!!!

A HEROIN ADDICT THAT THINKS HE'S BEEN ASKED ABOUT HEROIN AND NOT GLAND HORTS MASTRONAUTS

AND/OR AGAINST GOLD HATS ASTROMEN

Shh... I think they are in the house. Call the police.

MARYWEATHER T. SNOPPLE
HEIR TO THE SNOPPLE BEVERAGE FORTUNE

....

We know you're here, Maryweather! Show yourself or I'll burn your house down and drink your Snopple!

SCARY MAN WHO IS OWED A TON OF MONEY BY SNOPPLE

....

. . .

MARYWEATHER T. SNOPPLE
HEIR TO THE SNOPPLE BEVERAGE FORTUNE

....

I really love this comic book, but I truly hate the way that Ryan draws cow heads. Use some damn reference!

IRRITATED BAWB ROSS
PAINTER OF TREES AND EVERYTHING SURROUNDING TREES

....

Well honestly, Detective, I have no idea why those men were in my house. All I knew is that I had to survive, no matter the cost.

MARYWEATHER T. SNOPPLE
HEIR TO THE SNOPPLE BEVERAGE FORTUNE

....

Alright, Maryweather. Just do me a favor and don't leave the country until we get this all sorted out. There seem to be some holes to fill.

DETECTIVE STEPUNIE LAMBILLZO
INVESTIGATING DETECTIVE FOR THE SNOPPLE HOMICIDE CASE

....

I think this book mutated the way I think about animals. That there Ryan Browne guy sure makes 'em look hot!

SOME GUY WHO IS NOT ALLOWED NEAR MY CAT

....

One-way ticket to Costa Rica, please. Say, you don't accept Snopple Value Bucks, do you?

MARYWEATHER T. SNOPPLE
HEIR TO THE SNOPPLE BEVERAGE FORTUNE

....

Maryweather killed our best men! There is no way we are gonna let that Snopple bitch get away with this!

VENGEFUL MAN WHO IS OWED MONEY BY MARYWEATHER

Sometimes life is grand! *Sound of slurping Snopple Piña Colada Strawmonade out of a coconut.*

MARYWEATHER T. SNOPPLE
HEIR TO THE SNOPPLE BEVERAGE FORTUNE

....

This series doesn't deliver on Browne's promise of "heavy laser sword usage." Not a single laser sword to be found.

GOREGED LEWKISS
PIONEER OF THE AMERICAN DREAM FOR LASER SWORDPLAY

....

Life's pretty great here in Costa Rica. The one thing they don't have here is an all-natural fruit fusion beverage. Hmm...

MARYWEATHER T. SNOPPLE
HEIR TO THE SNOPPLE BEVERAGE FORTUNE

....

Facts have come to light in the Snopple homicide investigation that lead us to believe that Maryweather Snopple has fled the country.

DETECTIVE STEPUNIE LAMBILLZO
INVESTIGATING DETECTIVE FOR THE SNOPPLE HOMICIDE CASE

....

I've got more important things to do than read this book. Those deep sea fish aren't going to catch themselves!

STRESSED-OUT DEEP SEA FISHERMAN

....

Any information as to the whereabouts of Ms. Snopple will be met with a large cash reward by the Police Department.

DETECTIVE STEPUNIE LAMBILLZO
INVESTIGATING DETECTIVE FOR THE SNOPPLE HOMICIDE CASE

....

When we find Maryweather we will kill the hell out of her! I have my best men scouring the globe to bring her to justice!

VENGEFUL MAN WHO IS OWED MONEY BY MARYWEATHER

....

Ladies and Gentlemen of Costa Rica! I, Sally Sauceberry, would like to announce the debut of the world's greatest all new multi-fruit flavored beverage, Phrutopia!

MARYWEATHER T. SNOPPLE
HEIR TO THE SNOPPLE BEVERAGE FORTUNE

RYAN BROWNE

(Pronounced Brown) was once confused with a 40,000 pound, endangered silverback gorilla. He is, in fact, a wild baboon wearing an ill-fitting gorilla mask who can see the future of certain crocodiles who are currently under-employed.

When Ryan was young, he excelled at being smaller than he now currently is. Now he is enormous, larger even than what you are right now picturing. Actually, take what you are picturing, size-wise, and quadruple it. Now forget your new picture of Ryan's physique because I was lying. Ryan is, in reality, quite small. He is capable of crushing old Raisinettes with just one hand, but this takes considerable effort.

Once upon a time, Ryan worked with adequate effort to become a professional baseballman. This, as you can guess, did not work out. BUT, as you cannot guess, he was incredible at fielding ground balls exclusively between his legs. He would throw caution to the wind, spread his legs, and field screaming line drives and short hop grounders with little to no regard for the safety of his genitalia. Ryan is currently childless.

For a little while, Ryan ate only horse meat. This caused his horrible smell and the loss of almost all of his friends to other people who didn't smell horrible because they ate mostly vegetation.

There was a time when Ryan thought about pursuing a career in sanitation and in walrus-wrangling vehicle maintenance. In the end, he discovered that a walrus was not what he had thought it was, and that, in fact, he had been thinking of a manatee the entire time. Disappointed and homeless, Ryan shifted his career goals towards manatee-wrangling vehicle maintenance, but then discovered there were no such vehicles.

Ryan did not taste pasta until the age of 65—or, at least, that is his goal, since he is currently 63 years old.

The first time Ryan flew in an aeroplane was last weekend. He has not been seen since.

Oh wait, there he is. Sorry. He was partially obscured by that walrus-wrangling vehicle.

At one point, Ryan had actually constructed his own town for the sole purpose of having a place to store his loose bark collection. "Browne Towne," as it was called, never got past the building phase because he couldn't convince Steve Harvey to be the mayor.

While considered by most to be clinically hyper-obese, Ryan still wears a 28-inch waist. It's one of the great mysteries of the world, and Ryan asks that you not talk about it.

Ryan hopes you have enjoyed this second volume of Golf Hotter Astroturf. If you were not aware that there was a first volume before this, then you have screwed up mightily and must immediately purchase the first volume from Image Comics. Thank you for your patience and your ability to tolerate confusion.

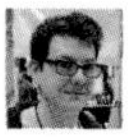

TINY PHOTO BY
SEAN DOVE

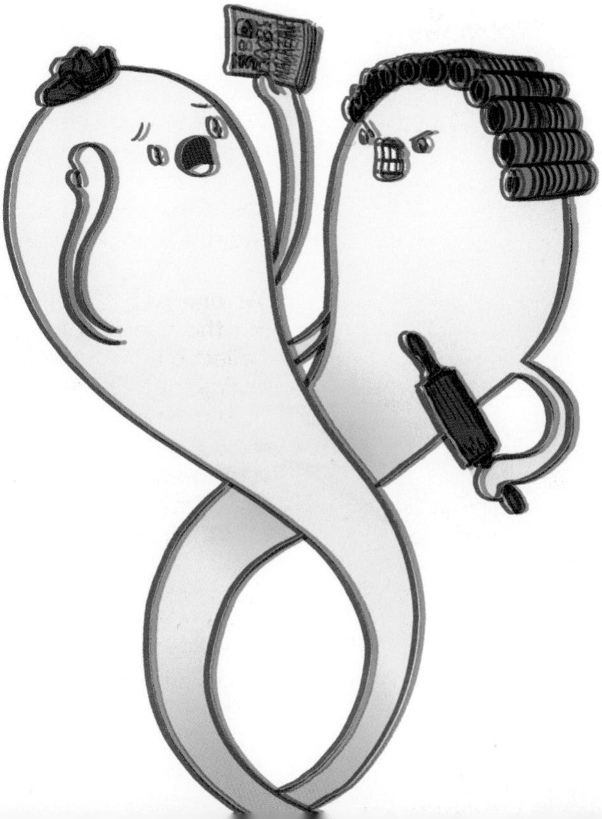

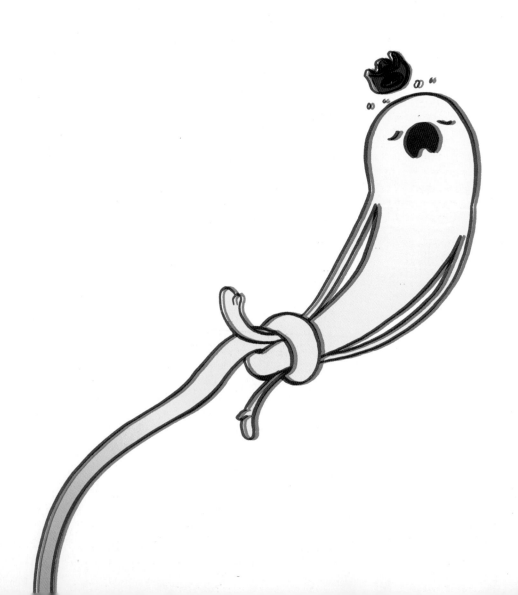